Transactional Lawyering

Transactional Lawyering

An Experiential Approach to Communication and Problem-Solving

Julie A. Ryan

ADJUNCT PROFESSOR OF LAW
GEORGETOWN LAW

ADJUNCT PROFESSOR
LOYOLA LAW SCHOOL, LOS ANGELES

PARTNER
ACCELERON LAW GROUP, LLP

CAROLINA ACADEMIC PRESS
Durham, North Carolina

Library of Congress Cataloging-in-Publication Data

Names: Ryan, Julie A., author.
Title: Transactional lawyering : an experiential approach to communication
  and problem-solving / by Julie A. Ryan.
Description: Durham, North Carolina : Carolina Academic Press, LLC, 2019. |
  Includes bibliographical references and index.
Identifiers: LCCN 2019006344 | ISBN 9781531004743 (alk. paper)
Subjects: LCSH: Commercial law—United States. | Legal composition. |
  Negotiation in business—United States. | Attorney and client—United
  States. | LCGFT: Textbooks.
Classification: LCC KF889.85 .R93 2019 | DDC 651.7024/3400973—dc23
LC record available at https://lccn.loc.gov/2019006344

e-ISBN 978-1-5310-0475-0

Carolina Academic Press
700 Kent Street
Durham, North Carolina 27701
Telephone (919) 489-7486
Fax (919) 493-5668
www.cap-press.com

Printed in the United States of America

Contents

Table of Practice Notes

Preface

When I first began teaching lawyering skills in 2008, I had been a practicing transactional attorney at major international law firms for more than 10 years. I was immediately struck by how most courses—and the law school curriculum in general—were focused primarily on litigation, and by how little I had been aware of what I was missing when I was a law student. This was especially true of skills-based courses. Yet, almost half of law students go into transactional practice after graduation, often with little insight or exposure to what transactional practice even is.[1]

In addition, I felt more emphasis was needed on preparing our students to communicate effectively in the increasingly globalized practice of law. Lawyers of today—especially transactional lawyers—frequently represent clients in transactions that span different legal systems, cultures, and languages. To succeed in this environment, they need to bring with them into practice a minimum level of cross-cultural competence.

I set about creating an upper-division transactional lawyering-skills course, called Advanced Legal Writing for International Business Lawyers, to address this perceived gap in course offerings. The course, which I was gratified to find proved to be extremely popular with both J.D. and international LL.M. students, evolved into the idea for this book.

This book is intended primarily to serve as a template and principal text for professors interested in teaching a simulation-based advanced legal writing or lawyering skills course. But it might be equally useful as supplemental reading for a business-law-oriented practicum or clinic, or any other business-law class on topics such as international business transactions, M&A, negotiations, and contract drafting as a guide to some of the practical aspects involved in business law and cross-border transactions. It can also serve as a useful reference guide for junior lawyers as they enter practice.

This book does not presume students will have taken business organizations or other prerequisites. Thus, it adapts well to teaching both J.D. and international LL.M. students. When I teach my course, I typically hold half of the spaces in the course for international LL.M. students.

What makes this book unique is its holistic approach: from the first chapter, the reader is immersed into the role of a first-year associate, exposed to realistic matters in the form and substance a junior lawyer will likely encounter in practice. It goes beyond the technical aspects of legal writing or contract drafting in the abstract to expose the

---

1. Lisa Penland, *What a Transactional Lawyer Needs to Know: Identifying and Implementing Competencies for Transactional Lawyers*, 5 JOURNAL OF THE ASSOCIATION OF LEGAL WRITING DIRECTORS 118, 118 (Fall 2008).

reader to writing, thinking, and problem-solving in the context of transactional lawyering as a whole. Becoming a competent transactional lawyer requires more than being able to draft a contract or a client letter (although these are of course important skills); it requires a shift in viewpoint and overall approach.

As much as it can, this book takes the student reader out of the classroom and into a simulated law-firm environment. It promotes learning through doing, practice over theory, and understanding through context. Although the book focuses primarily on a law firm context and the role of a junior associate at a law firm, the concepts and skills apply to any context.

Law school trains law students to think like—and even as—lawyers, but not necessarily as transactional lawyers. My hope is that this text fills this critical gap for law students and others interested in transactional or business law.

I could not have created the course that was the genesis for this book without what I learned from pioneers in the field of transactional lawyering and global legal skills. Sincere thanks to those who forged the path and inspired me to write this book: Tina A. Stark, Richard K. Neumann Jr., Mary-Beth Moylan, Cynthia Adams, Mark Wojcik (and the wonderful Global Lawyering Skills conference he has created), Alicia Alvarez, Paul Tremblay, Deborah McGregor, Elizabeth Fajans, Shannon Trevino, and Therese Maynard.

I would also like to thank Carolina Academic Press's anonymous reviewers for their many insightful comments; Kristen Konrad Tiscione, for sparking my interest in legal writing while I was a student in her class at Georgetown Law; my husband, Kevin, for telling me I should write a book; and Carol McGeehan, for convincing me I could.

Finally, I am grateful to the many students who have taken my classes over the years and who have taught me so much.

About This Book

The primary objectives of this textbook are to provide you with practical insight into transactional lawyering and to help you learn the skills necessary to effectively communicate in this practice setting, such that you will be able to confidently apply and adapt these skills to any situation or assignment. In completing the exercises in this textbook and other tasks assigned by your instructor, you will learn to think and act *as* a transactional lawyer. So, when the partner calls you into her office on day one, you are ready.

Integrated Approach: Communication, Knowledge, and Problem-Solving

Being a transactional lawyer requires more than knowing the substantive law or having theoretical or actual knowledge of business. It involves several integrated components—a cocktail consisting of one part communication, one part substantive knowledge, and one part problem-solving. The accomplished transactional lawyer blends each of these attributes into every interaction, whether with a partner or senior associate, the client, or opposing counsel.

A transactional lawyer who is an expert in a substantive area of law will not be able to provide her client with the best advice if she is unable to effectively communicate what the law is and how it applies to the client. Similarly, a naturally proficient writer will not be much help to his client if he does not have a firm understanding of the underlying law or legal issue. And the best legal knowledge and communication skills are of little value if the lawyer cannot appreciate the practical consequences of any given legal advice.

In our increasingly globalized world, one additional ingredient to the recipe for being an effective transactional lawyer exists that is often overlooked: cross-cultural competency. Lawyers of today, especially transactional lawyers, frequently represent clients in transactions that span different legal systems, cultures, and languages. Junior lawyers must be prepared to adapt their communication skills to any context, whether helping a client in Texas negotiate a transaction with a New York company, representing a California manufacturer in the acquisition of a factory in Malaysia, or assisting an Irish software company conduct its initial public offering in the United States.

Experiential Approach: Learning through Simulation

This book uses simulations to replicate the experience of a first-year associate in transactional practice at a law firm, exposing you to the types of transactions, demands, and forms of communications you will likely encounter as a new lawyer, whether you are part of a big law firm, in-house counsel team, boutique firm, or other setting.

In addition to building concrete drafting and other skills, the simulations your instructor will guide you through are designed to help you learn what questions to ask and have the confidence to approach any assignment.

Although we will touch on contract drafting concepts, this text focuses on written and oral communication skills in the broader sense. You will learn how to translate and comment on contracts, but also how to draft emails, office memoranda (formal and informal), client letters, comment letters, and bullet point lists, and to engage in discussions and meetings with partners, clients, and opposing counsel.

Holistic Approach: Learning in Context

From the first chapter, you will be immersed in the role of a first-year associate, exposed to realistic matters in the form and substance you will likely encounter in practice. This text goes beyond the technical aspects of legal writing or contract drafting in the abstract to expose you to writing, thinking, and problem-solving in the context of transactional lawyering as a whole—to being a "practice-ready" first-year lawyer.

Emphasis on Transactional Law

The emphasis of this book is on transactional lawyering. Chapter 1 examines in more detail what we mean by transactional lawyering, and how it differs from other types of law practice. Many of the skills focused on in this text are important for any kind of lawyer. But we examine each of these skills through the lens of a transactional lawyer.

Focus on Law Firm Setting

The general premise of this book asks you to assume you are an associate at a law firm. I recognize that many of you may choose alternate career paths. However, using a law firm setting facilitates exploring a wide range of transactional lawyering activity and provides valuable exposure and insight, whatever your ultimate path. References to junior *associates* can in most cases be substituted equally with junior *lawyers*.

How to Get the Most Out of This Book

If you are reading this textbook as part of a law school course, I recommend completing the assigned reading for each week prior to that week's class, as this will help you more easily follow the in-class discussion.

As you come across terms or concepts with which you are not familiar, refer to the Practice Notes located at the end of each chapter. You may also want to refer to the Glossary, for definitions of key terms. or Appendix A, which contains Practice Area Overviews that provide summaries of selected practice areas, for a deeper understanding of the materials and additional practical insight and explanation.

Try to complete as many of the In-class Exercises as possible and consider each of the Questions for Discussion as you go through each chapter (unless otherwise directed by your instructor), as these are designed to illustrate and clarify the theoretical discussion.

At the end of each chapter, you will find either a Simulation Exercise or Writing/Negotiation Project. The Simulation Exercises are designed to reinforce the materials covered in that chapter. The Writing and Negotiation Projects ask you to delve deeper into the subject matter and are designed to be completed over several weeks using materials that will be provided to you by your instructor.

PART I

Fundamentals

Chapter 1

....

Overview of Transactional Practice

This chapter defines what we mean by transactional practice. It starts by identifying the scope and hallmark characteristics of transactional practice and goes on to explore the diverse range of activities that are performed by transactional lawyers, as well as the numerous practice areas that fall under the transactional-practice umbrella.

By the end of this chapter, you will be able to:

- Demonstrate knowledge of what transactional practice is — and is not
- Recognize the scope and breadth of transactional practice
- Differentiate among typical transactional lawyering activities

....

It's your first day as a summer associate—or perhaps as a newly hired first-year associate—in a transactional practice group at a major law firm. One of the senior partners asks you to stop by her office so that she can bring you up to speed on a transaction she is working on.

As you are reading this text, you've already accomplished one or possibly two years of law school. Or you may have already earned a law degree from another country. You may or may not already have had some work experience. But how prepared are you for that meeting with the senior partner? Do you have the necessary communication skills to walk into the partner's office and inspire her confidence in your ability to complete whatever task she assigns? Are you going to be familiar with the context? Will you understand what your role is and how it fits into the transaction as a whole?

....

What Is Transactional Practice?

To be effective in transactional practice, you need to understand what transactional practice encompasses. To do this, we first must define what we mean by a "transaction." Most of us have a common understanding of the term: every time we buy something, or exchange something of value, we are engaging in a transaction. For example, if I agree to give my daughter an ice cream if she cleans her room, I am entering into a transaction (albeit probably not a smart one from a parenting perspective). The defining characteristic is that we have each agreed to give something in exchange for something else.

The definitions of "transaction" in MERRIAM WEBSTER include the following: "something transacted; especially: an exchange or transfer of goods, services, or funds . . . an act, process, or instance of transacting . . . [or] a communicative action or activity involving two parties or things that reciprocally affect or influence each other."[1]

In the legal or business context, the quintessential example of a transaction is a deal; transactional lawyers often refer to themselves as "deal lawyers." Large deals between public companies are frequently in the news: mergers, acquisitions, and joint ventures are all common forms of deals.

Deals are business agreements negotiated between parties for their mutual benefit. They are a form of transaction and make up a large part of transactional practice. But not all transactions are deals. A deal connotes an element of negotiation. For example, if I enter a store and purchase a product, I am engaging in a transaction. But it is not really a deal unless I start negotiating for a lower price.

Hallmark Characteristics of Transactional Practice

Transactional practice involves transactions. But what does it mean to *practice* in this area? A transactional lawyer does not *transact*—that is the role of the actual parties to the transaction. What does a transactional lawyer do? The following characteristics help define what it means to practice transactional law. Transactional practice is:

- *About communication.* A transaction is a communicative action. It follows that transactional practice is about facilitating communication. This communicative function is the cornerstone of transactional lawyering, and the central focus of this text. To be an effective transactional lawyer is to be an effective communicator.

- *A distinct form of lawyering activity.* Transactional lawyering is distinct from other forms of legal practice. The foundational skill set for all lawyers is the same: the ability to identify legal issues, engage in critical thinking, research and analyze legal doctrine, and apply that legal doctrine to specific facts. But not all lawyering activity is the same. Beyond this basic paradigm, the skills, knowledge, acumen, and mindset required of lawyers in different practice areas are more nuanced.

  The Cambodians have an expression: "same same but different." When you ask for one thing, say a blue piece of cloth, and they offer you a green piece of cloth, they assure you that it is "same same but different." The equivalent can be said of lawyering in different practice areas: it's all somewhat the same, but also different. The types of legal issues that arise, the lawyer's role, and even the type of client are all influenced by the area in which the lawyer is practicing. This is perhaps most apparent when comparing litigation to transactional practice. The litigator and transactional lawyer often have very different perspectives.

> *Illustration:* **Transactional Practice versus Litigation Practice Perspective**
>
> CleanCo, Inc., a manufacturer of soaps and lotions, is interested in expanding its business to include perfumes. CleanCo's main competitor, ScentCo, Inc., has a successful line of proprietary scents based on the extract of certain tree bark. CleanCo is working on developing a scent derived from jacaranda tree extract but has not had much success. It decides it needs more expertise and starts discussions with ScentCo's head of research and development, Sam Sniff.
>
> Sniff informs CleanCo that he signed a noncompete with ScentCo that he believes would prevent him from working for CleanCo. CleanCo calls a litigation attorney and asks for advice about the risk involved in violating the noncompete. The litigation

---

1. MERRIAM WEBSTER, available at http://merriamwebster.com (last visited Sept. 12, 2018).

attorney will likely start by examining the facts—in this case the language of the non-compete and the relevant circumstances—and then compare the facts to those in precedent cases to predict the potential outcome if ScentCo were to seek to enforce the noncompete against Sniff.

In sum, the attorney would be predicting who would win, based on the parties' past actions. Traditionally, when we talk about common law legal analysis, this is the paradigm we are referring to: the more similar the facts to those in precedent cases (and the more cases there are), the more likely the result will be the same as in those precedent cases (or vice versa).

Now let's assume that instead of seeking to recruit Sniff, CleanCo decides to approach ScentCo about a possible joint venture. CleanCo calls its law firm and speaks with a transactional lawyer. Where does the transactional lawyer start? She starts by ascertaining the facts: what, if any, terms have the parties discussed, what would be included in the venture, and other issues.

But that's where the similarity ends. She does not need to compare the parties' past actions to precedent. In fact, little relevant past actions or precedent will exist. Nor does she need to predict who will win. Rather, she needs to look *forward* to determine what actions to take to best achieve her client's future goals.

- *Focused on the goal of "win-win."* The example above also illustrates the mutual gain aspect of transactional lawyering. This characteristic is relatively easy to grasp: parties enter into a transaction because they each believe they will derive some benefit. By contrast, in litigation, one party's win generally means the other's loss. Situations do arise in litigation where both parties "win" to some extent. For example, in a case with multiple claims, some may be decided in one party's favor and some the other, or the parties may reach a settlement. But the mindset of litigation at the outset tends to be focused on victory to the other party's detriment, whereas in transactional practice winning is not viewed as being mutually exclusive.

  A simple analogy illustrating this distinction can be made to a slice of pizza. In litigation, both parties are arguing over who gets the last slice. Typically, the winner gets the slice and the loser gets nothing (unless they can reach a settlement and they each get half). In the transactional context, the parties are looking for exchange or compromise. For example, the person who gets the last slice must do the dishes for the next two days. Both parties walk away feeling as if they "won" something and are mutually satisfied with the result. Of course, some crossover exists. Let's go back to the settlement scenario where each party gets half of the last slice. Does a settlement look more like a litigation matter, where one party loses and the other wins, or more like a transaction, where both parties negotiate for mutual gain? The answer is: a little of both.

- *Forward-looking.* Another critical characteristic of transactional practice is that it is forward-looking. A forward-looking approach may not be intuitive to most law students because of how they learn about the law and legal reasoning. Most substantive knowledge in law school (at least in the United States and other common law jurisdictions) comes from reading cases, which arise in litigation. This creates two issues. First, by limiting the context to litigation, this approach distorts the law student's understanding of how law is applied outside of a litigation context. Second, it encourages the student to look backward to predict how the law will be applied.[2]

  In transactional practice, not only will many of the issues confronting the transactional

---

2. Alicia Alvarez & Paul R. Tremblay, Introduction to Transactional Lawyering Practice 3 (2013).

lawyer not have been litigated, but they will not yet have arisen. The transactional lawyer is less constrained by the past; the focus generally is on what actions the parties should take going forward to reach a desired result. This is not to say that the transactional lawyer does not engage in legal research or common law analysis. For instance, in the joint venture scenario discussed above, the transactional lawyer may want to look at cases on the enforceability of joint venture agreements to guide her drafting of the transaction documents. But the overall emphasis is on what the parties can do going forward to achieve their objectives, and on anticipating and avoiding potential future issues.[3]

Put another way, case law can tell you what happens if a party refuses to pay the purchase price in a contract, but not how to negotiate the purchase price.[4] Accordingly, as we will see in later chapters, in advising a client on a transactional matter, the transactional lawyer must develop skills beyond traditional legal analysis.

- *Voluntary in nature.* Another hallmark of transactional practice is that the parties come together voluntarily, out of a desire for a mutually satisfactory result.[5] This is not always the case in other practice areas such as litigation (where often the party being sued becomes involved against his will).

- *A form of advocacy.* The underlying objective in representing a client in a transaction is to generate value and minimize the risk of conflict. In this way, transactional practice is still a form of advocacy, and the transactional lawyer still needs to zealously represent the best interests of her client.

- *A problem-solving activity.* Finally, and perhaps most important, transactional lawyering is about problem solving. It's about understanding your client's wants and needs, the other side's concerns, and finding a mutually satisfactory result that maximizes the benefit and minimizes the risk for your client. This brings us full circle to the other characteristics of transactional practice: it is difficult to solve your client's problems (or fully understand what needs to be solved) without effective communication, forward-looking analysis, and seeking to maximize value and minimize conflict.

What Transactional Practice Is Not

Transactional practice can also be defined by what it is not. Transactional practice is not litigation. The orientation in a litigation scenario is retrospective. It's important to know what happened in the past to develop a theory of the case. The focus is on the facts that have already occurred and what they evidence as having happened. It's about telling a story. In transactional practice, the orientation is fundamentally different. While transactional lawyers do not disregard the past, it can be less determinative of outcome. The facts are the client's goals, issues, and any agreed terms. As we will explore, the way you will use these facts in transactional practice is very different from a litigation context.

Transactional practice is also not a zero-sum game. In an adversarial situation, for one person to win, the other must lose. In transactional practice, both sides win; the result of a transaction is greater than its parts.

Transactional practice is not limited to contract drafting, although drafting, reviewing, and negotiating contracts and agreements form an integral part of what a transactional lawyer does, and represent a common medium through which transactional lawyers communicate.

---

3. *Id.* at 4.

4. Case law may be instructive in drafting the provision so that it will be enforceable, such as suggesting specific terms of art or avoiding specific ambiguity, but likely will be unhelpful in formulating the exact deal terms you are looking to create.

5. Alvarez, *supra* note 2, at 1.

Finally, both the lawyer and client should understand that transactional practice is not a guaranty that conflict will not arise. Rather, it is an exercise in identifying, anticipating, preventing, and overcoming hurdles.

Transactional Law Clients

Another distinguishing mark of transactional practice is the nature of the clients. Because of the win-win focus of transactional law practice, clients enter into a transaction expecting to leave it happier than when they entered. This affects the relationship you will have with your client. In addition, the parties on either side of a transaction often will have an ongoing relationship. Your representation may continue beyond the initial transaction, morphing over time. For example, you may represent a start-up company with its initial fundraising. Upon completion of the financing, the two parties—the company and the initial investors—will continue to have a relationship. Your role will shift from advising on the financing to perhaps helping the company with employment agreements, vendor and customer contracts, real estate, and other ongoing corporate matters.

Typical Transactional Lawyering Activities

What constitutes a transaction includes an extremely broad range of activities—from deals such as mergers, asset sales, and joint ventures, to regulatory compliance or essentially any form of agreement or promise. Transactional practice is equally broad in scope, encompassing many practice areas. Some examples include corporate, tax, real estate, entertainment law, intellectual property law, securities, capital markets, finance, banking, employment, regulatory compliance, trusts and estates, and mergers and acquisitions, to name a few. Can you think of any other examples? Although each of these can be quite specialized areas of practice, they all fundamentally involve transactions of one form or another. This means that each of these practice areas draws on overlapping fundamental skills and tasks. Some examples of typical tasks include:

- *Due diligence.* Due diligence is conducted in a variety of transactions, including corporate, securities, real estate, and merger and acquisition transactions. Due diligence involves identifying and reviewing documents to ascertain the accuracy and completeness of representations and warranties made by the parties regarding a transaction, identifying potential risks, and managing that risk. The scope and form of due diligence depends on the type of transaction and which party you represent. For example, if you are representing a buyer who is looking to purchase all the operating assets of a sports-drink manufacturer, what information would likely be important in confirming the value of what your client is acquiring? If the sports drinks are based on a proprietary recipe, would you want to confirm the seller's rights to that proprietary information? If so, what documentation would you likely want to examine? Due diligence is discussed in greater depth in Chapter 11 and in the Practice Notes in Chapter 8.

- *Drafting, reviewing, and negotiating contracts or other agreements.* Contracts and other written agreements form a significant part of what transactional lawyers do. Virtually all transactional practice areas involve some form of contract drafting and negotiation.

- *Regulatory review and compliance.* Transactional lawyers may also be responsible for monitoring, reviewing, and complying with regulatory requirements. For example, securities lawyers must ensure that any offering of securities complies with relevant securities laws, and will also be responsible for preparing and coordinating any required filings with the relevant regulatory bodies. Employment lawyers will often be called upon to advise on compliance with labor laws and other regulatory requirements. Tax is another example of a transactional practice area heavily dependent on regulatory expertise.

- *Entity formation and corporate governance.* Business transactions are largely engaged in by entities. Thus, entities tend to make up a significant part of a transactional lawyer's clients. In addition to seeking advice on specific transactions, these entities will often look to their transactional lawyer to assist with the legal aspects of being an entity, such as advising on board of directors and shareholder matters and preparing corporate filings. In other instances, the transactional lawyer will assist in forming the entity or a new subsidiary in connection with a proposed transaction.

- *Coordinating the deal process.* Whether drafting and maintaining a formal closing checklist in an M&A deal or keeping track of documents and signatures in a securities filing, the transactional lawyer is often in the role of general contractor, responsible for overseeing the various components and parties involved in the transaction. In a complex acquisition, this may mean coordinating review and input from more specialized lawyers and other professionals, such as employment law experts, accountants, or tax lawyers.

- *Communicating with the client.* Communicating with the client is a critical part of being a transactional lawyer. It can take many forms—from letters, in-person meetings, and conference calls, to emails and texts.

"Big-Law" versus Small Firm Practice

Do these typical activities vary based on the size of the law firm? It depends. Although the types of tasks tend to fall into the same categories, the size of the law firm and how it is structured can impact the scope of each lawyer's expertise and how a client project is assigned. For example, in a large firm with delineated practice groups, you may be assigned to a specific practice area and will develop a deep expertise in that one area. When a client project comes in, the lead partner on the transaction will staff the project based on what area of expertise is needed.

Recall CleanCo and its proposed joint venture with ScentCo. At a large firm, an M&A lawyer might take the lead on drafting the joint venture agreement, while a lawyer from the employment law practice area might draft any needed employment agreements or advise on any employee-related issues. Someone from the tax department may be brought in to advise on tax issues. Each lawyer will work on their discrete piece of the transaction, with the lead partner coordinating the team.

In other firms, you may be part of a general corporate department that handles all types of transactions and may not have the same level of siloed subject-matter expertise. In smaller firms, you might have one lawyer who takes the lead on all aspects of the transaction, perhaps with the assistance of one or more junior associates. Even in a smaller firm, however, it is common practice (and probably advisable from an ethics standpoint) to bring in specialists to review and perhaps draft and negotiate specific documents or provisions. Instead of relying on in-house capabilities, the smaller firm will likely outsource this review to another small firm or independent lawyer. A smaller firm may not have an intellectual property or tax lawyer, as it may not have enough intellectual property or tax business to keep a specialist busy full time. But it will likely have a relationship with another firm that specializes in intellectual property or tax that it can bring in to consult.

For purposes of the simulations and exercises throughout this text, I have assumed the reader is a general corporate associate at a law firm. However, the techniques and skills these exercises seek to hone are applicable to any context, whether you start as a junior tax associate at a large firm, a small-firm corporate generalist, or part of an in-house legal team. The substantive law and issues you will deal with may vary, but the goal of this text is to help you develop skills that you are able to adapt to any transactional practice setting.

FOR DISCUSSION:

1. Can you think of types of transactions that you have encountered? What about a lease for an apartment? Is that a form of transaction? Is it a deal? What about employment contracts?

2. Many law firms have designated separate departments (also known as practice areas). Some examples of common departments are corporate, capital markets, real estate, tax, antitrust, litigation, appellate litigation, employment law, trusts and estates, and intellectual property. Which of these do you think involve transactions? Can you think of some of the transactions you might encounter in any of these practice areas?

3. Assume you have been practicing for four years advising clients who have developed software applications in negotiating software license agreements with end users. You have been contacted by a potential client who wants help negotiating a license for certain trademark and branding rights relating to a fashion line. Are there any ethical issues? What if you are approached by a potential client who needs help negotiating the acquisition of a software developer?

Exercise 1.1

Work in pairs to consider the following two scenarios and the questions that follow:

Scenario 1: Your client owns a small business that is expanding and rents some office space to house its growing number of employees. One week after your client moves into the space, the landlord rents the space directly above to a music studio. The noise is making it impossible for your client's employees to get their work done.

Scenario 2: Your client owns a small business that is expanding and wants to rent some office space to house its growing number of employees. It has found what it thinks is the perfect space and comes to you to help it negotiate the lease.

In each scenario:

    What is the legal issue you need to analyze?

    What is your first step?

    What is your goal?

    What is the lawyer's role in each of these scenarios? How is it the same? How is it different?

PRACTICE NOTES

Sorting through Common Practice Areas

We talk about securities law, capital markets, and mergers and acquisitions as common practice areas, but what are they and how are they related? Securities law deals with the legal aspects of holding, buying, selling, and disclosing ownership interests in companies (referred to as securities). Securities can be made up of equity, debt, or something in-between.[6] The quintessential form of security is

---

6. Section 2(a)(1) of the Securities Act of 1933, as amended, defines the term "security" as "any note, stock, treasury stock, security future, security-based swap, bond, debenture, evidence of indebtedness, certificate of interest or participation in any profit-sharing agreement, collateral-trust certificate, preorganization certificate or subscription, transferable share, investment

shares of stock.[7] The principal regulatory agency governing the buying and selling of securities in the United States is the Securities and Exchange Commission (SEC). Capital markets typically encompass any type of corporate financing (raising money for operations or specific projects), including the offering and sale of securities. Practitioners in this field typically represent entities ("issuers") that want to issue securities to raise money (referred to as "capital"), holders of securities seeking to sell their securities, or investment banks that underwrite and sell securities on behalf of issuers. Mergers and acquisitions—or M&A—involves at its essence the buying and selling of companies, businesses, assets, or securities. Each of these practice areas contains a myriad of transaction types and issues. For a more detailed discussion of each of these, refer to the Practice Area Overviews in Appendix A.

Ethical Considerations in Being a "Jack-of-All-Trades" Transactional Lawyer

The rules of professional responsibility in most jurisdictions require that a lawyer have a minimum degree of competency to represent a client. Rule 1.1 of the California Rules of Professional Conduct,[8] for instance, states that "A lawyer shall not intentionally, recklessly, with gross negligence, or repeatedly fail to perform legal services with competence." Rule 1.1 defines "competence" in any legal service as applying the "(i) learning and skill, and (ii) mental, emotional, and physical ability reasonably necessary for the performance of such service."[9]

Rule 1.1 goes on to state that competency can be achieved by "associating with or, where appropriate, professionally consulting another lawyer whom the lawyer reasonably believes to be competent," or by "acquiring sufficient learning and skill before performance is required."[10]

Because of the broad scope of transactional practice, much of what we do as transactional lawyers to satisfy the competency standard, especially for those of us working in smaller firms or in-house, is to "acquire sufficient learning and skill" through researching the substantive area(s) of law relevant to a transaction, learning from precedent documents, or bringing in specialized counsel, such as tax or employment counsel. Junior associates, in addition, will often rely on consultation with more senior attorneys within the firm.

At its core, the competency standard recognizes that lawyers are trained to solve problems and to think about how the law is applied to any set of circumstances; every deal is a new deal in some way. Thus, even if you are more comfortable with a given area through repeated exposure, this does not mean you cannot be competent in other areas. But this does not alter the fact that, as transactional lawyers, each time we start on a new transaction, we have a duty to ensure we have acquired sufficient knowledge to be competent to advise the client.

Conclusion

Transactional practice is broad in scope, encompassing diverse practice areas, from real estate to securities laws; from intellectual property to commercial transactions. What most distinguishes transac-

---

contract, voting-trust certificate, certificate of deposit for a security, fractional undivided interest in oil, gas, or other mineral rights, any put, call, straddle, option, or privilege on any security, certificate of deposit, or group or index of securities (including any interest therein or based on the value thereof), or any put, call, straddle, option, or privilege entered into on a national securities exchange relating to foreign currency, or, in general, any interest or instrument commonly known as a 'security', or any certificate of interest or participation in, temporary or interim certificate for, receipt for, guarantee of, or warrant or right to subscribe to or purchase, any of the foregoing." 15 U.S. Code s.77b.

7. Although the Securities Act defines "security," it leaves some room for interpretation. *See* SEC v. Howey, 328 U.S. 293 (1946) (formulating a four-part test for determining whether an investment contract is a security). *Howey* involved the sale of tracts of land on a citrus farm and remains the gold standard for determining whether new forms of investment constitute securities. It may even determine the fate of digital tokens and other cryptocurrencies. *See also Howey, infra* Chapter 7, note 5.

8. Cal. Rules of Prof. Conduct 1.1, *available at* http:// www.calbar.ca.gov/Attorneys/Conduct-Discipline/Rules/Rules-of-Professional-Conduct/Current-Rules/.

9. *Id.*

10. *Id.*

tional practice from litigation or other practice areas is its forward-looking, problem-solving approach, as well as its focus on mutual gain. These unique characteristics underpin how a transactional lawyer should approach any transaction or task. An effective transactional lawyer must be able to communicate effectually with her client and with other lawyers in a manner that is at the same time persuasive and collaborative. In the following chapters, we will look in greater depth at the transactional lawyer's role, some of the fundamental communication skills that every transactional lawyer should master, and how to strike the correct balance when communicating in different contexts.

SIMULATION EXERCISE #1

You are a junior associate at Ryan & Associates. A senior associate comes by your office and asks you to help her with a task that she was just assigned by a partner for Simple Beverage Corp., one of the firm's existing clients.

She hands you a set of notes she took when she met with the partner, outlining concerns that Simple Beverage has regarding a distribution arrangement it is considering. She asks you to prepare a bullet point list of steps that might be taken (documents that could be drafted or actions that could be taken on behalf of the client) to address each of the concerns raised by Simple Beverage. She tells you there is no need to do any research; the goal is to just get a broad sense of what would be needed so that the partner can advise the client as to potential time/legal costs. She will take your draft set of bullet points and finalize and incorporate them into an email to the partner. She tells you that she needs you to complete the task within 48 hours.

Notes from meeting

- Our client Simple Beverage Corp. has some concerns regarding a proposed distribution arrangement with Bevco Ltd.
- Simple Beverage is a start-up company that is manufacturing a line of specialty juices and waters made with all-natural ingredients.
- Bevco, Ltd. is an established distributor of soft drinks with a well-established distribution network throughout the U.S. and Canada.
- Simple Beverage has the following concerns/questions:
  - Bevco is asking Simple Beverage a lot of questions about its business model and product. Simple Beverage wants to know if it should be concerned about giving them too much confidential information, and if there is a way to protect against Bevco disclosing Simple Beverage's information to competitors.
  - Before spending money on drafting a distribution agreement, is there a short document we can prepare that sets out the basic deal terms (price, minimum quantities, etc.)?
  - Bevco has told Simple Beverage that Bevco has distribution channels into all Canadian provinces, with warehouse facilities in at least 50 cities in Canada and the U.S. How can we be sure this is true?
  - Bevco also told Simple Beverage that Simple Beverage might need to apply for certain licenses depending on which states and/or provinces it distributes products into. How can we determine what these are and whether they would apply if Simple Beverage is limiting manufacturing operations to California?
  - Bevco is also suggested that instead of a distribution arrangement, they might want to consider forming a joint venture. Simple Beverage would be open to this but would want to get some more information on Bevco's customers and financial condition. What is the best way of going about this?

Chapter 2

· · · · · · · · · · · · · · ·

The Transactional Lawyer's Role

In this chapter, we turn to the role of the transactional lawyer. We examine the line between the business and legal aspects of a transaction, and how a transactional lawyer can add value to a business transaction. This chapter also introduces deal terminology and other concepts that a junior associate will be exposed to when entering practice.

By the end of this chapter, you will be able to:

- Differentiate between business and legal issues
- Evaluate the role of a lawyer in a business deal
- Engage in a problem-solving approach to a given legal issue
- Distinguish between advising and counseling

· ·

You have been at your new firm for about six months when you are assigned to work with a new client. The client is seeking advice relating to starting a new business providing online group financial planning services to companies and their employees. The founders of the new business are expert financial planners, having worked in the industry for many years, but are relatively inexperienced in terms of running a business. They have identified a potential investor and are looking for advice on how to proceed.

How do you know what kind of advice you should be providing this client? Is there a clear line between legal and business decisions the client will need to make? Are you competent to advise the client if you have no experience with their business?

· ·

Issues and Terms

You probably had to engage in "issue-spotting" in law school exams or identify the "Issue Presented" in a legal writing memorandum in your first-year legal writing class. For those of you who were taught legal writing using the "IRAC" paradigm, you will recall that the "I" in "IRAC" stands for "Issue."[1]

---

1. For those unfamiliar with the term, IRAC (or one of several variants, including IRREAC, CRAC, and CREEAC) is a paradigm commonly used in U.S. law schools (and in bar preparation courses) to help law students learn to approach and organize their written common law legal analysis logically and cohesively. It stands for Issue, Rule, Application, and Conclusion. The IRAC paradigm starts by having the writer identify the issue(s) to be addressed, identify and explain the relevant legal rules, apply those rules to a given set of facts, and end with a conclusion summarizing the preceding analysis. The CRAC version has the writer start with the conclusion and is commonly used in guiding persuasive writing. Chapter 6 provides a brief overview of these paradigms in the context of transactional writing.

Issues

In a transactional setting, an issue also refers to an item (a piece of the transaction) that has yet to be decided. It may not be contentious but is nonetheless something that needs to be addressed for the transaction to go ahead. Issues can be defined broadly or narrowly. For example, in the introductory scenario, one issue might be how the investor will invest in the business. How much money is he willing to contribute? What does he expect in return? More narrowly, issues such as how the money will be paid and when will need to be determined.

Terms

Once the parties have decided how an issue will be addressed, it becomes a term.[2] Terms are issues that have been decided (or at least proposed) either as a result of negotiating and deciding an open issue, or by being unilaterally proposed, in response to or in anticipation of, an issue.[3]

The agreed terms then need to be memorialized in a document. Once incorporated, they are referred to as the terms (or provisions) of the document (usually a contract or other agreement). For example, if the parties above agree that the investor will invest $1,000,000, payable in two installments of $500,000, these are terms. Perhaps the investor will propose further that the second installment will be payable only upon the business reaching specified revenue goals (sometimes referred to as milestones). In this scenario, these terms will likely be memorialized in a stock purchase agreement. Whether these terms will be legally binding (i.e., whether your client will be able to take legal action against the investor if he does not comply with these terms), and under what conditions, are additional issues that will need to be flushed out by the lawyer and converted into terms. The lawyer's role is to ensure that the terms are memorialized accurately, unambiguously, and consistent with the parties' intent (Chapter 3 examines this aspect in greater depth).

Proposed terms can sometimes generate new issues. In the example above, has the company agreed that the payment of the second installment of $500,000 be conditioned on certain milestones? The conditioning of the second payment is now a new issue. The parties' resolution of this issue will in turn likely generate new terms to be added to the agreement—clarifying, revising, or replacing the originally proposed term.

Issues and terms are inexorably intertwined, highlighting the recursive nature of negotiating a transaction. Many practitioners use "issue" and "term" interchangeably. For example, a lawyer might email his client a list of "open terms to be discussed." The key is to understand the fundamental conceptual distinction between something that needs resolution and the agreed or proposed resolution itself. In its simplest form, an issue represents the "question," and the term the "answer." An answer may generate more questions, to which more answers will be needed.

Business versus Legal Issues

As transactional lawyers, we next need to differentiate between business and legal issues.[4]

How to Distinguish between Business and Legal Issues

The dividing line between business issues and legal issues can be murky. Business issues tend to be those that relate to the commercial aspects of a transaction. For example, in an acquisition, business

---

2. Richard K. Neumann, Jr., Transactional Lawyering Skills: Client Interviewing, Counseling, and Negotiation 3 (2013).

3. In other contexts, "term" can also mean a period of time.

4. See Neumann, supra note 2.

issues might include how much is going to be paid, what is being acquired, and how the different assets are valued. In an employment contract, business issues would include the salary and the employee's responsibilities. In a lease agreement they would include the rent, the available square footage, and permitted uses. Legal issues, on the other hand, relate to how the agreed business terms are documented, protected, and enforced.

In her seminal article, *Thinking Like a Deal Lawyer*,[5] Tina Stark suggests five categories of business issues that commonly recur in transactions: money, risk, control, standards, and endgame, and that most business issues arguably fall into one or more of these categories, each with different corollary legal issues.

Why the Distinction Matters

Distinguishing between business and legal issues helps define the transactional lawyer's role. Prior business experience can certainly be advantageous and will likely help you better understand the client's issues and goals; but remember, you are being engaged in your capacity as a lawyer to provide legal advice; focusing too heavily on business issues can cause you to miss key legal issues and undermine the value of the legal services you are being paid to provide.

In addition, understanding the distinction allows the transactional lawyer to look at the transaction from the client's perspective; by separating legal issues from business issues, the lawyer is better able to recognize the practical consequences of a given legal solution, enhancing the lawyer's ability to problem-solve, a fundamental component of a transactional lawyer's role.

Initially, these two rationales seem inconsistent: on the one hand, I am saying the lawyer needs to know what the business issues are to avoid focusing on them, and on the other, I am arguing that the value of the lawyer comes from recognizing and understanding the business issues in a deal. But these are easily reconciled. The experienced transactional lawyer will recognize and anticipate the business issues and consequences that may be present or could arise in a transaction, but will also be able to identify the corollary legal issues and offer legal solutions.

As lawyers, our primary role is not to negotiate business issues (unless specifically agreed with or requested by the client) but to translate them into legal issues. For every business issue, the transactional lawyer needs to determine the corollary legal issue(s).

Identifying Corollary Legal Issues

How do transactional lawyers determine the corollary legal issue(s)? Let's take the first category of business issues the Stark article identifies: money.[6] The amount of the purchase price in an acquisition is a business issue, but how and when the purchase price is paid are typically legal issues the lawyer should address.

The degree of risk in a transaction is another business issue.[7] A risk is something that exposes a party to negative consequences. For example, the risk of liability for environmental damages caused by a manufacturing operation, or the risk that the other party will not make payments or deliver what it has agreed. The lawyer's role is to ensure adequate legal protection against each identified risk (in the form of prevention, mitigation, and remedies), while at the same time enabling the client to achieve its business goals. The lawyer needs to balance these competing interests. You can do a good job of protecting your client against a risk, but at what cost? For example, in an acquisition, a principal business risk is that the value of the assets being acquired is less than what the buyer negotiated.

---

5. Tina L. Stark, *Thinking Like a Deal Lawyer*, 54 J. Legal Educ. 223 (2004).

6. *Id.*

7. *Id.*

The best protection against this risk is to not buy the assets, but the cost would be the loss of the deal. Instead, the client will look to the transactional lawyer to identify legal mechanisms that mitigate the risk while still allowing it to proceed with the deal.

We look in more detail in Chapter 11 at some common forms of legal mechanisms (referred to commonly as protective devices) that can be incorporated when drafting a contract, including due diligence, representations and warranties, affirmative and restrictive covenants, conditions to closing, and remedies such as termination and indemnification.[8]

Determining the appropriate protective device requires the lawyer to exercise judgment as to which risks are more likely and the client's tolerance for those risks. Other factors that can determine how much and what form of protection is needed include:

- the size of the transaction (the smaller the transaction, the less is at risk);
- the relationship between the parties; and
- the severity of the potential consequences.

---

*Illustration: **Balancing Risk and the Cost of Protection***

Let's consider two different scenarios.

- In scenario 1, the client is negotiating a distribution contract for the sale of its widgets in Canada worth approximately $40,000 per year.
- In scenario 2, the client is negotiating the acquisition of a $50,000,000 manufacturing business based in South Africa.

In the first scenario, the biggest risk is likely that the distributor does not sell sufficient product. Ways to address this risk might include adding in a termination right for the client, ensuring that the contract is nonexclusive, or confirming the distribution channels through some due diligence prior to signing the agreement.

In scenario 2, the dollar amount at risk is larger, at least initially. In addition, several things could go wrong. For instance, the value of the business could be significantly less than what was bargained for, the deal could be blocked by regulatory approvals, or the business could have substantial unknown liabilities. If any of these risks materializes, the client could stand to lose a significant amount. Thus, you would likely spend more time negotiating deal protection devices in the second scenario and engaging in in-depth due diligence.

FOR DISCUSSION:

Try to come up with as many deal protection devices as you can for the above scenarios. Which of your suggested protection mechanisms are preventative? Which act more to mitigate the risk? Do any act as remedies?

---

8. See Glossary and Chapter 11 for explanations of these devices.

Addressing Other Categories of Business Issues

Other categories of business issues that can arise are whether a party should have the right or obligation to take certain action (control), and how hard the parties need to try to perform those obligations (standards).[9]

Controls, standards, and risks are interrelated. The lower the standard required to perform an action, the higher the risk of nonperformance. Conversely, the higher the perceived risk, the more control a client might want. The effective transactional lawyer will balance the client's desire for control with its tolerance for risk.

The legal issue, then, is how to qualify an obligation to mitigate the risk by defining the standard. Consider an individual agreeing to sell a piece of equipment. Is there a difference between "I will sell you this equipment in good condition" compared with "I will *use my best efforts to* sell you this equipment in good condition"? Yes; in the first iteration, if the equipment is not in good condition when the buyer takes possession, the seller bears the full risk because it assumed an unqualified obligation to deliver the equipment in good condition. In the second iteration, provided the seller used *best efforts* to protect the equipment from damage, the buyer assumes the risk that something could happen to the equipment before it is delivered. The use of the term *best efforts* qualifies the obligation of the seller and partially shifts the risk from the seller to the buyer.[10]

Additionally, what is the intended result of the transaction? What happens if one of the parties does not honor its side of the bargain? What rights does the other party have? Does the aggrieved party have the right to terminate the contract, or to walk away? Is the party entitled to damages? These are business issues. How the lawyer ensures the right to walk away or the right to receive damages are some of the corollary legal issues.

It can be helpful to think of business and legal issues as a continuum, with some issues in the realm of either business or legal, and others falling somewhere in between:

Figure 2.1

Business versus Legal Issue Continuum		
BUSINESS ISSUE	⟵————————⟶	LEGAL ISSUE
The amount of consideration	The type of consideration	Purchase price mechanism; closing mechanics
Risk of unwanted liabilities	Which liabilities are going to be expressly assumed	Scope of representations and warranties/indemnities/conditions/other protective devices
Obligations agreed to by the parties	What happens if obligation not met	Confirming the legal obligations of the parties; obligations versus rights
The ability to terminate an agreement	Reasons for terminating	Mechanism for terminating and legal consequences; conditions to closing; indemnities

---

9. *See* Stark, *Thinking Like a Deal Lawyer, supra* note 5.

10. See the discussion in Chapter 11 on contractual building blocks for a fuller understanding of how these provisions are used.

FOR DISCUSSION:

Your client, ABC, Inc., is negotiating the purchase of all the shares of stock of Target Co., a company based in the United Kingdom, for $200,000 cash. You circulated the first draft of a stock purchase agreement to Target Co.'s lawyer. Target Co.'s lawyer has responded with a mark-up of the agreement, including adding in a provision that ABC will be responsible for paying all Target Co.'s "legal and accounting fees relating to the negotiation of the transaction contemplated hereunder."

On its face, this seems to be a business issue; it goes straight to the heart of what ABC will have to pay. As the lawyer on the deal, how and what do you advise the client? Recognizing this as a business issue is the first step. But how do you solve the problem without focusing too heavily on the business issue? Let's break it down:

1. Are you qualified to advise the client as to whether this is a good or bad deal?
2. Are you qualified to advise the client as to whether they can afford to spend this money?
3. How can you help the client make this business decision?
4. What are the corollary legal issues?
5. From a legal drafting perspective, what could you suggest that might provide some additional comfort?

Exercise 2.1

Work in groups to review the following issues and determine whether each is a business issue or a legal issue. If a business issue, what might be the corollary legal issue? What would be the proposed legal solution?

- In an asset purchase transaction in which you represent the seller, the purchaser is seeking to have the purchase price paid over a two-year period instead of a lump sum at closing.
- The parties to a lease agreement want to make sure any notices under the lease are delivered via certified mail or facsimile.
- The seller of goods under a commercial contract wants the agreement to be governed by the California UCC.
- In an employment contract, the employer wants to be able to terminate the employee at any time, with or without a reason. The employee has countered this with a proposal that if he is terminated without cause, he is entitled to four months' severance.
- In an acquisition of a retail hardware business, the buyer wants to make sure that the seller bears the risk of any loss of inventory prior to closing.

Understanding the Role of a Lawyer in a Business Transaction

We now look at the role of a transactional lawyer more broadly. The effective transactional lawyer needs to listen to the client's business goals and concerns and translate them into a legal construct. But her role does not end there. The role of a business lawyer can be broken down into four components that make up the acronym S-A-N-E:

[S] Spot the Issues

The first task of a transactional lawyer is to figure out what legal issues are involved. You also need to identify the type of transaction. This will determine how it is structured and what documentation and steps are needed.

Illustration: **The Importance of Identifying the Type of Transaction**

Your client has come to your firm for advice regarding potential financing. What does that mean? Is it looking to raise money to fund operations or for a specific project? Is the client planning on issuing equity? Is it looking for a loan? Or perhaps what it is contemplating is some form of convertible debt. It could well be that the client does not have a clear idea yet of exactly what type of financing it is looking for. What is clear is that the structure and documentation for an equity financing is different from that needed for a loan, as is the negotiation process. For example, does the amount financed need to be repaid? Will the investors have the right to vote on certain decisions? Each of these can significantly impact the client's decision as to whether to proceed.

Your job is to flush out exactly what the client wants or—more precisely—needs, and determine the structure best suited to accomplish the client's goals. Only then can you begin to determine exactly what issues and steps will be relevant. Being able to distinguish between what the client wants (or says it wants) and what the client needs, and to effectively solicit the right information from the client to reconcile the two, are critical transactional lawyering skills that we will explore in greater depth in Chapter 4 (Fundamental Techniques) and Chapter 9 (Communicating with the Client).

[A] Assess and Strategize

The next step is to assess the parties' concerns and other issues you have identified, and to strategize ways to address them to optimize the desired result. This is the **what-when-where-how-why** phase. Spotting the issues, potential or otherwise, only adds so much value. The essence of your contribution as a transactional lawyer is being able to evaluate how important an issue is to your client in the context of what it is seeking to accomplish.

Remember that transactional practice tends to be forward-looking. This means problems and issues have not necessarily arisen. The effective transactional lawyer must anticipate and predict what and how significant the issues are going to be. She also needs to anticipate and understand the legal and practical consequences of any given action.

To take the example from above, if the client decides to proceed with a loan, what will the transaction look like and what will the consequences be? Does the client understand that required repayments may adversely impact its cashflow? Are there any tax consequences, and how would these differ in an equity financing? What are the disadvantages and advantages of the two? Your task is to help the client weigh the positives and negatives of any given course of action by advising the client as to what those potential positives and negatives might be, and to generate options for the client to consider.

[N] Negotiate

Negotiation, in its broadest sense, includes a broad range of communicative activities; everything from the point at which you conceptualize the options and strategies to achieve your client's goals until those goals are achieved. Much of what we do as transactional lawyers falls into this component. The most obvious form of negotiation is when the parties are sitting at a conference table (or perhaps on a conference call) hammering out a deal point, or on a phone call or emailing with a lawyer from the other side to try to get him to accept your changes to an agreement. But negotiation also occurs any time you draft an agreement or have a conversation with the other side. It is any attempt to bring about a result through discussion.[11]

In practice, these three components of the lawyer's role are not delineated; they are recursive, often occurring simultaneously or alternately. The transactional lawyer will shift back and forth between her various roles as the transaction proceeds. The process may begin with spotting the preliminary issues and identifying an initial approach. It may then proceed to drafting a term sheet or the agreement itself. The parties will then likely go back and forth discussing and revising the terms of the agreement. In some cases, this may result in spotting new issues that will need to be negotiated or having to reassess the approach.

[E] Execute

All the issue spotting, assessing, strategizing, negotiation, and documentation will not matter if the deal is not properly executed. Execution technically refers to the signing of legal documents, which then must be "delivered" to the other side. From the lawyer's perspective, it also encompasses everything needed to ensure the deal is properly carried out to completion.

For example, in an acquisition structured as an asset purchase, in addition to the asset purchase agreement that must be signed by both the buyer and the seller, what else needs to happen to effectively transfer the assets from the seller to the buyer? Most likely, you will need to prepare and have executed an assignment and assumption agreement. You may also need to obtain approvals and ensure the transfer of the purchase consideration. It is the transactional lawyer's role to ensure that these necessary elements are prepared and finalized in compliance with all applicable legal requirements.

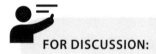

FOR DISCUSSION:

A client is starting a new business. It has received checks from three friends who are willing to invest in the business, and has meetings planned next week with potential customers. The client wants to be able to cash the checks so that it can start to hire employees in anticipation of securing a contract with the potential customers. Applying the SANE construct, what do you need to do? What are some of the potential issues? What options are available? What, if anything, needs to be negotiated at this point?

Adopting a Problem-Solving Approach

We have talked about the role of the transactional lawyer in terms of its various aspects: spotting issues, assessing and strategizing how to proceed, negotiating, and executing the transaction. Let's turn now to *how* you should approach each of these aspects.

As you saw in Chapter 1, transactional lawyering has distinctive characteristics, including commu-

---

11. Definitions of negotiate in the OXFORD ENGLISH DICTIONARY include: to "obtain or bring about by discussion[;]" to "try to reach an agreement or compromise by discussion[;]" and "to find a way over or through [an obstacle]." OXFORD ENGLISH DICTIONARY, *available at* https://en.oxforddictionaries.com/definition/negotiate.

nication, problem-solving, and forward-looking analysis. These fundamental characteristics guide how we, as transactional lawyers, approach any transaction.

Let's examine how these characteristics inform the transactional lawyer's approach using the following scenario. Assume you represent a client who is contemplating entering a lease for premises in which to operate a vegan café. The premises are in a small strip mall comprised of eight different storefronts. The client is considering this location because there are no other food outlets in the mall, no other vegan or vegetarian restaurant options exist nearby, and of the seven other tenants in the strip mall, one is a yoga studio and one is a pet clinic; the client expects to generate a fair amount of foot traffic from these two businesses alone. The client is not sure it would generate sufficient revenues in this location if it had to compete with another health-food restaurant. The landlord has told your client that it does not to rent to businesses that compete with its existing tenants. The client asks you to review the lease before it signs. You need to spot the issues, assess and strategize as to options, and negotiate any changes to the lease. What should your approach be?

Problem-Solving: Translating Business Issues into Legal Terms

The business issue for the client is clear: it does not want to have to compete for customers. But how do transactional lawyers ensure the client is protected? How do we solve this problem? We need to translate the business issue and the parties' discussions into legal terms.

Is it enough that the landlord has told your client that it does not rent to competing businesses? What is the landlord doing? He is making a promise that a fact is true. How do we document this in a way that provides our client with a legal remedy in the event the landlord is not telling the truth? We need to translate the promise into legal contractual terms. In this case, we need to include a *representation and warranty* in the lease that states that the landlord represents and warrants that it does not permit competing businesses to enter into leases concurrently. If this later turns out to be false, the client will have a legal remedy for breach of the representation and warranty.

The client did not ask you to draft a representation. Your job as the lawyer is to translate what the client wants into what the client needs in legal terms: to identify the corollary legal issue.

Communication and Forward-Looking Analysis

What other legal protection might you want to add to the lease to mitigate the risk? Could we have the landlord agree categorically that it will not lease any premises to a competing business during the term of our client's lease? This is called a covenant (a type of agreement). So now we have the landlord agreeing not to do something to change the accuracy of the fact it is representing. But does this raise any other issues? What constitutes a competing business? We need to include a definition of competing business to eliminate this issue. What does our client consider to be a competing business? Is there anything else our client is concerned about? What possible future issues can be preempted?

Advising versus Counseling

We have referred generally at this point to advising and counseling the client. But what is the difference between advising and counseling? Although the two terms are used somewhat interchangeably, they serve different purposes, in much the same way a college advisor performs a different role than a college counselor. In the college context, an advisor's role is primarily informational, whereas a counselor helps the student pinpoint and address specific problems.[12] In the same way, when a lawyer

---

12. *See* Terry Kuhn, Virginia Gordon, and Jane Webber, *The Advising and Counseling Continuum: Triggers for Referral,* 26 NACADA JOURNAL, 24–31, *viewed online* at http://www.nacadajournal.org/doi/pdf/10.12930/0271-9517-26.1.24) (suggesting that advising and counseling roles fall along a continuum) [last viewed Aug. 2, 2018].

advises a client, the lawyer is providing the client with information. For example, he might explain what the law requires, or what a contract provision means in terms of consequences. A lawyer counsels a client when the lawyer helps the client decide on a course of action. In either case, the lawyer is not making the decision for the client; rather, the lawyer's role is to help the client make an informed decision.[13]

Exercise 2.2

Discuss in pairs whether each of the following activities would fall under advice or counseling. Be prepared to explain why in each case. Is the issue in each case a business or a legal issue? Are you providing the client with information, a recommendation as to a course of action, or both?

1. The client asks you whether it will have to pay capital gains tax on the sale of its ownership interest in a subsidiary.
2. The client asks whether it should accept a proposal for a joint venture partner to limit the right to terminate the joint venture to termination for cause only.
3. The client asks you whether it should structure a proposed acquisition as a stock purchase or an asset purchase.
4. The client asks you what it can do to limit its liability in a proposed acquisition.
5. The client asks you if it should agree to provide a severance package to its CFO in renegotiation of the CFO's employment agreement.

PRACTICE NOTES

Use of Mark-Ups

When negotiating an agreement, lawyers typically use the redlining (also known as track changes) features available in most word-processing programs to mark their changes, comments, and suggestions directly into the draft agreement. This edited version of the draft agreement is referred to as a "mark-up." Upon receipt of the mark-up, the drafting attorney can easily view the changes and elect to accept or decline any change, or to further modify any suggested edit. The drafting attorney can choose to redline any changes to create a "cumulative mark-up" showing each party's changes (usually in a different color), or to create a "clean copy" and just track the changes as made against a prior draft. Although increasingly rare, some lawyers prefer to mark up documents by hand, and to either fax or email the comments in pdf form. The downside to this—or upside, depending on which side you find yourself—is that the other person cannot directly incorporate or modify the comments, but must manually input them into the document.

Deal Terminology: Asset and Stock Purchases

Many deals involve the buying or selling of companies or their assets. These deals, referred to collectively as acquisitions, can be structured several different ways. In an asset purchase, the buyer is acquiring from the seller a set of specified assets. An asset is any property or thing of value. It can be tangible or intangible. For example, machinery, inventory, and buildings are all tangible assets, as are

---

13. The advising-counseling continuum is discussed in greater depth in Chapter 9.

any customer or other contracts that have value. Examples of intangible assets include intellectual property rights and goodwill. In financial accounting terms, an asset is something the company owns that can provide future economic benefits and is included in the company's balance sheet.

The other common acquisition structure is a stock purchase, where the buyer acquires the shares of stock (units of ownership interest in a corporation) of a company (or if the company is an LLC or a partnership, the membership interests or partnership interests, respectively). If the buyer acquires all the outstanding shares of stock of a company, it becomes the new owner of that company (and of the assets owned by the company). If the buyer is an entity, it is referred to as the parent company.

In either structure, the process is similar: typically, the purchase agreement is negotiated and signed, but the assets or shares do not yet change hands. The parties must first assemble all the documents and other actions needed to legally transfer the assets or shares (for example, any shareholder consent, regulatory approvals, or assignments of contracts). Only once all this documentation is complete and ready to be signed does the transfer occur and money change hands. This is referred to as the *closing* of the deal. Up until this point, the assets or shares remain in the hands of the seller. When this period exists between signing and closing, the closing is referred to as a *delayed closing*. In some instances, such as when there are no significant actions to be taken to ensure legal transfer of what is being acquired, the signing and closing of the transaction can occur simultaneously.

Use of Closing Checklists

A single transaction can require numerous documents and actions to produce the desired legal effect. Clients will typically rely on their lawyers to keep track of them. The most effective way to do this is to create a closing checklist. A closing checklist is a table where you list each document and action needed to consummate a transaction. In addition to listing these items, a good closing checklist will also include a column that lists the responsible party for each item as well as any required signatures, and another column that tracks the status of each item. The checklist is updated as the deal progresses by updating the status column. See also the Practice Note in Chapter 12, and the sample closing checklist included in Appendix B.

Conclusion

A transactional lawyer wears many hats: problem-solver, advisor, counselor, scrivener, and negotiator. The transactional lawyer is the "SANE" person in the room. He or she is the person responsible for overseeing and coordinating the transaction process, both as a whole and in managing and often taking the laboring oar in completing each step of a transaction—from spotting and assessing the issues, to drafting and negotiating the legal terms. In performing her role, the transactional lawyer needs to be cognizant of the distinction between legal and business issues and to be able to effectively communicate with the client and other parties involved in the transaction. In Chapter 3, we turn to the specific skills a junior transactional lawyer can develop to effectively take on this role.

SIMULATION EXERCISE #2

You receive the following email from a partner at your firm. Prepare a response.

Julie Ryan

From: Julie Ryan jryan@ryanassoc.com
Sent: January __ 1:00 PM
To: Junior Associate
Subject: Expanding Sales into Colombia—Brainstorming ideas

Junior Associate:

We have a client (Vivitel) who manufactures components for flat-screen televisions and other similar products using proprietary patented technology. Vivitel is a major player in the U.S., with sales in almost all 50 states. However, most of its competitors also market their products overseas, allowing them to significantly increase their sales. Vivitel wants to start expanding beyond the U.S. It has heard that Colombia has a burgeoning television-manufacturing industry, with several small, family-owned manufacturers. It is thinking of expanding its sales in Colombia, with the hope of further expansion into other South American countries. I understand that Colombia has a favorable foreign investment regime, including tax incentives, free-trade zones, competitive labor rules, and strong protection of intellectual property rights. In addition, its economy has been experiencing stable, moderate growth. With over 35 million inhabitants, it is the second largest population in South America. The current exchange rate between the U.S. dollar and the Colombian peso is relatively stable at 1:3,045. Our client is concerned about reports of ongoing violence relating to drug cartels and common street crime but has heard this problem is centered in and around Bogotá, the country's capital, and that the coastal port cities (where the main free trade zones are located) report very low crime rates.

Without doing any additional research at this point, I would like you to generate some ideas about how best to accomplish the client's goal of expanding sales of its products into Colombia. Specifically, I would like you to come up with 2 possible different ways to achieve this goal (i.e., 2 different structural alternatives). Also, what are 2 possible legal issues and 2 possible business issues? Please email me with a bullet point list of what you come up with. I do not need any detailed discussion at this point; I want to use these bullet points to brainstorm. Please email me your list within 48 hours.

Thanks,
Julie

Julie A. Ryan
Ryan & Associates
299 Valley Avenue
3rd Floor
Los Angeles, CA 90009
Tel: 213-510-5000
Email: jryan@ryanassoc.com

Chapter 3

....

The Role of the Junior Transactional Associate

This chapter explores the role of a junior transactional associate at a medium- to large-sized firm. It will identify the typical activities a junior associate will likely encounter, and how she can contribute value to any transaction.

By the end of this chapter, you will be able to:

- Crystallize your understanding of the value a transactional lawyer brings to a transaction
- Articulate what makes a good junior transactional associate
- Add value to any project to which you are assigned
- Perform a task with an understanding of how it fits into the overall transaction

....

It's your first month at the firm. You have been asked by a senior associate to help him review a set of documents relating to a large deal he is working on for a partner. He informs you that the client is the borrower of a $500 million syndicated debt financing that it is in the process of negotiating. He has his assistant email you a document that is titled "Draft Indenture," with instructions to "review and summarize potential events of default." Do you know where to start? Do you fully understand the context, and how this assignment fits into the transaction as a whole? What questions might you ask the senior associate to ensure you understand your task and can perform it in a way that adds value?

....

How Do Transactional Lawyers Add Value to a Business Deal?

Much of what we are involved in as transactional lawyers relates in some degree to business. Yet most lawyers have not trained in business, ever started their own business, or worked in sales. Many of us did not take a single business course in college. What unique value can a transactional lawyer bring to a business transaction?

In the litigation context, most proceedings and documents follow specific legal doctrine and forms that require legal expertise and knowledge; for instance, how to comply with the relevant jurisdiction's civil or criminal procedure, or how to differentiate binding from persuasive legal authority. These are tasks that fall traditionally and almost exclusively in the realm of those trained in the law; in fact, unless you are representing yourself, you must be admitted to the relevant bar to appear before the court. The expertise and qualifications required in this context are thus relatively unique to lawyers, in much the same way as the expertise required to perform surgery is unique to a trained surgeon. A layperson can certainly acquire some know-how, but the results would be mixed at best.

In transactional practice, although you must be trained as a lawyer and licensed by the relevant bar to practice law, the line between engaging in business and the practice of law (and business and legal expertise) is harder to define: a businessperson may have handled enough contracts to feel comfortable negotiating her own agreements, and the Internet abounds with information on how to form an entity and fill-in-the-blank forms.[1] Of course, these do not replace the advice of a trained lawyer, but where self-help options are available, hiring a lawyer can seem an unnecessary expense. It is thus critical as a transactional lawyer to understand what value you are adding to a business transaction. From the client's perspective, why does the client need a lawyer as part of the business transaction?

We looked in Chapter 1 at the broad range of transactions you might encounter as a transactional associate, from the purchase or sale of a business and advice regarding regulatory compliance, to entity formation, negotiating employment or other agreements, to protecting intellectual property.

The value transactional lawyers can add to any of these transactions is relatively consistent, regardless of industry, practice area, or transaction type. Following are some of the qualities that differentiate a transactional lawyer and the value she brings to a business deal:

- *Cognitive and analytical skills.* As with a litigation attorney, the cognitive and analytical skills honed in law school are a fundamental aspect of the transactional lawyer's ability to add value. Being able to identify potential legal issues, engage in critical thinking, extrapolate information and discern between relevant and irrelevant details, and to research answers and solutions to problems is a unique skill set. For instance, a client with a successful business wants to expand to Internet sales. Are there any legal requirements or impediments? The client will look to its lawyer to be able to come up with the answer.

- *Experience-based knowledge and judgment.* Clients tend to rely on their lawyers' experience with similar transactions. The longer you practice, the more transactions you will be exposed to, and the better you will become at recognizing and being able to advise the client as to what is "typical" or "common" in a specific transaction, and what they should or should not try to negotiate. For example, what is a typical royalty fee? How many weeks' vacation is customary in an executive employment agreement? What period is reasonable for a noncompete in connection with the sale of a business?

- *Writing skills.* Transactional practice is, above all, an exercise in effective communication. Much of what we do as lawyers is write. Drafting contracts and other legally binding documents requires practice and skill; understanding how each provision relates to every other provision, the importance of word choice, and how the language addresses the statutory or other legal requirements, are fundamental to drafting an effective agreement that accurately reflects the parties' intent and achieves the desired result.

- *Negotiation skills.* As with writing skills, these form part of the overall ability of a well-trained transactional lawyer to communicate effectively in any context, with any counterparty. Many of our communications as lawyers, written or oral, are forms of formal or informal negotiation. The transactional lawyer must be skilled at adapting her content, tone, and style to persuade her listener (or reader).

- *Legal perspective.* Most businesspeople recognize the importance of having someone provide

---

1. For example, online companies such as LegalZoom market a range of legal documents that customers can personalize without having to necessarily hire a lawyer, including wills and trusts, business formation documents, copyright registrations, and trademark applications.

a legal perspective in a transaction. They often have a good sense of the business issues and what they want to achieve but will rely on the lawyers in the room to tell them if it can be done legally (or more often, *how* it can be done).

- *Organizational skills and attention to detail.* Transactional lawyers often serve as gatekeepers in transactions, responsible for coordinating the various aspects of a deal. The lawyer's critical thinking and training plays a role here: it gives her the ability to break down an issue or problem into discrete, logically connected parts. Training also teaches us the significance of paying attention to detail. Changes to a single word, or a misplaced comma, can prevent a contract from being enforceable.[2]

- *Reputation and integrity.* Finally, lawyers are bound by a strict code of professional responsibility and ethics. This can make it easier for the parties on each side of a transaction to trust that the other is negotiating in good faith and provides comfort in relying on information disclosed by the other party. This reliance often is documented in the form of a legal opinion.

Exercise 3.1

Work in pairs or small groups to research the following topics, using any online source:

1. How to form a special purpose company in Delaware
2. Whether an interest in a limited liability company (LLC) is considered a security under federal law and in the jurisdiction in which you are based
3. The typical break-up fee in a public company merger
4. Significant regulations governing oil and gas drilling in the U.S.

How difficult was it? How did you start? How did you narrow down the topic? How did you know how to approach this task?

What Makes a Good Junior Transactional Associate?

The qualities and skills described in the preceding section are all qualities a junior transactional associate needs to develop, but what value can you add as you develop these skills? How can you stand out to a busy partner or senior associate? The single most valuable contribution a junior associate can make is saving the partner or senior associate time. A junior associate can achieve this goal in several ways:

- *Know your partner's preferences.* Make sure you have a clear understanding of how much initiative the assigning partner or senior associate wants you to take. Does he want you to check in periodically, or only if you have questions? Is he easily accessible for questions or does he prefer you to figure things out for yourself? What role does he want you to play? Does he expect you to contact the client directly, or to go through him? Understanding how the partner views your role in the big picture is critical to understanding how to be most effective in that role.

---

2. One well-known example is a misplaced comma in a contract that resulted in a million-dollar judgment in a lawsuit between Bell Aliant and Rogers Communications. Ian Austen, *The Comma That Cost 1 Million Dollars (Canadian)*, NEW YORK TIMES (Oct. 26, 2006), *viewed online* at http://www.nytimes.com/2006/10/25/business/worldbusiness/25comma.html). Myriad other examples exist.

- *Hone your research skills.* As a junior associate, you likely will not be expected to advise the client on a complex structure, or to be the lead negotiator on a deal. But you will be expected to assist whomever that person is to be able to negotiate with complete and accurate information as to what the underlying law and facts are; your job is to arm them with that information.
  - *Identify the issue.* Research in a transactional law context is a little different than in a more traditional litigation context (with which you are likely more familiar from your first-year legal writing course). Remember that transactional practice is forward-looking. Often the problem has not yet occurred. Before you can research how to solve a problem, you need to be able to identify what the problem might be.

Illustration: **Identifying the Issue**

A client comes to your firm asking for help in suing a seller for a breach of representation arising in an asset purchase transaction. Your research mandate is apparent: you will need to research the elements needed to prove a claim for breach of representation, as well as possibly looking for cases with similar facts on which you can rely. Now, let's assume the client comes to your firm to help it negotiate an asset purchase transaction. Is it clear what needs to be researched, if anything? You first need to anticipate any problems that might arise. For example, are there any facts the client is particularly concerned with that should be addressed in the purchase agreement? If so, you may want to research language for crafting a pro-buyer provision that addresses those facts.

  - *Organize, triage, and synthesize.* Don't just give the partner what she can find herself. It is not helpful for a partner if all you do is provide a printout of a case or a link to a website. The partner's time costs too much to spend it reading lengthy cases or treatises. The partner may sometimes want to read it for herself, but don't assume she will; your job is to read the sources and synthesize the results for the partner. Your research results should be organized in such a way that the partner can easily digest the crux of the research results. She can then choose whether to review anything in more detail.
  - *Avoid unconscious assumptions.* Learn to recognize what you don't know and avoid making faulty assumptions that can misdirect your research or render it too high level to be of use. Take a step backward. For example, if you are being asked to research whether an agent of a broker-dealer needs to register as a broker-dealer, first make sure you understand exactly what the issue is. What do you need to understand? How about what is meant by a *broker-dealer*? Is there a regulatory framework that governs broker-dealers? What general area of the law is involved?[3] You might not be able to charge all this research time to the client, but conducting this type of background research will benefit you in other ways by allowing you to become more informed and to ultimately deliver a more useful product.
  - *Think outside the box.* Keep an open mind when researching an issue. You want to be precise in terms of answering the issue posed, but avoid being too literal when formu-

---

3. See the Practice Note at the end of this chapter discussing this topic.

lating your research. To take the example immediately above, why does the partner want you to research whether an agent must register as a broker-dealer? What is the underlying issue? Are we representing the purported agent or the broker-dealer? Is there a broker-dealer already in place? Is the agent an employee? Does it matter? The key here is not to go off on a tangent in your research but to avoid tunnel vision, which can lead you to produce results that are too narrow to be useful. If your answer is yes, can you expand? Are there any exceptions or specific requirements that might need further analysis to ensure your results are accurate?

See the Practice Notes at the end of this chapter for additional practical research tips.

- *Be efficient.* Efficiency is not synonymous with speed. Although efficiency can promote speed, speed does not necessarily promote efficiency, especially if it leads to carelessness or incompleteness that later needs to be corrected. An efficient junior associate is one who takes the time needed to perform a task accurately and completely while minimizing unnecessary steps or distractions and without getting "stuck in the weeds." This requires focus on the task at hand and a solid understanding of what the task is (and what it is not). This ties into the next point: understanding the big picture.

- *Take time to understand the big picture.* Make sure you understand what the overall transaction is and how your task fits into it. If you are not familiar with the type of transaction or documentation, do some research to bring yourself up to speed. It is also acceptable to ask questions to clarify where your task fits. For example: "Just so I am sure, this due diligence is relating to an asset purchase, correct?" Most partners will appreciate your attempt to understand the overall context and your effort to focus your work product on exactly what is needed. Recall the scenario in the introduction to this chapter: the associate is handed an indenture and asked to review it. What research could you perform, or questions could you ask, to improve the quality of your contribution? Do you know what purpose an indenture serves?

  Familiarizing yourself with a new topic or transaction structure takes time and can therefore seem counterintuitive if you are focused on being efficient. But taking the time to fully understand what you are doing will likely make you more efficient, especially over time. Recognize that, at the beginning, it will likely take you longer to do things. The more you can immerse yourself into the underlying topic, however, the more quickly and efficiently you will be able to conceptualize and categorize the issues.

- *Keep focused on the client.* In addition to understanding the big picture—the view from 40,000 feet—you also need to stay grounded in who you represent: who the client is, and the client's concerns, goals, and bargaining position. You may not have much interaction with the client, but you will not be efficient without some understanding of which side of the transaction you represent. Who your client is and what it wants matters in terms of the partner's purpose for having you complete a task.

---

*Illustration: **Adopting Correct Perspective***

You are asked to research and summarize whether an agent must register as a broker-dealer (see discussion above on "thinking outside the box"). If your client is the agent, the purpose is likely to determine what, if any, regulatory requirements the client will need to satisfy. If the client is the broker-dealer, it could be to advise the client as to whether it should hire an individual as an agent, or it could be to advise the client on how to structure a new broker-dealer business. Either way, you need to understand the

> big picture—what a broker-dealer is and what regulations are applicable—and whom you represent. You might organize your summary differently depending on whether the client is the agent or the broker.

- *Excel in written communication.* You can generate great research, but if you are unable to summarize your findings in an organized, logical, easy-to-read format, it will be of limited use. Writing that lacks cohesiveness or contains grammatical or spelling errors also can adversely affect the credibility of the writer. Ambiguity can result in unintended consequences. This is true of a formal memo or a quick email. In the following chapters, we will be focusing on fundamental writing skills and applying them in a variety of forms.
- *Improve your oral communication skills.* Effective oral communication requires more than the ability to express yourself verbally: it involves being aware of nonverbal cues and engaging in active listening. Oral communication skills are discussed in more depth in Chapter 8.
- *Pay attention to detail.* If the junior associate is not paying attention to detail, errors will slip through the cracks. Chances are, as a junior associate, you have less expertise, skill, and instinct than other lawyers on the team. Add value by paying attention to the details that these more experienced lawyers may miss, whether it's because they are too busy managing the client, focused on negotiating complex deal points, or because they expect you to be paying attention.

  This task is not easy. Details are not as exciting or as glamorous as talking a client through structural options or sitting down to negotiations with the other side. But these can't happen without someone keeping track of the details. A common example is where a senior associate will ask a more junior associate to review a revised draft of an agreement to make sure all the previous comments have been incorporated correctly by the other side.

  The other aspect of being detail-oriented involves how you report your research or other findings to the partner. Your job is to provide the partner with the right amount of detail to enable her to effectively advise and counsel the client. For example, in the above scenario relating to the need to register as an agent of a broker-dealer, the general rule is that, in most states, an agent must be registered. But are there any exceptions that may apply? Might this be a critical detail that if omitted could result in the partner providing the client bad advice?

- *Finally, use your best judgment.* Judgment comes with experience but, at a minimum, be aware of who you are communicating with, what their basic expectations are, what your role is, and act accordingly. If in doubt about whether to put something into an email, call a client, or circulate a draft document to the other side, don't. Busy partners do not want to constantly worry about what a junior associate might say or do; they want to work with associates who demonstrate sound judgment.

Alternatives to "Big-Law"

In describing the attributes of a junior associate, I have framed the discussion in the context of a medium-to-large law firm. But these attributes are equally important in a smaller firm or other environments. In fact, in smaller firms, the ability of a junior associate to write well and understand a deal with minimal supervision is essential: smaller firms lack the bandwidth to staff deals with layers of different levels of associates.

What may differ is who will be supervising the junior associate's work in these other environments, and how big a role the junior associate will play. But the value a junior associate is expected to contribute is the same.

Exercise 3.2

A junior partner has asked you to send him a bullet point list outlining the factors that may trigger broker-dealer registration. The partner tells you that he needs this research for a client who wants to engage a finder to assist in identifying potential investors in a real estate project the client hopes to develop.

Work in pairs to formulate responses to the following: (1) What is the big picture? (2) What is the client's likely goal? (3) What should be the starting point for your research? (4) What additional information do you need to fully understand the assignment? Once you have formulated responses to these, draft a set of bullet points that responds to the partner's request.

PRACTICE NOTES

Building Experience-Based Knowledge

A junior associate will not have much personal prior experience on which to base her advice to the client. But experience can be institutional. In a larger firm, especially, lawyers can and should draw on their collective experience, whether through sharing subject files (see Practice Note on page 107) or sending an email asking if anyone has experience with a similar set of circumstances. Lawyers also build knowledge through participating in ongoing legal education, conferences, and state bar committees. Finally, a transactional lawyer should also keep abreast of business news. Try reading business publications such as the Wall Street Journal or the Financial Times or subscribing to news feeds related to your practice area to absorb information in context.

Research Tips

You likely have spent a fair amount of time conducting legal research, either for law school classes or perhaps as a summer associate. In doing so, you probably relied on a legal research tool, such as Westlaw or Lexis, or perhaps an online practice guide, such as The Rutter Guide, Matthew Bender, or BNA. These are all excellent sources. In the transactional practice context, however, it can be more difficult to formulate an initial search, either because the issue you are trying to solve has not been litigated, or because you are still trying to anticipate what the issues might be. Thus, you may find it helpful to start with alternative sources to help you frame your search. Examples include law firm client alerts and blogs; materials published by legal organizations, such as the Association of Corporate Counsel, the American Bar Association, and the various state bars; regulatory and government agency websites, such as sec.gov and ftc.gov, or state departments of corporations or secretary of state websites. For precedent document forms, try document databases, such as Westlaw's Practical Law, onecle.com, and lawinsider.com. These are all searchable online.

Regulation of Broker-Dealers

I have used a few examples in this chapter that involve broker-dealers.[4] I use this topic as an example as it is a highly regulated yet somewhat gray area of law that often requires both traditional analysis of statutory and case law and forward-looking problem solving. The U.S. Securities Exchange Act of 1934 (the federal statute governing the secondary trading of securities in the United States, including

---

4. I use the term *broker-dealer* in this text to refer to securities broker-dealers. Brokers also exist in other contexts, such as real-estate brokers. Although some of the concepts may be similar, these other forms of brokers and the regulatory regime to which they are subject are beyond the scope of this text.

the regulation of securities broker-dealers), defines a broker as "any person engaged in the business of effecting transactions in securities for the account of others."[5]

Section 15 of the Exchange Act requires registration with the Securities and Exchange Commission (SEC) of all broker-dealers using interstate commerce or the facilities of any national securities exchange to effect transactions in securities (with certain exceptions). The Exchange Act, FINRA[6] rules, and each state's corporations code prescribe an extensive scheme of regulation for broker-dealers.

Certain Exchange Act provisions and rules apply to all broker-dealers, whereas others only apply to those required to be registered with the SEC (not all broker-dealers are required to be registered with the SEC, based on size and other factors). Issues commonly arise in determining whether someone is acting as a broker-dealer (i.e., whether that person meets the definition), and whether and to what extent the various regulations apply. The guidance on these issues is derived from a variety of sources, including statutes, case law, practice guides, and SEC no-action letters[7] and interpretive guidance, among other sources.

Conclusion

In this chapter, we looked at why clients involve lawyers in transactions and at the value a lawyer adds, whether through legal training, experience, reputation, or perspective. We then turned to look more specifically at how a junior associate can add value to a transaction despite a lack of experience. We examined the importance of honing fundamental research and written and oral communication skills, and of developing a deeper understanding of the transactional law context, the players, and the purpose of any given task. In the next few chapters, we turn to how to improve these specific skills and to practice applying them in context.

 SIMULATION EXERCISE #3

You receive the following email from a partner at your firm. Prepare a response.

Julie Ryan

From: Julie Ryan jryan@ryanassoc.com
Sent: January __ 10:05 AM
To: Junior Associate
Subject: Issue with upcoming merger

Junior Associate

I am currently negotiating the terms of the acquisition by our client of a company in Finland. The parties have not yet decided whether this will take the form of an asset purchase, stock purchase, or merger. As I expect they will want to move quickly once they do decide, I am starting to think of what representations and covenants we will want to put into the agreement. Our standard form documents typically include the following provisions. I am not sure if they are necessary in our

---

5. Section 3(a)(4)(A) of the Securities Exchange Act of 1934, 15 U.S.C. § 78c(3)(a)(4)(A).

6. FINRA (Financial Industry Regulating Authority) is a self-regulating organization (SRO) authorized by the U.S. Congress to regulate the broker-dealer industry for the protection of investors.

7. No-action letters are published responses provided by the SEC to individuals who ask the SEC to review a proposed action to determine whether the SEC would likely take enforcement action against the individual if the individual proceeded with the stated course of action. The individual is asking the SEC to confirm whether a given action violates a specific provision of the federal securities laws. These no-action letters are informative and persuasive but are nonbinding.

case. As it has been a while since I have looked at these, I would like you to summarize for me the basic requirements and applicability of each of the following regulations:

- Hart-Scott-Rodino (HSR)
- Bulk Sales
- Foreign Corrupt Practices Act (FCPA)

For your information, I have attached sample language addressing each of these regulations from our subject files. I do not want to bill the client for this, so please do not do too much research on any of these; some quick Internet research should be sufficient. I do not need you to determine whether they are applicable; I can do that.

Please get this to me within 48 hours. Email is fine.

Thanks,
Julie

Julie A. Ryan
Ryan & Associates
299 Valley Avenue
3rd Floor
Los Angeles, CA 90009
Tel: 213-510-5000
Email: jryan@ryanassoc.com

This email message and any attachments are being sent by Ryan & Associates, LLP, are confidential, may be privileged, and are for the sole use of the intended recipient(s). Any unauthorized review, use, disclosure, or distribution is prohibited. If you are not the intended recipient, please contact the sender immediately by replying to this email message and destroy all copies of this email message and any attachments.

Attachment:

Foreign Corrupt Practices Act Compliance. No Seller Party has, directly or indirectly, in connection with the Seller's business, made or agreed to make any payment to any person connected with or related to any Governmental Body, except payments or contributions required or allowed by applicable law. The internal accounting controls and procedures of Seller are sufficient to cause Seller to comply with the Foreign Corrupt Practices Act.

HSR. Seller and Buyer will each make as promptly as possible the filing it is required to make under the Hart-Scott-Rodino (HSR) Act with respect to the transactions which are the subject of this Agreement and each of them will take all reasonable steps within its control to cause the waiting periods required by the HSR Act to be terminated or to expire as promptly as practicable.

Bulk Transfer Laws. Buyer acknowledges that Seller will not comply with the provisions of any bulk transfer laws of any jurisdiction in connection with the transactions contemplated by this Agreement.

Chapter 4

....

Fundamental Writing Skills
for Transactional Lawyers

To be an effective transactional associate, you must be able to convey information as accurately, completely, and efficiently as possible. This chapter examines some of the fundamental writing skills underpinning effective legal writing. Many of these skills also apply in the litigation context; thus, you likely will have come across some discussion of these skills in your first-year legal writing course. Consistent with the general theme of this book, however, this chapter approaches these skills from the perspective of a transactional lawyer. This serves two main purposes. First, it provides a helpful review of fundamental techniques that apply to any kind of legal writing. Second, by taking these familiar concepts and reformulating them in a transactional lawyering context, it provides additional insight into the transactional lawyering paradigm.

By the end of this chapter, you will be able to:

- Recognize the role of effective communication in transactional lawyering
- Employ fundamental writing techniques to improve your writing
- Edit your own writing for conciseness, clarity, and precision
- Consciously engage in reader-centered writing

....

You recently performed some research for one of the partners at your firm. Impressed by what you found, he has asked you to draft a memo summarizing your research that he can potentially share with the client and other attorneys at the firm. This will be the first memo you have drafted at the firm. You want to make a good impression, but how are you going to synthesize 50 pages of research into a memo that will show the partner you can write well?

....

Common Forms of Communication Used by Transactional Lawyers

Perhaps the most recognizable form of written communication for a transactional lawyer is the contract. A contract is a form of agreement. Much of what a transactional lawyer does in terms of spotting and assessing issues, problem-solving, and negotiating and executing a transaction (i.e., the SANE acronym from Chapter 2) can be reduced to writing in the form of a contract or other written agreement. The written agreement is the transactional lawyer's principal tool for communicating the terms of a transaction.

There are myriad forms of agreements beyond the traditional contract, including letters of intent, term sheets, letter agreements, and memoranda of understanding, Transactional lawyers also communicate through a variety of other forms, oral and written, including:

- memoranda
- correspondence
- emails
- video conferences
- meetings
- telephone calls
- interoffice messaging applications[1]

We will be looking at each of these forms in more detail in the ensuing chapters. Regardless of form, the underlying fundamental techniques are the same.

What Is Communication?

Communication is the expression of a thought or idea. It is a process of encoding and decoding messages; of putting thoughts, ideas, and feelings into a set of symbols, such as words, to create a message (encoding), which then must be perceived and interpreted (decoding).[2] We communicate using words, but also through sounds, signs, and behaviors. Most importantly, for an idea to be communicated, it must be received by someone other than the person expressing it. Communication is a two-way street; its effectiveness turns on how accurately it is interpreted by the person receiving it.

Many things can interfere with communication between the expression of the thought by the sender and the interpretation by the recipient. At the most rudimentary level, the recipient could have trouble hearing what the sender is saying, is not paying attention, or speaks a different language. If you have ever played the game telephone, where each person whispers a message into the ear of the next person down the line until the last person announces the message, you will recall that often the message at the end bears little resemblance to the original message. This illustrates how easily an intended expression can become garbled. But more abstract interferences arise as well. For example, the recipient's own perceptions and beliefs can influence how the recipient interprets a message.

In the legal realm, miscommunication can be costly. Part of the lawyer's role is to counteract the natural interference that occurs in communication to minimize the risk of misinterpretation. We will look at how to do this in oral communications in Chapter 8.

---

1. One example of this type of messaging application is Slack (http://slack.com).

2. William B. Gudykunst and Young Yun Kim, Communicating with Strangers: An Approach to Intercultural Communication 6 (2d Ed., McGraw Hill, 1992).

Communicating Effectively in Writing: Starting with a Strong Foundation

For the remainder of this chapter, we are going to focus on improving the efficacy of written communication. Let's turn first to the three fundamental techniques of effective legal writing: clarity, conciseness, and precision.

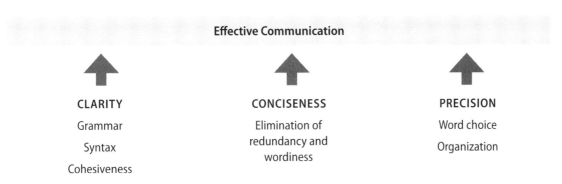

Effective Communication

CLARITY	CONCISENESS	PRECISION
Grammar	Elimination of redundancy and wordiness	Word choice
Syntax		Organization
Cohesiveness		

Clarity

Clear writing says what it means and means what it says, eliminating ambiguity or doubt in the reader's mind as to what the writer intended. It eliminates as much interference as possible so that the interpretation by the reader matches the intended meaning.

How can you increase the clarity of your writing?

Use Short Sentences

No one will ever judge you because your sentences are too short. If your reader is going to have trouble following your sentence, break it into two. The shorter your sentences, the less interference between expression and meaning. Nothing is wrong with a lengthy sentence if done correctly, but there is less room for error in a short sentence.

Compare the following sentences:

(1) *We are attaching the most recent draft of the agreement.*

(2) *We are attaching, along with the various documents signed by the parties, a copy of the most recent draft of the agreement as prepared by us in connection with the transaction.*

Sentence (1) leaves little room for misinterpretation and is much easier to follow. Sentence (2) loses the reader about halfway through; it is too long and unwieldy.

Logically Connect Sentences and Paragraphs

Some of the tools for making these logical connections include topic strings, signposts, and transitions.

• *Identify topic strings.* Consider this example from a nine-year old's journal entry:

   I like dogs. My favorite ice cream is vanilla. Today school was boring.

   What is the logical connection among these three sentences? Is there one? In her mind there may be, but it is not apparent to the reader. The problem is that the *topic*[3] of each sentence is different. Thus, the writing appears "choppy" and lacks cohesiveness.

---

3. The topic of a sentence is not the same as its subject (although it can be). Think of the topic as the first noun or noun-phrase in the sentence; what (or whom) the sentence is about. The remainder of the sentence is the *comment*—what the

To make the writing more cohesive, the topic of each sentence should logically follow from the previous sentence, either by repeating the topic or linking the topic to the comment from the prior sentence.[4] This may require reformulating the sentence, moving sentences around, or perhaps adding an introductory sentence that connects the sentences that follow. For example, the journal entry could be revised as follows:

> *Some of my favorite things are dogs and ice cream. My favorite ice cream is vanilla. I also like school, but today was boring.*

Note how the underlined topics are repeated or relate to the comment in the prior sentence. This creates a cohesive flow that guides the reader.

- *Incorporate signposts and transitions.* As with topic strings, signposts and transitions provide logical connections between sentences and paragraphs to ensure a cohesive and coherent flow. Examples include:

  - thus
  - moreover
  - therefore
  - however
  - on the other hand
  - in addition
  - finally

Each of these signals to the reader how to connect the sentences or provides a "transition" from one thought to the next, allowing the reader to understand where you are taking her next.

Exercise 4.1

Modify the following paragraph using topic strings, signposts, and transitions to make the paragraph more cohesive:

The law governing the use of finders in securities transactions is unclear. Our client has some concerns about its proposed transaction. I have researched the issue as requested. Finders can be used only in very limited circumstances. The client should not pay any commission. The transaction will involve the sale of approximately 5,000 shares of common stock. It wants to use a finder to help it identify potential investors.

Use Plain English

Legalese tends to obscure meaning. In fact, in 1998, the U.S. Securities and Exchange Commission (SEC) promulgated its plain English rule requiring issuers filing registration statements with the SEC to write the cover page, summary, and risk factors section in plain English.[5] In describing the purpose of its rule, the SEC stated:

> Full and fair disclosure is one of the cornerstones of investor protection under the federal securities laws. If a prospectus fails to communicate information clearly, investors do not re-

---

sentence has to say about the topic. Edward Finegan, Language: Its Structure and Use 273 (7th Ed., 2015).

4. These are sometimes referred to as "topic strings." *Id.* at 275. For additional discussion on topics and enhancing cohesiveness, *see* Joseph M. Williams & Gregory G. Colomb, Style: Lessons in Clarity and Grace, 68–81 (Longman, 10th ed.).

5. Final Rule: Plain English Disclosure. SEC Release No. 33-7497 (January 28, 1998).

ceive that basic protection. Yet, prospectuses today often use complex, legalistic language that is foreign to all but financial or legal experts. The proliferation of complex transactions and securities magnifies this problem. A major challenge facing the securities industry and its regulators is assuring that financial and business information reaches investors in a form they can read and understand.[6]

Despite this recognition by the SEC and others that legalese thwarts effective communication, lawyers still cling to legalese such as "heretofore" and "forthwith," whether out of habit or a false sense that it engenders credibility. That does not mean that you should adopt legalese.

---

*Illustration: **Plain English***

Following is an example of a risk factor in an SEC filing drafted using legalese, and a revised draft of the same provision using plain English:

Competition

The lawn care industry is highly competitive. The Company competes for commercial and retail customers with national lawn care service providers, lawn care product manufacturers with service components, and other local and regional producers and operators. Many of these competitors have substantially greater financial and other resources than the Company and may use said resources to adversely affect our ability to compete.

Because we are significantly smaller than the majority of our national competitors, we may lack the financial resources needed to capture increased market share.

Based on total assets and annual revenues, we are significantly smaller than the majority of our national competitors: we are one-third the size of our next largest national competitor. If we compete with them for the same geographical markets, their financial strength could prevent us from capturing those markets.

For example, our largest competitor did the following when it aggressively expanded five years ago:

- launched extensive print and television campaigns to advertise their entry into new markets;
- discounted their services for extended periods of time to attract new customers; and
- provided enhanced customer service during the initial phases of these new relationships.

Our national competitors likely have the financial resources to do the same, and we do not have the financial resources needed to compete on this level.

In its final rules, the SEC provided significant guidance on what it meant by plain English, stating that issuers should at a minimum use "(i) short sentences; (ii) definite, concrete, everyday language; (iii) active voice; (iv) tabular presentation of complex information; (v) no legal or business jargon; and (vi) no multiple negatives."[7]

---

6. *Id.*
7. Securities Exchange Act Rule 421(d), 17 C.F.R. 230.421(d).

Thus, instead of referring in a memo to:

the above-referenced matter regarding said contract forwarded under cover of my email dated _____, 2017.

you could refer simply to

the [insert name of matter] matter regarding the contract that I emailed to you on _____, 2017.

Use Correct Grammar

Grammatical errors can create ambiguity that can lead to misinterpretation, with potentially significant legal consequences. For example, consider the differing legal obligations between the following two provisions:

(1) *Distributor agrees to order merchandise and sell the Products*
(2) *Distributor agrees to order, merchandise, and sell the Products.*

In the second version, the obligation of the distributor to merchandise the products is clear; in the first version it is ambiguous as the word "merchandise" can also be interpreted as a noun.

Unclear pronouns are another common grammatical pitfall. Consider the following sentence:

Although the seller will provide both a representation and an indemnity, we would like to ensure that it guarantees it.

To what or whom do each of the references to "it" refer? Is it clear?

Using correct grammar enhances your credibility. If your writing contains grammatical errors, the reader may assume either that you do not understand the rules of grammar or that you were careless. Either way, this does not inspire confidence in your ability to provide complex legal advice and pay attention to detail.

Pay Attention to Syntax

Remember, the goal is to make your writing as clear and straightforward as possible to allow your reader to accurately interpret what you are trying to communicate. The following techniques are simple enough to practice and can greatly enhance the clarity of your writing:

- *Place the subject and verb close together.* For example, note the placement of the subject (*the parties*) and verb (*will commence*) in this sentence:

  <u>The parties</u>, as soon as reasonably practicable after the execution of this Letter of Intent, and consistent with the terms set forth in this Letter of Intent, <u>will commence</u> to negotiate, in good faith, a definitive merger agreement.

  Now consider this revision:

  <u>The parties</u> <u>will commence</u> to negotiate in good faith a definitive merger agreement as soon as reasonably practicable after the execution of this Letter of Intent. The definitive merger agreement will be negotiated consistent with the terms of this Letter of Intent.

  In the first version, the reader has forgotten who the subject is by the time she gets to the verb and will likely have to re-read the sentence. In the revised version, the subject and verb are not only closer together, but are placed at the beginning of the sentence, making it immediately clear to the reader who will do what. Note that the revised version also breaks the sentence into two shorter sentences and eliminates legalese to further enhance clarity.

- *Avoid nominalizations.* Nominalizations are verbs used as nouns. They typically require additional verbiage and can thus create unnecessary interference in the communication of the idea. In addition, nominalizations shift the verb from specific to more abstract. For example:

  (1) *The parties reached an agreement.*
  (2) *The parties agreed.*

The verb "to reach" in (1) less clearly describes the specific action than the verb "to agree."

- *Use parallel structure for lists and series.* For example:

  (1) *The parties will need to sign the agreement, file the appropriate form, and issue the shares.*
  (2) *The parties will need to sign the agreement, the appropriate form must also be filed, and they should issue the shares.*

In (1), each of the three items is expressed using the same pattern of speech. Version (2) does not use parallel structure for each of the three items and the sentence thus appears disjointed and confusing.

- *Don't misplace or "dangle" modifiers.* Modifiers add description and, when used correctly, can enhance communication. But they need to be placed correctly to modify the intended word. For example:

  Being ready to sign the deal, the lawyer will circulate the purchase agreement to the parties.

Who is ready to sign the deal? The parties, not the lawyer. Yet, by misplacing the modifier in this way, the writer is describing the lawyer, not the parties. How could you rewrite this sentence to correct this confusion?

A dangling modifier is missing the target of the description altogether:

  Having agreed, the contract was signed.

The contract cannot agree; the writer must be referring to the parties, but the parties are not mentioned. Thus, the reader cannot be sure. How could this sentence be revised?

Use Thesis Sentences to Begin Each Paragraph

Of all the recommendations in this section, this may be the most impactful to the clarity and readability of your writing. A thesis sentence is not the same as a topic sentence. A topic sentence tells you what the paragraph is about:

  In this paragraph, we will discuss thesis sentences.

A properly crafted thesis sentence lets your reader know exactly what the *point* of your paragraph will be:

  Thesis sentences are an effective tool.

Headings and subheadings may sometimes serve as the thesis sentence for a paragraph. Look back at the paragraphs in this section. Can you identify the point of each paragraph from the first sentence or subheading?

This section summarizes some useful grammatical and other techniques for enhancing the clarity of your writing. It is not intended to be a comprehensive lesson on grammar. Your responsibility as the writer is to make sure that your writing is as grammatically correct as possible. There is no substitute for careful proofreading and for checking your grammar against a reference guide.[8] When in doubt, keep it simple: the shorter, more straightforward your sentences, the clearer they will likely be to your reader and the more effective your communication. If you have to re-read a sentence three times to understand it, your reader likely will, too!

Exercise 4.2

Read through the following sentences and identify any issues with clarity. How can you revise each sentence to increase its clarity?

1. The assertion that a buyer who is purchasing only selected assets of a seller does not succeed to all the liabilities of the seller well-founded in case law.
2. Pursuant to the provisions of the contract, the aforementioned parties shall use best efforts to obtain the necessary consents.
3. Company will until such time, as said agreement expires, pay the royalty fee.
4. Due to the fact that the agreement was not signed, it is unclear what the parties' obligations are.
5. The user agrees that all confidential information, including any and all writings, charts, customer lists, intellectual property and drawings provided by the licensor, shall be kept confidential by the user.
6. There appears to be three main elements under Cal. Corp. Code 25601.1 to qualify as a finder: it must be a natural person; services can only be provided to an issuer in a transaction that does not exceed a securities purchase price of fifteen million dollars ($15,000,000) in the aggregate; and complying with the specific requirements set forth therein.

Conciseness

Forgive me for having written such a long letter, for I had not time to write a short one.

— Cicero[9]

When asked about the amount of time he spent preparing speeches: "It depends. If I am to speak ten minutes, I need a week for preparation; if fifteen minutes, three days; if half an hour, two days; if an hour, I am ready now."

— Woodrow Wilson[10]

Excess verbiage clouds the meaning intended to be expressed. It creates interference that can prevent the reader from accurately interpreting the information being communicated. As a writer, it will always be easier to write using as many words as come to you, but this does not make it easier for your reader. Conciseness takes time; the fewer words used to express an idea, the longer it takes

---

8. One useful reference is Bryan A. Garner, The Redbook: A Manual of Legal Style (2d ed. 2002).

9. This quote has been attributed in one form or another to several different sources, including Blaise Pascal, John Locke, Benjamin Franklin, and Henry David Thoreau.

10. Suzy Platt & Library of Congress Congressional Research Service, Respectfully Quoted: a Dictionary of Quotations Requested from the Congressional Research Service 244 (Library of Congress, 1989) (digitized by Google. Inc. and made available courtesy of HathiTrust) (citing Josephus Daniels, The Wilson Era; Years of War and After, 1917–1923, page 624 (1946)), *available at* https://babel.hathitrust.org/cgi/pt?id=uc1.31822004082384 ;view=1up;seq=1.

to boil the expression down to its essential parts. This is what makes editing and revising so important.

Conciseness does not mean oversimplification.[11] It does not mean cutting out relevant information. A short piece of writing can be wordy, and a lengthy piece of writing can be concise. Rather, conciseness refers to the elimination of any extraneous word, phrase, sentence, or paragraph that does not contribute to the reader's understanding, without sacrificing clarity.

Following are some key techniques for editing for conciseness:

- *Eliminate metadiscourse.* Metadiscourse refers to talking about what you are going to talk about. It adds no additional meaning, just extra verbiage. For example:

    (1) *I am writing to advise you that we are in receipt of your letter of June 23.*
    (2) *In my opinion, the company would be best served by choosing structure A.*

  Without metadiscourse these become:

    (1) *We are in receipt of your letter of June 23.*
    (2) *Structure A is [probably] the better alternative.*

- *Take your audience into account.* In determining what information is necessary or relevant, consider your audience. For example, if you are emailing a summary of a statute to a partner who is familiar with an area of law, you will not need to include as much detail as if you are emailing the information to a client.

- *Use the passive tense deliberately.* Only use the passive tense if you have a good reason for using it. Consider the following two examples:

    (1) *The contract was signed by the parties on December 15.*
    (2) *The parties signed the contract on December 15.*

  The second sentence uses fewer words and is visibly shorter. Is the use of the passive necessary in the first sentence? Does it add anything to the meaning? Not really. Now let's assume the next sentence in the paragraph reads:

    (3) *It was prepared by Seller's counsel.*

  Is there a reason to use the passive here? In either case, the passive makes sense as the topic "it" (referring to "the contract") is referring directly to the subject (sentence (1)) or comment (sentence (2)) of the preceding sentence (see discussion on topic strings on page 37). Thus, the use of the passive here works to connect the two sentences. Starting the sentence with "Seller's counsel" would introduce a new topic and lack cohesiveness.

- *Eliminate redundancy.* Saying something twice, using multiple words with the same meaning, or adding unnecessary adjectives or intensifiers does not make what you are saying more persuasive; in fact, it can have the opposite effect. In a famous courtroom scene from the movie *A Few Good Men*, the defense attorney objects to a question being asked of her witness. The judge overrules the objection, to which the defense attorney replies that she *strongly* objects. The judge gives her a withering look and her co-counsel mocks her for thinking that the addition of the word "strongly" would change the judge's mind in any way.[12]

---

11. Kevin J. Fandl, Lost in Translation: Effective Legal Writing for the International Legal Community (2013).

12. A Few Good Men (Columbia Pictures 1992).

Examples of redundant expressions include:

- *the following items below*
- *but nevertheless*
- *the reason for this is because*
- *collaborate together*
- *revert back*
- *still remain*
- *first and foremost*

Redundancy can be hard to spot, as it can creep into our writing almost out of habit. Look for words and phrases that, if you deleted them, would not alter the meaning of your sentence. For example, in the phrase "*during that period of time,*" is "*of time*" necessary? Look also for words that repeat the meaning of other words, such as "*brief summary*" (the word *brief* is implied in the meaning of *summary*). Historically, legal writing is rife with redundancy: *free and clear, any and all,* and *true and correct* are good examples. If you are drafting a document based on precedent, look for and eliminate these. One caution: make sure you understand the legal significance of each word you are deleting. For example, in an indemnification provision in a contract, is the expression "*indemnify and defend*" redundant, or does each term have a distinct legal meaning?

Look also for phrases that can be replaced by a single word, or negative phrases that can be reworded in the affirmative.[13] For example: *despite the fact that* (even though); *in the situation where* (when); and *it is possible that* (may); *not different* (similar); *not many* (few); and *not include* (omit). The affirmative uses fewer words than the negative and simplifies what the reader must interpret.

Editing Tips

Following are some practical tips for targeting your editing to spot redundancy and other issues in your writing:

- Look for sentences that begin with "there is/are." Chances are, you can rephrase more concisely. For example: "*There are several issues raised by the Seller's comments*" becomes "*The Seller's comments raise several issues.*"
- Look for words that are common "fillers," such as *really, actually,* and *basically.*
- Look for adjectives and intensifiers.
- Check the beginnings of your sentences for metadiscourse.
- Check your writing for use of the passive tense.

Illustration: **Concise Editing**

The following shows how the first paragraph of a memorandum can be edited for conciseness.

Original version:

As previously discussed in your office last week, the following memorandum provides below a brief summary of the research that I conducted in relation to the transaction proposed to be completed by our client, ABC, Incorporated. There are two parts to this memo. In Part 1, you will see a discussion of the relevant law that I think is possible may be applicable

---

13. Williams & Colomb, *supra* note 4, at 101.

to our client's situation. In Part 2, I will discuss how I think we can use my research to provide the client with a response.

Edits:

As ~~previously~~ discussed ~~in your office last week, the following memorandum provides~~ below *is* a ~~brief~~ summary of ~~the~~ *my* research *regarding* ~~that I conducted in relation to the transaction proposed to be completed by~~ our client, ABC, Incorporated*'s proposed transaction.* ~~There are two parts to this memo. In~~ Part 1~~, you will see a discussion of~~ *describes* the relevant law that ~~I think is possible~~ *may* ~~be applicable to our client's situation~~ *apply.* ~~In~~ Part 2 *analyzes potential responses to the client,* ~~I will discuss how I think we can use my research to provide the client with a response~~ *based on my research.*

Final version:

As discussed, below is a summary of my research regarding our client, ABC, Incorporated's proposed transaction. Part 1 describes the relevant law that may apply. Part 2 analyzes potential responses to the client based on my research.

The illustration above represents just one way to render the original paragraph more concise. If you were editing the writing, you may have chosen to leave in some words or eliminate others. Can you identify why the final version eliminates the words that it does? What would you do differently, if anything?

As a writer, you may sometimes deliberately choose to structure a sentence in a less concise way, or to leave in a word that may not be absolutely necessary, whether out of concern for clarity, emphasis, style, or time (note the use of the word *absolutely* here: Is it necessary? If not, why do you think I left it in?). Sometimes you may not be able to catch every instance. Your reader likely will not notice an occasional lack of conciseness. Remember, concise editing is more a means to an end—to communicate as effectively as possible—than a goal in and of itself.

FOR DISCUSSION:

Consider the following quote by Nathaniel Hawthorne in his literary masterpiece, *The Scarlet Letter:*

> It contributes greatly towards a man's moral and intellectual health, to be brought into habits of companionship with individuals unlike himself, who cares little for his pursuits, and whose sphere and abilities he must go out of himself to appreciate.

This is beautiful prose, but what does it mean? How can you encapsulate the key terms and relevant details without altering the meaning?

Precision

Imprecise word choice can inadvertently alter the legal obligations of the parties. It can also create ambiguity, which in turn may affect the legal enforceability of a provision or agreement.

Illustration: **Precision**

Your client is agreeing to purchase shares in a new company. Your client tells you he wants to be sure the company will buy his shares back if, after three years, he decides he wants to cash out. This is known as a right of redemption. You happen to have a well-drafted precedent share purchase agreement form that contains a redemption provision. You send the redemption language to the lawyer for the company and ask her to include it in the agreement. The language you provided her states: "The Company may redeem the shares at any time following the fourth anniversary of the date of this Agreement." Have you adequately addressed your client's concerns? The answer is no. First, under the language you provided, he will have to wait four years instead of the desired three to have his shares redeemed. Second, the use of the word "may" creates a right, not an obligation. Thus, as drafted, the company has the right, but not the obligation, to redeem the shares. This one word makes a big difference.

Word Choice

Deliberate word choice is a significant component of precision. Some words are legal "terms of art." Thus, you not only need to be sure you are using the word that best represents your intended meaning, but also that you are using the word correctly. For example, the terms *representation*, *opinion*, and *execution* all carry specific meaning in legal drafting. Making a representation in a contract (see Practice Note and other materials in Chapter 11 discussing representations and warranties) creates a specific remedy for the party relying on that representation. If the parties do not intend to create that remedy, they should be careful when using the term "representation." Similarly, lawyers should be careful about referring to advice as an opinion; an opinion carries with it a legal connotation to which specific rights and remedies attach.

Organization

Bullets, numbering, and use of headings can be effective tools for ensuring accurate interpretation, as can organizing your thoughts from general to specific, and demonstrating the hierarchy between your points.

Illustration: **Organizational Techniques**

The following uses the organizational techniques described above to present the same information:

Techniques for precision include:

1. Word choice
    a. Using correct words
    b. Using words correctly
2. Organization
    a. Going from general to specific
    b. Use of headings
    c. Numbering
    d. Bullet points

e. Demonstrating hierarchy between points
- Through use of multilevel numbering
- Through use of tabs and paragraphs
- Through use of signposts and transitions

Exercise 4.3

Look for wordiness, lack of precision, faulty parallelism, metadiscourse, redundancy, ambiguity, lack of conciseness, misplaced modifiers, unclear pronouns, or other errors in the following excerpt. Then rewrite the paragraph using the techniques for clarity, conciseness, and precision. Once you have completed your revised paragraph, switch with your neighbor. What did he or she do differently? Which version is easier to understand? Why?

As it pertains to the matter you discussed with me last week, having spent a significant number of hours reviewing the relevant and pertinent sources on the given subject matter, you instructed me to report to you once I had completed my review of said subject matter, the client should be advised that in order to proceed with the transaction with the buyer as contemplated by it, he should structure the proposed transaction as an asset purchase in light of the concerns raised by them.

Using Defined Terms

Two schools of thought exist as to the use of defined terms. On the one hand, in a lengthy memorandum or complicated contract, defined terms can be helpful, especially if you are going to make repeated references to a term and cannot do so succinctly. For example, in a confidentiality agreement, you will likely want to ensure that "intellectual property" is part of the information that must be kept confidential. But if you simply refer to "intellectual property" without defining it, have you been sufficiently precise as to avoid ambiguity? Are the parties clear as to what comprises "intellectual property"? Probably not. Thus, you will likely need to include a definition of what the parties mean by "intellectual property."

On the other hand, defined terms can make a document unwieldy, especially for a nonlegal reader. For every defined term, the reader must look back to where it is first defined to verify the correct meaning of the term. Defined terms can also be unnecessarily distracting to the reader. If a term can be abbreviated without creating ambiguity, a defined term may be unnecessary.

Illustration: Determining whether Defined Terms Are Necessary

In a three-page memo regarding a proposed acquisition by ABC Construction Company, Inc., of a company called Century Cement, Ltd., where Century Cement, Ltd., is a wholly owned subsidiary of Century Holdings, Ltd., you can probably shorten the company names to ABC, Century Cement, and Century Holdings without creating a defined term for each; the reader is clear about which company you are referring to. But what if ABC Construction is planning on creating a subsidiary, ABC Cement, Inc., to hold the assets of Century Cement? And what if your memo is a 10-page memo discussing the allocation of liabilities in an acquisition between the buyer and the seller? Now it might be helpful to define the various parties using terms that will be useful in your analysis. For example, you could define ABC Construction as the "*Buyer*," ABC Cement as "*Buyer SubCo*," Century Cement as the "*Company*," and Century Holdings as the "*Seller*."

Defined terms are typically included either: (1) in a separate definitions section at the beginning or end of the agreement, or (2) scattered throughout the document. Under this second approach, the term should be defined the first time it is used. Common practice is to place the defined term in parentheses immediately following the term or description being defined. Typically, the defined term will be in quotation marks, and will be formatted distinctly, such as bold, underline, or italics (or any combination of these). For example, the term *intellectual property* might be defined in either of the following ways:

In a Defined Terms section:

"*Intellectual Property*" means any intellectual property used or held for use by Company in connection with its business and all goodwill associated therewith, including, without limitation, all URLs and domain names, and any and all other inventions, art work, designs, photos, logos, product formulations, processes, patents, trade names, trademarks, service marks, copyright, other works of authorship know-how, improvements, procedures, discoveries, designs, customer lists, customer and contact information, trade secrets and other intellectual property.

The first time it is used in the document:

2.1 Seller agrees to sell, and Buyer agrees to acquire, substantially all assets of the Company, including any intellectual property used or held for use by Company in connection with its business and all goodwill associated therewith, including, without limitation, all URLs and domain names, and any and all other inventions, art work, designs, photos, logos, product formulations, processes, patents, trade names, trademarks, service marks, copyright, other works of authorship know-how, improvements, procedures, discoveries, designs, customer lists, customer and contact information, trade secrets and other intellectual property ("*Intellectual Property*").

Once you provide a definition for a term, you can refer to that defined term elsewhere in the document. Thus, the next time you refer to "intellectual property," you do not need to repeat the definition. You would simply refer to it by the defined term. This saves space and ensures the term is defined consistently for each use. Typically, you indicate use of a defined term by using initial capitals:

The Seller represents that (i) it owns or has the right to use all Intellectual Property; (ii) the Intellectual Property does not infringe on the rights of any third parties; and (iii) . . . .

Once you define a term, use that term consistently throughout the document to avoid ambiguity. But only use the defined term where it is applicable. For example, if you refer later in the agreement to intellectual property without capitalizing it, the reader will assume that you are referring to intellectual property that does not fall under your definition of Intellectual Property.[14]

---

14. See the discussion below on Grice's 4 maxims of communication, which presupposes that readers will assume a writer intends to be unambiguous. In this case, the natural assumption would be that if the writer had intended to refer to the defined term, she would have used the capitalized defined term.

FOR DISCUSSION:

Assume you have incorporated the definition of Intellectual Property above in an asset purchase agreement. You want to add a provision that states the seller has not infringed on the intellectual property of any third parties. Should this use of intellectual property be capitalized? What if you want to include a provision that the Seller will ensure that each of its employees signs an assignment agreement relating to any intellectual property developed by the employee during his or her employment?

Presentation and Style

Clarity, conciseness, and precision are like road signs; they eliminate ambiguity and vagueness in much the same way as a "no left turn" sign clearly, concisely, and precisely tells a driver not to turn left.

These techniques need to be packaged into a reader-friendly and appropriate format, using consistent style and presentation. Regardless of how salient your legal reasoning, sloppy presentation will interfere with the communication process, in much the same way as a road sign splattered in mud may not be legible. We will look at presentation and style in context in Part II.

Reader-Centered Writing

Recall that communication is a two-way street. When we express a thought, the purpose is to convey the meaning of that thought to another, who must perceive and interpret that expression. How we perceive and interpret is influenced by who we are: our context, personal experiences, and culture all shape how we view the world and how we "decode" communications.[15] Thus, if you want your message to be accurately interpreted, you must consider your reader's perspective. The goal of any legal writing is to communicate your thoughts such that the recipient has no doubt as to the message you intend to convey.

To do this, you need to know your audience and write to that audience. According to linguist Paul Grice, when interpreting an utterance, the listener assumes that the speaker has complied with several principles ensuring that conversation is a cooperative activity. The same arguably applies to written communication. Grice identified four principles (referred to as maxims) for ensuring efficient communication based on this theory, which have been widely cited:[16]

Figure 4.1

Grice's Four Maxims of Effective Communication

QUALITY — the assumption that what is being said is truthful and accurate

QUANTITY — the assumption that the information being communicated is no more than is necessary

RELEVANCE — the assumption that the information being conveyed is relevant

MANNER — the assumption that speaker or writer is intending to be clear and unambiguous

---

15. *See* Gudykunst & Kim, *supra* note 2, at 32–27.

16. *See, e.g.,* Richard E. Grandy and Richard Warner, *Paul Grice*, The Stanford Encyclopedia of Philosophy (Edward N. Zalta ed., Winter 2017), *available at* https://plato.stanford.edu/archives/win2017/entries/grice/.

These must be measured from the perspective of the reader: what information will your *reader* deem to be of quality, of sufficient quantity, relevant, and unambiguous? Let's look at each of these maxims in the context of transactional legal writing:

- *Quality*: If you state in an email that you are attaching a revised draft of an agreement incorporating all comments received since the prior draft, the reader assumes that everything she is reading is accurately stated.
- *Quantity*: To take the same example from above, if you add that you have spoken with your client, the reader will assume this is a necessary piece of information. What might the reader interpret this to mean? Is there a way to make the meaning clearer?
- *Relevance*: Information (or words) can be relevant but still be unnecessary to the communication, and vice versa. In the above example, what if you add a request that the other party confirm whether they have any questions or comments? The other party responds as follows: "*Thank you for this revised draft. Our client is traveling in India right now but is interested in closing the deal by the end of the year.*" As the recipient of this information, you start by assuming this is both necessary and relevant. But is the location of the client's travels relevant? Possibly, perhaps to indicate that communication may be difficult. Is it necessary?
- *Manner:* Manner requires the speaker to be clear, brief, and organized, and to avoid obscurity of expression and ambiguity. In the above example, does the other party's response satisfy the maxim of manner? No. In fact, it seems to deliberately avoid a clear response. This renders the communication less effective, as you must now infer from the statement the answer to your direct question.

The difficulty is in parsing out information that may seem necessary, relevant, or accurate to *you* as the writer because you know what you are trying to communicate. For each word, phrase, sentence, or paragraph in your writing, ask: "Does my reader need to know this? Will my reader understand the relevance? Will this be clear to my reader?"

Cross-Cultural Considerations

The same maxims apply in a cross-cultural context, with the caveat that what a reader may consider necessary, relevant, or accurate or unambiguous may differ depending on cultural norms and expectations. For example, being too direct can seem disrespectful in some cultures. The rhetorical preference in those cultures might be to lead up to a point more indirectly. In American English, this "meandering" often equates to what we would view as metadiscourse, or excess verbiage. Culture therefore defines whether this verbiage is viewed as necessary or relevant. Remember, these maxims are viewed from the perspective of the listener/reader. Recognize that this point of view may be skewed by cultural preferences if your listener/reader is from a different culture.

....

PRACTICE NOTES

Term Sheets and Letters of Intent

Term sheets are commonly used in business transactions to summarize key business terms agreed to by the parties and to flush out any significant issues or areas of disagreement. They can also be referred to as Letters of Intent (LOIs) or Memoranda of Understanding (MOUs). Each serves the same basic purpose. Typically, term sheets are not intended to be binding; rather, they serve as a starting point for drafting the definitive transaction documents. The same applies for LOIs and MOUs. The terms included will depend on the type of transaction and what each party views as essential to the deal (commonly described as the "material" terms). The materiality of a term is subjective, and each party to a transaction may have different views of what is material. Each party will have certain expectations that, if not realized, would cause that party to not want to enter into the transaction (or at a minimum to renegotiate other terms to make the transaction worthwhile in the party's view). Identifying these material terms early in the process is critical, before the parties start spending significant time and resources in drafting and negotiating the definitive documentation. It is much more cost-effective to identify these major negotiation points in a two- to three-page term sheet than waiting to do so in the draft of a 40-page purchase agreement. Drafting and using term sheets and LOIs are discussed in more detail in Chapter 11.

Federal Agencies Relevant to Transactional Practice

We refer in this chapter to the U.S. Securities & Exchange Commission (known as the SEC). The SEC is one of several federal agencies that regulates activities and promulgates and enforces laws and rules relevant to transactional practice. The SEC regulates the offer and sale of securities in the United States. It has broad rulemaking and enforcement power, including under the U.S. Securities Act of 1933, the U.S. Securities Exchange Act of 1934, the Trust Indenture Act of 1939, the Investment Advisors Act of 1940, the Investment Company Act of 1940, and more recently the Sarbanes-Oxley Act of 2002, the Dodd-Frank Wall Street Reform and Consumer Protection Act of 2010, the Jumpstart Our Business Startups Act of 2012 (the JOBS Act), and the Tax Cuts and Jobs Act of 2017.[17]

Typical transactions that might involve the SEC or compliance with any of these regulations include mergers, acquisitions, syndicated debt offerings, private placements, tender offers, proxy solicitations, public offerings (IPOs), employee incentive arrangements, and some real estate transactions.

Other relevant federal agencies and regulations include the Internal Revenue Service (IRS) and the Internal Revenue Code of 1986, the Department of Justice (DOJ), and the Federal Trade Commission (FTC). The DOJ and the FTC share jurisdiction under the Hart-Scott-Rodino Antitrust Improvements Act of 1976 (HSR), relating to pre-merger filing requirements, as well as other antitrust regulations under the Sherman Antitrust Act of 1890 and the Clayton Antitrust Act of 1914. Other agencies you may encounter in transactional practice include the FDA, the EPA, the FCC, and OSHA.[18]

You should familiarize yourself with the websites for these various agencies, which often provide useful forms, tips, regulations, and other information that can help you identify and address potential legal issues that may arise in a transaction.

Conventions for Formatting Documents

Precedent and subject files are a resource not just for content, but also for formatting and style conventions. Look at documents prepared by other lawyers in your firm. Pay attention to the details:

- Are they typically double-spaced?
- Are the paragraphs block-indented?
- Are the margins full- or left-justified?
- Are defined terms highlighted in bold, italics, underline, or some combination?
- How are headings and subheadings formatted? Do the documents use automatic style features such as autonumbering of sections, or are these done manually?
- In a contract, does the numbering follow a particular style (1.1, 1(a), II.A, etc.)?

---

17. Congress is currently considering legislation referred to as the JOBS Act 3.0, which aims to go beyond the original JOBS Act to jumpstart the initial public offering market by reducing filing and compliance costs, among other provisions.

18. These acronyms refer to the Food and Drug Administration, the Environmental Protection Agency, the Federal Communications Commission, and the Occupational Safety and Health Administration.

- Are any specific forms of footer or header used?
- Is there a specific font?

Most firms have their own style. Most also follow basic conventions, such as omitting the page number on the first page of a document, and using a relatively standard font, such as Times New Roman 12 point or Arial Narrow 11 point.

Conclusion

The skills and techniques described in this chapter are fundamental to any kind of writing you may engage in as a transactional lawyer. The more clear, concise, and precise your writing, the more effective it will be at communicating information to your reader. Your job is to make your writing as easy as possible for the reader to interpret, with as little room for misinterpretation as possible. This entails not only carefully and critically drafting and editing your writing, but doing so with an understanding of your reader's perspective. As you hone these skills in the practice exercises included in each chapter, you will be sculpting your writing to make it more effective.

SIMULATION EXERCISE #4

A senior associate has sent you the following email. Prepare a response.

Senior Associate
_____

From: Senior Associate seniorassoc@ryanassoc.com
Sent: January ___ 10:05 AM
To: Junior Associate
Subject: California securities law — new section 25102.2

Junior Associate:

Some new filing requirements were added a few years ago to the California securities laws. I have attached below the relevant section containing these new requirements. I need you to summarize the requirements for a presentation I am doing for the State Bar on Saturday. Feel free to tabulate and/or break into more than one part if you deem sensible:

> 25102.2 The commissioner shall require any issuer that is engaged in the business of purchasing, selling, financing, or brokering real estate, and that relies upon an exemption authorized by subdivision (e), (f), (h), or (n) of Section 25102, or subdivision (p) of Section 25100, for an offering which involves the offer or sale of securities to any person who is not an accredited investor, as defined in Regulation D of the Securities and Exchange Commission (17 C.F.R. 230.501 et seq.), in a transaction that is not registered pursuant to the Securities Act of 1933, to provide additional information regarding the nature of the proposed offering on a form prescribed by the commissioner. This information shall include the names of the issuer's officers and directors in the case of a corporation, managers in the case of a manager-managed limited liability company, members in the case of a member-managed limited liability company, general partner in the case of a limited partnership, or persons performing similar functions, in the case of other types of issuers, the offering disclosure documents provided to prospective purchasers, a list of all state and federal licenses required to further the purposes of the

investment, and the names of all licensed persons that will undertake those activities. (Added by Stats. 2012, Ch. 669, Sec. 5. Effective January 1, 2014.)

As I mentioned, I am presenting on Saturday, so please get this to me within 48 hours. Email is fine.

Thanks,
Senior Associate

Senior Associate
Ryan & Associates
299 Valley Avenue
3rd Floor
Los Angeles, CA 90009
Tel: 213-510-5000
Email: seniorassoc@ryanassoc.com

Chapter 5

Cross-Cultural Considerations

This chapter considers in greater depth some of the cross-cultural considerations highlighted throughout this text. In cross-cultural contexts, additional barriers to effective communication exist, whether due to differences in language, cultural expectations, or behavioral norms. Developing an increased awareness and appreciation for cultural differences and these potential barriers can increase a transactional lawyer's effectiveness whether communicating with a partner, the client, or the other side.

By the end of this chapter, you will be able to:

- Demonstrate an understanding of culture and cross-cultural similarities and differences
- Assess your own level of cross-cultural competency
- Engage in cross-cultural communications

Your New York-based law firm represents a Norwegian oil-rig construction and management company. The company is considering entering into a joint venture with an Indonesian petroleum exploration company to conduct exploration operations off the coast of Papua New Guinea. The partner asks you to prepare the due diligence materials the client will be required to deliver in connection with the transaction. He informs you that you will need to review documents at the client's offices in Bergen, Norway, as well as in Pascagoula, Mississippi, where the client is currently constructing two of its rigs. You will also need to conduct due diligence on the Indonesian counterparty, which is based in Jakarta. How should you prepare? Are there any special considerations for how you will interact with the individuals you will be meeting in each of these locations? What differences and similarities might you expect?

What Is Culture?

There are many different definitions of culture. Essentially, culture is the lens through which a group of individuals views the world. It's the package of beliefs, traditions, and values that inform how we behave and how we interpret the behavior of others. In its broadest sense, this includes how we communicate, both in terms of style and the language that we use.

Culture should not be conflated with nationality or origin, although they do overlap. It is both broader and narrower than each of these. For example, within the United

States, many different cultures and subcultures exist. People from different parts of the country use different terms to describe the same thing (for instance, use of the word "pop" in the Midwest and "soda" in the Northeast) and prioritize different values and beliefs. The relevant point is not that one view is right or wrong, but that these values are embedded in our cultural identity and shape how we see the issue.

Relevance of Cross-Cultural Communication for Transactional Practice

The ability to communicate across cultures is relevant to transactional practice for two main reasons. First, in our global economy, business transactions increasingly comprise a cross-border component.[1] Most major law firms have offices overseas and commonly represent clients in transactions that span more than one country. Cross-border transactions are not limited to large firms. Even in smaller, regional firms, it is increasingly common to encounter transactions where at least one party involved is from a different country. Second, cross-cultural differences can arise even in domestic transactions. In the example at the beginning of this chapter, the lawyer will need to overcome culture-based barriers to communication in Pascagoula, Mississippi, in much the same way as he will in Bergen, Norway, or Jakarta, Indonesia.

Barriers to Cross-Cultural Communication

Barriers to communication exist even when communicating within the same cultural group. Failure to engage in active listening, absence of nonverbal cues, lack of clarity or precision in word choice, or any other number of external factors can interfere with the message being conveyed. These barriers are amplified in a cross-cultural setting. Principal barriers include:

- *Language*. Words represent the main tool we use to communicate ideas to others. Thus, it stands to reason that one of the principal barriers to communication in the cross-cultural context is language. If you have ever traveled overseas, you likely will have run into this issue. If you do not speak the same language, it can be difficult to make yourself understood or to understand others. In our own language, we can understand what someone is saying even if we don't hear every word. It can be harder for non-native speakers to "fill-in-the-blanks" in this way. Speaking more slowly and engaging in active listening when communicating with a non-native speaker can help mitigate this barrier.

- *Context*. Context refers to the predominant norms, beliefs, values, and rules of a culture that influence how individuals in that culture perceive the world and communicate with others. These contextual variables are sometimes referred to by linguists as "dimensions of cultural variability."[2] We know that different cultures communicate differently. To communicate effectively across cultures, however, we need to understand not only what those differences in communication style are, but *why* those differences exist. Failure to understand that the other person might see things differently—and that such other perspective might make sense to that person—can hinder effective communication. Identifying these dimensions of cultural variability can help us understand why and how people from other cultures might see things differently.

    One of the key dimensions of cultural variability focusing on cultural differences in the

---

1. *See* Jane E. Smith, *Minimizing Risk: Best Practices in Managing Cross-Cultural Concerns in Global Contracting*, 8 The ABA Guide to Int'l Bus. Neg.: A Comparison of Cross-Cultural Issues and Successful Approaches 159 (James R. Silkenat, Jeffrey M. Aresty, Jacqueline Klosek Eds., 3d ed. 2009).

2. Gudykunst & Kim, *supra* Chapter 4, note 2, at 42.

communication process itself, introduced by anthropologist E.T. Hall in 1976, is the concept of low- and high-context cultures or communication.[3] In a high-context culture, much of the message comes from context, including relationships and nonverbal cues. The listener must draw appropriate inferences. In a low-context culture, the information is primarily conveyed through actual words. Individuals from low-context cultures tend to be more direct and explicit in their communications.[4]

Another important dimension is the emphasis we place on individuals versus the collective. Individualistic cultures tend to prioritize individual goals, whereas more collective cultures tend to promote the interests of groups, such as a family or tribe.[5] Other dimensions include how we react to uncertainty, how power is distributed within the culture, and our approach to gender differences.[6]

The use of eye contact, how we greet another individual, the value we place on personal relationships versus merit, and even the notion of time are culture-specific;[7] what may be considered appropriate or mean one thing in one culture can mean the opposite in another. The same can be true of what it means to be fair, logical, or objective.

Recognizing that these variables exist and influence how we communicate can minimize the barriers that otherwise might impede effective communication. On the other hand, ethnocentrism—viewing the world and other cultures through your own lens in which differences are perceived as "wrong" as opposed to different—can inhibit your ability to properly interpret others' behavior or response.[8]

- *Expectations.* Closely connected to context, this category relates specifically to cultural norms and values of a given culture, such as customs and rhetorical preferences. For example, the degree of respect shown for a superior (or a client), the directness with which we write or speak, and the degree to which a statement is true or false, can be culturally specific.

*Illustration: **Cross-Cultural Barriers***

You represent a German manufacturer. In-house counsel has asked you to participate in a meeting with a Venezuela-based potential distributor of its products. The representatives of the Venezuelan distributor arrive 30 minutes late. Once they arrive, they offer no apology, but ask if anyone would like some coffee and begin to warmly shake hands while patting you on the back. Your client appears affronted by the tardy arrival of the Venezuelans and the intimacy of the handshakes. He reticently shakes hands, sits down at the table and says, without smiling, in English, "We are not here for coffee. We would like to focus on winning the deal." The Venezuelans stop in their tracks and look equally affronted. Neither side intended to offend the other. Each party is exhibiting different cultural norms and expectations. For example, they have different no-

3. *Id.* at 44.

4. *Id.* at 44–45. For additional reading on the topic of cultural dimensions; see also Geert Hoftede, Cultural Consequences: Comparing Values, Behaviours, Institutions, and other Organizations Across Nations (2d ed. 2001).

5. Gudykunst & Kim, *supra* Chapter 4, note 2, at 42–43.

6. *Id.* at 45–48.

7. *Id.* at 49–50.

8. *Id.* at 5.

tions of time.[9] They also have different customs for greeting others and for respecting personal space, and place differing importance on the value of forming a personal relationship. The Venezuelans seem to want to engage your client to get to know him a bit more; your client, on the other hand, is more focused on negotiating based on facts and merit alone. Finally, language barrier issues also come into play; did your client mean "winning the deal" or did he mean to say "agreeing"?

FOR DISCUSSION:

Assume you are working with a client based in France. To be spelled correctly, the E in the client's name requires an accent. The partner tells you to place the accent over the E "from front to back." Which of the following two examples shows the accent going "from front to back"?

É   OR   È

Did everyone in the class agree? How could the partner have communicated more clearly?

What Is Cross-Cultural Competence?

If culture is the set of learned beliefs, traditions, and values that shape our view of the world around us and our behavior, what is cross-cultural competence? Does it require us to completely modify our own values and behavior to mimic those of any given culture?

The short answer is: no. Imagine a meeting between a Japanese businessman and the head of a small nomad tribe in Bhutan. Imagine if the Japanese businessman arrives in traditional Bhutanese dress and starts speaking in Bhutanese, while the Bhutanese leader appears in a business suit and speaks in Japanese. Neither party would likely expect this, and it would probably hamper the effectiveness of the meeting. What if the Japanese businessman arrives in normal business attire but tries to address the Bhutanese leader using the traditional Bhutanese greeting, and the Bhutanese leader for his part perhaps bows in the Japanese custom? These "nods" to the other's culture could go a long way toward facilitating communication between the parties.

Cross-cultural competency does not mean becoming someone you are not. Rather, it means adapting your language, tone, and behavior in a way that facilitates communication. It allows you to recognize cross-cultural differences and adapt how you communicate and behave to ensure the other party will interpret your communication as intended.[10] It is not about being comfortable communicating with individuals from a culture with which you are familiar or have studied, but about communicating effectively with people from *any* culture.[11]

---

9. Venezuelan culture (and Latin American culture in general) is polychronic; individuals typically have a less rigid sense of time and promptness. German culture, on the other hand, is monochronic, taking time commitments seriously and preferring to do one thing at a time. *See* David Binder et al., Lawyers as Counselors: A Client-Centered Approach 34–39 (3d ed. 2011) and David A. Victor, *Cross Cultural Awareness*, The ABA Guide to Int'l Bus. Neg.: A Comparison of Cross-Cultural Issues and Successful Approaches 143–57 (James R. Silkenat, Jeffrey M. Aresty, Jacqueline Klosek Eds., 3d ed. 2009).

10. *See* Maureen Watkins, *Intercultural Competence*, in Mary-Beth Moylan & Stephanie J. Thompson, Global Lawyering Skills 22 (2013).

11. *See generally*, L.J. Rasmussen & W.R. Sieck, *Culture-General Competence: Evidence from a Cognitive Field Study of Prof'ls who Work in Many Cultures*, Int'l Journal of Intercultural Rel. (2015), *available at* http://dx.doi.org/10.1016/j.ijintrel

Different theories exist on how to achieve cross-cultural competence, although most recognize different levels of competence.[12] Below is a common categorization:

Level 1: self-awareness. The first level is understanding your own culture; being aware of your own beliefs and values and how they shape your behavior and communication. We all have an unconscious understanding, but without conscious recognition of our biases and proclivities, it can be difficult to recognize differences in how others act and view our behavior.

Level 2: awareness of differences. At this level there is an understanding that not all cultures think or act alike, and that the beliefs and values we rely on in our culture may differ in other cultures.

Level 3: sensitivity. This refers to the ability to view cultural differences without necessarily judging them; understanding that there may be valid beliefs and/or values underpinning a behavior or attitude that makes sense for that culture, even if it does not make sense through our own cultural lens.

Level 4: adaptation. This involves being able to adapt the way we present information to consider the different linguistic and cultural backgrounds of the other person.

To be effective in a cross-cultural situation, a transactional lawyer should strive for at least the third level of cultural competence; the more sensitive a transactional lawyer is to the fact that differences in communication and interpretation exist, and that no one "right" interpretation exists, the more able that lawyer will be to minimize any barriers to communication.

Again, this does not mean learning everything there is to know about every culture we might encounter. Rather, it involves being perceptive to verbal and nonverbal cues, and being cognizant that your listener or reader may have a different perspective.

Illustration: **Levels of Competence**

Assume you are a U.S. lawyer meeting with a CEO of a company based in Pakistan. Level 1 competence might involve you being aware that in the United States, we tend to be direct and fairly informal. At Level 2, you would recognize that this might offend someone from a more formal culture such as Pakistan. At Level 3, you might appreciate that formality and indirectness play a role in how the parties in that culture become comfortable enough to do business. At Level 4, you may choose to be less direct and more formal. For example, you may dress more conservatively, bow slightly when shaking hands, and avoid launching straight into your negotiation points.

.2015.03.014.

12. *See, e.g.,* THE SAGE HANDBOOK OF INTERCULTURAL COMPETENCE (Darla Deardoff Ed., 2009); Susan Bryant, *The Five Habits: Building Cross-Cultural Competence in Lawyers*, 8 Clinical L. Rev. 33 (Fall 2001) (discussing the importance of learning cross-cultural communication skills for lawyers); Mercedes Martin & Billy E. Vaughn, *Cultural Competence: The Nuts & Bolts of Diversity & Inclusion*, STRATEGIC DIVERSITY & INCLUSION MANAGEMENT 31–36 (DTUI Publ. Div.) *available at* https://diversityofficermagazine.com/cultural-competence/cultural-competence-the-nuts-bolts-of-diversity-inclusion-2/ (proposing a definition of cultural competence with four components: awareness, attitude, knowledge, and skills); and J. Johnson, T. Lenartowicz & S. Apud, *Cross-Cultural Competence in Int'l Bus.: Towards a Definition and a Model*, 37 J. INT'L BUS. STUD. 525 (Jul. 2006), *available at* https://doi.org/10.1057/palgrave.jibs.8400205 (proposing a definition of cross-cultural competency in the context of international business and a model for developing in individuals).

Stereotyping

In discussing cultural identities and preferences, I am by necessity generalizing. Be wary of stereotyping, however. Every person will act to some degree in accordance with his or her cultural identity but also in accordance with his or her own individual personality. In addition, cultural identities are becoming increasingly blended due to globalization.

FOR DISCUSSION:

Jot down answers to the following questions: (1) What is the main way you show politeness/deference to another person? (2) What is the most valuable characteristic in a business lawyer? (3) Your brother owns a printing company. Your client needs to print some prospectuses. Is it ethical to suggest they use your brother's company? Does it make a difference if you receive commission on the deal? What dimensions of cultural variability might affect your responses? How do your responses differ from those of your classmates?

Cross-Border Transactions

We turn now to address these cross-cultural considerations in the practical context of a cross-border transaction by examining the following two questions: (1) is a transactional lawyer in the United States expected to know the laws of other countries? and (2) is that transactional lawyer expected to modify his or her behavior to conform to the client's cultural expectations?

- *Extent of Expected Knowledge.* As a U.S.-trained attorney engaging in a cross-border transaction, to what extent should you be familiar with the law of the other involved countries? For example, if you are representing a client on a deal with a Thai company, do you need to understand Thai contract law? Do you need to know what it takes to make a contract enforceable under Thai law? How about what a Thai contract looks like? The answer is: it depends, but make sure you know what you don't know. The most important step is recognizing that Thai law might govern, and that Thai contract law might treat enforceability differently. You also need to think about other implications of conducting a deal in Thailand. For example, are there any restrictions on doing business with foreign entities? Is it a civil or common law jurisdiction? Might this have a bearing on how the parties negotiate? This does not mean you need to have intricate knowledge of Thai law (nor that you should advise the client on matters of Thai law); but you should have an idea of what questions to ask local Thai counsel.

  Your task is to educate yourself with basic awareness of the types of issues and cultural and legal differences to be able to ask the right questions and to seek the right additional assistance. Of course, if you are frequently involved in deals in a country, you should become familiar with the specific laws, terminology, and general requirements for that jurisdiction. For example, once you have completed a few deals in the United Kingdom, you should know that the "closing" of the transaction in the United Kingdom is called "completion," and that most transactions are subject to stamp tax. But do not let this create a false sense of security. Unless you are licensed to practice in that country, you are not qualified to provide the client legal advice as to the applicability of the law in that country. Thus, in most instances, if local law is going to be implicated, you will need to retain local counsel.

• *Expected adaptation.* Is a U.S. attorney expected to modify her behavior to conform to client's cultural expectations? Let's go back to our Thailand example. If you are going to a meeting in Thailand, is it expected that you dress like the client or engage in certain social norms? If you are a female in a Muslim country, should you wear a headscarf? How much are you supposed to adapt your behavior? Again, the answer is: it depends; you need to use your judgment.

As with knowledge of the law, it comes down to awareness. You should be mindful that the way you behave might elicit a different reaction coming from someone from a different culture than what you would expect in your own culture. For example, in the United States, grabbing someone by the shoulder as you shake their hand and say: "How're you doing?" is a friendly gesture, but it could be offensive in other cultures. But this does not mean you need to avoid handshaking altogether, even if the other culture typically bows. Take your cues from the other people in the room; if everyone is bowing, then perhaps you might want to forgo a handshake and bow.

In some situations, both sides can be trying to accommodate the other's culture. Most of the world is more attuned to cultural differences and sensitivities than in the United States; thus, you may find that when you enter a meeting the other parties will already be adapting to the U.S. way of doing business. For example, in Japan, instead of bowing, a Japanese client might instead shake your hand. You need to assess the degree to which you want to show the other person that you understand that customs may be different. The whole point is to enhance communication and to minimize barriers. Just a little awareness can help to make sure what you are seeking to communicate is interpreted as you intended.

Terminology Used in Cross-Cultural Communication

There are many theories on cross-cultural communication, some of which are mentioned earlier in this chapter. A detailed discussion of these theories, although relevant to improving your cross-cultural communication skills, is obviously too broad to fit into a single chapter of a textbook (or even a single textbook!). The sources cited throughout this chapter provide a more in-depth look into some of these theories and concepts for those interested in additional reading. For our current purposes, highlighted here are a few of the more common concepts that can be helpful when applied to cross-cultural communication in transactional law practice.

Language as a Reflection of Culture

Does culture reflect language or does language reflect culture? Anthropological linguists have debated this question for centuries. One often-cited theory on this question is the Sapir-Whorf hypothesis, which posits that the structure of a language determines the speaker's perception and how she categorizes her experiences.[13] Consider the United States and England. The United States was founded primarily by the English. The two countries speak the same language. Yet the English language has developed differently in each country, with differences in vocabulary, grammar, accent, intonation, and spelling. But the cultures are also distinct—the level of formality, fundamental values, and beliefs are different, although they share some fundamental characteristics. How did these differences evolve? Which came first, the changes to language or behavior? And why? Was it the influx of immigrants adding new vocabulary and behaviors? Or was it the new environment?

---

13. Gudykunst & Kim, *supra* Chapter 4, note 2, at 153–54.

High Versus Low Context

Cultures can be classified as high or low context.[14] In high-context cultures, communication tends to rely more heavily on visual and vocal cues (the nonverbal aspects of communication) to interpret meaning.[15] Communication in this type of culture tends to be less direct, leaving the listener or reader to perceive the intended meaning. This carries over into the importance placed on relationships in high-context cultures; the better you know a person, the better able you are to interpret their nonverbal cues. In low-context cultures, communication relies more on the verbal aspects—the words themselves.[16] Directness is key: say what you mean and mean what you say.

Rhetorical Preferences

Rhetorical preferences refer to the way individuals from different cultural and linguistic backgrounds prefer to receive information.[17] For example, U.S. readers prefer direct, concise writing; they like to see the conclusion up front, and then have the explanation follow. In other cultures, readers prefer when the writer leads the reader gradually to the conclusion. Directness can be perceived as disrespectful and can lower the writer's credibility in the eyes of the reader.

> **Exercise 5.1**
>
> Work in pairs to identify a list of high- versus low-context cultures. Are there any that surprise you? Why? Do you know anyone from any of the cultures you have identified? How well does the description fit?

Conclusion

In the increasingly global practice of law, the ability to communicate effectively across different cultures is fundamentally important. Transactional lawyers should strive for a minimum level of cultural competence that allows them to anticipate, recognize, and adapt for cultural differences in language, nonverbal communication, rhetorical preferences, behavior, values, and beliefs. The more aware a transactional lawyer is of the potential for these dimensions of variability, the better able she will be to minimize barriers to effective communication.

SIMULATION EXERCISE #5

You receive the following voicemail instructions from a partner:

"Draft an email to our Russian client postponing our meeting scheduled for Friday at 9:00 a.m. because I have a meeting with another, bigger client and my daughter is in a play that evening. See if you can set something up for Wednesday or Thursday of next week.
    The client's name is Maksim Kuznetsov."

In drafting your email, take into consideration the client's likely cultural background and rhetorical preferences. What level of formality should you adopt? How direct should you be?

---

14. *Id.* at 44.

15. *Id.* at 44–45.

16. *See id.*

17. *See* Anne Enquist & Laurel Currie Oates, Just Writing: Grammar, Punctuation, and Style 297–302 (3d ed. 2009) (containing a chart of rhetorical preferences).

PART II

Communication in Context

A

Communicating with the Partner or Senior Associate

Chapter 6

· · · · · · · · · · · · · · · · ·

The Formal Office Memo in Transactional Practice

This chapter marks the beginning of our look at communication in context, and the first of three chapters focused on interoffice communications. It starts with the traditional form of interoffice memorandum (or memo, as the term is commonly used), applying and going beyond the fundamental techniques discussed in Chapter 4 within a transactional law context.

By the end of this chapter, you should be able to:

- Differentiate between the purpose and format of a transactional practice memorandum and a traditional litigation practice memorandum
- Compose a full interoffice memorandum
- Apply research techniques and fundamental writing skills in context

· ·

The partner recently gave you a research assignment regarding a regulatory compliance issue that she wants turned into a formal memo she can refer to in formulating her advice for the client, and that she can possibly share with the client and others at the firm. You have done the research, and you have been working on honing your fundamental writing skills. But how do you know what form the memorandum should take? The last memo you wrote was in your law school legal writing course, and that was about whether the client could sue for attractive nuisance. You can't see how the memo format you used in that class could be useful in your current situation—or could it?

· ·

The Shift to Transactional Writing

Most of what you have learned in legal writing thus far has likely been in the context of litigation (predictive office memos, briefs, and motions). As discussed in more detail below, the shift to a transactional context involves a change in both focus and overall objective.

Transactional Office Memorandum: Beyond the Traditional Law School Memo

As a first-year law student, you likely learned to draft office memoranda following a rigid structure. For instance, you were likely instructed which sections to include in your memo and how to label them (such as the Question Presented, Brief Answer, and Discussion sections). You also may have been taught to present your analysis adhering to an analytical paradigm, such as "IRAC" (Issue/Rule/Application/Conclusion) or "CREAC" (Conclusion/Rule/Explanation/Application/Conclusion). This structure is helpful for students first learning to draft legal memoranda. Most students come to law school unfamiliar with common law analysis—reading and analyzing cases, synthesizing rules of law, and applying those rules to specific facts. Adhering to a formal structure in their writing helps students practice these new analytical skills while keeping their writing well-organized, coherent, and clear.

Expanding Beyond IRAC

Once you have mastered the basic paradigm for presenting legal analysis in a clear, concise, and precise manner, you can deviate from the paradigm *if it makes sense to do so*. Remember, using a basic IRAC or other formulaic structure in your memo is not wrong; these paradigms are still useful bases for organizing your thoughts and ideas and are likely familiar to your supervising attorney. But as you become a more advanced legal writer, it becomes less important to adhere to these paradigms with the same rigidity, provided you can otherwise ensure your writing remains effective (and unless, of course, your supervising attorney or firm has indicated that he or she prefers you to use one of these paradigms).

Adopting a Transactional Focus

A less rigid approach makes sense in transactional practice. As a transactional attorney, you may find attempting to adhere too rigidly to a formal IRAC-type structure makes it difficult to provide the assigning attorney a clear answer to the issue(s) you have been asked to address. This is because the IRAC family of paradigms, and most of what you learned in first-year legal writing, is litigation-focused. The goals of written analysis in litigation are different from those in transactional practice. The objective of an office memo on a litigation matter is to look back to the facts and outcomes in precedent cases and predict the likelihood of a similar outcome in your client's case, based on a series of facts that have already occurred. Thus, litigation analysis tends to be case-driven and "backward-looking," with the overall goal of predicting outcome based on past events.

In transactional practice, your analysis will be more forward-looking; the aim generally is to advise the client on what facts would most likely lead to a desired outcome. You may rely on precedent to help you make your determination; often, however, little precedent exists.[1] Your goal is not so much to *predict* outcome as it is to find a way to *achieve* a desired outcome.

Figure 6.1

Difference in Focus	
LITIGATION	**TRANSACTIONAL**
Goal = to avoid/succeed in litigation	Goal = to close mutually satisfactory transaction
Focus = likelihood of achieving goal based on existing fact	Focus = what can be done to best achieve goal by overcoming existing facts and/or creating new facts
→ PREDICTING OUTCOME	→ PROBLEM-SOLVING

---

1. Commonly, issues facing a transactional attorney have not been litigated in the past because they are not the types of issues that give rise to disputes; rather, they tend to relate to strategic business decisions and/or dispute avoidance.

Relation between Purpose and Focus

Keep in mind the purpose for which the supervising attorney will use your memo. Consider the following example. The supervising attorney has told you he has a client looking to hire two individuals. The client would like to hire these individuals as independent contractors (instead of employees) and wants your firm's advice as to whether it can do so. The supervising attorney asks you to summarize the test for determining whether a person is an independent contractor or an employee, and the penalties for misclassification.

In a litigation-focused memo, you typically would set out the legal test and then apply that legal test to the known facts to predict the likelihood that the individuals would be deemed misclassified.

In a transactional setting, your review of the law will be in the context of future action. As with a litigation-focused memo, you will want to start by setting out the legal test. Instead of focusing on predicting outcome based on known facts, however, you will want to provide the supervising attorney with the information necessary to be able to generate options for the client going forward to avoid potential misclassification issues. For instance, you may want to include a checklist of recommended steps for ensuring that a person is an independent contractor or emphasize the factors from the test that are most significant.

This does not mean you should automatically go beyond the specific instructions of the supervising attorney. You will need to use your judgment as to what your supervising attorney expects (or you can ask her). Even if you determine that your assigned task is limited to simply stating the law, however, you should keep in mind how the supervising attorney will likely be using that information.

Illustration: *Focus Reflects Purpose*

Taking the above example, the discussion section of your memo might read in part as follows:

Litigation purpose:

Whether an individual is classified as an employee or an independent contractor depends on several factors. These factors include whether: (1) the company has the right to control how the worker does her job; (2) the worker provides her own tools and pays her own expenses; 3) the worker receives any employee-type benefits; . . . . No one factor is dispositive. *Smith v. Jones, [citation omitted].* In *Smith, [discussion of precedent facts omitted].*

In our case, the worker likely will be classified as an employee given that the company plans to control how and when the worker provides the services and will receive employee-like benefits. The company is requiring the worker to be at the office between the hours of 9:00 am and 5:00 pm, and to comply with the instructions of the department manager in performing her assigned tasks. In addition, the worker will be entitled to two weeks' paid vacation. Similar to the worker in *Smith* who was classified as an employee when he had set office hours, had to report to a senior manager on a daily basis, and was entitled to participate in the company's profit-sharing plan, these facts likely are sufficient to trigger classification as an employee.

Transactional focus:

Whether an individual is classified as an employee or an independent contractor depends on several factors. These factors include whether: (1) the company has the right to control how the worker does her job; (2) the worker provides her own tools and pays her own expenses; (3) the worker receives any employee-type benefits; . . . . No one factor is dispositive. *Smith v. Jones, [citation omitted].*

In order to minimize the risk that the worker be classified as an employee, the company should adhere to the following guidelines [*possible footnote citing to key facts in Smith*]:

(1) Allow the worker to set her own hours;
(2) Ensure that the worker retains discretion in how he will perform the required services;
(3) Include a provision in the independent contractor agreement that makes clear (1) and (2);
(4) Limit the worker's eligibility for employee benefits such as vacation time, sick leave, and profit-sharing plans.

These are simplified examples for illustration only. But note how both examples start the same, where they begin to differ, and how these differences in focus reflect the differing purposes.

Regardless of purpose or focus, your memorandum must make sense from the reader's perspective. However you structure your memo, be methodical and logical. Take your reader through each step. You know where you are going, but does the reader?

Comparison of Format and Content

This shift in focus and purpose manifests itself also in terms of micro-organization and content. The chart in Figure 6.2 illustrates the key differences with respect to traditional memo[2] sections and content:

Figure 6.2

Traditional Litigation-Focused Memo Component	Transactional Memo
HEADING	A proper Heading remains important in a transactional memo. Generally, the heading should include \<To\> \<From\> \<Date\> and \<Re\> lines. Many firms have specific templates you can use. Regardless of format, your Heading should look professional and make consistent use of spacing and tabulation.
INTRODUCTION	This also remains a useful section in a transactional memo. It should briefly summarize the issue being addressed, introduce the parties, and outline any key considerations. You may also want to include a brief roadmap (see below). You may also include a brief statement of the question presented and your brief answer (if you do not include these in a separate section—see below).

---

2. I use the term *traditional memo* to refer to the IRAC-structured litigation research memo typically used in first-year legal writing classes. Readers may have been exposed to a variety of other formats, but I believe it instructive to use the "classic" form as a basis for comparison, as this is the form used by most litigation practitioners.

Traditional Litigation-Focused Memo Component	Transactional Memo
QUESTION PRESENTED/ BRIEF ANSWER	In a litigation memo, the Question Presented identifies the legal issue or question and salient facts.[3] The Brief Answer provides a succinct answer to the Question Presented, often highlighting key legal elements relied on in drawing a conclusion.[4] Depending on the length of the memo, these sections may or may not be necessary in a transactional memo. This is especially true of the Brief Answer. Both can often be summarized more informally in the Introduction. For example, you can incorporate the Question Presented in the Introduction of a memo by starting with: "*You have asked me to analyze whether . . . .*" Unlike in a traditional litigation memo, you do not need to phrase the Question Presented or Brief Answer in terms of the salient facts or legal elements; rather, try to state them more succinctly.
STATEMENT OF FACTS	In a traditional litigation memo, the goal of the Statement of Facts is to tell the reader a story of what happened. Because past facts are less relevant to a forward-looking transactional analysis, a formal Statement of Facts may not always be necessary and, if included, should generally be more concise than in a litigation memo. Often, the facts can be summarized in the Introduction. The key is to provide your reader with facts sufficient to support your analysis and avoid gaps in reasoning, including any stated goals or preferences the client may have expressed. For example, in a memo discussing the advantages and disadvantages of a stock purchase versus an asset purchase, a crucial fact might be whether the purchaser is concerned more with avoiding successor liability or more with ensuring it acquires all the assets of the business. Without this basic information, the reader must make an inferential leap to reach your conclusion (that one structure is better than the other). Ask yourself what facts and assumptions are relevant to your analysis of your client's options going forward. As with a more traditional memo, you will still need to state the facts objectively and organize them logically. Generally, a topical, rather than chronological, organization makes more sense.

3. For example, in a memo discussing the likelihood of success in a misappropriation of trade secrets claim, the Question Presented might read: "Did the defendant misappropriate trade secrets when he had access to the plaintiff's customer phone numbers on a confidential basis and used those numbers to contact customers after he had left the company?"

4. For example, in the same memo described above, the Brief Answer might read: "Yes, the defendant likely misappropriated trade secrets given the customer lists were not generally known by or readily ascertainable to competitors, plaintiff took reasonable steps to protect the information, and in using the lists the plaintiff violated his duty to maintain the secrecy of the customer lists."

Traditional Litigation-Focused Memo Component	Transactional Memo
DISCUSSION	This will still constitute the body of your memo. Your Discussion section may not necessarily follow a rigid IRAC or IRREAC paradigm. You should determine the most appropriate organization and content. The individual components that generally comprise the traditional Discussion section are discussed separately below.
Umbrella Section/ Roadmap	Depending on what you include in your Introduction, it can be a good idea to start your Discussion with a brief umbrella section or a "road map," especially if you are addressing multiple issues or rules with multiple elements. It can be as simple as a single sentence. The goal is to provide your reader with an overview of the structure of your discussion—where you will be taking the reader. If you did not include a Brief Answer section or an overall conclusion in your Introduction, you may want to include one here.
Rule/ Rule Explanation	You generally will want to start with a clear, synthesized statement of the relevant law (the legal rules). However, because the purpose of a transactional memo is less about predicting outcome based on past litigation, you may find you need to include less traditional rule explanation (summarizing the facts, reasoning, and holdings in prior cases).[5] This is especially true with issues that have not been litigated previously. For instance, you may have been asked to analyze whether your client should structure its new business as a corporation or a limited liability company. Not only has there likely been little litigation on this issue (and thus little case law), but a detailed explanation of the facts of another case is not likely to be helpful. On the other hand, in a memo addressing whether a sale of securities will violate securities laws, a much-litigated topic, a brief discussion of the outcome-determinative facts in precedent cases may well be helpful. Similarly, in a memo examining whether a purchaser of a business will be deemed to have successor liability for the debts of the seller, it can be helpful in explaining the test for whether successor liability attaches to include specific examples of cases in which it did or did not attach. You can then use these examples to support your advice to structure the purchase in a way to avoid the pitfalls that occurred in those prior cases.
Application Section	This is where the greatest divergence occurs between a traditional litigation-focused memo and a transactional memo. Your analysis in a transactional memo will generally be less about predicting outcome based on past facts and more about defining future options. In many instances, given the forward-looking nature of advice in a transactional setting, the factual circumstances to which the rules would eventually apply have not yet been created. Thus, rather than applying the legal rules to a set of existing facts, you may need to propose a factual scenario that you then apply to the set of legal rules.

5. See the sample litigation memo in Appendix B for examples of rule explanation.

Traditional Litigation-Focused Memo Component	Transactional Memo
Application Section, *(cont.)*	Fact-based analogies and distinctions are effective in supporting predictions based on precedent. They consequently tend to be less relevant in forward-looking transactional memos. However, to the extent you are analyzing an issue that has been litigated in the past, these can still serve as a powerful tool for supporting your recommendations. In addition, law-based analogies and distinctions can also be useful. For example, in a memo discussing whether membership interests in a limited liability company constitute "securities" for purposes of securities laws, an analogy to the treatment of limited partnership interests (on which there is more established guidance) could be effective.

A word of caution: the fact that you may need less factual comparison to support your arguments does not mean your analysis should not be in-depth. The depth of your analysis should be appropriate to the task you have been assigned, the nature of the issue/law, and the specific instructions you have been given.

Finally, if you do not opt to follow an IRAC format, make sure you continue to organize your analysis, and each paragraph, logically and methodically, starting each paragraph with a thesis sentence, organizing your thoughts from general to specific, and using transitions and other tools when needed to ensure clarity and precision.[6] |
| CONCLUSION | Your reader will generally expect a brief conclusion at the end of your memorandum. Your conclusion should succinctly state your overall recommendation. It can also be a good idea to close with an invitation to let you know if the supervising attorney has any questions or would like you to take any additional action. |
| CITATIONS | Litigation memos tend to be prepared in connection with pending or threatened litigation. Because a litigation memo may serve as the basis for the supervising attorney's arguments before the court, proper and accurate in-text citation is crucial. Of course, identifying the source of your information remains important in any practice area, but in transactional memos, your citation to these sources can be placed in a footnote or endnote (see the Practice Note at the end of this chapter). |

Techniques that Continue to Apply

Notwithstanding the differences outlined in Figure 6.2, many of the fundamental techniques applicable to the traditional office-memo format are equally applicable when drafting a transactional office memo. The aim should be to build on and refine these fundamental techniques within the transactional law context. Some of these key fundamental techniques that apply to both are highlighted in Figure 6.3:

---

6. A useful way to think about your organization is to start each paragraph with a thesis and then use the remaining sentences in that paragraph to support your thesis (these can be analogies, explanation, or express inferences).

Figure 6.3

Effective Techniques that Still Apply

✓ **DO** organize your memo logically. Your reader needs to be able to follow your reasoning; poor organization, inferential leaps, and lack of cohesiveness all limit the readability of your memo and adversely affect your credibility. If you are addressing multiple issues, address each issue separately.

✓ **DO** keep your tone objective, with appropriate hedging. You should be careful to present the entire picture. The underlying purpose of an office memo should still be to educate your reader.

✓ **DO** present the applicable legal rules (i.e., the relevant law) for your reader before you show your reader how those rules apply to the facts of your client's case (unless you have a specific reason otherwise). To increase readability, formulate the rules from general to more specific.

✓ **DO** synthesize the various cases and other authorities to provide your reader with an accurate summary of the law on your issue. Simply listing a series of rules from a set of cases or other sources is not particularly helpful to your reader; he or she could easily read these. The value comes from the effort you put into accurately and concisely synthesizing the various rules.

✓ **DO** be consistent in your use of terms in formulating your rules and any rule explanation, and in subsequent application of those rules to your client's facts (mirroring the key terms from the rules throughout).

✓ **DO** mirror where possible the structure and order of the rules in your Application. For example, if you present the rules as A, B, and C, you should generally discuss them in that same order.

✓ **DO** use thesis sentences to start each paragraph. These are extremely effective in keeping your writing—and your reader—focused.

✓ **DO** use headings if you think they are helpful in organizing the content of your memo and in directing the reader.

✓ **DO** engage in reader-centered writing.

✓ **DO** pay attention to the overall presentation and appearance of your memo; it should be polished and professional-looking, with appropriate font type and size, pagination, and spacing.

✓ **DO** use techniques such as signposting, transitions, and topic strings to maximize the cohesiveness and readability of your memo.

✓ **DO** review your memo for conciseness, clarity, and precision. This includes eliminating excess verbiage, legalese, and irrelevant information from your writing.

✓ **DO** proofread your memo carefully to eliminate typographical, spelling, and grammatical errors.

FOR DISCUSSION:

Appendix B includes a traditional litigation-focused office memo relating to a potential breach of contract claim arising from a guaranty, compared with an office memo for the same client, but in this case *prior to* entering into the guaranty and focusing on a transactional issue. Compare these two memos. What is the same, what is different? Can you identify each of the traditional memo sections in the transactional memo?

The Writing Process

Although focus and purpose may vary, the writing process itself is the same as with any other form of memo. It is a recursive process, starting with the gathering of information. You will need to gather various types of information:

- *Background information*: any facts, the parties, the relevant industry, any key terms that are industry- or client-specific, and the basic context (the big picture).
- *Relevant substantive concepts*: the general area of law involved and the principal legal issues. Don't forget any related substantive areas of the law, such as contract drafting, that may be relevant.
- *Procedural concepts*: the formulation of your initial research inquiry and the scope of the assignment.
- *Assignment instructions*: the specific instructions for completing the task. Do the instructions provide clues for how to limit your research and focus the scope of your memo?
- *Precedent materials*: any precedent documents have you been provided, or that you should try to locate.

As you are gathering this information, you should begin to write, and to gain a deeper understanding of the subject matter, which in turn prompts the need to gather more information, which further deepens the understanding. As this is occurring, you should be reviewing, As you begin writing, you may want to briefly review Chapters 1 through 5 to recall the principles, concepts and techniques for effective communication.

Once you have an initial draft of your memorandum, it is important to go back through and re-read and revise your memorandum to ensure you are communicating the information as effectively as possible.

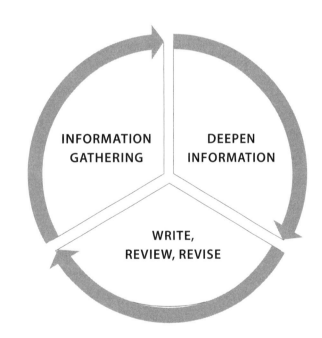

You may need to re-read your memo several times, each time looking at different aspects: organization, technique, content, formatting, grammar, and conciseness. These can be grouped into three main areas:

1. *Organization and technique*: Is your memo well organized? Have you made effective use of the fundamental techniques for effective writing?
2. *Content*: Have you answered the questions you were asked completely and accurately? Have you provided sufficient depth of information and analysis? Have you adequately synthesized the information? Have you included all relevant parts of your analysis (including a recommendation or conclusion)?
3. *Tone*: Does your memo use the correct tone? Is it professionally presented?

Figure 6.4 provides a useful checklist for this process:

Figure 6.4

Checklist for Preparing a Transactional Office Memorandum

I. ORGANIZATION/TECHNIQUE

☐ Is your memo logically organized?

☐ Have you included all relevant sections, and can the reader easily spot them?

☐ Have you made effective use of headings, if necessary?

☐ Have you made effective use of fundamental techniques such as thesis sentences, mirroring, topic strings, signposting, and transitions?

☐ Is your writing as concise as possible, eliminating all excess verbiage, wordiness, and irrelevant details?

☐ Is your writing clear (including elimination of unnecessary legalese)?

☐ Is your writing precise (including proper hierarchy among points/elements)?

☐ Have you checked your memo for overall coherence, both within and between paragraphs?

II. CONTENT

☐ Have you started with an appropriate introduction? Have you included a road map?

☐ Have you properly identified the relevant business and legal issues?

☐ Is your description of the law correct?

☐ Is your analysis of the law correct?

☐ Have you gone into the appropriate depth in describing and explaining the law?

☐ Have you gone into the appropriate depth in analyzing the law as it pertains to the client's concerns?

☐ Is your analysis properly focused on the correct issue(s) and instructions?

☐ Have you adequately synthesized the law and your reasoning?

☐ Have you included sufficient facts and other details?

☐ Have you included a recommendation or conclusion?

III. TONE/PROFESSIONALISM

☐ Have you included a proper heading?

☐ Is the overall tone of your memo objective?

☐ Have you added value for the supervising attorney (how will your memo help the supervising attorney better advise the client?)?

☐ Have you exercised appropriate legal judgment?

☐ Is your writing reader-centered?

☐ Have you proofread your memo for typographical, spelling, and grammatical errors?

☐ Have you checked your memo for proper citation form and formatting?

☐ Have you printed out your memo and examined it for overall professional appearance and readability?

Exercise 6.1

Use the checklist in Figure 6.4 to review the transactional office memorandum included in Appendix B. Can you find examples of how the memorandum satisfactorily addresses each of the points on the checklist? Are there any that the memorandum does not adequately address? If so, how would you suggest revising the memorandum?

Researching the Transactional Office Memorandum

Unless you have expertise in a topic, a transactional office memo still likely requires you to engage in research. Chapter 3 included techniques for honing your research skills in the context of transactional practice. As with any research task, before you begin, you first need to identify the scope of what you are being asked to do:

- What are the specific legal issue(s), to the extent identified?
- What are the business issues?
- What is the overall context: who are the parties, your client, the transaction, the industry?
- What is the underlying substantive context? What general area of law is implicated?
- What is the purpose of the memorandum?

The answers to these questions help you frame your research. For example, assume you are asked to research whether your client needs to obtain shareholder consent. Why is the consent needed? What is the business transaction that will need to be approved? Who is your client? Is the client the buyer or the seller, or in some other role? Are there alternative ways to structure the transaction in which consent may or may not be needed? Is the client open to different structural alternatives? How does the partner intend to use the results of your research? You may need to conduct additional background research to prepare to research the ultimate issue. For example, do you understand the substantive area of law? Do you need to understand more about the client's industry to determine what, if any, regulatory issues might arise?

Once you have started the research process, the results will guide you on how to structure the memorandum. How is the relevant law organized? Does it have a series of elements? Or a list of factors that need to be individually analyzed?

Finally, remember that much of what you will be researching in transactional practice may not have been litigated, and thus little or no case law may exist. In other instances, you may have no fully formed legal issue; you may just be presented with a business issue that you will need to translate into a relevant legal issue. For these reasons, it can be helpful to start with alternative research sources to help frame your research (see the Practice Note on page 31).

Exercise 6.2

Working in groups, research the following issue:

Your client owns membership interests in a California limited liability company (LLC)[7] and wants to sell those interests. Are the membership interests securities for purposes of federal and California securities law?

One half of the group should rely solely on Google or other Internet search engine; the other half should use only Westlaw or Lexis. What result? How many of you arrived at the same results? Which sources would you cite?

PRACTICE NOTES

Employees versus Independent Contractors

The illustration on page 69 involves classifying someone providing services as an employee or independent contractor. Why does classification matter? This distinction is in fact an important one that can have significant tax and other consequences, including onerous fines. Yet many clients resist following their attorneys' and accountants' advice on this issue. Companies, especially start-ups, will often prefer to engage individuals as independent contractors. The primary reason is that it allows the company to minimize costs associated with being an employer and the need to comply with minimum wage and other employment regulations. Problems arise when someone is classified as an independent contractor, but the relationship has the earmarks of an employee relationship. The test for whether someone is an employee or a contractor is a factual one and varies from state to state.[8] The best practice is to err on the side of caution: if a relationship bears any of the characteristics of an employment relationship, lawyers will typically advise the client that the potential cost of misclassification is likely not worth the risk.

Triggering Securities Laws: Why It Matters Whether Something Is a Security

We make numerous references throughout this text to determining whether something is a security. The definition of a security is discussed in the Practice Notes at the end of Chapter 1. But why does it matter if something is a security? The offer, sale, and purchase of securities is highly regulated at both the federal and state levels in the United States. Transactional attorneys, even if not specializing in securities laws, need to be able to spot potential securities law issues. For example, an asset purchase transaction may seem on its face to have nothing to do with securities laws—by definition, the parties are buying and selling assets, not securities. But what if the buyer is paying part of the purchase price by issuing some of its stock to the seller? This would constitute a securities offering. Failure to comply with applicable securities laws could jeopardize the entire deal. For additional discussion of securities laws, see the Practice Area Overview in Appendix A.

---

7. See Practice Note on different entity types at the end of Chapter 9 for an explanation of LLCs.

8. California is one of several states to recently have made it more difficult for companies to classify individuals as independent contractors. A 2018 California Supreme Court case held that to classify someone as an independent contractor, the company must show the worker is "free from the control and direction of the employer", performs work that is outside the company's "core business," and usually engages in "an independently established trade, occupation or business." Dynamex Operations West, Inc. v. Superior Court, Docket No. S222732 (Apr. 30, 2018).

Conclusion

The principal struggle in drafting a transactional memorandum is to break away from litigation-focused application of the law. Often, you will have few facts with which to frame your analysis. Standard litigation legal analysis—the prediction of outcome based on existing/past facts—is less pertinent. Instead, your focus will be more on problem-solving and option-generating. The next major hurdle is deciding how to structure the memorandum. Notwithstanding these differences, many of the fundamental organizational and memo-writing skills you learned in law school apply, regardless of how sophisticated the legal issue. In the next chapter, we will look at how these fundamental skills apply to less formal forms of communications within the law firm.

....

WRITING PROJECT #1: Drafting an Office Memorandum

Follow the instructions and information provided to you by your instructor for completing a six- to eight-page office memorandum. This project is designed to allow you to practice the skills and apply the concepts covered in Chapters 1–6.

Chapter 7

Other Forms of Written Communications in Transactional Practice

This chapter takes us beyond the traditional memorandum to discuss effective writing techniques as well as appropriate format, tone, and content for a variety of other forms of writing you will likely encounter as a junior associate in a transactional (business law) practice, including short-form memos, bullet points, emails, and other "informal" communications.

By the end of this chapter, you will be able to:

- Demonstrate how to adapt in-depth research and analysis on a topic for a variety of formats, including short-form memos and bullet point summaries
- Identify which format is most appropriate in a given context
- Compose professional email correspondence
- Engage effectively in quick-turnaround research and analysis assignments

A harried senior associate sticks his head into your office and asks you to help him with an urgent project. He is in the middle of a deal closing. One of the parties has raised a legal issue at the last minute, and the partner on the deal has asked the senior associate to find someone to do some "quick research" and prepare a short summary of the relevant law. He wants to use the summary to decide how big an issue it really is, and as support for any advice he gives the client. You recently prepared a 10-page memo for another partner that took you two weeks to research and write. The partner wants this by the end of the day. How detailed does the summary need to be? How much research is enough to constitute what the partner has in mind by "quick research"? How formal does your summary need to be? What format should it be in? How much explanation do you need to include? These are all questions you will likely need to figure out quickly if you are to get the partner what he needs by the deadline.

Overview of "Informal" Communications

Often, you will not be expected to prepare a formal memorandum to document your research on an issue. Instead, you may be asked to prepare a shorter, more informal summary, such as a short-form memo, a set of bullet points, an email, or handwritten notes. You may also be instructed to limit the amount of time you spend researching. These types of work-product are commonly referred to as "quick-turnaround" assignments.

Your supervising attorney may ask you to do some "quick research," or to "see what you can find without putting in too much time." In other instances, the supervising attorney may specifically tell you that he or she does not want a lengthy memo, just "an informal memo" or "some bullet points." Other times, a partner may indicate she just wants you to send her the information in an email.

Regardless of form, the fundamental characteristics of effective legal writing remain pivotal. In fact, these skills are arguably even more important in a shorter piece of writing than a longer, more formal piece. A longer piece of writing affords the writer the luxury of being less selective in choosing what information to include. This is not to say that the writer of a longer piece should not strive for conciseness and clarity. But the more room the writer has, the less risk she will omit a salient piece of information. Anyone who has had to write a college application essay in 500 words or less will have experienced the pressure of saying as much as you can in as few words as possible.

We turn now to some of the more common forms of quick-turnaround communications that you may be asked to prepare to examine how these fundamental characteristics apply.

The Short-Form Memo

A short-form memo is similar in format to the full-length office memo described in Chapter 6, and all the same considerations apply. However, as the name suggests, it will be shorter (generally no more than three to four pages). This format is one of the most useful in transactional practice, as it lends itself well to the types of legal issues being analyzed. Many of the traditional sections found in a litigation memo, or a full-length transactional office memo, can be omitted.

Eliminate Formal Memo Sections

You normally do not need to include formal memo sections, such as the "Question Presented," and "Brief Answer" sections.[1] These concepts can be incorporated into your introduction. You may likewise decide to omit any discussion of the facts. If you are relying on key facts, or making fundamental assumptions, however, you should provide some indication to your reader that you are aware of and relying on a given set of facts. For instance: "*Based on the facts provided by [client] during this morning's meeting, . . .*" or "*For purposes of this analysis, I have assumed that . . . .*"

You can omit or minimize the number of section headings. The shorter the piece of writing, the less necessary formal headings are to break the writing into sections. Instead, you can use transition words and signposts to guide your reader. For example, instead of a heading such as "*Statement of Facts,*" you can start a new paragraph with "*The facts upon which our analysis is based are as follows,*" and instead of "*Conclusion,*" a paragraph that commences "*In conclusion, ...*"

The key is to make a conscious decision about what headings and sections are needed. You can and should use headings if you think they will aid readability or clarity.

Limit Rule Explanation[2]

Although you should still include a complete description and analysis of the relevant law, this can be condensed. One way to condense your discussion of the rules is to shorten or eliminate your explanation of the rules, or by explaining only the most relevant portions. Another effective technique for shortening your rule explanation is to use parentheticals. The following two excerpts in Figures 7.1 and 7.2 illustrate this technique.

---

1. Chapter 6 describes each of the traditional memo sections and their respective purpose.
2. See Chapter 6 for a brief discussion of rule explanation.

Figure 7.1

MEMORANDUM

Attorney Work Product — Do Not Produce

To: SDO/RDJ/File
From: JAR
Re: [Client}: Research Concerning Meal and Rest Period Issues
Date: May 7, 200_

Per your request. this memo analyzes (1) employers' recordkeeping requirements with respect to meal and rest periods, and (2) the consequences of an employer's failure to comply with meal period recordkeeping and requirements.

For purposes of this analysis, I have assumed the company is located solely within the state of California. I have also assumed that the company employs at least 50 employees.

Relevant Law

Under Section 7 of each of the California IWC wage orders, among other things, every employer is required to keep accurate time records reflecting when each employee begins and ends each work period, including when each employee begins and ends their respective meal periods. Meal periods during which all of the employer's operations cease need not be recorded.

It is the employer's responsibility to keep accurate records of the time that the employees work, including meal periods. If the employer fails to maintain accurate time records, the employee's credible testimony or other credible evidence concerning his hours worked is sufficient to prove a wage claim.

The burden of proof is then on the employer to show that the hours claimed by the employee were *not* worked. Absent such showing by the employer, the employee may establish that he/she was not given and or did not take the requisite meal period. For example, in *Anderson v. Mt Clemens Pottery*, (1946) 328 U.S. 680, 687–88, employees at a 1200-employee, quarter-mile-long pottery plant were entitled to compensation for time spent clocking in, walking to their stations, and preparing to start work (such as turning on their machinery), where the exact times punched in and out were rounded to the nearest quarter hour. Even though the employees could not prove the exact amount of time it took, it could be reasonably inferred that there was an approximate minimal amount of time the employees were required to be on the premises and the employer was unable to establish the precise amount of time worked or negate the reasonableness of the inference.

In Figure 7.1, the last paragraph explains the shift in the burden of proof with a detailed explanation of what happened in the *Anderson* case. Consider how this rule explanation might be useful in a litigation context, where perhaps an employee has sued for missing wages, to help analogize or distinguish the facts of the current case to those of *Anderson* to argue that the same—or different—result should apply.

Recall the primary purpose of a litigation office memo: to educate the reader as to the law and predict outcome based on legal precedent and analysis of the law. The function of detailed rule explanation in this context allows the writer to: (1) convince her reader that her interpretation of the law is correct, and (2) predict outcome with as much certainty and credibility as possible by directly comparing like facts in the precedent case.

In the transactional context, what is the likely purpose of this memo? Remember the forward-looking aspect of transactional practice. A likely purpose is to advise the client as to proper employee record-keeping practices to put in place, or perhaps to evaluate existing procedures at a company your client is looking to acquire. In either case, although the specific factual context of the precedent cases can be helpful, it is not immediately critical. It is not *wrong* to include litigation-style rule explanation in a transactional memo, but—especially in a short-form memo—it is likely not going to be the key focus for your reader. Consider now this revised excerpt of the same memo:

Figure 7.2

MEMORANDUM

Attorney Work Product — Do Not Produce

To: SDO/RDJ/File
From: JAR
Re: [Client}: Research Concerning Meal and Rest Period Issues
Date: May 7, 200_

Per your request. this memo analyses (1) employers' recordkeeping requirements with respect to meal and rest periods, and (2) the consequences of an employer's failure to comply with meal period recordkeeping and requirements.

For purposes of this analysis, I have assumed the company is located solely within the state of California. I have also assumed that the company employs at least 50 employees.

Relevant Law

Under Section 7 of each of the California IWC wage orders, among other things, every employer is required to keep accurate time records reflecting when each employee begins and ends each work period, including when each employee begins and ends their respective meal periods.[1]

It is the employer's responsibility to keep accurate records of the time that the employees work, including meal periods. If the employer fails to maintain accurate time records, the employee's credible testimony or other credible evidence concerning his hours worked is sufficient to prove a wage claim.

The burden of proof is then on the employer to show that the hours claimed by the employee were *not* worked. Absent such showing by the employer, the employee may establish that he/she was not given and or did not take the requisite meal period. *Anderson v. Mt Clemens Pottery*, (1946) 328 U.S. 680, 687–88 (explaining where an employer keeps inadequate or inaccurate time records, and the employee produces sufficient evidence to show the amount of work for which he was not paid as a matter of just and reasonable inference, employee is entitled to damages, even if approximate, if the employer fails to establish the precise amount of time worked or negate the reasonableness of such inference).

---

1. Meal periods during which all of the employer's operations cease need not be recorded.

Note the use in the last paragraph of the parenthetical explanation to further clarify the rule, without the factual detail contained in the first example.

Edit for Conciseness and Clarity

As with longer forms, do not confuse conciseness with superficiality. To be of use, a short-form memo must still contain sufficient information to achieve its purpose and to not be misleading.

The goal is to strike the correct balance between which details to include or omit. Brevity and depth of analysis are not mutually exclusive; rather, the difference comes more in how much detail you provide on the surface.

Illustration: **Striking the Correct Balance While Editing the Short-Form Memo for Conciseness**

Following are three sample excerpts from a short-form memo that describes the available exemptions from registration for an offering of securities:

Sample 1: Several exemptions maybe available. Rule 506(c) is probably the best option as it allows for general solicitation if all investors are accredited investors.

Sample 2: Several exemptions may be available under Regulation D, which provides a safe-harbor from registration if certain requirements are met. Two different Regulation D exemptions might apply: Rule 506(b) and Rule 506(c).

- Under Rule 506(b), the two principal requirements are: (1) there can be no "general solicitation" and (2) the issuer must reasonably believe that the securities are purchased by no more than 35 nonaccredited investors. Additionally, the offering must comply with the general requirements under Rule 501 and Rule 502, including integration, information requirements, and limitations on resale.
- Rule 506(c) allows for general solicitation if: (1) the issuer takes "reasonable steps" to verify that all purchasers are "accredited investors"; (2) the issuer reasonably believes they are, at the time of sale, accredited investors; and (3) the requirements of Rule 501 (definitions), 502(a) (integration) are met. The SEC has provided some guidance on what constitutes "reasonable steps."
- Both exemptions are also subject to "bad-actor" disqualification in Rule 506(d).

Sample 3: Several exemptions may be available. Rule 506(c) is probably the best option as it allows for general solicitation as long as all investors are accredited investors. Rule 506(c) states that to qualify for exemption under this section:

- Sales must satisfy all the terms and conditions of §§ 230.501 and 230.502(a) and (d).
- In addition, all purchasers of securities sold in any offering under this section must be accredited investors. The issuer shall take reasonable steps to verify that purchasers of securities sold in any offering under this section are accredited investors.
  - The issuer shall be deemed to take reasonable steps to verify if the issuer uses, at its option, one of the following nonexclusive and non-mandatory methods of verifying that a natural person who purchases securities in such offering is an accredited investor; provided, however, that the issuer does not have knowledge that such person is not an accredited investor:

1. Reviewing any Internal Revenue Service form that reports the purchaser's income for the two most recent years (including, but not limited to, Form W-2, Form 1099, Schedule K-1 to Form 1065, and Form 1040) and obtaining a written representation from the purchaser that he or she has a reasonable expectation of reaching the income level necessary to qualify as an accredited investor during the current year;

2. Reviewing one or more of the following types of documentation dated within the prior three months and obtaining a written representation from the purchaser that all liabilities necessary to make a determination of net worth have been disclosed: bank statements, brokerage statements and other statements of securities holdings, certificates of deposit, tax assessments, appraisal reports issued by independent third parties; consumer report from at least one of the nationwide consumer reporting agencies; or written confirmation from one of the following persons or entities that such person or entity has taken reasonable steps to verify that the purchaser is an accredited investor within the prior three months and has determined that such purchaser is an accredited investor: a registered broker-dealer; an investment adviser registered with the Securities and Exchange Commission; a licensed attorney who is in good standing under the laws of the jurisdictions in which he or she is admitted to practice law; or a certified public accountant.

Hopefully you immediately recognized that Sample 3 is too in-depth to be helpful in the context of a short-form memo. At the same time, it lacks sufficient breadth by focusing only on one specific exemption. The problem with Sample 3 is not that the information is incorrect, but it includes either too much or too little.

You should also have recognized that Sample 1 does not provide enough information to allow the reader to be able to use the memo to inform herself or to advise the client. It also makes unclear whether the writer has sufficiently researched and understood the issue. The key is to sacrifice excess verbiage, not content.

Sample 2 strikes the right balance between sufficiency and brevity. It informs the reader of all the available options, with enough detail to: (1) convince the reader that the writer has a thorough understanding and (2) allow the reader to accurately determine how each exemption might apply. It also presents the information precisely and clearly. Additional details can always be provided, as needed, or attached as an appendix.

Bullet Point Summaries

Bullet point summaries are an increasingly favored format for busy transactional partners and senior attorneys.

Purpose

The utility of bullet point format is that it increases readability, aids in organizing your thoughts in a logical manner, and demonstrates the relationship between your points without further explanation. As with a long-form or short-form memo, the purpose is still to inform and educate the reader, but in a way that can be more easily digested.

Technique

When preparing bullet points:

- Keep them concise:
  - Avoid unnecessary detail
  - Eliminate metadiscourse and excess verbiage
- Use indents to indicate hierarchy/relationship between points
- Place each separate idea in a separate bullet point
- Use white space to increase readability
- Organize logically (e.g., general to specific)
- Employ parallel structure where possible
- Be consistent with use of punctuation and sentence structure:
  - Complete sentences versus clauses
  - Initial capitalization
  - Punctuation between points
- Try to limit to one page (or one screen if in an email)

As with all writing, drafting bullet points is a recursive process. Start with an idea of the points you want to make, then go back and fill in additional points, subpoints, and details as needed. The level of detail needed in each bullet point, as well as the formality (such as whether to use complete sentences) will depend on your audience. For example, is your reader knowledgeable about the subject matter? Is he someone you communicate with on a regular basis? Is your bullet point summary likely to be circulated to a broader group? It will also depend on purpose. Are you summarizing research on a legal issue, outlining steps that need to be taken, or perhaps requesting information or input?

Fundamental Writing Skills

The use of bullet points does not excuse poor grammar or syntax, or lack of clarity, conciseness, or precision. Bullet points, if used effectively, can improve your writing—but only if you draft each bullet point with these concepts in mind. Bullet points should convey to the reader that the writer took the time to understand, think through, and synthesize each point.

FOR DISCUSSION:

Following are three different examples of bullet points summarizing the requirements for forming a corporation in Delaware for a senior associate who is unfamiliar with Delaware law.

Which of these three examples is more effective, and why? Which is least effective? In reaching your conclusion, consider the following questions: (1) Is there sufficient detail to provide the reader with enough context as to what each point means? (2) Do they include unnecessary detail? (3) Are the points logically organized from general to specific? (4) Is the relationship between the various points (the hierarchy) clear? (5) Is the grammar and syntax consistent throughout? (6) Is there any excess verbiage? (7) As the reader, do you have a clear sense of exactly what the steps would be? (8) Do the bullet points read as if the writer fully understood the law? (9) Any other reactions?

Example #1: Following are the requirements for incorporating in Delaware:

- We first need to file the certificate of incorporation with the Secretary of State of Delaware and pay the filing fee of $89.
- Before filing the certificate of incorporation, the desired name should be reserved to ensure it is available
  - Must contain one of the enumerated words (such as corporation, ltd., etc.)
  - The name must be included in the certificate of incorporation
- Preparation of by-laws—do not need to be filed
- Certificate of incorporation must include certain mandatory provisions; the rest are optional
- The fee is based on the number of pages
- We will need to obtain an agent for service of process.

Example #2: To incorporate in Delaware, there are 5 separate documents/actions that must be completed:

- Certificate of Incorporation
  - Must be filed with the Delaware Secretary of State by incorporator
  - Filing Fee - $89 for first page plus $9 per each extra page
  - Mandatory provisions include:
    - name of corporation
    - business purpose
    - authorized shares
    - name and address of agent for service
    - name and address of incorporator
  - Optional provisions enumerated in DGCL §102(b), including, among others:
    - provision creating, defining, limiting and regulating the powers of the corporation, the directors, and the stockholders, or any class of the stockholder
    - provision eliminating or limiting the personal liability of a director to the corporation or its stockholders for monetary damages for breach of fiduciary duty as a director,
- Obtain Agent for Service of Process
- By-Laws—these do not need to be filed, but should be approved by the Board of Directors
- Action of Sole Incorporator—must appoint initial Board of Directors
- Organizational Meeting—to adopt by-laws, authorize issuance of shares, open bank accounts

Example #3: The following list summarizes the requirements necessary for incorporating a company in the State of Delaware:

- The requirements are set forth in the Delaware General Corporate Law ("DGCL") starting at Section 101.

- DGCL §101 states that the certificate of incorporation needs to be filed by the incorporator with the Secretary of state. It must include certain mandatory information, such as the name of the corporation and the authorized shares, and the business of the corporation. It shall be sufficient to state, either alone or with other businesses or purposes, that the purpose of the corporation is to engage in any lawful act or activity for which corporations may be organized under the General Corporation Law of Delaware, and by such statement all lawful acts and activities shall be within the purposes of the corporation, except for express limitations, if any
- Under DGCL Section 102, the name of the corporation must contain one of the words "association," "company," "corporation," "club," "foundation," "fund," "incorporated," "institute," "society," "union," "syndicate," or "limited," (or abbreviations thereof, with or without punctuation), or words (or abbreviations thereof, with or without punctuation) of like import of foreign countries or jurisdictions (provided they are written in roman characters or letters).
- In addition to the mandatory matters required to be set forth in the certificate of incorporation described above, the certificate of incorporation may also contain any or all of the matters listed in DGCL §102(b). See attached.
- The company will also need to prepare by-laws and hold an organizational meeting.

Exercise 7.1

Using the sample short-form memo included in Appendix B, convert the information into bullet point form. Working in pairs, one of you should assume you are preparing the bullet points for an experienced senior associate. The other should assume you are preparing the bullet points for a client who is unfamiliar with securities laws. Compare your results. How did your intended audience affect how you formulated your bullet points? Which one contained more detail? How did you organize the points?

Informal/Quick Summary

Similar to a short-form memo, a "quick summary" is often less formal. In fact, it can often be presented directly in the body of an email. Characterized by: (1) the time it takes to complete, and (2) the scope and depth of its content, the quick summary will usually require limited research and a quick turnaround—usually no more than a couple of hours. Typically, a quick summary is intended to be a preliminary analysis, and will be followed up by additional, more in-depth analysis if needed.

Purpose

Partners and senior attorneys are under significant pressure to reduce costs and respond quickly to clients. A long-form interoffice memorandum is a luxury for which many clients, especially transactional clients, are unwilling to pay. In addition, a partner may not have time to read a lengthy memo, especially if he is not sure the deal will progress in that direction.

Unlike in litigation, where an accurate and complete prediction as to outcome is essential to move forward with filing documents with the court, the purpose of a research memo in a transactional context tends to be more about providing the partner with a general idea of an area of law, or to help identify a range of potential solutions for a transaction that may or may not proceed. This is not to say that accuracy and completeness do not matter—you should always try to be as accurate and complete as possible within the confines of the work-product you have been asked to produce—rather, a transactional attorney has more flexibility to revisit any relevant issue in greater depth if and when a solution is agreed upon and the parties begin to move forward with documentation.

Context

Recall Simulation Exercise #3 in Chapter 3, which asked you to summarize the basic requirements and applicability of certain contract provisions. The instructions directed you to "not do too much research," and that "some quick Internet research should be sufficient." This is a prime example of the quick summary form.

You were also given clues as to the context—or big picture—in which to frame your assignment; you were told that the parties had still not decided on a deal structure, the partner was "starting to think" about what provisions to include, and that she wasn't going to bill the client. These all suggest the partner was looking for preliminary analysis. She needed enough information to understand the scope of the relevant law and any key requirements, but likely was not looking for much detail in terms of whether the law would be applicable.

The exercise also told you that "email is fine," although deliberately did not specify whether you should present your summary as an attachment or in the body of the email. This required you to use your judgment. Quick summaries lend themselves well to either approach. Look for clues and ask for clarification if you are not sure. The partner specifically said that "email is fine." How was she planning on using your analysis? Was she just using it to quickly educate herself? Did she need your analysis in a separate document? Do not give your supervising attorney more than he or she wants. Is it likely that she will be reviewing on a phone or other handheld device? If so, is it easier for her to have the analysis directly in the body of an email?

Technique

How do you determine how much information is sufficient? Can your analysis be too high level to be useful? At what point are you including too much detail? The key is to: (1) understand the purpose of this type of communication, and (2) recognize the contextual clues as to what the partner is looking for.

Most quick summaries can follow the same format. We will use the topic of the sample short-form memo included in Appendix B to illustrate the format. To recap: our client holds membership interests in a limited liability company (LLC) that engages in real estate investments. It is looking to sell its membership interests. The partner informs you that she is not sure if the membership interests will constitute "securities" for purposes of federal securities laws (and could thus require securities law compliance analysis). She wants you to see if you can find anything informative on this issue.

A quick summary of this issue could be organized using the template in Figure 7.3:

Figure 7.3.

Template	Example
Start by repeating the specific question you have been asked to address:	You have asked whether membership interests in a limited liability company constitute "securities."
Follow this with a short answer:	The short answer is yes, courts generally deem membership interests to constitute securities, particularly when the LLC is manager-managed.
Include any specific facts determinative to your analysis:	My understanding is that in our case, the LLC is manager-managed.
Follow with a brief analysis:	An interest in a limited liability company is a security when the investors in the LLC invest money with the expectation of profits solely from the efforts of others. This ultimately turns on whether and to what extent the day-to-day management of the company is vested in one or more managers, and what, if any, control the members have to restrict the manager's power. In the client's case, although there are some limited veto rights, the day-to-day management of the company is vested in a managing member, and the managing member has the sole right to make all "major decisions."
End with an overall conclusion, consistent with your short answer:	Thus, although we could argue that the veto rights of the members allow them to participate in the management of the company, the more conservative view is that because the majority of decisions will be made by the managing member, the LLC interests will likely be deemed to be securities. We should therefore advise the client on complying with relevant securities laws.

Compare this content to the short-form memo in Appendix B. Note how the crux of the information and conclusion are the same. Note also how, to present the information in the condensed format described above, the writer will have still had to go through the same analysis as they would in preparing the short-form memo.

Depth of Analysis in Informal Communication

Your analysis in a short-form memo, bullet point summary, or quick summary should be as succinct as possible. However, your underlying analysis should be sufficiently thorough to ensure you are providing an accurate and complete account of the relevant law. It is good practice to prepare a separate memo to the file with your rule development, tracking your research and rule synthesis. That is, you still need to go through the same process as with a more traditional memo, but without the need to "show your work." A good analogy is an iceberg. Only the tip of an iceberg is visible above the water, but any good ship captain knows that the bulk of the iceberg lies beneath. The same is true

SUMMARY

UNDERLYING
ANALYSIS

of a summary—what the reader sees is the narrow result of the broader effort and analysis that supports it (much as the summary above would need to be based on the longer short-form memo from Appendix B).

Skimming Versus Diving

Conciseness does not preclude depth of analysis. Distinguish between skimming the surface of an issue and understanding it in sufficient depth such that you can summarize it for the reader. How do you know how deep the partner wants you to go? How do you balance the partner's express instruction that she does not want you to spend too much time on an issue with making sure you deliver her accurate and useful information? Ultimately, being able to effectively "skim" an issue comes with practice. As a junior associate, you will likely need to dive deeper into an issue than the partner may require to arrive at the same result as a more seasoned attorney. For example, if the partner asks you to summarize the Rule 701[3] securities exemption requirements, you may need to spend an hour or so on your own time researching securities laws in general before you understand enough to be able to effectively complete the assigned task and render a succinct summary.

Drafting Professional Email Correspondence

Increasingly, written communications in legal practice are in the form of an email. The benefits of email are significant: it allows cost-effective, real-time communication anywhere in the world. But email can also pose traps for the unwary. Most issues arise when the writer forgets that email in a business or legal setting is still a form of written communication. Another issue is the ease with which emails can be forwarded to large numbers of individuals, literally at the touch of a button. Thus, the best way to approach email correspondence is to treat email as a form of formal written communication. What you put in an email needs to be just as carefully considered as what you put in a letter or a formal memorandum.

As with all other forms of written communication in a legal setting, you are creating a record: the content of email is discoverable, and remains so, long after you have clicked "send." In addition, the goal of effective communication remains the same as with any other form of legal writing: to convey a message to the reader that will be interpreted by the reader as accurately as possible. Finally, emails, however brief, can create a lasting impression.

Purpose

Transactional lawyers rely heavily on email correspondence because of its versatility—it allows for almost instantaneous sharing of files and documents and for communications to be sent at any time of the day or night. Accordingly, emails are relied on for a variety of purposes:

Email as a Cover Note

Each of the characteristics of email correspondence described above can provide huge advantages in the context of negotiating a business deal, which typically involves drafting and negotiating numerous documents simultaneously in a short amount of time. Before email (not that long ago!) transactional lawyers negotiating deals would either sit around a table manually making edits to

---

3. Exemption for Offers and Sales of Securities Pursuant to Certain Compensatory Benefit Plans and Contracts Relating to Compensation, 17 C.F.R. §230.701. Under federal securities laws, offerings of securities must be registered, unless they can satisfy an applicable exemption. Rule 701 is commonly used in connection with the issuance of stock options and other equity compensation to employees.

documents or faxing back and forth comments marked by hand. With the advent of email and more advanced word processing programs came the ability to edit and share documents electronically.

Thus, a principal purpose of email correspondence in transactional practice is its use as a conveyance medium; the email represents a "cover note" to accompany a piece of writing—for example, an email attaching a memo or comments to an agreement.

Email as a Substitute

In other instances, an email can replace another form of writing altogether. Its purpose in this case mimics the purpose of the form of writing it is replacing. For example, an email can be used in lieu of a memo or a letter, or to present a bullet point summary or quick analysis. In these instances, the writing should follow the technique relevant to the form being replaced.

Email as Conversation

In other cases, email correspondence is used to replace an in-person or telephonic conversation. This use of email runs the greatest risk of inadvertent breakdown in communication. The tendency to treat it as conversation lulls the writer into a false communication context. In an actual conversation, the speaker can rely not just on the spoken words to convey his intended meaning, but also on tone and nonverbal cues (more about this in Chapter 8). Email can easily miscommunicate tone, and cannot convey nonverbal cues; thus, the reader can only interpret what is being said by the words themselves. Hence, when engaging in email "conversation," refrain from lapsing too far into conversational language; err on the side of formal writing.

The other peril with email is being lulled into a false sense of security when the person you are conversing with is a friend or close colleague. Tone can easily be misconstrued in email; what might be friendly banter in person could be construed as offensive in written form. Moreover, emails can be forwarded. A good rule is to assume that any email you send can and will be forwarded to others.

Technique

As with all other forms of writing, the same fundamental techniques, including the core techniques of conciseness, clarity, and precision, apply to drafting the substance of an email. In fact, they can be even more critical. Let's examine these techniques in the context of email correspondence, focusing on tone, format, and content:

Tone

- Remain professional. Because emails are generally brief and lack nonverbal cues found in face-to-face communication (or the tone of voice and pace of conversation on the telephone), tone can be difficult to master. Make deliberate choices about the words you use and how you phrase your sentences. Consider the following example:

  A partner emails you to see if you would have time to help with reviewing due diligence files on a pending deal. You have just been assigned by another partner to a deal that requires you to leave that afternoon for Houston for all-day meetings. Which response uses the correct tone?

  Sorry. Can't.

  Sorry. Heading to Houston.

  Sorry, but I don't think I will be able to. I was just asked to fly to Houston this afternoon for the XYZ deal. If it can wait until my return on Friday, however, I would be happy to try to help.

I am so sorry. I always learn so much when working with you and greatly admire you. I will try to find a way to get rid of my other projects to assist you on this deal.

The first and second answers are too abrupt, and make it sound as if you are just not interested, never a good impression for a junior associate to convey. The fourth answer lacks professionalism and doesn't really answer the question. The third answer strikes the correct tone while providing a clear, unequivocal answer that is still polite and professional.

- Give thought to the appropriate salutation. Do you know the person well enough to use their first name?
- Do not send an email while angry or emotional. Before sending an emotional email, try to think about whether you would say the same thing to the person's face and how you would feel if you received the email. Draft the email and then let it sit for a while. Once you are calmer, you can reassess whether your tone is appropriate.

Format

- Keep your style formal, including proper syntax, grammar, punctuation, and formatting. As with other forms of written correspondence, typographical, grammatical, or other errors reflect poorly on your credibility. Avoid common abbreviations found in personal emails (such as "u" instead of "you"), contractions, and colloquialisms.
- Edit and spell-check.
- Avoid using emoticons (☺). Limit your use of exclamation marks and ALL CAPS.
- Use a professional signature block with your contact information and a privilege notice.
- Take the same care with an email that you would for a letter; re-read the email before sending.

Content

- Keep the content short, clear, and readable.
- Make sure the substance is accurate and clearly explained. In doing so, be sensitive to any confidential information (remember, emails can be forwarded).
- Keep your email short. Every word of the email should be necessary. Try to keep your email to one screen length. Once a reader has to start scrolling, the more difficult it is for the reader to absorb the information. Moreover, many clients simply stop reading. If your message is too long, consider creating an attachment.
- Use bullet points or headings to help make the information easier to read.
- Highlight key information, such as deadlines.
- Start with your main point up front (people tend not to scroll all the way down when reading emails).
- Don't forget to add a confidentiality warning as a part of your standard signature. Most firms will have their own standard form.

....

PRACTICE NOTES

Top 10 Do's and Don'ts of Professional Emails

1. *Think twice before sending.* Does the email make sense? Is your reader going to understand it in the way you are intending? Remember the lack of nonverbal cues; humor and sarcasm do not translate well. Also, you need to assume your email may be forwarded. Is there anything included that you would not want anyone other than the recipient to see?

2. *Resist the urge to respond immediately with legal advice.* Take the time to think through what you are being asked and what the response should be, especially if it is a complex issue. A useful technique is to set aside time to respond when you have time to focus fully. Once you have drafted your response—or any email for that matter—re-read it carefully. If you don't know the answer, don't feel obligated to give one anyway. It is better to have an accurate answer in two days than an immediate response that is wrong.

3. *Respond promptly.* How can this piece of advice be reconciled with point #2 above? Point #2 cautions against responding too quickly, before thinking through the response. However, if the response is going to take you some time to research, it can be a good idea to respond briefly to let the sender know you have received the email and are working on it. You can then follow up with a more substantive response without the pressure of immediacy created by email. It is better to respond that you are working on an answer than to provide the wrong answer.

4. *Resist letting your inbox overflow.* Having too many emails in your inbox is not productive for two main reasons: it can make you feel overwhelmed; and it can cause you to lose track of emails that require your attention. Instead, try to keep your inbox to between 20 and 50 emails. One easy way to accomplish this is to create folders. Once you have dealt with an email, move it to the relevant folder. Be selective, however; only save emails that need saving. Try to get into the habit of deleting emails that require no further follow-up and do not contain information that you may need in the future.

5. *Be judicious in responding if not the direct recipient and using "reply all."* If you are copied on an email, consider whether the sender is expecting a response from you or is merely keeping you informed. Unnecessary responses clutter inboxes. The same is true with "reply all." Before selecting this response, consider whether everyone included on the email needs to see your response.

6. *Keep it short.* Work on the assumption that the recipient will not read anything beyond the initial screen and will skip lengthy blocks of text. This reflects how we read online. If an email starts to get too long, consider whether an attachment might be more appropriate.

7. *Pay attention to the subject line.* When responding to an email, make sure the subject line reflects the content of your response. The subject in a chain of emails can morph over time. Updating the subject line can facilitate finding the email later if you need to search your (hopefully) uncluttered inbox. It also helps the recipient decide how quickly to open the email. An email that has "*Lunch on the 25th?*" in the subject line connotes a different time-sensitivity than "*Project Aspen —final draft for review.*"

8. *Err on side of formality.* Recall that your writing will create an impression and that you do not know who else will see your email. In work-related emails, err on the side of formality, even if you are on close terms with the recipient. Do not be lulled into a false sense of comfort by a partner's casual tone. The partner may email you: "*Hey — got those drafts for me yet?*" If you have a good working relationship with the partner, the temptation may be to respond: "*Yeah — hold on—grabbing them now and will shoot them down to you.*" A more appropriate response might be: "*Yes. I will bring them down to you now.*"

9. *Avoid including unintended recipients.* Avoid inputting email addresses until after you have completed drafting. This helps avoid inadvertently sending before you have finalized the draft. In addition, be careful in your use of cc and bcc; only copy those people on an email that need to be on the email. In addition, blind copying recipients (bcc) may not realize they have been blind-copied. As a safer alternative to bcc, you can forward the sent email to these recipients.

10. *If in doubt, DON'T.* If you are not sure whether you should put something into an email, don't. Pick up the phone, or send an email suggesting a phone call.

Understanding Entity and Ownership Structures

I mention companies repeatedly throughout this text. But what do I mean when I refer to a company? What is a company, in concrete terms? Is it the same as a business? Sometimes. A business is a commercial activity. You can operate a business as yourself, or with one or more partners. Or you can form a separate entity—something with a separate legal existence—through which to operate. I refer to an entity in the generic sense as a company. Common entity forms are corporations, limited partnerships, and limited liability companies (LLCs). Each has different characteristics and unique advantages and disadvantages that should be considered in determining which form of entity is most appropriate to your client's business.

These three entity types share two key characteristics: (1) separation of management and ownership (the persons who own the company are not involved in day-to-day decision-making); and (2) limited liability (to differing degrees).

In a corporation, owners are referred to as shareholders (or stockholders), and the management of the corporation is in the hands of the board of directors (and by delegation, to officers). In a limited partnership, the owners are the limited partners, and the general partner manages the affairs of the partnership (although the general partner will also have an ownership stake). In an LLC, the owners are known as members. The affairs of the LLC can be handled either by the members (this is referred to a member-managed LLC), or by one or more managers, who may or may not also be members (a manager-managed LLC).

Owners hold their ownership interests in "pieces" or percentages. In a corporation, these are expressed as shares; in a partnership, as limited partnership interests; and in an LLC, as membership interests or membership units. Under U.S. federal securities laws, shares are securities, subject to federal and state securities laws that govern their offer, purchase, and sale.[4] Whether partnership interests and LLC membership interests are securities is not as clearly defined. But the general view is any ownership interest held by a person not involved in the management of the entity likely is a security.[5]

Using Citations in Transactional Practice

You may have noticed in the sample memo on page 259 the writer included full citations in the text of the memo itself. Whether to include citations at all and, if so, whether to include them in the body of the memo, is a question of style and personal preference of the attorney for whom you are preparing the memo or other form of writing.

Generally, formal citations are less prevalent in transactional memo writing. The main reason for this is that legal analysis in transactional practice typically is forward-looking. Your goal is to problem-

---

4. The U.S. Securities Act of 1933 defines a security as: "any note, stock, treasury stock, bond, debenture, evidence of indebtedness, certificate of interest or participation in any profit-sharing agreement, collateral-trust certificate, pre-organization certificate or subscription, transferable share, investment contract, voting-trust certificate, certificate of deposit for a security, fractional undivided interest in oil, gas, or other mineral rights, any put, call, straddle, option, or privilege on any security, certificate of deposit, or group of index of securities (including any interest therein or based on the value thereof), or any put, call, straddle, option or privilege entered into on a national securities exchange relating to foreign currency, or, in general, any interest or instrument commonly known as a 'security,' or any certificate of interest or participation in, temporary or interim certificate for, receipt for, guarantee of, or warrant or right to subscribe to or purchase, any of the foregoing." 15 U.S.C. §77b(a)(1).

5. *See* SEC v. Howey, 328 U.S. 293, 298 (1946) (establishing a four-part test for determining whether an investment qualifies as an investment contract and thus a security, including whether there is: (1) an investment of money (2) in a common enterprise, with (3) an expectation of profits (4) derived from the efforts of others). This *Howey* test has over time led the SEC and the courts to focus on the degree of involvement of the investors in the management of the enterprise in determining whether an interest is a security.

solve and advise on action going forward. Thus, either no citable source exists, or the source is not relevant. This is especially true of case law, which will only exist for issues that have been litigated in the past. In the litigation context, the underlying statute or case law is critical to outcome; the lawyer's job is to convince the judge that her client should win, *based on* precedent. Thus, the judge and the lawyer on the other side need to be able to easily identify and refer to the cited sources to assess the strength of your arguments. The transactional lawyer's job is to find ways to achieve a result that complies with existing law, rather than to argue that a result is correct based on existing law. Both involve careful analysis of the law, but the emphasis is different.

Another reason is that citations provided in a transactional memo tend to be for internal use. Thus, it can be less important for the citations to be in correct format, provided the reader can easily identify the source. In litigation, citations will make their way into formal pleadings filed with the court, which must strictly comply with formatting and other rules, including proper citation format.

Of course, you should still rely on accurate sources where possible, and the partner reading your memo should be able to double-check the accuracy of your analysis for himself. For example, if you are describing the mandatory provisions that must be included in the articles of incorporation when forming a corporation in New York, the partner will likely expect you to include a reference to the relevant statutory provision. It is common to include citations in footnotes, where they are less distracting but still available.

Conclusion

Informal written communication will likely form a significant part of a junior transactional associate's daily tasks. The challenge is being able to adapt the fundamental skills and techniques to any form to communicate as effectively and efficiently as possible. Regardless of form, your writing should be professional in tone, concise, clear, precise, free from grammatical errors, purpose-driven, and reader-centered.

SIMULATION EXERCISE #6

A partner has asked you to do some quick research for her. She tells you that she has a client based in California who is considering an arrangement whereby he would introduce potential investors to a real estate fund. He would receive a commission based on the amount of investment from investors introduced by him. The partner tells you that she is pretty sure this would trigger securities broker-dealer registration requirements.[6] She recalls that there is an exception for "finders" (individuals who limit their activities to introducing investors) but can't remember exactly what the requirements are. She would like you to research and summarize for her in an email whether a person acting as a finder is exempt from the broker-dealer licensing requirements.

To help you get started, she forwards to you an excerpt from a California Bar Association e-bulletin she received:

New Rules Implementing Statutory Exemption from California Securities Broker-Dealer Registration for "Finders" Go into Effect

The California Department of Business Oversight has adopted final rules 10 CCR §260.211.4–§260.211.7 implementing California's exemption from broker-dealer registration for certain individuals acting as finders in securities transactions. The exemption,

---

6. See Practice Note on Broker-Dealers in Chapter 3 for background on broker-dealer regulation.

codified on January 1, 2016 at §25206.1 of the Corporations Code, provides long-sought clarification of the scope of allowable activities for finders in securities transactions in California and creates a streamlined regulatory framework in which finders can legitimately provide services. Most significantly, it permits finders who satisfy the requirements of the exemption to receive transaction-based compensation.[7]

She also provides you with the following suggested sources: two recent SEC No-Action letters[8] *and a guide published by the SEC:*

1. *Brumberg, Mackey, & Wall P.L.C.*, SEC No-Action Letter, Fed. Sec. L. Rep. (CCH) ¶[   ] (May 2010).
2. *Hallmark Capital Corporation*, SEC No-Action Letter, Fed. Sec. L. Rep. (CCH) ¶[   ] (June 2007).
3. *SEC Guide to Broker-Dealer Registration* (2008), available at https://www.sec.gov/reports pubs/investor-publications/divisionsmarketregbdguidehtm.html#II).

She also mentions that she has seen several articles online on the topic. You may do any additional research you consider necessary but should not spend more than one hour on additional research.

---

7. Julie Ryan, *New Rules Implementing Statutory Exemption from California Securities Broker-Dealer Registration for "Finders" Go into Effect*, STATE BAR OF CALIFORNIA BUSINESS LAW SECTION CORPORATIONS E-BULLETIN (July 6, 2017).

8. As we saw in the Practice Note on Broker-Dealers in Chapter 3, no-action letters are published responses provided by the SEC to individuals who ask the SEC to review a proposed action to determine whether the SEC would likely take enforcement action against the individual if the individual were to proceed with the stated course of action. In other words, the individual is asking the SEC to confirm whether a given action violates a specific provision of the federal securities laws. These no-action letters are persuasive but nonbinding.

Chapter 8

······················

Oral Communication in
Transactional Practice

This chapter turns to oral communication and the role it plays in transactional lawyering. We begin with a theoretical discussion of how oral communication works, and from there move on to exploring specific techniques for improving oral communication skills in general, as well as in specific contexts (including cross-cultural situations). Finally, no chapter on oral communication would be complete without a discussion of active listening and its role in effective communication.

By the end of this chapter, you will be able to:

- Effectively communicate in an in-person setting with other lawyers
- Participate with confidence in a teleconference, meeting, or other law firm group setting
- Recognize and accurately interpret nonverbal and other visual cues in oral communication
- Engage in cross-cultural communication by recognizing and adapting to cross-cultural differences

···

You have been working on due diligence in connection with a large merger in which your firm represents the acquiror. You are the most junior member of the team. The parties have agreed for the lawyers from both sides to meet next week for the next—and hopefully final—round of negotiations on the merger agreement. In anticipation of these negotiations, the partner in charge of the deal has called an all-hands meeting to go over any major issues that need to be addressed, as well as strategy. She mentions to you that she may call on you to outline any issues relating to your due diligence investigation. You know the due diligence inside out, and have perfected your due diligence report, but are nervous about speaking in front of a group of more senior lawyers. How much detail do you need to go into? What if they ask you questions to which you don't know the answer? How should you best prepare?

···

Face-to-Face (In-Person) Communication

Face-to-face communication is perhaps the easiest—and most difficult—form of communication for a junior transactional lawyer to master. On the one hand, you can use nonverbal cues, receive instant feedback on whether what you are communicating is being interpreted correctly, and adjust your message as you go. In this respect, you have a large margin of error. If you use the wrong word or ramble on, your listener may start looking confused or ask you to confirm what you just said. If you are paying attention and actively listening (more about this later), you can quickly correct the word or rephrase, ensuring the message is correctly interpreted.

On the other hand, written communication provides the luxury of being able to review, revise, and rethink what you are communicating before the other person ever sees it. How and what you communicate creates an impression on the listener. If what you are saying is disorganized, vague, or inaccurate—if the listener must repeatedly ask you to go back and rephrase or clarify—the impression likely will be that your understanding of the subject matter is disorganized, superficial, or incorrect, and the listener is likely to not have much confidence in what you are saying.

The goal is to communicate as effectively in person as in written communication, but with less time to think about what you are saying and how you are saying it. It seems like a tall order, but this chapter explores some techniques for becoming more confident, poised, and articulate in an oral communication setting. Before delving into these techniques, we first need to understand how oral communication works.

How Oral Communication Works

Understanding how oral communication works—how a speaker transmits a message to the listener—can help us become more effective. In his 1967 article, *Decoding of Inconsistent Communications*,[1] Albert Mehrabian argued that oral communication consists of three interrelated components: vocal, visual, and verbal. Although the article has been widely misinterpreted over the years,[2] the theory that oral messages are communicated through a combination of these three components is today broadly accepted. What role does each play?

- *Vocal.* Vocal refers to everything the listener hears *except* the actual words. It refers to things such as tone, inflection, and volume. For example, if someone is shouting, the listener will likely interpret that the speaker is angry or excited. Dogs are experts at interpreting vocal communication. The words you speak to a dog do not matter as much as the tone in which you say them. If you want to experiment with this theory, ask a dog if it wants a bath in the same tone of voice as asking if it wants a treat. Even though the dog may hate having baths, it will likely wag its tail enthusiastically—until it sees the water!
- *Visual.* Examples of this component include body language (such as leaning forward or crossing your arms), facial expression, eye contact, and movement or gestures. We often refer to these as nonverbal communication, or nonverbal cues. Both speakers and listeners emit these cues but are not necessarily conscious of doing so; the key is to notice them. For example, if I am teaching a class and see a student looking confused or beginning to look around the room, it communicates to me that the student is not understanding, or has lost interest in, what I am saying. By picking up on the visual cues, I can adjust what I am saying and how I am saying it (the verbal and the vocal components) to clarify the point I am seeking to communicate and to (hopefully) re-engage the student.[3]

---

1. Albert Mehrabian and Morton Weiner, 6(1) *Decoding of Inconsistent Communications*, J. PERSONALITY & SOC. PSYCH. 109 (1967).

2. See the author's website at http://www.kaaj.com/psych/smorder.html/.

3. Note that the visual component is lost when the conversation takes place over the phone. Thus, the verbal—and to a lesser extent the vocal—components take on added importance (some vocal cues are less apparent when not in-person, such as pauses or uncertainty).

- *Verbal.* Verbal refers to the actual words spoken. This component is perhaps the most obvious element of communication, and the one we think of as being the most important; after all, without words, how can we properly convey the intended message? But if we stop to consider how much we can communicate without words (for example, when communicating with someone who speaks a different language, or a child) we see that, while helpful at making our communication more precise, it is not necessarily the most significant component.

Lots of room exists for misinterpretation and miscommunication of any of these aspects of oral communication. It can be as simple as misreading someone's facial expression or hearing a word incorrectly. Thus, as natural and intuitive as oral communication may be, when communicating orally in a legal setting, try to put as much thought into what you are saying and how you are saying it as if you were writing it down.

Techniques for Becoming a More Effective Oral Communicator

The first step in improving your oral communication skills is in recognizing and understanding the significance of each of the three components described above. The more aware the speaker and listener are of these three elements, the more effective the oral communication. The next step is to become more conscious of your own word choice, as well as the vocal and visual cues you are providing.

Some specific techniques to practice:

Verbal:

- *Speak slowly and clearly.* This helps ensure that your listener hears the words correctly. It also allows you more time to think before you speak. Finally, it allows you time to notice the non-verbal cues being communicated by your listener (remember, communication is a two-way street).
- *Organize what you are saying from general to specific.* As with written communication, the more logically organized your thoughts, the easier it will be for the listener to understand. The tendency is to rush to make your point, but what information does your listener need first to put what you are saying into proper context? Remember, your listener may not have the same information you have and may be thinking about something completely different. For example, instead of walking into the partner's office and starting with: "*I don't think there are any exceptions we can use for that client you asked me about,*" you could say "*I wanted to get back to you on the [XXX] matter. You remember you asked me to look into whether there might be an exception we could rely on. Unfortunately, I don't think there is one.*"
- *Be precise, clear, and concise.* Make sure you are using correct terminology, stating your point as unambiguously as possible, and being as succinct as possible (without sacrificing clarity) to minimize interference with the intended message.

Vocal:

- *Maintain a calm and professional tone.* This may seem obvious, but it can be easy to get excited. In general, the calmer and more collected you appear to your listener, the greater the credibility of what you are saying.
- *Err on the side of formality.* As with email, we tend in conversation to slip into colloquialisms and shorthand. It is of course appropriate to strike a more conversational tone, but avoid crossing the line into offending someone with too familiar a tone. The best practice is to maintain a level of deference when speaking with a partner or supervising attorney.

- *Don't be afraid to pause.* Allow yourself time to think about what you are going to say.

Visual/Nonverbal:

- *Make eye contact.* This allows you to remain engaged with your listener and to be ready to spot the listener's nonverbal cues.[4]
- *Lean forward (if you are sitting at a table).* This indicates interest in what the other person is saying, as opposed to leaning back in your chair, which can signal indifference.
- *Use hand gestures, but in moderation.* Hand gestures can be helpful nonverbal cues, but they can also be distracting if overused. If you know you tend to "speak with your hands," try to moderate your gestures by consciously keeping your hands at your sides, or perhaps placing them on the table and either interlacing your fingers or placing one hand over the other.
- *Eliminate any distracting tics.* If you have a habit of clicking the top of your pen, leave it on the table. Other things to look out for are fiddling with hair, doodling, or tapping feet.
- *Smile.* Unless you are attempting to communicate anger or disappointment, try not to frown or scowl. Many of us do this when we are thinking but it can be easily misinterpreted.
- *Engage in active listening.* This facilitates communication by providing the speaker with appropriate cues and maximizing the accuracy of what is heard. Active listening is discussed in more detail below.

Finally, be prepared. If you know you are going to have to orally present the results of your research to the partner, outline what you are going to say in a couple of bullet points. Make sure you are as familiar as possible with what you are planning to talk about. The more prepared you are, the more confident you will feel, and the more you will be able to concentrate on communicating effectively.

Cross-Cultural Considerations

As if communicating orally is not hard enough, communicating in a cross-cultural context, orally or in writing, poses unique barriers. In Chapter 4 we examined how communication is a two-way street, with expression at one end, and interpretation of meaning at the other. Many things can interfere with the message in between. In a cross-cultural situation, added barriers such as language, context, and cultural expectations and norms can create additional interference.[5]

The most obvious barrier involves the verbal component (the language itself). Inevitably, if a language barrier is present, it will affect how precisely you can communicate. In this setting, you need to rely more on vocal and visual cues to convey the intended meaning. But these components pose barriers of their own. What may be attentive and engaging in one culture (for example, maintaining eye contact) can be interpreted as disrespectful or disconcerting in another.[6] Nodding or smiling can sometimes convey an unintended meaning. Speaking too forcefully—or too quietly—can connote the opposite of what is intended.

Moreover, different cultures place different emphasis on nonverbal and vocal cues. For example, in "high-context" cultures,[7] meaning comes more from how something is said (or what is not said); less attention is placed on the words themselves. In "low-context" cultures, the opposite tends to be true.

---

4. See discussion below on cross-cultural considerations. In some cultures, making direct or prolonged eye contact can be disconcerting or considered disrespectful.

5. See Chapter 5 for a more in-depth discussion of cross-cultural communication theory and techniques.

6. *See* Watkins, *supra* Chapter 5, note 10, at 25; Bryant, *supra* Chapter 5, note 12.

7. See Chapter 5 for an explanation of high-context and low-context attributes.

It is impossible to familiarize yourself with the communication preferences and subtleties of all the various cultures with which you may come into contact. The key is in being aware that differences exist and paying attention to the cues you receive.

FOR DISCUSSION:

How do you show politeness? How would you indicate to someone that a chair is free? That it is not free? How do you indicate you are interested in what someone is saying? How similar/dissimilar are your responses to those of others in the class?

Exercise 8.1

Working in pairs, try the following: (1) talk to your partner without making/breaking eye contact; (2) ask to borrow a book without being direct; (3) while your partner tells you about a recent vacation, try communicating that you find the story boring or interesting (your choice), using any combination of verbal, visual, and vocal cues. If you are the listener, what cues did you choose and why? If you are the speaker, how easily could you tell what the other person was thinking? What were the cues? Were they visual, verbal, or vocal?

Active Listening

> *"When you have a conversation, do you listen, or do you wait to talk?"*
> *"I have to admit, I wait to talk, but I'm trying hard to listen."*
>
> — Pulp Fiction[8]

Most people agree there are different types of listeners and different levels of listening. Terminology varies; I categorize them here as follows:

Level 1: Not listening. The listener at this level simply tunes out the speaker. The listener may be hearing the speaker but is not engaged in communicating with the listener: he or she is not attempting to interpret what is being said.

Level 2: Superficial listening. This type of listening refers to a listener who is not hearing every word because she is too busy interpreting and getting ready to respond: she is hearing the words but not really digesting them. This type of listening is especially problematic in a cross-cultural situation, as it can be harder for a non-native speaker to "fill-in-the-blanks" between what she hears and what the speaker is intending to be understood. The superficial listener is not taking the extra step to understand the context and to attempt to receive the message the speaker is trying to convey. For example, if I tell my children to put their electronic devices away and go to bed, they may just put their devices down, missing the context of my message: that it is bedtime. Similarly, if a partner asks you

---

8. Pulp Fiction (Miramax Films 1994).

to do something and you are listening while anticipating your response, you may tune out important context and other details.

Level 3: "Waiting to talk" listening. This type of listening is the lawyer's curse: we are too busy focusing on what we are going to say in response to listen carefully. This type of listener often cuts off the speaker, or relates what is being said to a prior, personal experience. Thus, the listener is not fully engaged in what the speaker is saying. This type of listening differs from superficial listening in that the listener is not tuning out what is being said; rather, this listener thinks or talks over the speaker.

Level 4: Active listening. Most of you should be familiar with this term. Active listening involves not just hearing but making sure you are understanding the message and the point of view of the speaker. Although scholarly views vary, most divide active listening into at least three elements.[9] Key elements include sensing, attending, and responding:[10]

- *Sensing*: being receptive to the speaker's visual and vocal cues in addition to the verbal cues (i.e., what the speaker is *not* saying).[11] This requires a degree of perceptiveness, especially in cross-cultural situations where visual and vocal cues might have different connotations. It can help to take notes as the speaker is talking to allow you to listen attentively without the concern of missing a point to which you want to respond or a follow-up question you want to ask.
- *Attending*: sending messages back to the speaker to show that you are actively listening.[12] The most common of these include leaning forward, nodding, providing verbal cues (such as "uh, huh," or "go on"), and other signals that show the speaker you are listening attentively.
- *Responding*: giving the speaker feedback to minimize any miscommunication. Feedback can be in the form of repeating parts of what the speaker is saying (we do this when taking down phone numbers) or recapping or clarifying, using phrases such as "to confirm," or "from what I understand." For example, when the client says: "We want to buy a company but are concerned with liabilities," effective responding might be to ask a clarifying question, such as: "So I am getting this right, you are most concerned with liabilities? Anything in particular?"

Exercise 8.2

Listen to the recording played by your instructor. Work in pairs to draft an email summarizing the main points of the recorded conversation.

In completing the exercise, also try to identify what type of listening is going on between the parties on the recording. How can you tell?

---

9. Harry Weger Jr., Gina Castle Bell, Elizabeth M. Minei & Melissa C. Robinson, *The Relative Effectiveness of Active Listening in Initial Interactions*, 28 Int'l J. of Listening, 13, 14 (2014), *available at* https://doi.org/10.1080/10904018.2013.813234; *see* John Barkai, *How to Develop the Skill of Active Listening*, 30 Practical Lawyer 73 (1984), *available at* https://ssrn.com/abstract=1437265; *see also* https://www.mindtools.com/CommSkll/ActiveListening.htm (last visited Sept. 18, 2018).

10. Mary-Beth Moylan & Stephanie J. Thompson, Global Lawyering Skills 100 (2013); Sheila Steinberg, An Introduction to Communication Studies 77 (Juta 2007).

11. Albert Mehrabian, Nonverbal Communication (Transaction Pub. 1972).

12. Moylan & Thompson, *supra* note 10, at 100.

Managing In-Person Communications with Partners and Other Senior Attorneys

Oral communication in a law firm setting often occurs when a partner or senior associate asks you to stop by her office to discuss an assignment. Never go into a partner's office without a pen and paper. This shows you are prepared. Taking notes will help you engage in active listening and ensure that you have the information you will need later when you sit down to start working on the assignment.

Try not to leave the partner's office without understanding exactly what you have been asked to do. It is better to be sure of what you are doing than to waste time doing the wrong thing. Most partners—this author included—prefer a junior associate to ask questions if she has any doubt as to what the task is. A busy partner would rather invest an extra five minutes going over instructions for an assignment than two hours fixing what you turn in.

Some questions you can ask when being given an assignment include:

- When do you need this by?
- In what format would you like this?
- Who should I bill my time to?
- Do you want me to limit my hours?

Other questions will depend on the assignment. Make sure you engage in active listening; paying close attention to what the partner is and is not saying, nodding or giving some sign that you understand what you are being told (or that you don't understand something), and responding—repeating key points, clarifying, or asking follow-up questions. For example, if the partner tells you she wants you to review a purchase agreement for inconsistencies with the term sheet, you might respond: "Should I limit my review for inconsistencies with the term sheet, or would you like me to flag other issues I see, as well?" Or: "How would you like me to mark the inconsistencies—in a memo, or directly on the purchase agreement?"

FOR DISCUSSION:

Consider the following email chain forwarded to you from a partner, relating to a start-up client, TrustCo. We know that Max is a potential venture capital investor who is considering investing in the client. What clues do you have as to what you are being asked to do? What information do you need to know to complete task efficiently? What questions might you ask the partner?

Fwd: TrustCo NDA Redlined

Partner partner@ryanlaw.com   Tue, Jan 31 at 6:18 PM
To: Junior Associate <juniorassoc@ryanlaw.com>

See below — please review and let me know if you see any major issues.
— J

On Tue, Jan 31, Beth Jones <bjones@trustco.com> wrote:

Julie —

We had just used the older NDA provided by our former attorney. Can you do a quick review please? Want to get this back to him ASAP.

Best,
Beth
CEO

On Tue, Jan 31, Max Smith <max@capitalco.com wrote:

Beth —

Just received the NDA back from our attorneys with a few minor comments:

1) The NDA you sent was unilateral, so we edited to make mutual
2) We shortened the duration to a more reasonable period
3) We removed the binding arbitration clause
4) Minor tightening of language elsewhere

Please let me know your thoughts so we can get this signed up and get started on due diligence.

Max

Participating in Meetings and Other Group Settings

Participating in internal law firm meetings can be daunting for a junior associate. What is the accepted protocol? Is there a place you should sit? Does anyone know who you are? How much should you plan on speaking? Can and should you ask questions? The answer to all of these is: it depends. The key is to read the room, and to prepare as much as possible beforehand. Following are some useful techniques for any situation:

- *Greet your neighbor.* Make eye contact with the person sitting immediately to either side of you. If you don't know them (and assuming the meeting hasn't already started) introduce yourself. If it's a small table, you may want to do the same with the person sitting across from you. By "breaking the ice," you open the lines of communication between you and these other individuals, who may be more inclined as a result to explain protocol to you or to include you in conversation.

- *Engage in active listening.* Try not to tune out. You never know when the conversation might turn around and suddenly, someone asks you: "What do you think?" It can be embarrassing if you have to ask, "About what?"

- *Be prepared to speak.* If you know you may be asked to respond to questions, bring any relevant materials with you. If they are voluminous, have them tabbed for easy reference, or you may want to prepare a bullet point outline of key points for yourself.

- *Be prepared to NOT speak (unless called for).* Depending on your role in the transaction and the seniority of the other participants, you may be expected to be a silent observer. Be wary of jumping into the conversation unsolicited, especially if you are not sure of what is being discussed. Of course, if you have information you think would be helpful, then you should probably offer it. For example, as the junior associate on a deal, you may be the person with the most in-depth knowledge of due diligence materials. If one of the partners at the meeting asks whether there are any issues with assigning contracts, you may be the best—or only—person to answer the question accurately.

- *Don't forget your fundamental communication skills.* If you are called upon to speak, organize your thoughts, speak clearly, deliberately, and precisely, make eye contact, eliminate any nervous tics (to the best of your ability), and keep your tone professional.

PRACTICE NOTES

Subject Files

The discussion question above asks you to consider what information you would need to review a nondisclosure agreement (NDA). Part of the issue for a junior associate is in knowing what you don't know. How can you determine what should or should not be in an NDA (or whether and how a provision should be revised) if you have never drafted or negotiated an NDA? Most transactional lawyers build up subject files over time—each time they work on a form of document, they save a copy into an indexed subject file. When they are asked to draft a similar document for a client, they can easily access prior forms. As a junior associate, it can help to find a more senior associate who has a decent subject file built up. In addition, most firms have a centralized document database that is searchable. Each time you are exposed to a new form of document from a reliable source, save it to your own subject file. When naming the document for your subject file, try to use as descriptive a name as possible that will help you identify the most appropriate form for later use. For example: "Short-form APA-Pro-Buyer," or "Mutual NDA-NY law."

Due Diligence

We refer to due diligence throughout this text. Due diligence is a task commonly assigned to junior associates. But what is it, exactly? Due diligence is an investigative process, most common in a mergers and acquisitions context, pursuant to which the buyer ascertains information about the seller. The purpose is threefold: (1) learn about the business being acquired; (2) discover actual and potential problems or liabilities; and (3) frame the representations and warranties the seller will be asked to make.

The side conducting the due diligence inquiry provides a due diligence checklist containing a list of all items it would like to review. Typical categories of items include corporate matters (certificate of incorporation, share registers, minutes), contracts, customers and vendors, employee matters, litigation, environmental matters, intellectual property, financial information, and regulatory matters. The other side will typically provide the responses (mostly in the form of copies of documents) in a data room. Most data rooms are now electronic, using a document sharing program to organize responses and allowing the buyer to review the documents.

Once the data room has been populated, the junior associate's task is to review each document, identifying and summarizing key issues. The issues that need to be spotted will vary depending on the category of document, the type of transaction, and whom you represent. The junior associate will then prepare summaries of each set of documents, and eventually a complete due diligence report summarizing the information gleaned from the investigation, including highlighting any potential problems or liabilities.

We discuss drafting due diligence checklists and reports in more detail in Chapter 11.

Conclusion

Being an effective oral communicator is an important component of being an effective associate. To be an effective oral communicator, you need to understand how communication works and to develop an awareness of the barriers to effective communication. Learning to speak clearly; to organize your thoughts; to regulate your tone, volume, and nonverbal signals; and to engage in active listening are all critical in minimizing barriers to effective oral communication.

SIMULATION EXERCISE #7

The partner stops you in the hall and thanks you for the research you recently prepared for him but tells you he doesn't have time to review it. Instead, he asks if you can stop by his office to give him a quick summary. Using the research you prepared for Simulation Exercise #3, prepare a brief oral presentation to the partner summarizing the results of your research.

Your instructor will provide additional information regarding the logistics of your presentation, the use of visual aids, and whether you will present individually, or in small groups.

B

Communicating with the Client

Chapter 9

....

Introduction to Client Communications and Meetings

In this chapter, we turn to the second of our three communication contexts: communicating with the client. Much of what we have learned thus far continues to apply in this context, with additional nuances. This chapter starts by looking at communicating with the client in the broader sense: how to engage in client-centered lawyering and distinguishing between advising and counseling. It then moves on to look at client meetings and other forms of in-person communication.

By the end of this chapter, you will be able to:

- Practice client-centered lawyering
- Distinguish between advising and counseling clients
- Prepare for and participate in a client meeting

....

You have been working at your firm for several months and have been involved with several different transactions. The partner for whom you do most of your work has commended you on a due diligence report you recently completed on one of her deals, and thinks you are ready to take on a larger role on her next project. She mentions that she will expect you to have more direct contact with the client. You are excited to be given the opportunity to take on more responsibility but are nervous about having to interact with the client. You are just a junior associate. How should you even address the client? What if you say the wrong thing? What if you give the client the wrong advice?

....

Overview

Most of the fundamental communication techniques discussed in the context of communicating with partners or senior associates apply equally to communicating with clients. Using the correct tone, making effective use of vocal, verbal, and visual cues, and engaging in active listening all contribute to effective communication and to minimizing miscommunication.

Beyond these fundamental communication techniques, however, communicating effectively with clients poses additional challenges. Recall our discussion in Chapter 4 on reader-centered writing and the four maxims of effective communication: quality, quantity, relevance, and manner. As with other audiences, to effectively communicate your message to your client, you must ensure that the information you provide and how you present it matches your client's assumptions as to the accuracy, relevance, and sufficiency of that information.

One of the more difficult aspects of client communications for junior associates to master is determining how much technical detail to provide clients. Most clients do not have legal backgrounds and can be an extremely diverse group, from experienced businesspeople, to unsophisticated entrepreneurs, to experts in their field. Generally, unless the client is also a lawyer, it is not particularly helpful to the clients to provide them with detailed legal analysis, quoted statutory language, or citations. On the other hand, you need to make sure the client has sufficient information on which to base its decisions. Your job is to synthesize your legal analysis in a manner that will maximize its usefulness to the client. This is the cornerstone of client-centered lawyering.

Client-Centered Lawyering[1]

The best analogy to explain client-centered lawyering is patient-centered medical care. Traditionally, the view was that doctors knew what was best for their patients, and that patients, due to their lack of medical training, should defer to the advice of their doctor. There has been a push in recent years against this elitist view to allow a patient adequate information, presented in a way the patient—as a non-medical professional—can understand, so that the patient can make an informed decision.

The same is true in the legal profession. Because the lawyer knows the law and the client does not, the tendency is to decide what to tell or not to tell the client, make decisions for the client, and not give the client sufficient information to allow the client to make its own informed decision. Yet the client is the one who must live with the decision.

Consider this example of a doctor's communication with a patient:

> *"You have a non-small cell adenocarcinomas in your lower right lobe. I'm going to have my staff book you into the OR for next week and we'll take a look."*

If you are the patient, what do you do with this information? Panic, possibly. Can the patient be sure what it means? Is the patient able to make an informed decision? Who is making the decision? The doctor. It could be the best decision, but it is difficult to know for sure without understanding what he is proposing and what the options are.

Now consider this alternative:

> *"You have lung cancer. There are two types, based on how they look and how they grow: small cell and non-small cell. You have the second type. This type of cancer tends to spread more slowly than small-cell but can be harder to isolate. There are a number of different treatment options. . . . I would recommend option 'A' as I believe it can offer you the best chance of long-term recovery."*

In this example, the patient can understand what he is being told and is given a sense of what the options are, allowing the patient to make his own decision, with the guidance of the doctor. This is what we are striving for in client-centered lawyering.

Now let's look at two examples in the legal context:

---

1. This concept is widely recognized as having been first formulated in DAVID A. BINDER & SUSAN C. PRICE, LEGAL INTERVIEWING & COUNSELING: A CLIENT-CENTERED APPROACH (1977).

"I understand you want to acquire company X. I generally recommend a reverse-triangular merger. I'll have my associate start drafting the documents for you to review."

"I understand you want to acquire company X. Can you tell me a bit more about your goals in doing this? Are you interested in acquiring its entire operations? There are a couple of ways to go. One possible option is what we call a reverse-triangular merger. Are you familiar with this concept? This is where . . . ."

Hopefully, the difference between these two examples is evident. The second example provides the client with information that enables it to make an informed decision, without condescending.

Techniques for Engaging in Client-Centered Lawyering

How can we make sure we are engaging in client-centered lawyering? What techniques is the lawyer using in the above example?

- *Active listening.* She is engaging in active listening, using sensing and responding techniques to confirm her understanding of the client's actual concerns (for example, she starts with "I understand" and repeats the client's words).
- *Questioning.* Note how the lawyer is careful to ensure the information she is providing is accurate and sufficient, by verifying whether the client needs additional details and asking questions of the client. Asking questions enables her to more effectively advise the client: the more clearly identified the problem, the easier it is to solve and to generate options. Recall that generating options is part of the "A" of the "SANE" acronym used to describe the transactional lawyer's role in Chapter 2. The more skilled a transactional attorney is at listening to the client and drawing out the pertinent information, the more able she will be to accurately assess the issues and generate valid options or strategies.
- *Appropriate tone.* Note also how the attorney in the above example explains the information to the client without appearing condescending or pedantic by checking with the client whether the client is familiar with the concept. Watch verbal and visual cues, such as eye-rolling, sighing, or an impatient tone, which can also make you seem arrogant. No one appreciates arrogance, especially from someone they are paying to perform services.

Additional techniques that facilitate informed decision-making:

- *Know the client's business.* To be able to provide the client with relevant information, you need to understand the client's issues in context and to have a sense of the "big picture" from the client's perspective.
- *Determine information that is relevant or necessary.* What information will your client consider relevant to its decision? Is there any additional information necessary for your client to understand the relevant information? Avoid tangential information that does not fit into either of these categories. For example, when explaining the benefits and disadvantages of forming a corporation versus a limited liability company, you may need to start by explaining the concept of a board of directors and shareholders in a corporation ("necessary" information) to help your client better understand why a limited liability company can offer greater flexibility in structuring management and control ("relevant" information). But do you need to go into detail about how a board of directors is elected? Probably not at this stage (see also discussion below on *Selecting Information*).

- *Avoid legalese.* Although helpful in certain circumstances to ensure precise meaning is conveyed (e.g., use of the term "representation" or "warranty" in a contract conveys an exact legal meaning), unnecessary use of legalese can obfuscate meaning, especially when communicating with a non-lawyer. Where possible, use plain English.
- *Set out options and explain possible consequences.* Your client may not be aware of available options for addressing a legal issue and thus may have no frame of reference for making a decision. Consider the doctor-patient analogy. A doctor telling a patient she has a sprained ankle doesn't help the patient make an informed decision as much as providing the patient with recommended treatment options.
- *Fully answer the client's questions.* Engage in active listening, consciously focusing on understanding what the client is asking. Make it a habit to ask the client: "Have I answered your question?" or "Do you have any other questions?"

Illustration: **The Importance of Understanding the Client's Goals and Concerns**

Let's consider the following example. A client is seeking venture capital financing. In reviewing the proposal, the lawyer can see, based on her experience, that the terms being proposed are extremely onerous compared to typical financings. She counsels the client against accepting the deal but tells the client: "I'm just the lawyer. You are the one who must live with the decision. What you must ask yourself is how much of a risk is there that this investor will walk away if you push back, and what the risk is if you agree to his terms." She then advises the client as to what those risks might be. The client responds that this investor said he was willing to invest without the client, a start-up, necessarily having secured a contract to provide its services. To the client, this was worth agreeing to his terms. The lawyer hadn't known this about the investor before she engaged the client in the discussion. If she hadn't presented the client with all the risks, the client may not have remembered to mention this fact.

This illustration highlights the fundamental principle of client-centered lawyering: making sure you understand exactly what the client's goals and concerns are; not necessarily what the client tells you initially, but what you are able to draw out through questioning, active listening, and other techniques. Just as a lawyer may struggle to translate a legal concept into terms a non-lawyer can readily interpret, clients may not articulate their goals and concerns in the terms that immediately lend themselves to legal analysis: they must first be translated from "business speak" into "legal speak." For example, if a client tells you it wants to "incentivize" its employees, this can be interpreted into several different legal concepts: it could mean implementing a performance bonus, creating a stock option plan, or perhaps a direct issuance of stock. As in the medical context, if you fail to provide the client with sufficient information or to ask sufficient questions, you can miss crucial "symptoms."

Selecting Information

Finally, how do you know how much information is enough? Remember that, as the lawyer, you know what the law is and have done the necessary research, and you will also have an idea as to your recommendation. But does the client need to know every step, every element of the rule, every case? Likely no. Synthesize the information so the client has sufficient information to inform his decision while at the same time eliminating extraneous information that is likely to overwhelm or confuse the client. The exercise that follows allows you to practice striking the right balance.

Exercise 9.1

Work in small groups to discuss the scenario below and answer the questions that follow.

A new client informs you that she and two friends want to form a new company in California that will offer tax preparation services. Each of the three wants to have equal ownership and rights, but also wants to make sure they have limited liability. They are not sure if they want to form a limited liability company (LLC), as at some point down the road they might want to get acquired and have heard it is better to be a corporation for those purposes. Also, they understand that LLCs are not eligible to hold the required license for tax prep services. But they are concerned about all the formalities of owning a corporation.[2]

Here are two provisions of the California Corporations Code that discuss "close corporations":

- §158(a) "Close corporation" means a corporation, whose articles contain, in addition to the provisions required by Section 202, a provision that all of the corporation's issued shares of all classes shall be held of record by not more than a specified number of persons, not exceeding 35, and a statement "This corporation is a close corporation."

- §300(e) The failure of a close corporation to observe corporate formalities relating to meetings of directors or shareholders in connection with the management of its affairs, pursuant to an agreement authorized by subdivision (b), shall not be considered a factor tending to establish that the shareholders have personal liability for corporate obligations.

Is this a good option for the client? How would you communicate this option to the client? What information do you need from the client before you can determine if this is a viable option? How do you explain it to the client? Are there any drawbacks? How do you allow the client to make an informed decision about whether to elect close corporation status?

In-Person Communication with Clients: Using Questions to Elicit Information

A critical technique to employ in in-person communications with clients is questioning: asking the right questions, in the right way, using the right language. Ideally, your questions should progress from general to specific, narrowing the information being provided by the client down to the precise information you need to be able to determine, and advise the client on, potential options.

Generating appropriate options is difficult without confirming basic factual assumptions. In Writing Project #1, you were asked to perform legal analysis in general terms, based on a set of assumptions. The next step you will be asked to complete in Writing Project #2 is to take that analysis and tailor it to the client's specific situation, based on information you will ascertain from the client, using questioning and other oral communication techniques described later in this chapter.

---

2. For additional background discussion on entity types and corporate formalities, see the Practice Note at the end of this chapter.

Advising Versus Counseling

We sometimes use the terms *advising* and *counseling* interchangeably, but they are distinct. Moreover, the distinction is pivotal in learning how to engage in client-centered lawyering.[3]

Advising

Advising a client involves explaining how the law or a legal document applies to the client's situation.[4] This is where you educate the client and arm her with the information sufficient for her to make an informed decision. In its most simple form, you are telling the client: "This is what the law says."

Counseling

Counseling a client involves guiding the client in her decision-making process.[5] This does not mean making the decision for the client; rather, it refers to objectively explaining the options and potential consequences of each option and answering any questions the client may have. When counseling a client, you may be asked to make a recommendation as to which option you would suggest and why, but the crux of counseling a client in a client-centered way is in the presenting of the options. This is telling the client: "Based on the law, these are your options and the potential consequences of each."

Counseling involves plugging client-specific facts and concerns into your analysis of the law or document.

Illustration: **Using Client Facts to Counsel Clients**

Your advice to the client regarding available exemptions from registration for a proposed offering of securities might include an explanation of the general rule (that all offerings must be registered) and a summary of the most common exceptions. Before you can counsel the client as to which option or options are available, however, you likely will need to confirm some additional relevant information. For instance, how much money does the client plan on raising? How many investors? Are the investors all located in the same state? Once you have gathered this information, you can start to assess with more specificity how the law might apply, and to start generating potential options and strategies to achieve the client's goals.

Recursive Process

The advising and counseling process is recursive. In generating options, you may discover another legal issue is implicated that requires further analysis, which may in turn need to be explained to the client before you can counsel the client on options. In other instances, the facts and the client's concerns can change, necessitating a completely different approach. Thus, it is important to maintain open lines of communication with the client throughout the process.

---

3. Neumann, *supra* Chapter 2, note 2, at 53.
4. Binder & Price, *supra* note 1, at 5.
5. *Id.*

Illustration: **The Difference between Advising and Counseling**

Your client is a surgeon who operates a wound-care clinic at a hospital. In doing so, he administers the clinic, supervises the nurses and technicians, and sees patients. His contract with the hospital states that he is an independent contractor. He is nearing retirement and has been having health issues. He comes to you because he is concerned the hospital will terminate his contract before he is ready to retire and wants to be able to prevent them from doing so. You review the contract and see that it states: "This contract may be terminated by the hospital at any time upon three months' notice, with or without cause, for any reason or no reason." No other provision of the contract seems to contradict or qualify this statement in any way.

Your *advice* to the client will likely be that the hospital can in fact terminate him at any time, as he fears. It is not what the client wants to hear, but the client needs this information to make an informed decision. What might you *counsel* the client? You might suggest possible strategies for renegotiating the contract, such as a part-time solution. Or perhaps you could negotiate a severance package for the surgeon to step down early. Another option would be to do nothing. In counseling the client, you will want to ask any questions that might help identify viable options, such as how long the client thinks he wants to continue to practice, or whether he is more concerned about the potential loss of income or control of the clinic.

Additional Tips for Effective Advising and Counseling

Following are some best practices as well as traps to avoid when advising or counseling a client:

- Avoid the urge to provide the client with a definitive answer if you are not sure. Clients will often pressure you for a black-and-white answer when one may not exist. If necessary, tell the client "it depends," or "I'm not sure; I would need to do some more research."

- Explaining options does not mean raising objections. Telling the client it should or should not do something is not counseling. Of course, instances occur in which you need to be clear that a proposed course of action or inaction is not a good idea, such as if it would violate the law or clearly jeopardize the client's objectives. But it still must be the client's decision. Your job is to help the client see that your recommendation is the right decision. Instead of saying: "You should not do X," effective counseling might be: "I strongly recommend against doing X, because if you do, here are the consequences."

- Be wary of telling the client what it wants to hear, instead of what it needs to be able to make an informed decision. We want to please the client, but omitting negative information or agreeing with the client without voicing reservations can backfire. It is always better to give the client accurate and complete information, even if the client does not end up following your recommendation.

- Consider your client's likely understanding of the law and business issues. In many instances, if you are a junior associate at a medium-to-large firm, your client will be a corporation or other entity, and your individual point of contact at the company may be a sophisticated businessperson or an in-house lawyer.[6] In other instances, particularly at a smaller firm, your

---

6. It is important to distinguish between a corporate client and its individual representatives in terms of whose interests you represent.

client may be a relatively unsophisticated entrepreneur or small business owner. If you are in-house, your clients will be the businesspeople at your company. You will want to tailor your advice and how you present it accordingly.

- Be mindful of cognitive bias, both on the part of your client and yourself—interpreting information in a way that matches existing interests or preconceived notions.[7] In clients, this can manifest itself in the client assuming the first piece of advice the client receives is correct, and everything else is wrong. Lawyers are also susceptible to cognitive bias. We tend to structure transactions based on our experience with prior transactions. This is not wrong, but avoid adhering to a particular deal structure just because it worked before without consciously assessing whether it makes the most sense in the current context.

FOR DISCUSSION:

Assume a lawyer has a client who wants to consummate a reverse merger[8] based on the advice from its financial advisor. One of the main problems with a reverse merger is that the company becomes public without having raised any money or with any public market for the shares. The lawyer does not explain this to the client, but merely tells the client it is a bad idea. Meanwhile, the client's financial advisor pushes the client to move forward. The client insists on going ahead with the reverse merger, only to have to undo it several months later.

1. Which of the potential pitfalls described above is taking place here? Why is the client so set on moving forward with a reverse merger in this scenario?
2. How could the situation have been prevented?

Cross-Cultural Considerations

As discussed in Chapter 5, people from different cultures see the world through varying perspectives,[9] influenced by their respective culture's norms, values, and rules. These factors influence not only how we communicate, but also our attitudes toward power and relationships, including how we view the role of lawyers (especially that of transactional lawyers). The cultural identity of your client will impact: (1) how your client perceives the distinction between advising and counseling; and (2) whether and to what degree your client expects to receive advice, counsel, or both. For example, a senior executive from China might not expect to receive—and in fact might be offended by—counseling from a junior associate. On the other hand, a Mexican business owner with whom you have developed a working relationship may be less interested in receiving advice, preferring you to take more of a counseling role (and possibly to make certain decisions on his behalf).

---

7. *See* Russel Korobkin & Thomas S. Ulen, *Law and Behavioural Science: Removing the Rationality Assumption from Law and Economics*, 88 Cal. L. Rev. 1051, 1101 (2000); *see also* Ian Weinstein, *Don't Believe Everything You Think: Cognitive Bias in Legal Decision Making*, 8 Clinical L. Rev. 783 (2002–2003).

8. See discussion of reverse mergers in the Practice Notes at the end of this chapter.

9. The Cultural Detective®, https://www.culturaldetective.com (last visited Sept. 18, 2018), an online resource for developing cross-cultural competency in business, refers to these perspectives as "lenses" through which individuals view the world and their relationships with others.

Client Meetings

Client meetings can occur in person, by phone, or via videoconference. They can occur in large groups or one-on-one. They can be formal or informal. The purpose, preparation, and techniques, however, are largely the same.

Purpose

The purpose of a client meeting is typically twofold: to obtain needed information from the client, and to provide information to the client. Following are some of the benefits of a client meeting over written communication in achieving this purpose:

- A meeting can help build rapport. It enables you and the client to engage in small talk and develop a human connection; to "put a face to a name." As humans, this interpersonal interaction can be critical in facilitating communication by enhancing our ability to more accurately interpret the other person's intended meaning.
- On a more concrete level, meetings can be an effective forum for problem-solving and option-generating. In written communication, each person must express an idea in turn, and then wait for the other person to interpret and respond. In a meeting, this process can happen instantaneously. It also is easier to interject clarifications and questions: the communication is more fluid.

Illustration: **How Meetings Facilitate Problem-Solving**

Assume you email a client a memo that lists out three potential options. The client may respond via email that it is not sure it understands the benefits of one of the options. Upon receiving this email, you might respond with an explanation. The client then responds with its choice of option. Now let's consider this scenario in the context of a face-to-face meeting. You would explain the three options, and the client might ask a question or two. You would respond, and the client may follow with additional questions. This back-and-forth may unearth concerns that the client may have been unable to articulate in its email, or may even cause you to discuss other potential options. Thus, the meeting would likely yield more productive results than an email exchange.[10]

Meetings provide the opportunity for real-time discussion that written communication cannot offer. Even email, which is virtually instantaneous, lacks the fully interactive nature of in-person communication.

---

10. This does not suggest that laying out the options in a written memo does not serve a worthwhile purpose. In fact, it can be helpful to send the client the memo in advance of the meeting so that the client has time to digest the information.

Techniques

The techniques for effective communication in a meeting are largely the same as in the other contexts discussed thus far. Specific techniques useful in a client meeting include the following:

- *Ask questions.* Client-centered lawyering means letting the client talk. The more the client talks, the more effective your problem solving will be. Asking the right questions can help guide the client to provide relevant and necessary information.
- *Be perceptive.* Pay attention to nonverbal cues and adjust your communication as necessary. If your client looks confused, stop and ask if the client has any questions.
- *Be prepared.* Know what you are going to say, even if it changes as the meeting proceeds. Do your homework: you should be familiar with the client, its business, the relevant law, and the contemplated deal terms and other facts. Have a list of questions or additional facts that would be helpful.
- *Be organized.* Prepare an agenda and have a clear idea of what you want to achieve in the meeting. Your objectives may evolve as the meeting progresses, but you should have a starting point to keep the discussion focused. A meeting that has no apparent agenda or where the discussion meanders too far off-topic will be less productive and can leave the parties wondering what, if anything, was accomplished. Effective means of keeping the meeting focused include:
  - Circulating an agenda beforehand
  - Recapping periodically, summarizing the discussion and any decisions
  - Referring to the agenda in between topics
- *Avoid overuse of laptops.* You may want to take notes during the meeting and a laptop can certainly be an efficient means of transcribing the discussion. But constant typing can be distracting and annoying. In addition, it can impede active listening and limit nonverbal communication, both critical aspects of effective in-person communication. If you must use a laptop, position it off to the side as opposed to directly between you and the client, and try to maintain eye contact as you type.
- *Do not steamroll the client.* Remember that your job is to advise and counsel the client, not to mandate to the client what the client should or should not do. Just because you have already determined the best course of action for the client, this does not eliminate the need to allow the client to reach the same conclusion on their own.
- *Avoid giving a detailed, overly technical recitation of the law.* Know your audience. Unless your client is a lawyer (and possibly even then) refrain from using legalese or quoting statutory language. Instead, paraphrase in plain English.
- *Maintain appropriate eye contact.* Make sufficient eye contact to demonstrate that you are paying attention to what the client is saying but avoid making the client feel uncomfortable (this can be difficult to balance in cross-cultural situations).

Formulating Effective Questions

Asking the right questions is critical to effectively performing the problem-solving role of a "SANE" transactional lawyer: incomplete or inaccurate information can make it harder to spot relevant issues, effectively analyze the law, strategize solutions, and negotiate on behalf of the client.

- Begin with broader, open-ended questions. This helps capture facts you may not know exist.
- Follow up with narrower questions that home in on potential issues or areas that need further clarification.

- Organize questions in logical order. Depending on the circumstances, a logical order might be chronological, or by topic.
- Prepare a list of facts you already know: do any warrant further clarification?
- Identify information that is relevant to application of any relevant law.

FOR DISCUSSION:

Look back at Simulation Exercise #1 in Chapter 1. The client now wants us to proceed with drafting a distribution agreement. What facts are already in our possession? What additional facts might be helpful when assessing potential issues or to clarify the parties' intent? Is there any relevant law we would need to apply? If so, what questions might help us determine how it should be applied?

Exercise 9.2

In this exercise, you will be asked to work in pairs, taking turns playing the role of the client and the attorney in the context of negotiating a potential distribution agreement between a U.S. manufacturer and a Brazilian distributor. Your instructor will provide you with some basic background, as well as some information specific to each client. As the lawyer, your task is to elicit as much information as possible from the client to allow you to negotiate the distribution agreement on the client's behalf.

Steps in Preparing for a Client Meeting

Preparing for a client meeting can be broken down into the following elements:

- *Identifying the goals for the meeting.* Your agenda should be based on achieving the desired goals.
- *Preparing background information.* This can include familiarizing yourself with the client, its business, the relevant industry, and the law; assembling facts received to date, any internal memos you may have drafted or other pertinent documents; compiling a list of potential questions; and preparing for any cross-cultural differences.
- *Formulating the agenda.* The agenda for the meeting should serve as an outline for both your preparation and the meeting itself. It does not need to be detailed; in fact, bullet point format can work well. The purpose of the agenda is to serve as a reference point to ensure you cover all necessary items and to keep the meeting organized and focused. In addition to your goals and any background information, the agenda should address each of the three main stages of any meeting:
    - *The opening.* This is where you welcome the client and build initial rapport by engaging in small talk. For example: "I hope you didn't have trouble finding the office," or "You have a great view." This is also where you can begin to summarize the purpose of the meeting and your understanding of the client's principal concerns or questions.
    - *The information gathering/counseling stage.* This represents the bulk of the meeting. Here you will use questions and active listening to elicit necessary information from the client, explain any relevant law, advise the client regarding options and their respective conse-

quences, and brainstorm potential strategies. You should also encourage the client to discuss any key business issues, as these may impact how you counsel the client.

○ *The closing.* End the meeting with a clear call to action, summarizing what has been discussed, confirming anything that has been decided, and articulating concrete next steps and timing.

Exercise 9.3

For this exercise, we return to the facts from Writing Project #1. The client in that case will be in town next week and would like to meet to discuss the advice you provided in your memo and to learn more about the potential considerations relating to each option you outlined. She is also interested in discussing additional possible alternatives before making a final decision. Based on the facts and information relied on in your memo and any additional information provided by your instructor, prepare the agenda for a meeting with the client. You may want to use the template in Figure 9.1:

Figure 9.1

Client Meeting Agenda Template

A. GOALS:
   a. _____
   b. _____
   c. _____

B. ORGANIZING THE INTERVIEW:
   a. Preparation
      i. _____
      ii. _____
      iii. _____
      iv. _____
   b. Opening
      i. *Welcome*
      ii. *Proposed agenda*
         1. _____
         2. _____
         3. _____
         4. _____
   c. Information Gathering/Counseling
      i. _____
      ii. _____
      iii. _____
      iv. _____
   d. Closing
      i. _____
      ii. _____
      iii. _____
      iv. _____
      v. _____

PRACTICE NOTES

Corporate Formalities

The exercise on page 115 refers to "all the formalities" involved in operating as a corporation. A corporation is a form of entity created by state statute (see Practice Note on Understanding Entity and Ownership Structures at the end of Chapter 7 for a discussion of entity types). Statutorily required corporate formalities in most states include: the holding of annual meetings of shareholders to elect directors; board of director meetings or consents to approve certain actions; minimum notice periods required to call a meeting of the board or of the shareholders; requirements governing minutes of meetings; establishing and adhering to by-laws; and maintaining shareholder and other appropriate records, among others. These can be expensive and time-consuming for a young company.

Why is it important to adhere to these formalities? One of the principal attributes of a corporation is the concept of limited liability, predicated on the notion that the corporation is an entity separate and apart from its owners. The owners—or shareholders—of a corporation have no personal liability for the debts and obligations of the corporation beyond the loss of their investment in the shares. Courts can disregard the separate entity, however, and allow recovery against the shareholders in certain circumstances (this is known as "piercing the corporate veil"). Failure to adhere to corporate formalities is a factor courts look to in determining whether to pierce the corporate veil.

Ongoing adherence to corporate formalities is also helpful upon a sale or other business combination: the buyer will want to confirm that the corporation is compliant with all relevant corporate formalities to ensure there are no potential issues; it can delay or even prevent the deal to have to retroactively "clean house."

"Going Public"

A company "goes public" when it files a registration statement with the SEC and registers its shares for public trading on a national exchange such as the New York Stock Exchange or NASDAQ. Being public means the company's shares are publicly tradeable. Anyone can buy or sell shares through the exchange on which the shares are listed. The principal manner of going public is to make an "initial public offering" or "IPO." In an IPO, an investment banker typically creates an initial market for the shares. Once its shares are publicly traded, a company must comply with the reporting and other requirements set forth in the Securities Exchange Act of 1934 (the "Exchange Act").[11]

Historically, the purpose of conducting an IPO is to raise capital by attracting new shareholders to purchase shares in the company, although this is not a requirement.[12]

Another way to go public is to conduct a reverse merger, where the nonpublic company merges with and into an existing public company (typically a shell company with no real assets or operations). The existing public company survives the merger but now holds all the assets and operations of the merged-out private company. Typically, a reverse merger is quicker and less expensive than an IPO and is less dependent on market conditions. The disadvantages of a reverse merger are that the private company: (1) will incur the expense of complying with the reporting and other regulatory requirements of the Exchange Act without receiving any additional influx of capital (unlike an IPO, in which the company receives the proceeds of the initial sale of its shares), and (2) will need to create a market for its shares.

---

11. 15 U.S.C. § 78a *et seq.*

12. For example, in 2017, Spotify Ltd. went public by listing its shares on the New York Stock Exchange without conducting an initial public offering.

Conclusion

Communicating with clients can be one of the most challenging components of being a lawyer. In some ways, lawyers and their clients speak different languages, and have different objectives when approaching a transaction. The key to overcoming these hurdles is to engage in client-centered lawyering: to seek to understand the client's concerns and allow the client to make its own informed decisions. The lawyer's responsibility is to be prepared, organized, perceptive, and to ask the right questions to properly advise and counsel the client.

SIMULATION EXERCISE #8

You receive the following email from the partner you worked with in completing Writing Project #1, asking you to prepare for an in-person meeting with the client. Your instructor will advise you as to the details of the client meeting and the issues you should cover in your response.

Julie Ryan

From: Julie Ryan jryan@ryanassoc.com
Sent: March __ 1:00 PM
To: Junior Associate
Subject: Preparation for next week's client meeting

Junior Associate:

As I mentioned, I will not be able to be at next week's meeting with the client. I therefore want you to be prepared to take the lead. I would like you to prepare some notes for the meeting so that I am sure you are on the right track. Your notes should cover the following two items *only*: (1) bullet points outlining the issue I mentioned to you; and (2) a list of *ten* questions you think we should ask the client. Please email me what you have within 48 hours.

Thanks,
Julie

Julie A. Ryan
Ryan & Associates
299 Valley Avenue
3rd Floor
Los Angeles, CA 90009
Tel: 213-510-5000
Email: jryan@ryanassoc.com

This email message and any attachments are being sent by Ryan & Associates, LLP, are confidential, may be privileged, and are for the sole use of the intended recipient(s). Any unauthorized review, use, disclosure, or distribution is prohibited. If you are not the intended recipient, please contact the sender immediately by replying to this email message and destroy all copies of this email message and any attachments.

Chapter 10

·············

Written Client Communications

Much of what we do as transactional lawyers is facilitate communication between parties. Our effectiveness in this role starts with how well we communicate with our clients. In this chapter, we turn our focus to written client communications, taking the fundamental writing techniques discussed in Part I and applying them to the client communications context. This chapter starts by looking at professional correspondence in general, followed by an in-depth discussion on client letters, including form, content, and tone. Although the materials focus primarily on the client-letter format, the principles discussed apply to any form of written correspondence with clients. The chapter ends by considering how to convert research and other written legal analyses into client-centered correspondence.

By the end of this chapter, you will be able to:

- Compose a professional letter to a client
- Convert an internal research memo into a client letter
- Prepare and respond to email correspondence with clients

···

The partner is so impressed with your research on a matter for the client he has asked you to summarize your research in a letter to the client. You are used to drafting memos, but you have never written a formal client letter. What format should you use? How formal a tone is appropriate? How much detail should you include? How long should the letter be? Is there a standard way to begin and end the letter?

···

Professional Correspondence in General

Professional correspondence is a common form of writing performed by business lawyers. It encompasses emails, cover letters, advice letters, demand letters, opinion letters, notices, comment letters, and transmittal letters, to name a few. The recipient of this correspondence can be a client, opposing counsel, a colleague, the court, a counterparty to a contract, a tenant, or a regulatory body or government agency.

Persuasive Writing

In most cases, effective professional correspondence is also persuasive. We generally think of persuasive writing as that performed by litigators when drafting briefs and motions for the court, but persuasion also comes into play in transactional practice. Just because a lawyer is engaged in transactional law, she is no less of an advocate for her client. As with court documents, the trick for the lawyer in drafting professional correspondence is to maintain credibility by striking an appropriate balance between advocacy and reasoned analysis.

Before You Begin Writing

Before putting pen to paper—or fingers to keys—consider the purpose and audience of your written communication. Some of the questions you should keep in mind are:

- Why are you preparing the letter, email, or memo?
- What is its ultimate purpose? Is it to educate the reader? To persuade the reader to take—or not take—a course of action? To provide advice or counsel the client? To serve as a record of your advice? All of the above?
- To whom is it being addressed? Who else might read it? Is the intended recipient a lawyer? An experienced CEO? A relatively unsophisticated founder of a start-up company? In-house counsel?

The answers to these questions should guide the choice of format, organization, content, depth of analysis, and tone of your writing.

Ethical and Other Considerations

As with other forms of written communication, anything a lawyer puts into a client letter or other correspondence has legal and ethical implications. In addition to providing needed information to the client, it also creates a record of the lawyer's advice.[1] Knowing when and how to put something in writing is a fundamental skill of the professional and ethical lawyer.

Your written communications can also make a lasting impression. Pay attention to detail and ensure your letter is polished and free of grammatical and typographical errors. Your correspondence should also be clearly organized and reader-centered.

With these general considerations out of the way, let us turn now to focus on client letters as a common form of professional correspondence.

Client Letters

The three integral facets of a professional client letter are: tone, format, and content.[2] Tone refers to the "voice" your reader will hear when reading the correspondence. Format refers to the way the communication is presented. Content refers to the substance of the communication. Each component is equally important in determining your reader's perception of what you are communicating.

Tone

- *Err on the side of formality.* Use professional language and structure, but do not fall into the trap of relying on legalese to convey formality and expertise. Although proper legal terminology may be appropriate or even necessary in some instances, excessive use of legalese can undermine the writer's credibility and create barriers to communication. Say things as simply

---

1. Mary-Beth Moylan & Stephanie J. Thompson, Global Lawyering Skills 122 (West 2013).
2. *See* Christine Coughlin, Joan Malmud Rocklin & Sandy Patrick, A Lawyer Writes 314 (3d Ed. 2018).

as possible, without lapsing into colloquialisms or too informal a tone. Remember, you never know who else might read your correspondence.

- *Adapt for your audience.* The appropriate tone will depend in part on your audience. For example, you may choose a more informal tone in a letter to a client who is a close friend but may adopt a more formal tone if the client is someone you do not know well or a senior executive.[3] The same consideration should be given to the client's background: you may want to include more legal terminology and refer to the source of the law if your client is in-house counsel. If your client does not have a legal background, you will likely want to limit the amount of legal terminology and use plain English.[4]

- *Be direct.* No matter what the conclusion and reasoning, your goal must be to answer directly the question or request posed by the client. If you cannot provide a direct answer, be direct by saying so, and then explain why there is no direct answer.

- *Be clear.* Use language that the client can understand and avoid vague legalese such as "aforementioned," "hereinafter," and "heretofore." In addition, avoid references to technical terms. If technical terms are necessary to be precise, explain them in the letter, unless you are confident that the reader will know the definitions. For example, if you are communicating with an unsophisticated client regarding a potential securities offering, when referring to "accredited investors," either define the term or refer instead to "investors who meet certain minimum income or wealth thresholds."

- *Be concise.* While clarity is the overriding goal of any legal writing, you also need to be concise whenever possible. Strive to reduce unnecessary verbiage without eliminating the substantive message.

- *Be considerate of your client.* Remember that your client has come to you for help. Respond to the client in a way that recognizes the client's concerns and needs.

Format

The format for any professional correspondence should be—in a word—professional. Among other things, this generally means adhering to standard conventions for professional correspondence. Standard conventions for a professional letter include the following:

Letterhead/ return address:	The first page of the letter should be printed out on preprinted letterhead. If you do not have letterhead, you should include your name and address at the top of the first page.
Confidentiality notice:	Depending on the sensitivity and type of information included in the letter, you may want to mark it as "*Confidential*" or as "*Attorney Work Product.*"[5] This statement should be added in the header at the top of the first page, and can also be repeated on each page, depending on your firm's protocol.

---

3. This distinction is discussed in Deborah B. McGregor & Cynthia M. Adams, The International Lawyer's Guide to Legal Analysis and Communication in the United States 256 (2008).

4. *Id.*

5. This language is deliberately mirrored on the attorney-work privilege doctrine, which is designed to protect a lawyer's advice from being discoverable in a lawsuit. *See, e.g.*, Cal. Code Civ. Pro. §2018.030(a). The impetus behind this doctrine is to allow attorneys to be able to advise their clients without fear that this advice could later be used against the client.

Date:	A letter should always be dated. The date is typically inserted below the sender's address or letterhead.
Recipient's address:	This should follow the date and should include the individual's name, title, and full address if known. Avoid typographical or spelling errors in the recipient's name, as these can adversely affect your credibility with, and even offend, the recipient before she has even read the contents of your letter. If you are sending the letter via email or fax, you should also include the email address or fax number and indicate that the letter is being sent by those means.
Subject line:	Although not required, it can be helpful to your reader to include a subject line that succinctly references the main topic or purpose of the letter.
Salutation:	How you address the recipient will depend on your relationship and the level of formality. If in doubt, err on the side of formality. For example: *"Dear Mr. Smith:"* Standard convention is to place a colon after the salutation.
Page numbers:	Always include page numbers in your letter. Omit the page number on the first page.
Closing and signature:	End the letter with a closing phrase, your printed name, and your signature. You may also want to include your title, depending on the circumstances. Typical closing phrases include: "Sincerely" or "Truly yours." In keeping with the professional tone of a client letter, you should generally sign your full name, unless you have a close personal relationship with the recipient. Always include your full printed name under your signature. For example:
	Sincerely,
	Julie
	Julie A. Ryan
	Traditionally, a letter should be signed manually (and if being delivered by mail, it should be an original signature). Electronic signatures are becoming increasingly frequent, however (see the Practice Notes at the end of this chapter).
Enclosures and copies:	Always indicate if you are enclosing any additional documents or materials with the letter, or if you are copying another recipient. The conventions for indicating enclosures or attachments is *"Enclosures,"* or *"Encl/"* with or without listing the specific enclosures. To indicate a copied recipient, use *"cc:"* followed by the name of the copied person. You can also include the person's title or affiliation if the recipient is otherwise unlikely to know who the individual is.
Paragraphs and spacing; overall appearance:	Professionalism is also conveyed by the overall appearance of the letter, such as efficient use of white space, tabs, and paragraphs. Either block paragraphs with a space in between each paragraph (the entire paragraph is flush-left), or indented paragraphs (the first line of each paragraph is indented) are acceptable. The key is to be consistent. The convention is to leave two spaces between each address, the date, and the salutation. Avoid fully justifying paragraphs, as this can cause the spacing between words to look uneven and be harder to read.
	Finally, you convey professionalism (and credibility) by carefully editing and polishing your letter. Typographical or grammatical errors in a letter tend to stand out and undermine your credibility.

Many firms have their own templates or precedent samples incorporating these conventions that you can use as a starting point.

Figure 10.1 is a sample of the first and last page of a letter advising a client on a legal issue. Note how the various conventions described above are incorporated, as well as the use of white space, paragraphs, and justification. A complete copy of this sample letter is included in Appendix B.

Figure 10.1

PRIVILEGED & CONFIDENTIAL
ATTORNEY-CLIENT COMMUNICATION

RYAN & ASSOCIATES, LLP
299 Valley Avenue, 3rd Floor
Los Angeles, CA 90009

March 15, 20__

James Ogden
Chief Financial Officer
Hudson Equity Group
1200 Company Way
Middletown, NY 11104

Re: Employee participation in securities offerings

Dear Mr. Ogden:

It was a pleasure meeting with you last week. As requested, set out below is a summary of broker-dealer issues relating to using employees of Hudson Equity Group to solicit additional investors for one of your funds. We recommend . . . .

[Body of letter]

Please let us know whether and how you would like to proceed. In the meantime, please let me know if you have any questions.

Sincerely,

/s/ Julie Ryan

Julie Ryan

Enclosures

Cc: Mary Jones

-3-

Content

The content of your letter will vary in terms of depth, scope, and organization, depending on the purpose of the letter.

Depth and Scope. A cover or transmittal letter may need to contain no more information than what you are transmitting. For example:

> *Attached for your review is a draft of the sales contract prepared in connection with the XYZ matter. I will call you to discuss any comments or questions.*

In other instances, the letter may serve to convey advice or to perhaps ascertain the accuracy of relevant facts. For example:

> *As requested, we have prepared a draft of the sales contract in connection with the XYZ matter, attached. In drafting the contract, we assumed [summary of key facts and assumptions]. In reviewing the contract, please note the following: [list key provisions/consequences].*

A letter summarizing research or recommendations may need to go into more depth: you may need to explain the legal basis for your advice to convince the client your conclusion and recommendation are valid. For example:

> *You asked us to advise you regarding the structural alternatives for your proposed relationship with XYZ company. Based on the facts discussed with you last week, we have identified two potential structures: (1) entering into a sales contract with XYZ, or (2) forming a joint venture with XYZ. For the reasons that follow, we would recommend entering into a sales contract. Under Delaware law, . . . [Explanation and analysis].*

Regardless of depth and scope, be wary of including specific case analysis or quoted statutory language. Present the information in more general terms if possible, omitting detailed information if it is not necessary to explain your conclusion and recommendation. This is not to say you should not have this detailed information at hand, either in a supporting research memo or in a note to the file. Recall the discussion in Chapter 7 relating to depth of analysis in informal communications. As with informal communications, your understanding of the law or issue and your underlying analysis should be sufficiently thorough to allow you to properly summarize your analysis and ensure your recommendation is accurately supported. You will see examples of how to achieve this balance in the remaining parts of this chapter.

Organization. Your letter should be logically and clearly organized. One way to ensure your writing is organized on a macro level is to break the letter out into sections or parts. Sections that generally make up the body of a letter or other correspondence are set forth in Figure 10.2.

Figure 10.2

Body of Letter	
SECTION	DESCRIPTION
Introduction	This is where you set the overall tone of the letter and introduce its purpose. You may want to refer to any specific question(s) the letter is addressing, and any prior communication with the client on the topic. For example: "*In response to your question whether . . . .*" or "*Following our conversation of January __ . . . .*" You may want to include your recommendation (or at least a summary) here or wait to include it at the end of the letter. For example: "*For the reasons that follow, we recommend . . . .*" You may also want to include a brief roadmap for your reader.

Statement of Facts	You may not always include a formal statement of facts. If you do not include this section, it is a good idea to at least refer to key facts in your Introduction, as it allows you to confirm your understanding of the facts and to direct the focus of the reader to the facts you deem determinative of outcome. Even if you state the facts to the client orally during a meeting, it is always a good idea to repeat those facts to the client—especially those legally significant facts on which you are relying—in written form. This gives your client the opportunity to clarify any misunderstanding about what actually took place and helps create a record of the basis for your advice.
Reasoning	The extent and nature of this section will vary depending on the context and the issue. In some instances, supporting case law can be unnecessary and distracting. On the other hand, you may decide your recommendations will be more persuasive if you summarize the law. Be prepared to eliminate (or relegate to a footnote) any supporting case law or legal argument that you think might undermine or distract from your explanation. However, it is good practice to be able to formulate the complete legal analysis (using the IRAC or CRAC paradigm), even if you later delete some of the sections from the final draft of your letter.[6] Most importantly, do not stop at explaining the law and the issues. Make sure you provide the client with options for achieving its goals and/or solving a stated problem if called for (recall the distinction between advice and counseling in Chapter 9). The key is to provide the client with sufficient information to allow it to make an informed decision as to how to proceed. Your relationship with different clients will of course vary: some clients require more guidance than others. But in most cases the client will appreciate your insight as to available options from a legal—if not business—standpoint.
Closing/ Recommendation	In the Closing of a client letter, you should: (1) answer explicitly the client's question or request, (2) provide your recommendation (if you have outlined a series of options for the client, you should include your recommendation as to which of several options you would recommend), and (3) invite the client to contact you. Sometimes your recommendation is not what the client wants to hear. If so: (1) be specific as to why the facts or your legal analysis led you to that conclusion (do not assume your client will have read your analysis or will make the necessary inference), and (2) try to generate one or more alternatives that might achieve a similar objective. For example, you may believe that a merger is impractical, but another form of acquisition may bring about some of the client's desired results. In this case, you might say: *"Given that the target company is a partnership, which will require conversion prior to any merger (and which will create additional costs), we would not recommend structuring as a merger. Instead we would recommend . . . ."*

In addition to macro-level organization, organizing your writing within each of these sections at the micro level (the organization within and between each sentence and paragraph), is pivotal to communicating effectively.

As you practice drafting client letters and commence Writing Project #2, in addition to referring to the materials in this chapter, I recommend reviewing some of the previous sections of this textbook focusing on organization, including the illustration of organizational techniques on page 46 and the office memo checklist in Chapter 6. Although these discuss organization in the context of interoffice communications, they apply equally to effective organization in client letters and other correspondence.

---

6. This need for formulating the underlying analysis in depth is discussed above in *Depth and Scope* and in Chapter 7.

Fundamental Writing Techniques

Having looked at how to select the appropriate tone, format, and content for client correspondence, let us now turn back to the fundamental writing techniques discussed in Chapter 4. You will now delve deeper into these skills to hone and adapt them for client communications.

Using Thesis Sentences: Start with the Point You Want to Make

Thesis sentences are arguably the most effective tool of an accomplished legal writer. Starting each paragraph with a thesis sentence can make your writing more concise, cohesive, and coherent, which makes it easier for your reader to follow. This makes your writing more informative and persuasive to your reader.

An effective thesis sentence is one that introduces the topic of the paragraph while also stating the writer's position. This is not the same as making an argument or stating a conclusion, although a conclusion may be a thesis sentence. An effective thesis sentence should not leave the reader asking: "so what?" It should include sufficient explanation to make the point clear to the reader. Consider the following three examples of the first sentence of the analysis section of a client letter on whether the client may risk successor liability under the "mere continuation" exception in a proposed asset purchase:

1. *An important factor in determining whether there has been a mere continuation is whether one or more persons were officers or directors of both companies.*
2. *You may be subject to successor liability under the mere continuation exception based on continuity of officers and directors because you intend to retain key management.*
3. *The mere continuation exception could expose you to liability because you plan to retain key officers and directors.*

Each of these three statements are thesis sentences. But do they all convey the same amount of information? In the first example, we learn that continuity of officers and directors is an important factor. Is the point clear, or will the reader ask: "so what?" If the reader is a client unfamiliar with legal analysis, does this sentence convey helpful information to the client? Probably not. Additional information will be needed to help make the inference clear to the reader. The third example, although it appears to provide an explanation, is a bit conclusory: it draws the inference between mere continuation and retention of key officers and directors but does not fully explain that retaining key officers and directors creates the requisite "continuity." The second example clearly and concisely presents and explains the writer's position, such that the reader has no doubt as to the point being made.

A useful technique for checking the effectiveness of your thesis sentences is to read the first sentence of each paragraph of your letter. If drafted effectively, these should read like an outline, with the first sentence of each paragraph showing the progression of your thoughts and ideas.

Signposts can also help guide your reader through the analysis. But these may not be necessary with cohesive thesis sentences. For example, a discussion of a rule might flow as follows. Note the signposts are optional due to the clear progression of the thesis sentences:

Paragraph 1: The general rule is . . . .
Paragraph 2: [*However,*] Exceptions to the general rule exist. First, ...
Paragraph 3: [*In sum,*] The most relevant exception in our case is . . . .
Paragraph 4: [*However,*] For this exception to apply . . . .
Paragraph 5: [*Thus*], To ensure this exception applies, we recommend . . . .

Organizing your Writing: Avoid "Starting in the Middle"

Using thesis sentences can help keep your writing logically organized in two ways: (1) it forces you to consider the connections between each of your paragraphs (remember, the first sentence of each paragraph should form an outline); and (2) it encourages you to start each paragraph and section "at the beginning." The tendency among novice legal writers is to be in such a rush to get to the point, to show that they have successfully analyzed a legal issue, that they forget to establish the proper context for the reader. This can feel to the reader as if the writer is "starting in the middle."

A simple but useful analogy is that of a child telling a parent about his day at school. The parent asks the child how his day went, and the child launches into an explanation: "*Well I'm upset because he got me into trouble because of the red crayon.*" Where is the beginning of the story? The parent can guess but needs to fill in the context. The parent might ask the child: "*Did someone take your crayon?*" The child might then respond: "*Jayden, he took my crayon.*" But still, where is the beginning of the story? Finally, the parent gets the child to start at the beginning: "*We were in art class and I got in trouble for talking because Jayden took my crayon and I turned around to ask for it back.*"

The same is true in drafting a client letter. You may be familiar with the law and the inferences that you have drawn in determining your advice for the client, but remember that the client will likely need you to explain your reasoning from a logical starting point.

FOR DISCUSSION:

Look back at the research topics used in Simulation Exercise #3. What was the logical starting point for explaining each of these to the supervising partner? Is the logical starting point different if you are asked to explain them to a client unfamiliar with the law? What might the starting point be for each of these?

Keeping Your Writing Concise, Clear, and Precise:
Say What You Mean (and Mean What You Say)

Letters to clients tend to be shorter than an office memorandum. They are typically one to three pages. This doesn't make writing a letter easier or less time-consuming. It can often be harder to keep a piece of writing shorter.

Strive to say what you need to say in as few words as necessary to ensure that you are clearly and accurately communicating information to your reader, and that your reader will interpret that information in the manner you intend.

Considering Your Audience: Stay Reader-Centered

Write for your audience. The effectiveness of what you are communicating should be measured from the perspective of the reader. Recall our discussion of Grice's maxims of communication in Chapter 4: your reader assumes that the information you include is relevant, necessary, and accurate, and that you intend to present it in as clear a manner as possible. For example, recall in Chapter 7 the sample language for a short-form memo describing the available exemptions from registration for an offering of securities. If in summarizing your research in a letter to the client you include a detailed list of the requirements for two different exemptions, the client will likely surmise that both of these exemptions are relevant to the client's transaction. If your advice is that only one of these exemptions is applicable, the client will be confused or (at the very least) wonder why you included details of the other exemption.

Editing and Polishing: Eliminating Typographical and Grammatical Errors

Finally, you should always carefully proofread any written communication that you send out to a client. Grammatical or spelling errors detract from the credibility of your writing and reflect a lack of professionalism. The checklist included at the end of this chapter provides a useful guide for proofreading your correspondence. See also Chapter 12 for a more detailed discussion on fine-tuning and proofreading in general.

Converting a Research Memorandum into a Client Letter

You may be asked to take an existing internal research memorandum and convert it into a memo or letter to the client. At this point, you might think the bulk of your work is done. You have already completed and synthesized the research, and hopefully have a solid understanding of the legal issues and how they relate to your client's concerns.

Generally, however, you will not want to simply forward the original memorandum to the client. It likely will contain information superfluous for the client's purposes. For example, you will want to eliminate any citations, as well as any references to specific cases or statutes, unless necessary for clarity or precision. You also likely will want to synthesize and condense any detailed analysis to the essential points.

Consider what information is necessary for the client to be able to make an informed decision. In most instances, the letter to the client should be an abbreviated, simplified version of the memorandum. You may also need to alter the tone and language. For example, consider the following introductory sentence from a research memorandum on whether LLC interests are securities:

> *While the definition of "security" under Section 2(a)(1) of the Securities Act of 1933, as amended (the "Securities Act") does not specifically refer to limited liability company interests, LLC interests may be deemed securities if they qualify as an "investment contract" under the Howey test.*

Does the client need all this information? Probably not. Thus, you may want to alter this introductory sentence to:

> *The LLC interests may be securities under federal securities laws if they qualify as an "investment contract."*

Does the client have enough knowledge to understand what the term "investment contract" means? If not, the client will be unable to make an informed decision. Thus, you may need to explain the term:

> *Whether something is an investment contract is based on the individual facts, but generally requires that there be an investment of money and reliance on the efforts of others to obtain a profit.*

Note how this explanation uses plain English to summarize the language from the *Howey* case.[7] Although the client will still need to rely on your legal advice as to whether the LLC interests are securities, she now has the information to enable her to draw her own conclusion and make an informed decision as to whether to follow your recommendation.

---

7. See discussion of the *Howey* case, *supra* Chapter 7, note 5.

Thus, the information included in the client letter is not always *less* than that included in your memo but may be *different*.

When to Send a Client a Letter or an Email

When should you put information to a client into a formal letter, and when is it appropriate to simply email the client the information? The decision turns on several factors, including: the length and depth of the analysis that needs to be communicated, the urgency, and the purpose of the communication.

When a letter may be more appropriate:

- If the information is going to be shared in a formal setting or as part of a formal procedure, such as in seeking board approval for a transaction;
- If the information to be communicated is complex or will take up more than a page or two;
- If the information is presented in tabular format or contains a lot of formatting. Often, formatting does not transfer well across different email programs: a table that looks perfect on your screen may be completely garbled when the recipient opens the email;
- If the client expects a certain level of formality;[8]
- If the information is highly confidential;[9] or
- If you are concerned about the information being forwarded.

When an email may be more appropriate:

- If time is of the essence, such as in the middle of closing a transaction;
- If you are communicating a succinct piece of information;
- If you know the client will likely be reading the information on a mobile device, while traveling, for example;
- If the client tends to be informal in communications, or typically communicates via email; or
- If the client is cost-sensitive.

A letter can also be communicated via email as an attachment. This transmittal method offers a useful compromise between the formality of a letter and the speed of communication of an email, and increasingly is becoming the main method of "sending" a letter. Some partners still like to follow an emailed letter with a mailed original but in the age of verified electronic signatures, this practice is becoming obsolete.

> **Exercise 10.1**
>
> Using the sample short-form memo in Appendix B, convert the information into a short email to the client. Working in pairs, one of you should assume that you are preparing the email for an in-house counsel. The other should assume that you are preparing the email for a client who is unfamiliar with legal matters. Compare your results. How did your intended audience affect how you formulated your email? Which one contained more detail? How did you organize the points? What information did you include/exclude?

---

8. This expectation might be based on the individual or may be culture-based.
9. Coughlin et al., *supra* note 2, at 292.

Cross-Cultural Considerations

Just as individual law firms and employers may have different preferences regarding format, content, and approach for interoffice memoranda and correspondence, so may individual legal cultures. For instance, in France, formal correspondence is traditionally concluded using a formal, formulaic closing.[10] You cannot be expected to learn all these different forms and customs. However, your responsibility as a business lawyer is to be mindful that different forms and customs may be preferred and expected, and to observe these customs where appropriate. For instance, if you are writing to a client who you know comes from a formal culture, you may want to adopt a more formal tone in your letter.

Checklist for Preparing and Proofreading a Client Letter

Once you have a draft of your client letter, go back through and re-read it to ensure you are communicating the information as effectively as possible. You may need to re-read your letter several times, each time looking at a different aspect: content, formatting, tone, grammar, and conciseness. Figure 10.3 provides a useful checklist.

Figure 10.3

Checklist for Preparing Client Letter

I. ORGANIZATION/TECHNIQUE

☐ Are your letter and each section logically organized?

☐ Have you included all relevant sections, and can the reader easily spot them?

☐ Have you made effective use of headings, if necessary?

☐ Have you made effective use of fundamental techniques such as thesis sentences, mirroring, topic strings, signposting, transitions, etc.?

☐ Is your writing as concise as possible? Have you eliminated excess verbiage, throat-clearing, wordiness, and irrelevant details?

☐ Is your writing clear (including elimination of unnecessary legalese)?

☐ Is your writing precise (including proper hierarchy among points/elements)?

☐ Have you checked your letter for overall coherence?

II. FORMAT/TONE

☐ Does your letter follow a professional format?

☐ Is your letter well-presented, using the appropriate font and spacing?

☐ Is your letter reader-centered, considering the client's educational, cultural, and business background?

☐ Does the letter directly answer the question or request posed by the client?

☐ Does your letter use the appropriate level of formality?

☐ Is your advice appropriately hedged?

---

10. A typical closing in a French business letter is: "*Je vous prie d'agréer, [Monsieur/Madame], l'expression de mes sentiments distingués.*" This translates roughly as follows: "Please accept, [Sir/Madam], the expression of my distinguished feelings."

    ☐ Is your tone professional?

    ☐ Have you proofread your memo for typographical, spelling, and grammatical errors?

    ☐ Have you printed out your letter and examined it for overall professional appearance and readability?

III. CONTENT

    ☐ Have you included an effective introduction, with a road map if appropriate?

    ☐ Have you included the appropriate level of factual detail?

    ☐ Have you gone into appropriate depth in stating and explaining the law?

    ☐ Is your statement of the law correct and logically organized?

    ☐ Have you included sufficient depth of analysis?

    ☐ Is your analysis supported by the law and known facts?

    ☐ Does your letter show a good grasp of the relevant business issues/consequences?

    ☐ Have you discussed available options?

    ☐ Have you provided a hedged assessment of which option would provide the best course of action for the client?

    ☐ Have you included a closing paragraph setting out the next steps and inviting the client to contact you?

PRACTICE NOTES

Electronic Signatures and the ESIGN Act

The Electronic Signatures in Global and National Commerce (ESIGN) Act, which was signed into law in 2000,[11] provides that electronic signatures are equally enforceable with paper signatures. Most states have similar laws. This allows for most correspondence and other documents to be sent electronically, without the need for "original" paper signatures. In transactional practice, it is increasingly rare to exchange paper signatures, even in connection with the closing of an acquisition or other deal, unless expressly required pursuant to applicable contract terms, or involving a deed or other document requiring notarization or other official seal.

The most common ways to collect and transmit binding signatures electronically include:

• Scanning a signed paper original into a pdf or other electronic format that can be forwarded via email;

• Using Docusign, HelloSign, or other online application to electronically request and affix signatures to documents. These programs allow you to upload the document(s) to be signed, select who the signatories will be, and indicate where each signature, date, or other information is required from each signatory. Each signatory then receives an email with a link to the document(s) to be signed and simply fills in each required field. Once all required signatories have signed, a pdf of the fully executed document can be saved, printed, and shared;

• Using the convention of inserting /s/ before a typed name in a signature block to indicate that person's intent to sign the document; and

---

11. 15 U.S.C. §96.

- Faxing signed paper originals. Note that most contracts expressly permit notices and other signatures to be sent via facsimile (fax).

When using either the scan method, the /s/ convention, or facsimile transmission, it is good practice to keep a copy of the original paper signature on file. When using an electronic signature platform, you will not have paper originals; however, these programs create a digital tracking number on each document. It can also be helpful for potential enforcement to include in any contract or other document that will be signed electronically a reference to the ESIGN Act. Finally, expressly allow for the document to be signed in separate counterparts. This allows the parties to sign separate copies of the same signature page instead of all parties having to sign the same original.

Following is a standard "counterparts" provision that includes electronic signatures:

> *This [document] may be executed in two (2) or more counterparts, each of which shall be deemed an original, but all of which together shall constitute one and the same instrument. Counterparts may be delivered via facsimile, electronic mail (including pdf or any electronic signature complying with the U.S. federal ESIGN Act of 2000, e.g., www.docusign.com) or other transmission method and any counterpart so delivered shall be deemed to have been duly and validly delivered and be valid and effective for all purposes.*

Conclusion

When communicating in writing with the client, whether in a formal letter or via email, adopting the right tone and format is crucial, in addition to the fundamental writing techniques discussed in Chapter 4. Drafting client letters poses unique challenges: the writer must keep in mind the purpose of the letter and her audience when selecting and organizing the content of the letter.

WRITING PROJECT #2: Drafting a Client Letter

Your instructor will provide you with materials and instructions for drafting a six- to seven-page client letter, based on the research you completed for Writing Project #1. This project is designed to allow you to practice the skills and apply the concepts covered in Chapters 6–10.

Chapter 11

....

Translating the Deal for the Client

This chapter brings us back to the beginning of this textbook, where we discussed how a transactional associate adds value to a business transaction by facilitating effective communication. In the intervening chapters, we examined the tone, format, and content of different forms of transactional legal writing and oral communication, and the importance of clarity, conciseness, precision, and other fundamental techniques in communicating effectively, regardless of context. In this chapter, we explore additional variations in form, and drill down the fundamental techniques discussed in earlier chapters to an even more practical level.

By the end of this chapter, you will be able to:

- Summarize a legal document for a client in plain English
- Translate the client's goals and concerns into legally binding language
- Recognize and evaluate the role of ethics in communicating with the client
- Identify and draft other forms of client communications

....

You are helping a partner represent the buyer in the acquisition of a manufacturing facility. You have been tasked with taking the lead on due diligence and the initial draft of the purchase agreement. This is your first time working directly with the client, and you are understandably nervous about making sure you ask all the right questions and have all the relevant information. At your initial meeting with the client, she tells you that she is not worried about environmental issues because the seller told her environmentally hazardous materials have never been used in the facility. How do you respond to this information? Do you accept the client's position and move on? Do you need to ask additional questions? What is the potential business risk? Are there any legal issues? How do you translate the seller's statement into language that will protect the client from a legal standpoint?

....

The Language of the Law

You may have noticed when you first arrived at law school that many of the terms you encountered were unfamiliar—you had to learn a whole new lexicon. How many times had you used the word "*tort*" before coming to law school? Did you "*sign*" or "*execute*" a letter? Whether you are a native or non-native English speaker, the language of the law is a new language you have had to master.

This language of the law goes beyond mere terminology: the way lawyers identify and approach issues, conduct legal analysis, and document information are all unique to the practice of law. For example, outside of the law, a person may "*agree*" to do something. Within the law, this is translated into a precise legal concept. The agreement may become a contract, letter of intent, promissory note, or take on some other legal form, depending on exactly what is being agreed, the terms, the law, and the parties.

Translating between Business and Legal Terms

One of the most important tasks a transactional lawyer undertakes is translating what the client wants into legal terms and, conversely, translating legal documents into terms that the client can easily understand, and which reflect the desired business deal. The lawyer in this role acts as a facilitator, enabling communication between the business and the legal sides of a transaction.

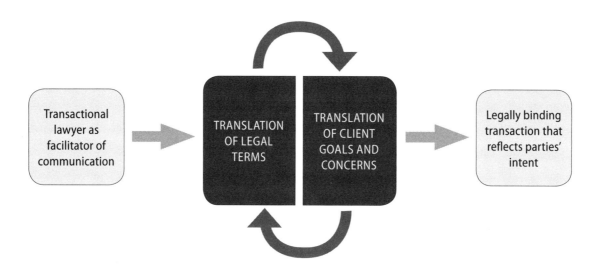

How a business deal is translated into legal terms will depend on how it is characterized.[1] For example, if two friends each put money into designing new software and begin to license it, what are the possible legal translations? Did they loan the business the money, or contribute to the capital of the business? Is the business a partnership, a joint venture, or another form? What happens to profits from the licenses? The parties may have an idea of what they intend, but this needs to be translated and properly documented to ensure the parties' expectations are legally protected. For example, if the parties intended the money to be repaid, the best characterization is likely that of a loan. In this case, the lawyer will draft loan documentation to ensure the appropriate legal protections apply.

Common Pitfalls

Translating the deal for the client can be one of the most difficult skills for a junior associate to master. A junior associate's lack of experience can mean she is less able to "spot" the appropriate characterization for what the client is seeking to accomplish. Junior associates are also less fluent in the language of the law, making it difficult to translate into clear terms for the client. Several specific pitfalls that can trip up a well-intentioned junior associate are:

---

1. See discussion on defining the structure of a transaction on pages 190–191.

- *Assuming underlying knowledge*. Know your audience. When translating a legal document for a client, don't assume your client is familiar with the relevant law. For example, in explaining a liquidated damages provision, you may need to take a step back and explain the legal rationale behind the concept of liquidated damages.

- *Misinterpreting the client's concerns*. This tends to happen when engaged in marginal listening. Don't be too ready to jump to your own conclusions about the client's concerns. Ask enough questions and listen carefully to the answers. Use active listening skills to ensure the terms the client is using accurately reflect his expectations. For example, a client entering into a joint venture may tell you he does not fully trust the other side. How should you interpret this? Is he concerned the other party will not act in good faith, or that they are hiding something? Does he want to be able to get out of the deal? Engaging in follow-up questions to flush out the client's actual concern will help you better identify what contractual provisions will best protect your client.

- *Being condescending*. Strive to provide the client with sufficient explanation of legal concepts without "talking down" to her. Again, know your audience: the more sophisticated your client, the less explanation he or she will need. A useful technique for gauging how much explanation is needed is to ask the client. For example: "*Are you familiar with [liquidated damages]?*" Another useful technique is to pay close attention to the terminology used by the client. A client investing in a company who refers to an "*8% pref*" as part of his desired deal terms likely is familiar with the concept of a preferred return and distribution waterfalls.[2]

- *Going into too much detail*. Avoid getting carried away when translating a contract or other legal document. You may be excited by how well the various provisions work together and your own understanding, especially if you drafted the contract. But resist the urge to explain how each provision works. The client will either quickly lose interest or may find it hard to distinguish issues that require her input from issues that do not necessarily require any action. The lawyer's role is to triage and synthesize the information that is relevant or necessary *from the client's perspective*.

Understanding the Basic Anatomy of a Contract

Much of what we translate into the language of the law in transactional practice is in the form of an agreement or contract. Although this text is not focused on contract drafting, a quick review the principal components of a standard contract (sometimes referred to as contract "building blocks") and the lexicon of contract drafting is helpful.

---

2. These are common terms used in venture capital and private equity financings and are included in the Glossary. See also the Practice Notes in Chapter 13.

Figure 11.1

Typical Contract Building Blocks

BEGINNING OF THE CONTRACT

Preamble:	Introduces the parties and the form of transaction
Recitals:	Offer a brief description of the transaction, highlighting key aspects and intent of the parties. Typically recitals are not binding, but can be used to interpret intent
Definitions:	Can form a separate section or be scattered throughout the agreement

OPERATIVE PROVISIONS

The Transaction:	Describes the actual components of the deal. Must understand the business deal to draft accurately
Consideration:	Should include type, amount, and timing
Deliverables:	All documents and information to be transferred at Closing
Closing Mechanics:	Timing, location, and constraints
Term:	The duration of the contract. Often combined with Termination (see below)

DEAL PROTECTION DEVICES

Representations and Warranties:	A statement as to an existing fact and a promise that that fact is true as of a certain point in time; promotes disclosure: party making the representation bears the risk of it being untrue or inaccurate
Covenants:	A promise to do (affirmative covenant) or not to do something (negative covenant). Sets out the obligations of each party and ensures the representations and warranties remain accurate and the bargained-for exchange occurs
Conditions:	Occurence that must be satisfied or waived before the transaction can close. These are commonly referred to as "walk-away rights" — if the condition is not met, the party relying on that condition is excused from consummating the deal
Remedies:	
Termination:	The right to end the contract before the expiration of its term
Indemnification:	Allows one party to seek reimbursement for loss or expense paid as a result of something the other party did, or the occurrence of certain circumstances
Damages:	Common law contract damages or liquidated damages
Equitable relief:	Remedy other than at law; for example, injunctive relief

END OF THE CONTRACT

Miscellaneous Provisions/Boilerplate:	Standard legal provisions addressing commonplace issues such as choice of law, severability, assignment, and amendment
Signature pages:	Where the parties to the agreement execute the agreement
Exhibits:	Typically include forms of ancillary agreements or other agreed information
Schedules:	Similar to exhibits, schedules tend to include lists of information that are too cumbersome to include in the main agreement, or that may be subject to frequent amendment

Most contracts incorporate these building blocks as a starting point, although not always in the same order or format. Each of these building blocks, and each provision within each block, must be tailored to reflect the specific deal terms negotiated between the parties.

Becoming familiar with these building blocks is important for several reasons:

- Each category of building block has different legal implications, including remedies for breach. Which concept you use to reflect a concern or negotiated term matters. For example, should a promise by one party be characterized as a representation, a covenant, a condition, or all three? What remedy is desired?
- Familiarity with the building blocks helps you structure your review of a proposed contract and how and what to negotiate. For example, in the representations and warranties section, you may want to focus on whether and to what extent the representations and warranties are "qualified," or how to "soften" covenants (see the Practice Note on Qualifiers and Softeners at the end of this chapter).
- You can use the building blocks as a starting point for drafting a contract, as well as for identifying useful precedent.

FOR DISCUSSION:

The text above mentions being able to "qualify" or "soften" representations and covenants. Presume a contract requires the seller to obtain all necessary consents. Does it matter if the contract states that the seller needs to use *best efforts* to obtain the consents, or *commercially reasonable efforts?* Which is the higher standard? What does this mean in practical terms for (a) the obligor, and (b) the recipient? [Hint: review the Practice Notes at the end of this chapter.]

Placement alone does not establish that a provision falls under a set building block or will be characterized in a certain way. The actual language of the provision is equally dispositive and should clearly indicate the intended legal characterization. Thus, absent a clear indication to the contrary, a provision stating the party "represents" that a fact is true will be treated as a representation, and a provision that states the parties "agree" will be treated as a covenant, regardless of where it is placed in the contract.

Finally, when drafting contract provisions, it is important to differentiate between rights and obligations of the parties. A right is a power, exercisable at the option of the holder and signaled by using the term "may," or "has the right." An obligation, on the other hand, is mandatory, and is indicated using terms such as "must" or "shall."

FOR DISCUSSION:

Look back at the hypothetical on page 21 involving a client who is entering into a lease in a strip mall for his vegan café. The client tells you he is concerned about having competing restaurants in the same mall, but the landlord has assured him that it does not rent to competitors of existing clients. Do you fully understand the client's concern? How can you translate this concern and the landlord's assurances into legally binding terms in the lease? You may want to refer to the sample contracts included in Appendix B.

Exercise 11.1

This exercise is in two parts.

Part 1: Review the contract and amendment your instructor will provide you, which you should assume you received under cover of the following email from the client:

Subject: FW: FX Contract

Can you take a quick look at this? Our concern is making sure that we get paid if the company gets their DOD grant. Best to just propose that Section 2B (we could change the bullets in the amendment to A and B) survive in Section 4? For a specific period?
Thank you.
- K

Working in pairs, answer the following questions:

1. What does the agreement relate to?
2. What is our client's role (our client is AS & Associates)?
3. What does the amendment change?
4. What, if anything, is unclear/ambiguous in Section 2?
5. What, if anything, is unclear/ambiguous in Section 4?
6. How would you explain any ambiguities to the client?
   (Focus on business issues/client's perspective)

Part 2: Your instructor will provide you with a revised amendment and an additional email chain. How would you translate this additional information for the client? How would you revise the contract to reflect your advice?

The Role of Ethics in Communicating with the Client

Throughout, this text has stressed the importance of effective communication as the cornerstone of adding value as a transactional lawyer. Clear communication with the client not only adds value, it also comports with the rules of professional responsibility and ethics both in and of itself and as a means of ensuring the client is equipped to make informed decisions. Following are excerpts from relevant rules from the Model Rules of Professional Conduct, which highlight the significance of communication in informed decision-making:

- Model Rule 2.1:

  In representing a client, a lawyer shall exercise independent professional judgment and render candid advice. In rendering advice, a lawyer may refer not only to the law but to other considerations such as moral, economic, social and political factors, that may be relevant to the client's situation.[3]

- Model Rule 1.4:

---

3. Rule 2.1 of the ABA Model Rules of Professional Conduct.

> *(a) A lawyer shall . . . [ ] reasonably consult with the client about the means by which the client's objectives are to be accomplished; . . . .*
>
> *(b) A lawyer shall explain a matter to the extent reasonably necessary to permit the client to make informed decisions regarding the representation.*[4]

- Model Rule 1.2:

> *(a) Subject to paragraphs (c) and (d), a lawyer shall abide by a client's decisions concerning the objectives of representation and, as required by Rule 1.4, shall consult with the client as to the means by which they are to be pursued . . . .*
>
> *[. . . .]*
>
> *(d) A lawyer shall not counsel a client to engage, or assist a client, in conduct that the lawyer knows is criminal or fraudulent, but a lawyer may discuss the legal consequences of any proposed course of conduct with a client and may counsel or assist a client to make a good faith effort to determine the validity, scope, meaning or application of the law.*[5]

- Model Rule 1.13:

> *(a) A lawyer employed or retained by an organization represents the organization acting through its duly authorized constituents.*
>
> *(b) If a lawyer for an organization knows that an officer, employee or other person associated with the organization is engaged in action, intends to act or refuses to act in a matter related to the representation that is a violation of a legal obligation to the organization, or a violation of law that reasonably might be imputed to the organization, and that is likely to result in substantial injury to the organization, then the lawyer shall proceed as is reasonably necessary in the best interest of the organization. Unless the lawyer reasonably believes that it is not necessary in the best interest of the organization to do so, the lawyer shall refer the matter to higher authority in the organization, including, if warranted by the circumstances to the highest authority that can act on behalf of the organization as determined by applicable law.*[6]

Rules 1.4 and 2.1 emphasize the importance of keeping the client properly informed and considering the client's situation when advising or counseling the client. Rule 1.4 makes clear that the lawyer has an obligation to inform the client about how the lawyer believes the client's objectives can be accomplished. This is the essence of client-centered lawyering. As the attorney, you have an ethical obligation to adequately explain to the client its options for achieving its goals, and the legal consequences of each option.

Rule 1.2 adds to this the concept that it is the client, not the lawyer, who should be making the ultimate decisions about a course of action. Note how Rule 1.2 addresses potential criminal conduct. What are the ethical obligations of the lawyer in this regard? Is it still the client who gets to make the ultimate decision?

Finally, Rule 1.13 raises a critical distinction. Often, although you will be communicating with individuals, your client will be the corporation or other entity for whom the individuals work. Although the interests of the entity and its individual representatives are largely aligned, this is not always the case.

---

4. Rule 1.4 of the ABA Model Rules of Professional Conduct.
5. Rule 1.2 of the ABA Model Rules of Professional Conduct.
6. Rule 1.13 of the ABA Model Rules of Professional Conduct.

In other instances, such as when advising a newly formed company, you may start your representation before the company is formed. In these cases, the line can be blurry as to whether you represent the entity, or one or more of the founders. Be clear in your own mind and in your communications with the client as to whom you represent. Why is this so important? What potential issues could arise? Look at Rule 1.13(b). What does this tell you about the need for a clear demarcation of the company as client?

What does compliance with these ethical rules mean in practical terms? We can draw two key practical conclusions: (1) the more you communicate with your client and the clearer and more precise those communications, the better; and (2) understanding the distinction between advising and counseling the client is imperative to ensuring that the client is making informed decisions.

In addition, be careful not to advise the client to take any action that circumvents the law. This line is easier to cross than you might expect, as the following hypothetical illustrates:

Illustration: **Ethical Dilemma**

A client emails you, asking if there is a way to pay someone a commission for acting as a finder (i.e., identifying and introducing investors) in a securities transaction. Under securities laws, a person who receives a commission for introducing investors typically is acting as a broker-dealer and must be registered, absent certain limited exceptions. The client thinks it has come up with a clever way to structure the relationship to avoid triggering the broker-dealer registration requirements. You think the proposed structure might work, but that there is a risk it may not pass muster. Ethically, how do you respond? There are two possible ways: the first is to respond that the client's proposed structure is workable, but stress that you would want to make sure it's done in a way that couldn't be deemed to be circumventing the registration requirements. The other is to advise the client that there are exceptions that may be applicable, provided the client ensures it complies with certain steps and with the caveat that the exception could be deemed not applicable.

FOR DISCUSSION:

What is the difference between the two responses in the above illustration? Is one more ethical than the other? Which one is allowing the client to make a more informed decision? The result is the same, but does one response suggest you are advising the client to circumvent the rules? Is this ethical?

> **Exercise 11.2**
>
> Working in small groups, discuss whether the following would be ethical and what steps could be taken to minimize the risk of any ethical violations:
>
> - Representing both members forming a limited liability company
> - Recommending your cousin's printing company to a client looking for a printer
> - Allowing your client to make a decision that you consider unwise
> - Allowing your client to make a decision that you consider immoral

Other Forms of Written Client Communications

Until now, we have focused primarily on memoranda, letters, and emails in discussing effective written communication techniques. Let us turn now to consider the techniques discussed in the context of specific sub-categories of these forms commonly encountered by junior associates in transactional practice.

Engagement Letters

An engagement letter is your contract with the client. You should not commence any work for a client without a signed engagement letter. Your firm may have other requirements and will also likely have a specific form that will need to be signed by a partner or other firm principal. As with any contract, the agreed terms need to be clearly and precisely laid out, including the scope of services to be provided, the identity of the client, the relevant fees, and the resolution of disputes. Clarity is vital in the context of an engagement letter, where the client's interests are arguably not aligned with those of the other party, in this case the client's own lawyer; signing the engagement letter should be as informed a decision by the client as possible.

Due Diligence Checklists, Memos, and Reports

Due diligence is a quintessential task assigned to junior transactional associates: a rite of passage akin to document review for a litigation associate. It is a critical component in most M&A transactions: issues discovered in due diligence can affect purchase price, liability, and even whether the deal proceeds. Thus, although seemingly a mundane task for a junior associate eager to be in the conference room negotiating the terms of a deal, due diligence is one of the most valuable ways a junior associate can contribute to the successful completion of a deal and should be conducted meticulously.

I describe due diligence in the Practice Note at the end of Chapter 8 as an investigative process used to obtain information about the other party to a transaction. In practical terms, due diligence is:

- asking questions
- to elicit responses and documents
- that help verify the relevant facts
- to manage the risk of a given transaction.

The more information you receive and the more you see of what the documents say, the more you can ascertain if the facts are what the other party represents them to be. The best analogy is to "looking under the hood" when buying a car.

Written communication in due diligence takes the form of one or more of the following:

- *Due diligence checklist.* The side conducting the due diligence inquiry will start the process by preparing a due diligence checklist containing a list of all items it would like to review. Your firm will likely have precedent you can adapt for any transaction. The type of information requested and the comprehensiveness of the checklist will depend on: (1) the complexity of the transaction and the parties involved; (2) the value of the transaction; (3) the type of transaction and industry; and (4) the risk tolerance of your client. For example, the purchase of $10,000 worth of stock in a newly formed company with limited operations by a seasoned investor will likely require a more limited due diligence checklist than a $20,000,000 merger with a highly regulated petroleum corporation.

- *Due diligence memos and reports.* A due diligence memo or report (these terms are used interchangeably) summarizes the results of your review of the answers and materials received in response to the due diligence checklist. A due diligence memo or report can be organized in many ways, depending in part on the categories of information reviewed. We will look at some of the techniques for organizing and drafting a due diligence memo below.

- *Email correspondence and follow-up due diligence.* Less formal than a checklist or a report, email correspondence can be useful when requesting follow-up information to an initial due diligence checklist, or to provide the partner or client with a quick synopsis of any significant issues.

Useful Techniques

The following techniques for drafting a due diligence memo are useful to learn, not only to enhance your ability to perform this task satisfactorily, but to hone your writing and organizational skills in general.

- *Be methodical in your review and note-taking.* As you review the documents provided, prepare summaries of each category of document. You may find it helpful to create a template for each category that lists out the key terms you are interested in. You can then fill in the template for each document you review in that category. This will help you to not miss important information, and more easily summarize your findings when the time comes to put together your memo. Try to include all possibly relevant terms, even though some may be inapplicable.

For example, when reviewing contracts, your template might include the following categories:

Summary: Contracts

Title, Date and Parties: _____

Purpose: _____

Term, Renewal and Expiration: _____

Consideration and Pricing Information: _____

Exclusivity/Territory: _____

Change of Control: _____

Default and Termination Triggers: _____

Consequences of Default or Termination:_____

Assignment: _____

Confidentiality Restrictions: _____

Restrictive Covenants: _____

Indemnities and Warranties: _____

Security: _____

Governing Law: _____

Other Comments: _____

And your template for reviewing organizational documents might include the following items:

Summary: Organizational Documents

Type of Document and Company Name: _____

Capitalization: _____

Properties of Each Class of Equity: _____

Pre-emptive Rights: _____

Transfer Restrictions: _____

Puts and Calls: _____

Dividends and Distributions: _____

Capital Calls: _____

Consents:_____

Number of Directors or Managers: _____

Restrictive Covenants: _____

Confidentiality Restrictions: _____

Other Rights of Equity Holders: _____

Anti-takeover Defenses: _____

Other Comments: _____

- *Determine a logical organization for your memo.* Does it make most sense to organize by category of document, most to least significant issue, time period, or other meaningful order?
- *Start by drafting the main points and headings and then go back and fill in as much detail as necessary.* For example, instead of working document-by-document and describing each one in turn, start with your initial headings, such as *Corporate Structure, Corporate Agreements, Commercial Agreements, Finance, Property, Employment*, and so on (you may want to track the categories used in the initial due diligence checklist). You can then go back and create sub-headings. For example:

Corporate Structure

- Organizational chart:
- Charter:
- By-laws:
- Certificates of good standing:
- Subsidiaries:

- *Be selective in the information you include.* You will need sufficient detail to allow the client or reviewing partner to easily identify red flags. But too much detail can obscure the issues and undermine the value of the due diligence memo. If you are unsure how much information to include, hedge your bets by including key points in the memo itself, and attach an appendix with more detailed summaries or copies of your original note-taking summaries. This allows the reader to access more detail if needed, without making the memo overly cumbersome.
- *Include an introduction section where you briefly summarize the parties, the transaction, and the scope and any limitations of the due diligence review.*
- *Following the introduction, include an executive summary where you can highlight any key categories of documents or issues.*

Exercise 11.3

Assume you represent ABC, Inc., a snack-food manufacturer. ABC is seeking to acquire Organa Corp., a California corporation that manufactures organic snack foods in California. ABC is interested in Organa primarily because it would like to capitalize on Organa's existing goodwill and distribution contracts to enter the California organic snack food market. You have been tasked with due diligence. As part of your due diligence investigation, you have received a copy of the form of distribution agreement used by Organa with each of its distributors (included in Appendix B).

1. Using the sample template for reviewing contracts above, prepare a summary of the key terms of this agreement.
2. What issues, if any, might you highlight in the executive summary of your due diligence memo? Why?

Letters of Intent and Term Sheets

Letters of intent (LOIs), term sheets, and Memoranda of Understanding (or MOUs) are documents prepared at the start of negotiation of a transaction. Their purpose is to outline the general terms of the transaction: a framework according to which the parties can negotiate the definitive terms of the transaction. Typically, these documents are nonbinding, although certain provisions, such as confidentiality and exclusivity, can be made binding.

LOIs, term sheets, and MOUs all serve similar purposes and carry the same legal significance, although they vary in appearance. As the names suggest, a letter of intent resembles a letter and a memorandum of understanding is drafted in the form of a memo. A term sheet typically is drafted as a list of terms. Which form is used is a matter of personal preference and custom. For example, most venture capital investors will prefer a term sheet, while a merger proposal will most likely be in the form of an LOI, and a joint venture proposal (especially one that involves parties from different countries) will be in the form of an MOU. For simplicity, I will use LOI to refer to all three forms.

The most common way a junior associate encounters one of these forms is when asked to review an initial draft of the definitive documentation for a transaction. The junior associate will be tasked with ensuring that the terms of the definitive documentation are consistent with the terms agreed in the LOI. Alternatively, a junior associate may be given a copy of an LOI and asked to prepare the initial draft of the definitive documentation for a transaction based on the terms of the LOI. In each case, the LOI serves as an intermediate step in translating the business deal into definitive legal terms, and, conversely, summarizing the transaction into key business points.

Not all transactions include an LOI; they can be superfluous in a simple transaction, or one with a very short time frame. Some of the commonly perceived advantages and disadvantages of using LOIs are summarized in Figure 11.2:

Figure 11.2

Letter of Intent: Advantages & Disadvantages

ADVANTAGES	DISADVANTAGES
• Memorializes key business terns and provides useful outline of structure of proposed transaction	• Risk that may be construed as binding, leading to liability if deal not consummated
• Ensures each party of the other's legitimate interest in proceeding	• Can trigger disclosure obligations of public companies
• Helps identify and resolve issues early on	• Can be difficult to renegotiate points outlined in LOI
• Can reduce likelihood of misunderstanding	• Can take time away from negotiating actual deal documents
• Can provide buyer leverage in obtaining necessary financing	• Can unintentionally create duty to negotiate in good faith
• Can be a way for buyer to obtain exclusivity for a specified time period	• Undue reliance

Figure 11.3 itemizes some of the common provisions typically included in an LOI for an acquisition:

Figure 11.3

Term	Possible details
Structure	The type of deal and the parties involved
Purchase Price	The amount, timing, and type of consideration, including any escrow, earn-out, and assumptions
What Is/Is Not Being Acquired/Assumed	List of what is being acquired/assumed, such as specific assets and specific liabilities, and what is expressly not included
Conditions	Typical conditions, such as material adverse change, due diligence, and obtaining necessary consents
Representations and Warranties	Typically, not detailed—usually refer to "customary representations and warranties to be included in definitive purchase agreement"
Covenants	Any specific agreements, such as employment, indemnification, or other
No-shop/ Exclusivity	Prohibits seller from negotiating with third parties during a specified period, usually the time Buyer negotiates for completing due diligence
Standstill	Requires the buyer to agree not to attempt to acquire a stake in target or make a hostile bid (used for public companies)
Confidentiality	May also incorporate by reference a prior nondisclosure agreement signed by the parties
Statement as to Nonbinding Effect	Confirms nonbinding nature of LOI, with carve-outs as needed

Exercise 11.4

Review the sample letter of intent and sample asset purchase agreement in Appendix B. Can you identify each of the above terms in the sample letter of intent? Can you identify where each of the terms in the letter of intent should be addressed in the purchase agreement? Will any changes need to be made?

PRACTICE NOTES

Representations and Warranties Reviewed

If you have taken a course in contract drafting, you are likely familiar with the concept of representations and warranties. These represent a common contractual building block—one of the fundamental sections in any contract. Representations and warranties are promises made by a party that certain facts are true as of a given point in time. Requiring the other party to a contract to make a representation or warranty serves several purposes: (1) it can help prompt disclosure of facts that may not have been readily apparent; (2) it allocates the risk between the parties; and (3) it forms a basis for indemnification, termination, or other remedy.

A party being asked to make a representation or warranty can provide the requested representation or warranty as presented, seek to modify or qualify the representation or warranty (using "qualifiers" or schedules), or refuse. For example, when buying a house, you may ask the seller for the following representation: "There are no easements on the property." This is a fact that may otherwise be difficult for you to ascertain through due diligence (although in most cases, easements are recorded). The seller can agree to the representation as is, in which case the seller then bears the risk of an easement that later comes to light.

The seller can also seek to qualify the representation. For example, the seller could change the representation to say: "*To seller's knowledge*, there are no easements on the property." Can you see how this shifts the risk arising from undiscovered easements to the buyer? The seller could also propose a schedule: "*Except as set forth on Schedule A*, there are no easements on the property." Schedule A would presumably list any easements, promoting full disclosure.

Finally, the seller could refuse to make the representation, in which case you would advise your client that it has the option to proceed relying solely on its own due diligence and assume the risk of undisclosed easements or walk away from the purchase. Once the representation is made, the seller has liability for any misrepresentation. Depending on how the contract is drafted, you could seek termination of the contract, indemnification, or other damages for misrepresentation.

Qualifiers, Softeners, and Other Terms of Art in Contract Drafting and Negotiations

Often, contract negotiations will center around subtle nuances in language that modify the degree of obligation and risk attributed to each party. The task of the transactional lawyer is to translate the agreed allocation of business risk and degree of obligation into binding legal terms. The most common mechanism for doing this is using qualifiers, or softeners. As the names suggest, these qualify or soften a contractual promise or obligation to shift some of the risk back to the other party. Examples include knowledge qualifiers, materiality, thresholds, and exceptions. For example, consider the variations of the same representation in Figure 11.4:

Figure 11.4

Flat representation (unqualified):

Seller represents that it has not violated any environmental laws or regulations This provides the buyer with maximum comfort—Seller is liable for any violation, known or unknown

Qualified by knowledge:

Seller represents that, to its knowledge, it has not violated any environmental laws or regulations Some of the risk is shifted back to the Buyer, as long as the Seller did not know of any violations

Qualified by materiality:

Seller represents that it has not materially violated any environmental laws or regulations This shifts the risk slightly to the Buyer for any violations that are not material. In both cases, the parties will negotiate the definition of "knowledge" and "materiality"

Qualified by exception:

Seller represents that it has not violated any environmental laws or regulations, except as set forth on Schedule 1.	This allows the Seller to expressly carve out known violations. Buyer must then assume any future liabilities associated with the disclosed violations, or choose not to proceed

Covenants are often softened by negotiating the degree of effort needed to satisfy the obligation. For example, a party might negotiate that it need only use *"best efforts"* or *"commercially reasonable efforts."*

Conclusion

In this chapter, we began to dive deeper into the practical aspects of communicating with the client. We looked at how to translate the client's desired outcome into legally binding terms and how to explain contractual terms or other legal terminology to the client. We also examined the role of ethics in deciding how and when to consult with the client when documenting a transaction. Finally, we looked in some depth at common forms of writing that a junior lawyer might be asked to prepare, such as due diligence checklists, reports, and letters of intent. In the remaining chapters, we shift to the third context covered in this text: communicating with lawyers on the other side of a transaction.

SIMULATION EXERCISE #9

You receive the following email from a partner at the firm. Your client, KL Shipping, is negotiating the acquisition of GTI, and has signed a confidentiality agreement. Review the referenced confidentiality agreement (located in Appendix B) and prepare a response to the client as instructed in the partner's email.

From: Julie Ryan jryan@ryanassoc.com
Sent: March ___, 10:05 AM
To: Junior Associate
Subject: KL Shipping — Confidentiality Agreement with GTI
Attachment: KL-GTI NDA

Junior Associate,

Attached is a copy of the signed confidentiality agreement between GTI and KL Shipping. The client has asked that we clarify the following questions regarding the agreement:

1. Is KL directly liable under this agreement to GTI's parent company, Gulf Shipping?
2. The definition of Confidential Information seems very broad. What about the terms of the purchase agreement between GTI and KL Shipping? Are those protected as confidential under the definition?
3. What about information provided by KL Shipping to GTI—is that protected under this agreement?
4. What does paragraph 2 mean? Can KL Shipping provide GTI's information to us, as its lawyers? What about the board of directors of KL? What about KL's CFO, who will be reviewing the financial statements?
5. How long will KL be bound by this agreement?

6. What does it mean in paragraph 5 that the Disclosing Party shall be entitled to "injunctive relief"?

7. Does this agreement bind KL in any way to proceed with the acquisition?

Please prepare a short email for the client responding to these questions in as simple and straightforward a manner as possible. Please forward the email to me <u>within 48 hours</u>. I will forward it on to the client once I have reviewed your answers.

Thanks,
Julie

Julie A. Ryan
Ryan & Associates
299 Valley Avenue
3rd Floor
Los Angeles, CA 90009
Tel: 213-510-5000
Email: jryan@ryanassoc.com

C

Communicating with Opposing Counsel

Chapter 12

....

Overview; Written Communications

This chapter marks the beginning of the third and final communication context covered in this text: communicating with lawyers outside of your law firm. It starts with exploring the different modes of inter-lawyer communication and then moves on to examine in-depth techniques for effective written communication, including letters, emails, and commenting on drafts.

By the end of this chapter, you will be able to:

- Assess the most effective mode of inter-lawyer communication
- Demonstrate the ability to adapt among communications with the client, partner, and lawyers on the other side
- Compose and respond to letters, emails, and other correspondence with other lawyers
- Evaluate, compose, and negotiate comments on draft agreements

....

You have been working on due diligence in connection with the acquisition by your client of a small software company. The senior associate on the deal drafted the initial version of the asset purchase agreement. Seller's counsel has reviewed the draft and has sent back a set of comments and revisions. The senior associate asks you to review the comments and determine whether there are any significant issues that need to be addressed. You identify several issues and discuss potential responses with the senior associate, who then asks you to draft an email to seller's counsel summarizing the issues and the proposed responses. He informs you that the client hopes to get the deal wrapped up and so does not want to get bogged down in lengthy negotiations. How should you go about drafting this email? What is the correct tone? How can you present the issues and solutions in a way that will facilitate closing the deal?

....

Overview: Lawyers Representing "the Other Side"

In most instances, the other lawyers you will encounter will be representing the party or parties on the other side of a transaction. I deliberately do not use the term "adverse parties." In a traditional litigation context, you will have a clear adverse party or parties. Transactional practice is less adversarial than litigation: the goal of any transaction is mutual gain, as opposed to win-lose. Thus, the interests of the party on the other side of a transaction may not be fully adverse to those of your client; in fact, they should be somewhat aligned. However, for ethical and other reasons, do not lose sight of the fact that the parties are still on different—if not completely opposite—sides, and that your role is still to advocate for your client's best interests.

This is true whether the parties are buyer and seller, landlord and tenant, or joint venture partners. The lawyer representing the other side will be advocating for his or her client to the best of his or her ability, and so should you.

The lawyer representing the other side of a transaction is commonly referred to as "opposing counsel," or by reference to the specific relationship of the parties to the transaction, such as "issuer's counsel," "buyer's counsel," or "lender's counsel." For brevity, I use the term opposing counsel.

Choosing the Most Effective Form of Communication

The overarching goal of communicating with opposing counsel in transactional practice is to negotiate the best deal for your client. What form of communication is most effective in achieving this goal? The answer, of course, is: "it depends." Several factors can influence how you choose to communicate with opposing counsel, which can change over the course of the transaction. Factors include:

- The relationship between the parties;
- The relationship between you and opposing counsel;
- The timing;
- The complexity of the subject matter of the communication; and
- Personal preferences.

These factors should seem familiar; we looked at them when discussing when to use email over more formal written correspondence. Let us now consider these same factors in a broader context. The table in Figure 12.1 below summarizes key characteristics of the main modes of communication between lawyers:

Figure 12.1

	Written communication (letters, mark-ups)	Email	Telephone	In-person (face-to-face)
TIME TO REFLECT:	Allows time for reflection and careful word choice	Allows time for thought in drafting	Easier to say the wrong thing	Similar to telephone conversation in terms of having little time to plan words
RISK OF MISCOMMUNICATION:	Some risk of ambiguity/ miscommunication	Easy to misinterpret as typically shorter and less carefully drafted; lacks nonverbal cues	Can minimize miscommunication but lacks visual cues	Lowest risk of miscommunication provided parties interpret nonverbal cues correctly and no other barriers to communication (e.g., language)

EFFICIENCY/RISK OF CONFRONTATION:	Avoids direct confrontation but more time-consuming; efficient for negotiating drafting details	Flexible and efficient; can send at any time; but can be time-consuming if dealing with issues that require significant back and forth	Efficient, depending on length of call and need to prepare and/or debrief; useful when dealing with specific issues as allows immediate response	Can become confrontational and can be time-consuming and expensive if travel is involved; can be efficient when dealing with big picture issues
RAPPORT-BUILDING:	Difficult to build rapport with other side	Some ability to build rapport	Better ability to build rapport	Greatest ability to build rapport

Know When to Switch Modes

Each of these modes offers distinct advantages and disadvantages, depending on the purpose of the communication at any given time. For example, at the beginning of a transaction, when building rapport is central, it might be more effective to have an in-person meeting or a conference call to introduce the parties. Once drafting begins, it can be easier to go back and forth with written comments and revised drafts; hammering out details or arriving at any concrete resolution in a meeting can be difficult, especially if several people are present. On the other hand, it can be easier to sit around a conference table and discuss big issues that are difficult to resolve without explanation. The parties can revert to email or telephone calls after the meeting to finalize any details.

Although efficient, and despite its popularity, email is perhaps the most problematic mode of communication. The exchange lacks both visual and vocal cues, such as body language and tone, which can impede the recipient's ability to accurately interpret what is being said. In addition, the shorter the communication, the more time it can take to be clear and precise; thus, some of the benefits of the immediacy of email are lost.

Long chains of back-and-forth emails can also create confusion. Once four or five emails have been exchanged on a point without resolution, it usually makes sense to pick up the phone and engage in conversation. Conversely, if a phone conversation or meeting becomes too heated, or you become deadlocked, it can be time to take a step back and agree to follow up with email, hopefully once emotions have cooled down. Nothing is wrong with saying: "*I don't think we are getting very far here, why don't we go back and summarize what we think the issues are in an email and then we can discuss?*"

Figure 12.1 does not include videoconferences, which serve as a hybrid between telephone and in-person meetings. The advances in videoconference technology offer huge benefits to transactional lawyers, as they allow for virtual in-person meetings without the time and expense of travel. However, and perhaps not surprisingly, videoconferences still lack some of the ability to build rapport and hash out big issues that an in-person meeting can offer. This is partly due to limitations on technology—it can be hard to hear, signals fluctuate, and so on. There is still no substitute for actual human interaction in communication.

Finally, in some circumstances it can be worthwhile to follow-up with an email summarizing a conversation or meeting. This can help memorialize a conversation and ensure that there is no misunderstanding. In addition, meetings often end leaving the details to be finalized; an email can be an efficient way to assign and confirm tasks to be completed. For example, a follow-up email might read: "*Further to our conversation this morning, to confirm, you will be providing us with copies of all board minutes. In the meantime, we will send you any additional due diligence queries, with the goal of com-*

pleting diligence by the beginning of next week." This makes clear what each party has agreed to do and sets a timeframe for completion. It also creates a record.

Written Communications

Most communication with other lawyers is in writing, whether a formal letter, an email, or comments on a document. The remainder of this chapter therefore focuses on techniques for communicating with other lawyers in the context of written communication. However, many of these techniques and considerations are also applicable to oral communication.

Fundamental Techniques

Written communications with opposing counsel take on the same general form as communications with a partner or a client, typically in the form of a letter or email. Less frequently, you may have a reason to use a memo format, or perhaps a bullet point summary. The same fundamental techniques discussed in the preceding chapters hold true for written communications in this context, including:

- *Clarity.* Your writing should be as unambiguous as possible (unless you have a conscious reason for being vague). Use short sentences and plain English, logically connect each sentence and paragraph using thesis sentences, topic strings, signals, and other techniques, and minimize any grammatical or syntax errors.
- *Conciseness.* Your writing should also be as concise as possible. Work on eliminating metadiscourse and other excess verbiage. Winding your way up to the point you are trying to make, especially if it is one on with which you know the other side will likely disagree, can be tempting. But this detracts from the persuasiveness of your writing.
- *Precision.* Use precise terms, headings, and other organizational techniques to present the information accurately and completely.
- *Reader-centered.* In addition, your writing should be reader-centered. The quantity, quality, and relevance of the information you include must be measured from the point of view of your reader.
- *Presentation and style.* Any written communication should always be professional in tone and presentation and use accepted style conventions.

> *Illustration: **Applying Fundamental Techniques***
>
> This first sentence of a letter to opposing counsel lacks clarity, conciseness, and precision:
>
> > *"In order to ensure the smooth completion of the transaction, I am forwarding to you under cover herewith our proposed initial comments to the foregoing documentation received from you earlier this week, as well as a copy of the regulations that we discussed with you."*
>
> Now consider the following rewrite of the same sentence:
>
> > *"We received your draft of the [name of document]. Please find attached our initial comments. We have also attached a copy of [name of regulation], per our discussion."*

Distinguishing Purpose and Audience

Correspondence with opposing counsel differs from correspondence with a lawyer within your firm or with your client in two main ways:

- *Persuasive versus objective purpose.* The goal of a letter to opposing counsel generally is to persuade the opposing party to agree to your desired result. When writing to a lawyer in your own firm or your client, although you ultimately want to persuade your reader to accept your analysis or advice, your principal goal likely is to educate or inform.
- *Friendly versus hostile audience.* Although transactional practice is less adversarial than litigation and many transactions are considered "friendly," the other side is still the other side. If you misstate a fact, misinterpret the law, or accidentally disclose information to a lawyer in your firm or the client, it may make you look bad, but the consequences will likely not be too far-reaching. These same errors in communications with opposing counsel could impact the negotiating power of your client and potentially thwart consummation of the transaction.

Setting the Tone: Balancing Persuasiveness and Collaboration

Transactional practice is not a zero-sum game. The goal in any transaction is to achieve the most favorable outcome for your client while doing your best to minimize any risks. At the same time, if the other side does not feel equally satisfied, you could end up with one of the following outcomes: (1) the other party could walk away from the deal, in which case no one wins; (2) the other party could push back, dig in its heels, or seek to renegotiate, making it more difficult to achieve the desired result for your client; or (3) the parties could end up in litigation.

How do you achieve the right balance? How can you persuade the other side that your proposal is acceptable without creating adversity?

The Transactional-Litigation Continuum

The distinctions between transactional and litigation practice and how these fall on a continuum of lawyering activity also have an impact on your correspondence with opposing counsel. For example, are you writing to opposing counsel to provide comments to a document in a friendly transaction, to put opposing counsel on notice that you are concerned with the other side's position or actions, or to propose a settlement of a dispute? The further along the continuum toward adversity, the more your interactions with opposing counsel will take on litigation-like features.

Striking the Right Balance

Consider the following three examples of an email from a lawyer to opposing counsel about the purchase of a drilling rig, seeking to negotiate greater comfort in the contract from the seller as to the maintenance history of the rig:

1. *I understand you may not be aware of any maintenance issues. However, we request that you consider including the following representations . . . .*
2. *We believe your client may be hiding maintenance issues. As you well know, federal environmental laws impose a broad duty on sellers of oil rigs to disclose any and all maintenance issues. Your client's blatant refusal to include even the most minimal representation as to the past maintenance of the rig . . . .*

3. *My client remains concerned regarding potential undisclosed maintenance issues. To reduce that risk, we would suggest adding the following representation, which we believe strikes a reasonable compromise . . . .*

Which version is more persuasive? In the first example, the lawyer appears defensive and weak. In the second, the lawyer appears accusatory—that tone is not likely to encourage anyone to want to compromise. In the third example, the lawyer appears professional and cordial while also appearing confident in her client's legal position.

Techniques for Persuasion

Negotiations, by definition, involve an element of adversity. Sometimes, you may need to stand firm. But when drafting correspondence to opposing counsel in a transactional setting, regardless of the circumstances, setting a collaborative tone is good practice.

Language that is obviously persuasive can often be ineffective at achieving a mutually satisfactory result. First, the reader recognizes what the writer is trying to do and may "subconsciously resist." Second, using language that is too argumentative can adversely affect the writer's credibility by making the writer appear too desperate.[1]

On the other hand, adopting too objective or conciliatory a tone can be equally unproductive. As your client's advocate, your goal is to convince others of your client's legal position. The aim is to strike a balance—persuasively argue your client's position while also appearing objective and reasonable.[2]

Following are some techniques that can help achieve the proper balance:

- *Let the facts speak for themselves.* As in a litigation setting, presenting the facts in such a way that allows the reader to reach your desired conclusion can be more persuasive than being overly argumentative.

- *Remain courteous.* No matter how contentious opposing counsel becomes, try to take the high road. Remember, the transaction is between your clients, not you and opposing counsel.

- *Provide sufficient explanation such that your argument appears objectively reasonable.* Make it difficult for the other side to take issue with your argument or request.

- *Avoid being overly defensive.* Offer support for your position without creating the impression that you do not believe it to be supported. For example, consider the following two examples:

    While we understand your client's reasons for not wanting to extend the term to two years, our client is concerned that one year will not allow sufficient time to develop the necessary distribution channels.

    We believe your client is making undue demands. Our client could obtain a two-year term with any other supplier and thus is justified in asking for two years here.

  The first provides a reasonable, objective explanation for the position, without being overly apologetic or self-justifying. The second suggests the change is based on a subjective feeling of unfairness.

- *Avoid qualifying your statements.* Instead of: "*We believe that this term does not address the concern of our client,*" state simply: "*This term does not adequately address our client's concern [for the following reasons].*"

---

1. Robin Wellford Slocum, Legal Reasoning, Writing, and Other Lawyering Skills 363 (2011).
2. *Id.*

- *Avoid overkill.* Use of superlatives like "obviously," and "clearly" adds little to the substance of your argument and can cause the other side to think you do not believe your argument to be obvious or clear.

FOR DISCUSSION:

Consider the following sets of alternative statements drawn from different cover letters. Which alternative in each case is more collaborative? Why? Which is more likely to result in easier negotiations?

Alternative A	Alternative B
Attached for your review and discussion is an initial draft of the asset purchase agreement for the proposed acquisition of TempAssist, Inc. ("Company"), as well as a preliminary closing checklist.	Attached is the form of asset purchase agreement that our client is willing to sign for the acquisition of TempAssist, Inc. by our client, as well as the closing checklist that sets forth the actions required of your client in order to close.
We note that the diligence files provided do not include any signed employee confidentiality agreements. Please confirm whether these have in fact been signed, and if so, please add to the data room.	The data room is missing any signed copies of any confidentiality agreements. This clearly needs to be rectified as soon as possible to our complete satisfaction.
The 30-day period to raise disputes relating to the final working capital calculations is unacceptable. We have changed it to 60 days.	We are concerned that the 30-day period required to raise any disputes relating to the final working capital calculation will not provide sufficient time for the accountants to resolve any issues. We are thus proposing this be changed to 90 days.
Regarding the exclusivity provision, our client is very concerned that without this, they might be exposed to unfair competition, especially as you do not have any current clients. Thus, we think our client is being extremely reasonable in asking that you not provide services to similar businesses, which would violate the spirit and intent of the transaction.	Regarding the exclusivity provision, we understand your concern regarding the ability to continue to service other clients who may be in a similar business. However, we note that your current list of clients does not include any competing business.
We look forward to hearing from you on these two points. In the meantime, please let us know if you have any questions/concerns with any of our other comments or would like to discuss	We trust the enclosed is satisfactory and await your client's signature within five days hereof.

| In the interest of time, I am circulating the attached prior to review by my client, subject to his review and approval. | My client has not yet reviewed the attached and so reserves the right to make further changes. |

Common Forms of Correspondence

The likely forms of correspondence you will be asked to draft as a junior associate are cover letters (or cover emails), letters of intent, emails, and comment letters.

Cover Letters

Cover letters and emails are used to transmit correspondence or other documents—for example, an email with an attached mark-up of an agreement, or a letter that accompanies a set of original documents. With the advent of electronic signatures and the ESIGN Act (see the Practice Note in Chapter 11), most correspondence is sent via email; only occasionally will a letter or other documents be sent via U.S. mail or courier, typically only if required to comply with a notice provision in a contract or regulatory requirements, or if sent in anticipation of litigation. Thus, you may find yourself drafting an email cover letter attaching a copy of a letter. For example, you may email opposing counsel a copy of a notice required under a contract.

Cover letters should follow the various conventions described throughout this text and should use a formal letter format (see Chapter 10). Figure 12.2 contains examples of the same cover letter drafted as a formal letter and as an email:

Figure 12.2

RYAN & ASSOCIATES, LLP
299 Valley Avenue, 3rd Floor
Los Angeles, CA 90009

March 15, 20___

Maura Smith
Dewey, Cheatham & Howe
123 Avenue of the Stars
Middletown, NY 11104

Re: Original Share Certificates

Dear Ms. Smith:

Further to our discussion of March 10, I am enclosing the original share certificates for TempAssist, Inc., duly endorsed in favor of your client, Tremont Holdings, LLC, pursuant to Section 4 of the Stock Purchase Agreement dated March 9, 2018.

I believe this is the only remaining outstanding deliverable. Please let me know if you believe additional information is required, or if you have any questions regarding the enclosed certificates.

Sincerely,

RYAN & ASSOCIATES, LLP

_____

Julie Ryan

Encl/

From:	Julie Ryan [mailto:jryan@ryanassoc.com]
Sent:	Monday, March 15, 20__ 12:54 PM
To:	'Maura Smith'
Subject:	RE: TempAssist, Inc. Share Certificates
Attachment:	Share Certificates

Dear Ms. Smith:

Further to our discussion of March 10, I am attaching the original share certificates for Temp Assist, Inc., duly endorsed in favor of your client, Tremont Holdings, LLC, pursuant to Section 4 of the Stock Purchase Agreement dated March 9, 2018.

I believe this is the only remaining outstanding deliverable. Please let me know if you believe additional information is required, or if you have any questions regarding the enclosed certificates.

Sincerely,

Julie Ryan

Julie A. Ryan
Ryan & Associates
299 Valley Avenue
3rd Floor
Los Angeles, CA 90009
Tel: 213-510-5000
Email: jryan@ryanassoc.com

This email message and any attachments are being sent by Ryan & Associates, LLP, are confidential, may be privileged, and are for the sole use of the intended recipient(s). Any unauthorized review, use, disclosure, or distribution is prohibited. If you are not the intended recipient, please contact the sender immediately by replying to this email message and destroy all copies of this email message and any attachments.

Letters of Intent

We discussed letters of intent in Chapter 11 in the context of communicating with the client. Although letters of intent are typically focused on key business issues and arise early in the deal process, the lawyers for each side will often draft and negotiate them. Thus, even though drafted from the perspective of the parties to the transaction, you should assume that the primary audience (or reader) is opposing counsel and, as such, letters of intent should be drafted with the same care and precision as with any other correspondence.

Emails

In addition to using emails as cover notes to accompany and transmit documents, email correspondence is commonly used as a substitute for a telephonic or in-person conversation. As when drafting emails to clients, be wary of adopting too casual a tone; strive to strike the correct balance between formality and conversation.

Even though the medium is conversational, email communication in a legal setting is still a form of written communication; it can create a lasting impression. In addition, unlike a traditional letter, emails can instantly be forwarded to many individuals. Thus, what you say and how you say it needs to be at least as carefully considered as what you put into a letter or a formal memorandum.

When substituted for telephonic or in-person conversations, email poses unique challenges: the lack of visual and vocal cues that form part of effective oral communication can hamper the reader's interpretation of the message being conveyed. Avoid humor and colloquialisms, as these can be easily misinterpreted. The same is true of any written correspondence, of course, but because email is viewed as a substitute for conversation, the effect is amplified and the writer should be more cognizant of how the reader might interpret what is written.

Figure 12.3 provides an example of an email adopting an appropriately formal yet conversational tone:

Figure 12.3

From: Robert Jacobs [mailto:rob@smithjones.com]
Sent: Monday, March 15, 20__ 12:54 PM
To: 'Julie Ryan'
Subject: RE: Introduction/Due Diligence

Julie,

My firm represents Archstone Capital Corporation, Inc. I'd like to schedule a call with you tomorrow if your schedule permits. The purpose of the call is mainly to:

- Introduce ourselves;
- Discuss due diligence (we'd like to get a sense of the corporate structure of Aztec so that we can tailor the due diligence request list we send);
- Drafting (we've been told you're drafting first draft of principal financing docs; we need to confirm that and discuss timetable. Also need to discuss ancillary documents and drafting responsibility/timetable);
- Anything else you think relevant at this point, such as any necessary third party consents you're aware of, etc.

I've attached a copy of the signed term sheet that our client sent us today.

Please let me know what your calendar looks like tomorrow, and we'll do what we can to make the time work.

Regards, Rob

Smith Jones LLP
Direct: 514-345-9090
Fax: 514-345-9091
Email: rob@smithjones.com

In Figure 12.4, the email is being used as a cover note to attach the original draft of a document for purposes of ongoing negotiations:

Figure 12.4

From: Julie Ryan [mailto:jryan@ryanassoc.com]
Sent: Monday, March 15, 20__ 12:54 PM
To: 'Robert Jacobs'
Subject: RE: Project Archstone: Draft Documents for Review and Discussion

Robert,

As discussed, attached for your review are (i) a draft stock purchase agreement and (ii) a draft restated certificate of incorporation which incorporate and accurately reflect all agreed terms as set forth in the term sheet signed by our respective clients. As you will see, these are both drafted in standard series seed financing form, taking into account any specifically negotiated terms.

In the interest of time, I am forwarding these documents to you prior to review by my client, and the attached thus remains subject to its review.

We are working on assembling the various documents requested in your due diligence checklist, and hope to have most if not all documents uploaded into an electronic data room for you by mid-week.

I am happy to discuss any questions/comments you may have on the attached documents via phone or email.

Best,

Julie Ryan

Julie A. Ryan
Ryan & Associates
299 Valley Avenue
3rd Floor
Los Angeles, CA 90009
Tel: 213-510-5000
Email: jryan@ryanassoc.com

This email message and any attachments are being sent by Ryan & Associates, LLP, are confidential, may be privileged, and are for the sole use of the intended recipient(s). Any unauthorized review, use, disclosure, or distribution is prohibited. If you are not the intended recipient, please contact the sender immediately by replying to this email message and destroy all copies of this email message and any attachments.

Note in each of the above the sender's use of a formal tone without legalese, bullet points for clarity and precision where necessary, and conciseness. Each email provides sufficient information for the reader to understand the exact purpose yet keeps it short enough to likely be read in a single screen. Note also how the sender includes complete contact information.

FOR DISCUSSION:

Look at the email examples in Figures 12.3 and 12.4. What do you notice about the subject line? How do they begin? What information is conveyed? What tone do they set? Why is there a sentence that refers to the documents being subject to client review? What does it mean in practical terms? How do the emails end?

Emails can also be used as substitutes for more formal correspondence, such as letters or memoranda. The decision to incorporate substantive content into the body of the email versus attaching it in document form to an email cover note depends on a variety of factors, including:

- The complexity of the formatting—a document requiring use of a spreadsheet or other tabular form may be hard to present clearly in the body of an email (and different email programs can distort the formatting);
- The complexity of the subject matter—if the information involves detailed analysis with numerous cross-references, it may be easier to attach it as a separate document that can be printed and read in hard-copy form;
- The length of the communication—readers tend to not read emails to the end, especially if they go on beyond one screen; thus, the longer the communication, the more advisable to include as an attachment;
- The individual preferences and relationships of the parties—as a deal progresses, the parties may develop a relationship in which emails become the accepted mode of communication, or a partner may have a particular preference; and
- The timing—the closer a deal gets to closing, the more quickly things tend to need to get done. Email can provide the necessary shortcut to exchanging information.

Figure 12.5 provides an example of an email being used as a substitute for a letter—in this case to communicate follow-up due diligence questions. The original due diligence request was sent in chart form as an attachment. Note the use of numbering, headings, and tabulations to aid in readability and clarity.

Figure 12.5

From: Robert Jacobs [mailto:rob@smithjones.com]
Sent: March 18, 20__ 12:54 PM
To: 'Julie Ryan'
Subject: RE: Project Archstone: Additional Due Diligence

Julie,

We have reviewed the due diligence documents that you provided, and we have the following questions and comments. In addition to the questions below, please also provide any additional documents that are created or have been discovered since the date of your last response.

Employees

1. Please provide a list of past and present employees and contractors. Confirm that each employee or contractor has signed an invention assignment agreement.
2. Provide a proposed list of employees that will participate in the bonus pool.

Corporate Documents

1. Please provide the Operating Agreement, and any amendments to the Articles of Organization, as well as any documents related to issuance of units.
2. There should also be member and manager consents, particularly authorizing the officers and managers (to the extent it is not covered by the operating agreement). I understand that these do not exist now—do you intend to ratify past actions?

Contracts

1. Please provide a customer list.
2. Are the contracts provided all contracts, or just current contracts? Are there older/expired contracts that have not been provided?
3. Do you have a list of companies with NDAs, and whether they have executed a standard form?
4. What is the status of the WhatsApp contract? It is in draft form. Are there other contracts that are under negotiation?

IP

1. Are there any other trademarks, other than the SGM registration?
2. Please provide additional information regarding the Confidential Information and Invention Assignment Agreement included in this folder. What was developed during this time period, and can you provide any other evidence of what, if anything, is assigned?

Best regards,

Rob

Robert Jacobs
Smith Jones LLP
Direct: 514-345-9090
Fax: 514-345-9091
Email: rob@smithjones.com

This email message and any attachments are being sent by Smith Jones, LLP, are confidential, may be privileged, and are for the sole use of the intended recipient(s). Any unauthorized review, use, disclosure, or distribution is prohibited. If you are not the intended recipient, please contact the sender immediately by replying to this email message and destroy all copies of this email message and any attachments.

Commenting on Drafts and Comment Letters

Reviewing and commenting on drafts of deal documents is a form of writing junior associates are frequently asked to perform. Typically, one side in a transaction will prepare an initial draft of the documentation required to consummate a transaction and will then forward the draft to the other side "for review and comment." The purpose of a comment letter, either in letter or email format, is to communicate to the other side any comments, questions, concerns, or discussion points stemming from the review.

Comment letters follow one of two formats: (1) self-contained, incorporating all comments to a document within the comment letter itself; or (2) as a cover note, in which case the comment letter will include some general comments and then refer the reader to an attached copy of the document, with any remaining comments marked directly on the document itself. This is referred to as a "mark-up" or "redline" (see Practice Note on use of mark-ups and redlines in Chapter 2).

In either format, a comment letter should follow the same guidelines as for any professional correspondence. It should be carefully organized, with precise references to the underlying documentation, and clearly drafted to eliminate any ambiguity. For example, the beginning of a comment letter on an asset purchase agreement might read:

> Each comment provides a concrete, specific description of the change requested, as well as a brief explanation where necessary.

We have reviewed the draft asset purchase agreement dated February 12, 2018 (the "APA") and have the following comments. Capitalized terms have the meanings as defined in the APA.

> The introduction clearly defines the agreement being reviewed, and clarifies the use of defined terms.

- *Section 2.1 Purchase Price: Please revise the amount of the Purchase Price to read "2.25 million" instead of "2 million," per section 4 of the term sheet.*
- *Section 2.4 Deliverables: Please add an additional paragraph (e) stating "copies of all employment agreements with Key Personnel."*

In addition, each comment is labeled by reference to the section number in the agreement and is presented in the order in which it appears in the agreement. This makes reviewing the comments easier for the other party and minimizes the risk of a comment being missed or incorporated in the wrong place.

In addition, it is important to engage in *triage*, making a conscious decision about: (1) which comments to include, and (2) how to word them.

Which Comments to Include

Commenting on a document is a form of negotiation. Sending the other side an exhaustive laundry list of comments can be counterproductive to the negotiation process. On the other hand, you should include all comments necessary to protect your client's interests; failure to raise comments in an initial draft can make it difficult to negotiate changes in later drafts. If no objection is raised to a particular issue, the other side assumes the issue is agreed. By raising the issue in subsequent drafts, it can seem as if the party is seeking to reopen "closed" issues, which can create mistrust and adversely affect the parties' willingness to work collaboratively.

Comments typically fall into one of four categories:[3]

- *Comments that fix errors or inconsistencies with the agreed business terms, or that eliminate ambiguities.* These comments should generally be included. The other side may agree to accept the comments as is or may propose modifications.

- *Comments relating to style.* For example, a suggestion to reword an obligation in the active instead of the passive voice: "*The Purchase Price shall be paid*" becomes "*The Purchaser shall pay the Purchase Price*."[4] This does not affect the meaning of the provision. Unless you believe the provision is unclear as is, you may want to consider omitting this type of comment. It will also depend on how many other comments you need to make—use judgment as to how many comments in the aggregate appear reasonable. Conversely, if you are controlling the draft and the other side makes one of these comments, you should probably accept it, unless doing so would create issues with clarity or other unintended implications.

- *Comments that seek to revise the terms.* If you are proposing changes that alter the original agreed terms—for example, inserting a requirement that the seller provide a guaranty that was not originally contemplated, make sure you provide sufficient explanation as to why your comment is reasonable and will not harm the other side's position (or why it is a fair exchange if it does).

- *Conceptual comments.* These tend to be more abstract, referring to the transaction or document as a whole—for example, a comment adding the principal shareholders of the selling company as parties to the transaction or proposing a solution to an issue that has yet to be addressed (i.e., how the parties intend to deal with employees after the closing of a merger). In making these types of comments, be prepared to justify your rationale or offer something in exchange.

In each case, make sure you identify the purpose of the comment and the substantive effect you are seeking. The same analysis should be performed when on the receiving end of comments to a document in determining whether to accept, modify, or reject each comment.

How to Word Comments

Comments should be carefully worded. The art of persuasion is in its subtlety. Depending on the circumstances, wording a comment politely, as a suggestion rather than a demand, can often yield better results. Note in the example on page 172 how each comment starts with the word "please," and takes care not to sound accusatory. How each comment is worded will also depend on its category:

---

3. George Kuney, in his book The Elements of Contract Drafting, introduces a method of categorizing comments received from opposing counsel in order to determine how to respond to those comments. George Kuney, The Elements of Contract Drafting, 60–61 (3d ed. 2011). In this instance, I use a similar method of categorization focusing on which comments a lawyer may want to include when reviewing a draft received from the other side of a transaction.

4. Note the use in this example of the word *shall*. Discussion abounds on whether and when to use *shall* or *will* and the historical difference in meaning. Be careful of commenting on use of the term; "shall" is widely used in contract drafting and in statutory language. Accordingly, it can seem nitpicky to change *shall* to *will* (or vice versa) and the other party may even disagree. Try to use the terms consistently in your own writing but limit commenting on their use in others' writing if it does not otherwise create ambiguity. For an interesting discussion of the use of *shall* in transactional documents, *see* K. Bishop, *When Shall Will Must May We Meet Again?* California Corporate and Securities Law Blog (2011), http://www.calcorporatelaw.com/2011/11/when-shallwillmustmay-we-meet-again [last visited Sept. 11, 2018].

greater deference may be needed to present a comment that seeks to revise a material term as opposed to a comment that addresses an obvious ambiguity.

Setting a collaborative tone at the outset of the comment letter can be constructive, either thanking the other side for preparing the initial draft (or for incorporating prior comments), or by indicating that your comments are minor (or if you are reviewing comments, that you have accepted a majority of the comments received).

Illustration: **Using Appropriate Tone in Comment Letters**

Following are two examples of an introductory paragraph of a comment letter drafted in the form of an email cover note: the first is drafted from the perspective of the reviewing party; the second is from the perspective of the side controlling the drafting (and thus receiving and incorporating the comments). Note the similarities in tone.

From: Ian Garzon
Sent: January 12, 20___ 2:15 PM
To: Julie A. Ryan
Cc: Michael G. Crowley; Elizabeth Banks
Subject: Project Archstone — Comments to Initial Draft Asset Purchase Agreement

Julie:

As discussed, following are our comments to the draft asset purchase agreement (the "APA") relating to the sale of assets of TempAssist, Inc. (the "Company") to a subsidiary (the "Buyer") of Zen Corporation ("Parent").

As you will see, most of our comments are fairly minor, with the exception of the following two comments highlighted below:

1. Deferred Purchase Price. Our understanding is that the parties agreed the deferred portion of the purchase price would not need to be secured. We have therefore deleted the provision relating to the guaranty in this section.
2. [. . . .]

From: Julie Ryan [mailto:jryan@ryanassoc.com]
Sent: January 14, 20___ 5:15 PM
To: Ian Garzon
Cc: Michael G. Crowley; Elizabeth Banks
Subject: Project Archstone — Revised Draft and Closing Checklist

Ian:

Thank you for your comments on the draft asset purchase agreement. Attached for your review and discussion is a revised draft incorporating all changes, as well as an updated closing checklist. For your convenience, I have attached both a clean version and a redline version marked to show the changes made against the prior draft circulated last Friday.

As you will see, we have incorporated most of your revisions. We have attempted to address your remaining comments in the attached draft.

[. . . .]

Exercise 12.1

This exercise is comprised of two parts.

Part 1: Your instructor will provide you with a copy of a draft agreement currently being negotiated for a client. The agreement contains comments from the other party. Your task is to: (1) review the comments from the other party and determine whether they relate to business or legal issues; and (2) formulate an email to the client describing the business issues.

Part 2: Your instructor will now provide you with the responses received from the client on each of the business issues you presented. Your task is to: (3) translate the client's responses into proposed revisions to the agreement; and (4) to determine which other revisions, if any, are necessary to address any legal issues and to give proper effect to the changes requested by the client.

Regulatory Agencies as Opposing Counsel

Much of this chapter assumes you are communicating with counsel on the opposite side of a deal. As you have learned, however, transactional practice is broader than just deal-making. The techniques and considerations discussed in this chapter and throughout this textbook apply equally to any task or circumstance a junior associate might encounter within the field of transactional lawyering, whether it be documenting a real estate transaction, handling employment matters, or drafting a trust.

One area that warrants specific mention in this chapter is regulatory review and compliance. Often, advice on regulatory matters such as tax, securities, antitrust, or environmental compliance is required as part of a deal or in handling a company's corporate governance matters. For example, you might be asked to determine whether a deal structure will comply with relevant tax laws, what disclosure needs to be included in a sale of securities, whether a pre-merger antitrust notice filing is required, or how to minimize the risk of assuming unwanted environmental liability.

In other instances, you may be tasked with complying with regulations; for example, preparing a registration statement for a securities offering, preparing an HSR[5] filing, or submitting a license application. In these cases, the lawyer on the other side will be a representative of the relevant regulatory agency. In these cases, formality, courtesy, professionalism, and a collaborative tone are essential. Be sure to know your audience and your client's goals and concerns.

Fine-Tuning Writing Techniques

You have had the opportunity by this point to practice various forms of writing commonly seen in transactional practice, in a variety of contexts. Effective use of fundamental writing techniques and consistent attention to detail remain paramount, whatever the audience, context, or format.

Regardless of how careful you are in drafting a document, natural tendencies can creep in, unnoticed. Learn to recognize your idiosyncratic tendencies. Do you tend to be verbose, or use metadiscourse? Perhaps you use too many commas or have a penchant for intensifiers.

---

5. HSR refers to the Hart-Scott-Rodino Antitrust Improvements Act of 1976. The HSR Act is a provision of the U.S. antitrust laws that requires parties to mergers or acquisitions in deals that meet certain requirements to file a pre-merger notification with the Department of Justice and the Federal Trade Commission prior to consummating the deal.

Some common issues to watch out for include:

- *Lack of logical organization.* Figure out what the beginning should be, from the viewpoint of your reader. If you are discussing how to structure an offering of securities to comply with a specific exemption, where should your starting point be? Do you start by describing the risks of failing to comply? The specific requirements of the exemption? Or do you need to start further back, by describing that an exemption is needed and then describing the exemptions that are available? Does it matter who your audience is? Remember, you have done the research and understand the legal context, but does your reader? Regardless of audience, try to start with the most general information and work your way down to more specific information.

- *Ineffective use of paragraphs.* Paragraphs that are too long, or that discuss more than one topic, can lack clarity and be difficult for a reader to follow. Try to keep your paragraphs short. Start each paragraph with a thesis sentence that lets the reader know what the paragraph will be about and connects the paragraph to the preceding paragraph(s).

- *Unclear/ambiguous sentence structure.* Read your writing out loud. If you have to read a sentence twice to make sure it's right, it is probably too long or contains grammatical errors. Common errors include run-on sentences, dangling modifiers, unclear pronouns, subject and verb being placed too far apart, and incomplete clauses. If in doubt, break a sentence into two or three.

- *Grammatical/punctuation errors.* These happen to the best of us, but they still reflect poorly on the writer and can undermine credibility. Be consistent with use of tenses and other grammatical constructs. The best way to check for these types of errors is to print your document out and read it. If you are unsure as to a grammatical or punctuation rule, consider altering the sentence to avoid the issue. You can also consult a style manual.[6]

- *Misspellings or incorrect word choice.* These can undermine your credibility and perhaps create ambiguity or even unintended legal consequences. Don't rely solely on spellcheck, as this will not catch incorrect usage. If in doubt, use a different word!

Proofreading

As discussed in Chapter 6, writing is a recursive process. Get in the habit of re-reading your writing at least once. The most effective is to re-read your writing several times, each time focusing on a different aspect. For example, on the first read, you might look for big-picture issues: consistent spacing, formatting, or missing thesis sentences. On the next read, you might look for spelling or grammatical errors. Next, you might work on editing for conciseness. Or you may focus on tendencies that you have identified in your writing. Figure 12.6 provides a useful checklist for organizing the proofreading process:

---

6. *See, e.g.,* Garner, *supra* Chapter 4, note 8.

Figure 12.6

Proofreading Checklist[7]

1. Have you included proper citations where appropriate?

2. Are the formatting and presentation consistent throughout?

3. Have you complied with any specific formatting requirements (at a minimum, is your format professional)?

4. Is your use of tense consistent and appropriate throughout?

5. Have you used the appropriate article with each noun?

   - If you are introducing "new" information to the reader for the first time, have you used an indefinite article?

   - If you are referring to something already mentioned or inferred, have you used a definite article?

   - Do your pronouns match the noun to which they refer in terms of gender and number?

   - Is it clear to which noun your pronoun refers?

6. Have you used short sentences (and eliminated any run-on sentences)?

7. Have you used plain English/eliminated legalese?

8. Have you eliminated any faulty parallelism?

9. Have you used thesis sentences and focused and chained topic strings effectively for point of view and cohesion within and between paragraphs?

10. Have you avoided passives other than where you have made a strategic choice? Clue: look for sentences that contain the verb "to be" and that do not start with an actor.

11. Have you checked for nominalizations and weak verbs? For example: "they entered into an agreement" versus "they agreed," and "made a decision" versus "decided." Are there any you can eliminate by revising the sentence?

12. Have you checked for wordiness?

    - Have you eliminated "throat-clearing" from your writing? Clue: look for sentences that contain phrases such as "the court held that," "there is," and "the fact that."

    - If you are over the page limit, look first for words you can eliminate, then clauses, then sentences.

13. Have you checked your writing for clarity?

14. Have you checked your writing for precision, including proper hierarchy among elements and use of definitions where appropriate?

15. Have you eliminated intensifiers such as "clearly" and "obviously"?

16. Have you eliminated any unnecessary references to "I" or "we"?

17. Have you used gender-neutral pronouns and nouns where possible?

18. Is each sentence complete?

19. Are the subject and verb of each sentence close together?

20. Is the subject of each sentence near the beginning of the sentence?

21. Try reading your draft aloud. Are there any sentences where you have to take a breath in the middle? If so, can you break it into two or more sentences?

---

7. This checklist is sufficiently comprehensive to allow you to use it for any type of writing. Not all items may apply in each case.

22. Have you included appropriate punctuation at the end of each sentence?

23. Have you checked for proper usage of commas, colons, and semicolons?

24. Have you read through your document at least twice, focusing on spelling and typographical errors?

25. Have you double-checked the spelling of the names of parties and key terms?

Finally: Have you read through your draft looking specifically for your weaknesses and tendencies?

Exercise 12.2

Using the checklist in Figure 12.6, review two pages of your own writing (for example, the memo you completed for Writing Project #1). How many errors can you find? Can you identify any tendencies in your writing?

PRACTICE NOTES

Ethical Issues When No Adverse Party

The nonadversarial nature of transactional practice can create inadvertent ethical issues. Rule 1.7 of the Model Rules of Professional Conduct states that a lawyer should not represent a client if that representation would involve a "concurrent conflict of interest."[8] One of the manners stated in the rule in which a concurrent conflict of interest exists is if the representation of one client would be "directly adverse" to another client.[9]

The rule goes on to allow representation when such a conflict exists, provided, among other requirements, that the lawyer obtains informed, written consent from each client and reasonably believes he or she will be able to represent each client diligently.[10]

If both parties' interests are aligned, can representation of one party be directly adverse to the other? If the parties are on opposite sides of a transaction, such as a lender and borrower, or a buyer and seller, the answer should be relatively easy: yes, even though both parties want the same result, they can certainly have competing interests. But what if there is no "opposite" side? For example, what if you are advising two founders on the formation of a partnership or limited liability company? Can you represent both founders? Should you?

The best practice is to either represent one or the other of the founders, or to represent neither and to serve as "company counsel." In either case, you should discuss it with the individuals to ensure that everyone is clear about who you will be representing. In most instances, the attorney will represent the to-be-formed company; the founders typically have limited funds, and the company will have immediate need for legal advice on its formation and initial capitalization.

If you decide to represent one or more of the founders, or switch at any time to representing the company, you will need a written conflict waiver from each of the founders to satisfy Rule 1.7.

---

8. Rule 1.7 of the ABA Model Rules of Professional Conduct.

9. *Id.*

10. *Id.*

Managing the Deal Process; Preparing a Closing Checklist

Part of your role in communicating with other lawyers on a transaction will be to coordinate the deal process itself. A typical deal process consists of the following stages:

1. *The initial approach*: the parties identify a potential opportunity to consummate a transaction. Lawyers are often not involved at this stage.

2. *The courting stage*: the parties start to explore their mutual interest in pursuing the transaction. This is the stage at which the parties will sign a nondisclosure agreement and letter of intent.

3. *The documentation and diligence stage:* the lawyers on the deal spring into action, drafting and negotiating the definitive deal documents and any ancillary documents, and conducting due diligence. This stage represents the bulk of the activity required to consummate a transaction. It culminates with the execution of the principal transaction documents.

4. *The closing*: this stage commences with the parties taking all the actions needed for closing, such as obtaining necessary approvals. It ends with the signing of any ancillary documents and the exchange of signature pages, documents, and other deliverables, including any consideration payable at closing. Once all these items have been exchanged, the deal is officially closed. In some instances, where no additional actions are needed, signing and closing can occur simultaneously, with all documents being signed and exchanged at once (this is known as a "simultaneous sign-and-close" deal; a deal with a period of time between signing and closing is known as a "delayed-closing" deal).

5. *Post-closing*: last but equally important, this stage involves cleaning up any loose ends, such as completing any necessary filings, and performing any post-closing obligations, such as payment of deferred consideration.

Closing checklists are an effective tool for managing this process. The role of a closing checklist is described briefly in Chapter 2. This Practice Note discusses how to create and use the checklist effectively.

To prepare a closing checklist, use a tabular format with at least three columns that list:

1. each document and action needed to consummate the transaction;

2. the person responsible for preparing or delivering each item; and

3. the status of each item, updated as necessary throughout the process.

Other useful columns to include are:

4. the persons who will be required to sign each document; and

5. the relevant provision of the main transaction document to which each item refers.

The checklist can be organized in any order, but most often starts with the main agreement, such as the purchase agreement, and then goes through the exhibits and schedules to that agreement. After this follow other ancillary documents, and anything needed to be addressed during the period between signing and closing, such as regulatory approvals and consents. Next come the closing documents themselves: the documents that are needed to legally transfer what is being delivered—for example, share certificates and executed assignments. Finally, the checklist should include any post-closing items, such as regulatory filings.

A closing checklist should be as detailed as possible. To ensure you have included all necessary items:

- Look at the contents of the main agreement: what documents are listed as exhibits or schedules? What covenants need to be performed? What about any deliverables? Each of these should be an item in the closing checklist.
- Make sure you understand your jurisdiction's statutory requirements, which will govern necessary filings and shareholder consents, as well as other potential regulatory steps.
- Cross-reference the results of any due diligence to determine whether any documents needed to address issues have been detected. For example, if due diligence reveals that certain contracts may need consent to be assigned, you should include those consents in the closing checklist.

A sample closing checklist is included in Appendix B.

Conclusion

This chapter began our focus on communicating with other lawyers. Transactional practice commonly involves dealing with other parties. Although these parties are not always on the "other side" of the transaction in the traditional sense, it is important to keep clear who you represent, and to advocate for your client's interests. The fundamental techniques for effective communication discussed in earlier chapters remain critical, adapted to the audience and purpose of communication in this context. In the remaining chapters, we will turn our attention to in-person communications with other lawyers, and the juxtaposition of oral communication and negotiation techniques.

SIMULATION EXERCISE #10

This exercise uses the materials from the in-class exercise on p.175. Respond to the partner's email instructions below. The referenced materials can be found in Appendix B.

From: Julie Ryan
Sent: March __ 12:00 PM
To: Junior Associate
Subject: Draft cover email — revised draft CY SPA

Junior Associate,

You will recall that last week we reviewed comments received from Seller's counsel on the share purchase agreement between Shaw Holdings and Sofia Lauden. I have attached a revised draft of the agreement, marked to show the changes we made incorporating those comments we were willing to accept.

I have also included below the original cover email received from Seller's counsel, Sandy Dee.

Please draft a short cover email to Sandy that we can use to attach our revised draft. In your cover email, please make sure you mention that:

1. we are attaching a revised draft, redlined to show the changes made;
2. this revised draft incorporates most of her comments;
3. we modified the reps and warranties for both parties, as we assume that was her intent;
4. the revised draft remains subject to review and final approval of our client; and
5. assuming the changes are acceptable, we will prepare a final version for signature.

You should also include a brief response to each of Sandy's three specific comments in her email (see below), indicating how we have addressed each concern. Feel free to include any additional information you believe is appropriate or necessary.

Please forward me your draft cover email within 4 days. There is no need to attach the revised draft, as I can attach it directly when I send out the email.

Thank you,

Julie

Julie A. Ryan
Ryan & Associates
299 Valley Avenue
3rd Floor
Los Angeles, CA 90009
Tel: 213-510-5000
Email: jryan@ryanassoc.com

---Begin forwarded email--

From: Sandra Dee [mailto: SDee@raklaw.com]
Sent: March __ 9:44 AM
To: jryan@ryanassoc.com
Cc: Brendan Long; Sofia Lauden [mailto:slauden@caymanyachts.com]
Subject: Purchase Agreement for Cayman Yachts (BVI)

Julie:

Attached are our comments to the draft agreement. Please make these changes and recirculate at your earliest convenience. In addition to the marked comments on the attached, we had the following additional concerns:

1. Clause 2.2 Consideration. The accountants suggest that the shares should be purchased for face value £100 and the buyer take on all existing liabilities/debts. This is due to only outstanding debt being Shaw Holding's loan/advance to Seller, it should also mean no tax liabilities for Seller.
2. Clause 5.6 Noncompetition. Seller is prepared to accept this time period and restrictions subject to the addition in the clause of compensation being payable by the Buyer equivalent to 75% of Seller's retainer/salary for the said 2-year period.
3. Clause 6 Indemnification. As it's suggested selling shares for face value only and the only debt of the Company being the loan/advance from Buyer, there should be no need for indemnification therefore this clause should be removed altogether.

I look forward to hearing from you.

Kind regards,

Sandy

Rain Allen & Kraft, LP
12424 The Strand
Tortola, B.V.I.
+284 0271 5544
sdee@raklaw.com

* *

Chapter 13

·················

In-Person Communications with Other Lawyers: Meetings and Negotiations

Most communication with other lawyers is a form of negotiation. This chapter discusses the various negotiation concepts, techniques, theories, and strategies in the context of lawyer-to-lawyer communication. In addition, it looks at the practical aspects of preparing for and communicating in in-person meetings with other lawyers.

By the end of this chapter, you will be able to:

- Apply various negotiation techniques in representing a client in a negotiation
- Plan and execute a negotiation strategy
- Identify issues that you should negotiate and how
- Engage in preparing for and leading a meeting with opposing counsel

··

You are working at a small transactional firm that handles start-ups and other early-stage companies. One of your firm's clients is seeking a $1 million investment from a group of investors. The parties have signed a term sheet, but now want the lawyers to document the deal. You and the lawyer representing the investor group have exchanged a set of drafts, but a couple of major issues remain to be worked out. Your supervising partner has suggested a meeting to try to resolve some of these issues. What is your first step? Do you have an idea of what your client is most concerned about? What if the lawyer for the other side is not willing to compromise? You are nervous because you lack any real experience. Should you march into the meeting and act as if you know what you are doing? Or should you let the other lawyer guide the conversation? How much cooperation should you be willing to give, and how much should you expect?

··

Negotiation as a Form of Communication

Regardless of how friendly a transaction, or how aligned the parties' interests, you should always be advocating for your client's best interests. To do this, you must persuade the other side to agree with—or at a minimum concede to—what you are proposing.

Chapter 12 focused on how to persuade through written communications. What about other forms of communication? What degree of persuasion is necessary in these other forms of communication? At what point does persuasion become negotiation?

Any time you communicate with opposing counsel, you are engaging in a form of negotiation to some degree. The amount of negotiation involved in the communication falls on a continuum that can be illustrated as follows:

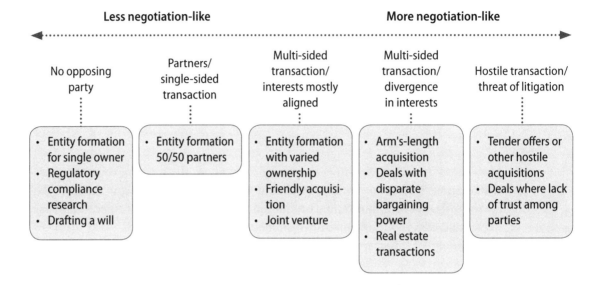

The term "negotiation" probably conjures up the scenarios toward the right of this continuum: formal negotiations around a conference room table where the parties bargain to maximize their interests, or where they may start to argue their positions. At the lower end of the continuum, you may not even recognize you are negotiating. At its essence, a negotiation is a discussion aimed at reaching an agreement. Thus, anytime you are communicating with opposing counsel to reach agreement on a transaction, whether on the specific wording of a provision in a document or what structure to adopt, you are negotiating.

The primary goal of negotiations with opposing counsel is to achieve the best outcome for your client. Other ancillary goals include building rapport and information gathering. In a way, these ancillary goals form the means to achieving the primary goal: the better your rapport with opposing counsel and the more information you glean, the easier it can be to negotiate a favorable outcome.

Exercise 13.1

Working in pairs, spend one to two minutes trying to convince the other person to take an action, such as switching chairs or giving you a piece of paper. Then compare the results. Did you start with a request or a demand? What was the initial response? Was there a counterproposal? Did it matter whether you thought the request was material, or something that wouldn't cost you anything? What was your initial approach? What nonverbal communication did you engage in? Did this make it easier or harder?

Exercise 13.2

Following are two different versions of a provision in a limited liability operating agreement involving three members, two of whom are founders and the third a new investor. As part of the business negotiations, the new investor is reviewing the terms of the operating agreement that will govern the members' rights and obligations.

- The first version is as originally proposed to the new investor
- The second version reflects the comments made by the new investor's counsel.

Working in pairs, with one person representing counsel for the founders and the other the counsel for the new investor, negotiate the final version of this provision. You may conduct research online to help you determine any common practices or standards.

Original Provision:

Duty of Loyalty. Each Member may engage in other business activities and may pursue business opportunities competitive with the business and operations of the Company without presenting any such opportunity to the Company or the Members, and the Company and each Member hereby waive any right or claim to participate therein.

Proposed Revision (underline reflects additional language,
strike-through reflects deleted language):

Duty of Loyalty. <u>Subject to Section 4.7 (Duty to Keep Confidential Information of the Company Confidential)</u>, each Member may engage in other business activities and may pursue business opportunities, <u>provided, however, that no Member will engage in other business activities or pursue other opportunities directly</u> competitive with the business and operations of the Company <u>or would otherwise create a conflict of interest</u> <u>without presenting any such opportunity to the Company or the Members</u> ~~and each Member hereby waive any right or claim to participate therein.~~

Role of the Transactional Lawyer in Negotiations

Chapter 3 discussed the attributes of a "SANE" transactional lawyer, and her role as problem-solver. In negotiations, the role of the SANE lawyer is to use her communication and problem-solving skills effectively and ethically to best achieve the desired result. The key in negotiations is to strike the right balance between spotting issues and creative problem-solving. This balance is encapsulated in the following four maxims:

1. *The goal is to reserve/maximize opportunity while minimizing or appropriately allocating risk.* Clients will be focused on the opportunity presented by the transaction, and less so on the risks. For example, in a manufacturing deal, the client may be focused on the favorable delivery terms he has negotiated. But what happens if the other party fails to meet the delivery schedule? The lawyer needs to be able to anticipate these types of risks or issues and identify legal solutions while preserving the benefit the client is seeking.

2. *Transactional focus is win-win.* Although the ability to spot issues and identify risks is always an important function, in negotiations, the emphasis is on being able to identify solutions: to enable the parties to reach a mutually satisfactory agreement rather than to put up roadblocks.

Look for ways to solve problems, as opposed to simply looking for problems. The transactional lawyer should facilitate, not hinder, the negotiations. A lawyer who fights back on every little point and seems to always be looking for reasons to scuttle the deal soon develops a reputation as a "deal-killer."

Of course, sometimes the best deal for your client is no deal, and the recommendation to the client will be to walk away. But the *client* should make this decision. The parties should never feel as if the deal did not happen because of the lawyers.

3. *The relationship between the lawyers can affect outcome.* A good working relationship between the parties' lawyers can facilitate the successful consummation of a transaction and allow both sides to feel satisfied with the result of negotiations. Conversely, a sour relationship between counsel can hamper the success of the transaction. This can make for an unhappy client even if the transaction closes.

4. *The lawyer is an intermediary, not a principal.* Above all, remember you are trying to achieve your client's goals, not your own. The transaction is between the parties, not the parties' lawyers. Maintaining a level of professional objectivity is critical, although not always easy. Negotiations feel personal. Opposing counsel could be difficult to deal with. Your client may instruct you to concede an issue you think is unfair to your client. Your role is to advocate for your client's interests and to strive to achieve your client's objectives, even if you dislike the other side. Remember, the client will be the one living with the result of the transaction.

Business versus Legal Issues

When negotiating issues in a transaction, distinguish between business and legal issues.[1] A room full of lawyers will not likely haggle over price without the clients being present. What you will be haggling over is how the money will be paid, what documentation will be required, and what the documentation should say.

Business and legal issues can cross over, however. When negotiating legal terms or proposing a resolution to a legal issue, be mindful of the practical consequences of the proposed resolution. For example, negotiating the language of an indemnity provision may seem to be a legal issue, but to the extent it limits the obligation of the indemnitor or the indemnitee's ability to recover, it becomes a business issue.

FOR DISCUSSION:

Consider the following legal issues. What might some of the potential business implications be?

- Adjusting the payment terms for a consulting agreement from 60 to 30 days following receipt of invoice.
- Allowing the seller in an asset sale to add "to the seller's knowledge" to its representation that there is no litigation pending against the seller.
- In a noncompetition agreement, adding an exclusion from the noncompetition obligation that would allow for investments in publicly traded companies that are competitors, as long as the investment does not exceed five percent.

---

1. Refer to the discussion on business versus legal issues in Chapter 2.

- In a stock purchase agreement, modifying the covenant to provide ongoing financial statements to the investor to be solely "upon request."

Does it matter which side you represent?

Concepts to Negotiate

The common concepts a transactional lawyer will typically negotiate fall into the following categories:

Standards[2]

The highest standard that can be negotiated in connection with a contract provision is unqualified commitment to perform an obligation. For example: "*The seller will obtain all third-party consents.*" If the seller fails to obtain the consents, it will be in breach of the agreement, affording the buyer appropriate remedies.

Once you accept anything less than this, your client is absorbing some degree of risk. For example: "*The seller will use commercially reasonable efforts to obtain all third-party consents.*" What happens if, despite its efforts, the seller fails to obtain the consents? The buyer now bears that risk. Assuming the buyer is not comfortable with absorbing all this risk, the lawyer's role is to seek ways to mitigate the risk. For example, the lawyer could counter by adding a condition to closing that requires all consents to have been obtained prior to closing.

Note how the discussion in the preceding paragraph is qualified with "*assuming* the buyer is not comfortable." Although the negotiation of the language and the use of conditions to shift risk among the parties is a legal issue, it carries consequences that may be a business issue for the client.

Whether the client expects to or should be consulted on an issue will depend on the nature of the issue, the client's background and risk tolerance, and the client-lawyer relationship. Some clients like to be involved in every detail; others expect you to handle everything and just alert them to major issues. Similarly, some issues are commonly negotiated, while others might be less customary. As a junior transactional lawyer, you will need to learn to use your judgment as to when you should check in with the client. Clear communication between lawyer and client, including active listening, can aid in making this determination. Remember, what may be acceptable to one client—or even the same client—in one deal, may not be in another.

FOR DISCUSSION:

The client tells you that the seller in an asset purchase being negotiated is supposed to pay off all outstanding debt before closing. What needs to be negotiated from a legal standpoint? Which provisions should the lawyer focus on? Is there any language that should be negotiated? What protections can be put in place? At what point do you think the client should be consulted?

---

2. *See* Stark, *Thinking Like a Deal Lawyer, supra* Chapter 2, note 5.

Facts[3]

When negotiating the terms of an agreement, identifying which party has knowledge of relevant facts is critical. If facts material to the value of the transaction for your client are difficult for your client to ascertain, your job is to try to flush out the truth and find ways to protect or compensate your client against any unknown or inaccurate facts.

In negotiating a contract or other agreement, the primary mechanism for addressing this issue is the use of representations and warranties. Negotiation of representations and warranties will turn on the results of due diligence, as well as the value at stake, the potential risks identified, and the relationship of the parties.

Illustration: **Negotiating Representations and Warranties**

Your client is acquiring a company for the value of its intellectual property for a purchase price of $80 million. In your due diligence inquiry, you come across several licenses relating to software and other intellectual property. The company assures you that none of this licensed intellectual property is essential to the operation of its business. This is hard for you to ascertain until your client starts operating the business. Thus, you will likely want to include representations that the company:

"owns all intellectual property necessary for the operation of the business."

The company, for its part, will want to minimize its risk, and may counter your proposed representation with a qualification that it:

"owns or has the right to use all intellectual property necessary for the operation of the business as currently conducted."

Can you see how this shifts the risk back to the buyer?

FOR DISCUSSION:

Using the illustration above, now consider a $500,000 transaction involving the purchase of an accounting practice. Is the representation regarding intellectual property needed? If so, how much effort should you expend on negotiating the language of the representation?

Exit/End Result[4]

The client will usually have an idea of how it wants the transaction to end or how committed a relationship it is seeking. For example, an investor in a joint venture will have a sense of when she expects to be able to sell her interests, would want other partners to be able to sell their interests, or perhaps seek a strategic buyer for the venture. A company entering into an employment agreement will have an idea of when it should be able to terminate the employee and on what conditions. A supplier will have thoughts about any minimum term or purchase amount on a supply agreement.

---

3. *See* Neumann, *supra Chapter 2, note 2, at 92.*
4. *See* Tina L. Stark, Drafting Contracts: How and Why Lawyers Do What They Do 191–209 (2007).

The lawyer's role is to ensure the relevant provisions of the agreement accurately reflect her client's expectations, close any potential loopholes, and incorporate the desired legal consequences. In addition, the lawyer's job is to determine what happens if the agreement is terminated.

Illustration: **Matching Business and Legal Issues**

Your client is a company looking to engage a consultant in exchange for cash and some equity in the company. Your client knows what value it believes the consulting services are worth and may have some preconceived ideas on other deal points. For example, he may tell you he wants to:

- limit the term of the agreement to one year, initially, and
- be able to terminate the consultant for cause.

Some of the legal issues you will need to determine and negotiate to give proper legal effect to your client's goals might include:

- the form and documentation for the equity portion of the compensation: should it all be payable at once, or should it be subject to vesting? Should there be any conditions attached to the issuance of the equity? How much equity equals the value your client has in mind?
- the definition of "cause," and
- whether the terms of the agreement can be renewed and by whom; what happens if the consultant does not provide the services as expected.

Exercise 13.3

This exercise contains two different scenarios:

Scenario 1 (Convertible Note): ABC Corp. has agreed to loan $500,000 to NewCo, Inc., in exchange for a convertible note[5] to cover operating expenses while NewCo tries to secure a $1 million preferred stock financing. The parties inform counsel that the note will carry six percent interest and will have a 12-month term. ABC would like the note to be convertible at its option at any time prior to maturity. NewCo would like conversion to be mandatory.

Scenario 2 (Asset Purchase): XYZ Corp. has agreed to acquire certain assets of CoolCo, LLC, relating to its marketing and branding business. CoolCo also engages in merchandising and advertising services, but these are not included in the purchase. XYZ has offered $10 million for all the assets relating to the desired business, payable over three years. It wants to make sure the business is worth the full $10 million and to be able to reduce the purchase price if it turns out to be worth less. CoolCo would accept payment of the purchase price over time but wants to make sure that XZY will remain obligated to pay the full amount as and when due.

Working in pairs, choose one of the two scenarios, and brainstorm what legal issues might need to be negotiated. Do these vary depending on which side you represent?

---

5. Convertible notes and preferred stock are common forms of security used in early-stage financing. See the Practice Note at the end of this chapter for a more detailed discussion of how these are used.

Miscellaneous Provisions

Most contracts and agreements include a set of miscellaneous provisions at the end of the contract relating primarily to legal issues. Clients typically will not have much input in these (or even read them), but this does not mean they are insignificant to the deal. These miscellaneous provisions (also known as "boilerplate") can have a significant impact, particularly if a dispute arises between the parties.

Many firms will have their own standard form of these miscellaneous provisions that will be incorporated into their standard forms of agreements. However, you still need to critically review in the context of your specific deal and revise accordingly. Similarly, when presented with an agreement drafted by the other side, do not overlook these provisions; many a negotiation has centered around them.

Examples of miscellaneous provisions include:

- Choice of Law and Venue
- Severability
- Assignability
- Entire Agreement
- Third-Party Beneficiaries
- Dispute Resolution
- Notices
- Expenses
- Counterparts
- Amendments and Waivers
- Remedies

Exercise 13.4

Choose three of the above provisions and locate a sample of each (see the Practice Note on page 31 discussing practical online sources for precedent documents and research). Working in groups, compare your results and compile answers to the following questions:

1. What type of transaction is involved?
2. Can you tell whether your sample provision is neutral or more favorable to one side or the other? If so, how?
3. Are there any terms or specific language that appear consistently in each of the samples?
4. Do any of the samples use significantly different language? If so, why do you think that is? (Hint: can you identify the context and the parties?)
5. What, if anything, would you change if you represented one party or the other?
6. What would the practical result be in the event of a contract dispute?

Defining the Structure of a Transaction[6]

What is the difference between a stock purchase and a merger? From the client's perspective, the result may be the same in business terms. But the choice of structure—how you define the transaction—can have significant legal, tax, and other consequences. It determines how you document the

---

6. *See* Neumann, *supra Chapter 2,* note 2, at 93 (discussing the significance of how lawyers "label" a transaction).

transaction, and thus the legal rights and obligations of the parties. The transactional lawyer must translate what the client wants in terms of result, and advocate for the structure and form that best achieves this result.

Be wary, however, of overstepping your role. Recall our discussion in Chapter 8 on the importance of client-centered lawyering. Do not change the business deal without client consent. If a choice of structure presents itself, for example, you should advise the client of the advantages and disadvantages of each structure, and possibly counsel the client as to which structure you recommend and why. But the ultimate decision belongs to the client.

Negotiation Theories and Strategies

This book is not intended as a text on negotiations, which can form the topic of an entire law school course. Our focus is on the interrelation of negotiations and communications among transactional lawyers. To effectively communicate with lawyers on the other side of a transaction is to effectively negotiate, and vice versa. It is helpful, nonetheless, to include a brief overview of some common negotiation theories and strategies.

Rights, Powers, and Interests

Three concepts widely recognized as critical to understanding how to effectively negotiate are rights, powers, and interests.[7] Each of these provides a form of justification for what you are seeking to negotiate.

- *Rights* demonstrate the legitimacy of your position.[8] For example, if commercially reasonable efforts are an accepted standard, it is reasonable to ask for this language to be included in a contract provision. Another example would be a statute that requires certain compliance. This gives you the right to ask for the compliance required by that statute, such as requiring that consummation of an acquisition be conditioned on receipt of antitrust clearance (known as HSR clearance). This clearance is required for transactions that meet certain thresholds. If your transaction exceeds this threshold, you should be able to negotiate the inclusion of this condition.

- *Power* reflects the ability to coerce without necessarily having the right.[9] A classic example of using power in negotiations is being a parent. No matter what argument the child comes up with, ultimately the parent can pull the "because I said so" card.[10] Power is derived from what you have that the other side wants. Typically, the bigger the player, the greater the power. But power can also come from skill and knowledge: for example, a small software company that has a revolutionary patent could have significant bargaining power with Apple or Microsoft. Finally, power can be derived from a party's willingness to walk away from the deal (see discussion on "BATNA" below).

- *Interests* relate to the underlying reasons for a demand or request: what the party is concerned about or wants.[11] For example, why does the seller in an acquisition want the buyer to pay the purchase price up front? One reason might be that the seller wants to make sure it gets paid.

---

7. *See, e.g.,* Neumann, *supra Chapter 2,* note 2, at 97–100.

8. *Id. at 98.*

9. *Id.* at 99.

10. Note that this could also be characterized as a right if we look at parents as having the right under the law to make decisions for their children.

11. Roger Fisher & William Ury, Getting to Yes: Negotiating Agreements Without Giving In 4–6 (2d ed., 1991).

Why would a buyer want to defer paying a portion of the purchase price? Perhaps because the buyer is interested in making sure the seller performs all its post-closing obligations before releasing the funds. As you will see below, understanding and focusing on the parties' interests can make a negotiation more effective.

Positional Bargaining Versus Interest-Based Negotiations

In their seminal book on negotiation theory, *Getting to Yes*, Fisher and Ury posit that there are two forms of negotiation: positional bargaining and interest—or principle-based—negotiations.[12]

Positional bargaining focuses heavily on rights and powers.[13] Each side comes to the table determined to stick to its original position, unwilling to compromise. The emphasis is on convincing the other side to accept your position—on winning. This should sound familiar: it describes one of the fundamental distinctions between transactional practice and litigation discussed in Chapter 1. Positional bargaining is not conducive to achieving the win-win outcome typically sought in transactional negotiations.

Interest-based negotiations involve the parties stepping away from their positions to focus on the interests underlying those positions and generating options that reach a middle ground, satisfying the interests of both sides, even if it means moving away from each side's initial position.[14] In the example above, where the seller wants to be paid up front and the buyer wants to delay payment, the middle ground might be to escrow a portion of the purchase price. Each party may be giving up its initial position, but by focusing on the underlying interests instead, the parties are able to achieve a mutually satisfactory result. In some cases, the parties may come to realize their underlying interests are the same. In the end, both parties want a deal that makes economic sense and allocates the risk in a fair way.

To be effective in interest-based negotiations, you need to determine: (1) your client's—and the other side's—underlying interests (what is driving their position and demands); (2) any objective criteria or standards against which to weigh each side's competing concerns, such as customary terms or agreed facts; and (3) options for satisfying the interests of both parties. In looking for options, you are seeking ways to "bridge the gap" between the parties' positions.

Interest-based negotiations are closely aligned with the core characteristics of transactional lawyering: the focus of both is on problem-solving that seeks to maximize the opportunities for both sides while minimizing risk.

BATNA[15]

BATNA, or the "best alternative to a negotiated agreement," is a negotiation concept that presupposes a point beyond which a party to a negotiation is willing to compromise; the point at which the benefits of going ahead with the deal are outweighed by advantages of one or more alternatives. Where this point falls depends on the available alternatives. The more alternatives a party has, and the more advantageous those alternatives, the better the party's BATNA. The better a party's BATNA, the greater that party's negotiation power, and the less likely that party will be willing to compromise.

---

12. *Id.*
13. *Id.*
14. *Id.*
15. *Id.*

Exercise 13.5

Break into pairs. Each of you will be representing a different side in a mock negotiation. Your instructor will provide you with confidential instructions depending on which side you represent. Using the term sheet and facts from Writing Project #1, negotiate the key terms of the transaction with your opposing counsel.

In-Person Meetings and Negotiations with Opposing Counsel

Preparing for and engaging in in-person communications with opposing counsel is similar in some respects to preparing for and engaging in a client meeting. Both involve the need for effective communication, problem-solving, and information gathering.

However, although both involve information gathering, instead of advising or counseling the other party, in a meeting with opposing counsel you are seeking above all to persuade and reach agreement. To do this, you will need to use some of the negotiation techniques discussed in this chapter. In addition, unlike in a client meeting where you are communicating on your own behalf, in a meeting with opposing counsel you are acting on behalf of your client.

Preparing for the Meeting or Negotiation

The key to an effective meeting with opposing counsel is proper preparation. Preparation includes the following steps:

1. *Set and control the agenda.* Have a clear idea of what topics you will cover and in what order, and what you want to achieve. What do you need to accomplish to deem the meeting successful or productive? Once in the meeting, strive to keep the discussion on track.

2. *Do your homework.* What are the key facts? What facts do you need to ascertain from the other side? What is your client willing to concede, if anything? What is the relevant law? You should be familiar with statutory provisions and case law that either support your position or present obstacles. Are there any specific industry concerns? What can you find out about the other party?

3. *Plan your strategy.* What approach will you take? (See discussion below on communication styles.) What is the relative bargaining power of the parties? What is your starting position on each issue? How will you present each issue? What is the underlying interest? Will you present your position first, or will you ask the other side where they stand? How will you respond to issues likely to be raised by the other side? What might those issues be?

Stages of a Meeting with Opposing Counsel

The typical stages, or components, of a meeting with opposing counsel include the following:

Figure 13.1

Component	Description
OPENING:	At the start of the meeting, it can be helpful to spend a few minutes establishing a rapport with the other side, commonly by engaging in small talk. This is where you set the tone of the meeting and determine whether and how you may need to adapt your communication style and approach.
INFORMATION EXCHANGE:	Don't forget to ask questions and gather information from the other side. Avoid being in a rush to get your point across. Watch for verbal and nonverbal cues. Engage in active listening. Don't be afraid to confirm information by repeating it back or asking follow-up questions.
VALUE EXCHANGE:	This is where you can start to make offers and concessions. Critical here is being aware of the anchor point[16] for the negotiation, staying focused on your client's goals and underlying interests, and looking for opportunities for compromise or bargaining.
CLOSING:	Concluding a meeting without having formulated the results in concrete terms undermines the value of the meeting (and makes it hard to justify the expense). Conclude the meeting with a summary of what was agreed (and the degree of commitment), what issues or actions remain open, who will be responsible for taking the next step, what that next step is, and the timing.

Negotiation Preparation Worksheet

Knowing your strategy going into a meeting with opposing counsel is critical. The worksheet in Figure 13.2 can be helpful in crystallizing this strategy and keeping you focused during the meeting or negotiation:

---

16. See discussion on anchoring on pages 202–03.

Figure 13.2

Negotiation Preparation Worksheet

PART I. BACKGROUND

    A. Issues/concerns identified:

Issue:	Relevant Term Sheet Provision (if any):

    B. Your client's BATNA (if any):

    C. Strategy/Approach (including any cross-cultural considerations):[17]

    D. Planned structure of negotiation (introduction, order of issues to be discussed):

PART II. INTEREST-BASED ANALYSIS

    A. Underlying Interests (in order of priority):

Your client:	Perceived interests of counterparty:

    B. Key facts/Objective standards (such as customary provisions):

    C. Options (think beyond the terms: consider whether you see any opportunity for log-rolling[18] or any way to bridge the gap between the parties' perceived interests):

---

17. Include also your planned communication style. For example, do you plan on using a collaborative or combative style? See discussion in Chapter 14 on communication styles.

18. Log-rolling refers to exchanging concessions to keep the deal moving forward. For example, a buyer might agree to a higher purchase price, but only if the seller agrees to allow the buyer to defer a portion of the purchase price.

PRACTICE NOTES

Equity Financings

Exercise 13.3 refers to convertible notes and preferred stock financings. These represent two common forms of nonpublic securities offerings commonly used by start-ups and other new companies to raise money (capital). Convertible notes are a form of debt security; preferred stock is a form of equity security. The principal differentiating characteristic between debt and equity securities is that a debt security contains a repayment obligation and does not afford the holder voting rights (although the terms of the note may include certain approval rights and preferred stock has some debt-like features). Both involve a degree of risk and are considered securities; thus, both are subject to securities laws.[19]

Convertible notes are convertible into equity securities (typically preferred stock) upon the occurrence of a trigger event, such as completion of a new round of financing or the sale of the company. The conversion can be at the option of the holder, at the option of the company, or automatic. If they are not converted, the notes will become due and payable upon the specified maturity date, typically with interest.

Preferred stock represents an equity ownership in a company that receives certain rights and privileges distinct from common stock. These can include liquidation preferences (which, in the event of a liquidation or sale of the company, entitle the holders of preferred stock to be repaid their initial investment before any common stockholders receive any share of the proceeds), protective voting provisions (where certain decisions require the vote of a minimum number of preferred stockholders), the right to select one or more directors, and the right to receive preferred dividends (based on a percentage of the amount invested versus the amount of shares held).

Conclusion

Negotiation at its core is a form of communication between two or more persons with their own interests and goals. Any time you seek to persuade another person to accept what you are proposing, you are engaging in a form of negotiation. Different degrees of negotiation exist: they can be friendly, hostile, or somewhere in the middle. Sometimes it won't feel like a negotiation—for example, when both parties' interests and goals are closely aligned. The better able you are to recognize where this alignment exists *and to effectively communicate this to the other side*, the easier the negotiation.

NEGOTIATION PROJECT: Preparing for and Engaging in a Negotiation

You will be assigned with a partner to play the role of lawyers representing one of two parties negotiating a transaction. You will receive confidential instructions depending on which side you are assigned. Using the instructions, prepare for the negotiation and complete a negotiation preparation worksheet. Do not share your confidential instructions with the other side. Live negotiations will take place in class.

---

19. Certain provisions of federal and state securities laws in the U.S. apply only to equity securities; because debt securities include a prepayment obligation, certain protections afforded to holders of equity securities are deemed to be less necessary.

Chapter 14

Additional Negotiation Techniques, Strategies, and Considerations

This chapter picks up where Chapter 13 left off to focus on different communication styles and their potential impact on the outcome of negotiations. It goes on to examine techniques for maximizing the effectiveness of negotiations between lawyers and how to avoid common pitfalls. The chapter concludes by exploring cross-cultural considerations.

By the end of this chapter, you will be able to:

- Weigh the most appropriate communication style to achieve the best outcome for your client
- Recognize and overcome cross-cultural barriers
- Effectively approach negotiations with difficult people
- Debrief a partner or client on the results of a negotiation
- Address the ethical issues that can arise in negotiations

You have just participated in a negotiation with opposing counsel on the sale of your client's printing business. The senior associate who was leading the negotiations was so impressed by your contributions in the negotiation that she has asked you to summarize what was agreed in a brief email to the partner and the client. Luckily, you took good notes. But are you sure as to what was decided for each point? Are there any open issues? How much information do you need to provide to the partner and the client? How should you organize your summary?

Communication Styles

In addition to the form of negotiation, the style in which you communicate can affect outcome. Communication styles form a continuum, ranging from collaborative to combative.[1] Each of us has natural tendencies that fall somewhere on this spectrum. External factors, such as differing circumstances and the communication style of those with whom we are communicating, can also affect how we communicate.

A combative style is best characterized as a battle of wills, where the person who holds out the longest wins. A combative negotiator seeks to maximize the benefits for his or

---

1. The terms used for these ends of the spectrum vary. *See, e.g., Brad Spangier, Competitive and Cooperative Approaches to Conflict,* Beyond Intractability (2003), http://www.beyondintractability.com (discussing cooperative versus competitive conflict styles).

her own side by convincing the other side to accept less, by gradually wearing the other side down. Typically, this type of negotiator starts with the highest initial position that is credible (or beyond) and discloses as little as possible.

A collaborative negotiator seeks to avoid conflict and is more willing to make concessions to reach agreement and preserve good will, and to develop a relationship of mutual trust and respect. Typically, this type of negotiator starts with a moderate offer and initiates concessions to create a moral obligation on the other side to reciprocate and to build the relationship.

Each end of the spectrum has potential disadvantages. At the combative end, there is a risk of ending in impasse. It can also harm the relationship between the parties and discourage exploring options. At the other end, collaborative negotiators can be vulnerable to more combative negotiators and concede more than necessary.

Following are some examples along the spectrum:

Collaborative

- *We understand your position, but have some concerns. Perhaps we can come up with a compromise that would address both our concerns.*

- *I want to find a solution, I do, but you've put me in a difficult position.*

- *We hear what you are saying, but we are not going to be able to convince our client to change her mind.*

- *That is unacceptable. We are not going to change our minds. You can either accept it or walk away.*

Combative

A combative style tends to be more aligned with positional bargaining. For the same reasons that interest-based negotiations tend to yield better results than positional bargaining, a more collaborative style similarly can be more productive. The more trust between the parties, the more likely they are to make reasonable concessions, especially where the relationship is ongoing.

Recall that communication involves speaking and listening. The communicative style of the speaker will to some extent depend on how it is perceived by the listener. The key is to make a conscious decision as to what style to adopt and to be cognizant of when you may need to shift more toward one end of the continuum or the other as negotiations proceed. Be wary of mirroring the other side's behavior. Just as two wrongs do not make a right, meeting a combative negotiator with a combative response can quickly derail negotiations.

Before sitting down at the negotiation table:

- Identify where you fall on the continuum: are you more of a collaborative or a combative negotiator? Are you willing to concede a point to avoid conflict? Or do you tend to stand your ground?

- Next, consider how much negotiation power your client has: how important is closing the deal for your client? How badly does the other side want what your client is bringing to the table?
- Finally, consider the relationship between the parties: is it expected to be ongoing? Strive to adopt a point on the continuum most conducive to achieving your client's goals.

Key Techniques in Negotiating Transactions

When negotiating a transaction, it can be easy to forget for whom you are negotiating and allow the negotiation to become personal. Remember you are representing your client and your client's interests. Of course, you have a vested interest in seeking the most favorable outcome for your client, but strive to maintain a professional detachment. Letting your personal feelings get in the way of de-escalating a disagreement between the parties can be a disservice to your client. The more you can approach the issues calmly, objectively, and logically, the more likely you will be able to: (1) interpret what the other side wants and why; (2) identify potential compromises or solutions that will satisfy both sides; and (3) convince the other side to accept what you are proposing.

The ability to remain objective and detached is one of the key advantages a transactional lawyer can bring to the negotiating table. This is easier said than done, of course, as it takes cooperation from both sides. But don't be afraid to lead by example and to take the high road.

Following are some techniques to keep in mind and pitfalls to watch out for when engaging in negotiations as a transactional lawyer:

Strike a Balance Between Over-Lawyering and Undue Compromise

A deal-breaking issue in one transaction may be less important in another. Your experience on prior deals can create an unconscious assumption (referred to as a cognitive bias) that once you have encountered an issue on a deal it needs to be addressed on all future deals. Learning from your mistakes is not necessarily a bad thing, provided you consider the context. For example, assume your client on a past deal needed to get out of a distribution deal because of a major earthquake and didn't have a *force majeure* provision. After that, you start including *force majeure* provisions in all your contracts. But is a *force majeure* provision always necessary? How hard should you fight to keep it in if the other side pushes back? Consider the context.

Don't over-lawyer or insist on provisions just because you should have insisted on them in the past. Learn to critically evaluate each issue being negotiated in the context of the deal. Ask yourself:

- What are the potential legal and business consequences if you cede the issue to the other side? How material are they to your client?
- How likely are any negative consequences to materialize?
- How do those consequences compare to those that might arise from other issues remaining to be negotiated?
- How much (dollar amount or otherwise) is at stake?
- Is there anything you might want to trade in exchange for giving in on the issue?

For example, in a $1 million transaction involving parties who have a long history of doing business together, you may be willing to include fewer representations than in a $100 million transaction with an unknown party. You may want to press for a covenant of the seller to preserve the goodwill of the business in a stock purchase where much of the value is connected to the existing customer contracts, but the same covenant may not be necessary where you are purchasing a manufacturing facility. You may be less inclined to spend time negotiating an indemnification provision if you know the other party has limited funds and is selling substantially all its assets, as opposed to a transaction in which the other party has substantial resources.

On the other hand, avoid conceding too much too quickly. If you believe a material concern exists and that you have a valid reason for negotiating an issue, you should use your best efforts to convince the other side of your position.

Make a Conscious Choice About How You Approach the Other Side to Concede or Compromise on an Issue

The goal is to convince the other side of your arguments. One approach is to *ask* the other side for what you want, supported by a reason:

> *My client is concerned that your client may sell us the assets and then form a new company and start competing. Thus, my client would like to include a noncompete to give it some comfort on this issue.*

Other times, it is necessary to draw a firm line in the sand and make a *demand* (a request that implies the party will only take "yes" as an answer):[2]

> *My client wants to include a noncompete.*

Junior associates are often fearful of not appearing confident or credible enough in negotiations. This is a valid concern. But you can be confident and still be civil. Being nice is not a sign of weakness, nor does it mean you are not advocating for your client. In fact, it can make you appear more self-assured. Conversely, being overly aggressive can undermine your credibility, and can cause the other side to be less willing to compromise, even when you make a valid point.

A similar choice occurs in responding to the other side's demands. You can choose to give a firm response:

> *No, my client will not agree to that.*

Or you could choose a more open-ended response:

> *I'm not sure my client will be willing to accept but I can check. If not, perhaps we can consider option X, which might provide you with similar comfort.*

The latter approach allows you to respond without committing but to still provide the other side with the sense that you are listening and hearing their concerns. Another alternative would be to agree, but to seek a concession, for example:

> *I think I can get my client to agree, as long as we can take out the wording that relates to [ ].*

Still another approach might be to seek something in return:

> *I can get my client to agree on that, but it will likely want to see the 30-day notice period put back into the agreement. Otherwise, my client will have no recourse if . . . .*

One approach is not necessarily better than the other, and a mixed approach may be appropriate. Whichever approach is selected should be based on a strategy that you have thought through ahead of time. You probably do not want to only make demands or only respond with firm responses. On

---

2. Neumann, *supra* Chapter 2, note 2, at 112.

the other hand, it would quickly become frustrating if every question and answer was vague and noncommittal.

Justify your Request or Refusal to Preempt Counterarguments

Note the justification in the last example above, supporting the requested exchange. Be prepared to justify each request, demand, or refusal. Letting the other side see that you have thought through the issue and have legitimate reasons for your position (and that you have considered their interests) helps show the other side you are not making demands just for the sake of making demands. Moreover, providing an objective reason can make it harder for the other side to justify refusing to accept your request.

Illustration: **Justifying Your Request**

In Simulation Exercise #10, the seller wanted to remove the indemnification provision, reasoning that the deal was not large enough to necessitate including the provision. The buyer's response was that it was not willing to remove the indemnification provision, because it was concerned with potential unknown liabilities. In this case, both sides engaged in justification. The buyer's justification was more compelling in this instance; it made it hard for the seller to insist that the buyer should take its chances for the sake of not including a provision that likely would not impact the seller.

Be Candid without Divulging too Much Information

An important component of successful negotiations is trust between the parties. Being candid with the other party can go a long way toward creating this comfort—it's hard to trust someone if you think he or she is hiding something. At the same time, however, be careful not to divulge information the client does not want to share, or that gives the other side too much leverage.

The decision to reveal information to the other side should be a conscious one, weighed against the relative pros and cons (and any ethical considerations—see below). Often, the decision as to what you can or should disclose needs to be made on the spot; good judgment, preparation, and client communication prior to the negotiation are critical in enabling you to make these decisions.

For example, let's suppose your client doesn't trust the seller and thinks it could be hiding liabilities. To account for this, you are seeking to include a strong indemnity and a parent guaranty. Do you tell opposing counsel that you need these protections because the buyer doesn't trust the seller? Will this set the right tone for cooperative negotiations? Likely not. A more tactful explanation might be that the buyer is concerned its board of directors will likely want a parent guaranty to approve the deal. Of course, you want to make sure that you are not being materially misleading or otherwise acting unethically (see discussion on ethics below).

Avoid Positional Bargaining, Chicken, and Deadlock

If you have ever witnessed a congressional debate, you will have seen examples of positional bargaining: lawmakers on each side of the aisle assert their respective positions without being willing to consider any compromise. The result of positional bargaining in Congress is either impasse and the bill fails, or one side wins based on the number of votes and the other side "loses."

Lawmakers tend to become more easily entrenched into positional bargaining because of how they are elected: they run for office based on their positions on key issues; once they are elected, they find themselves constrained by these positions. The system does not encourage compromise. As transactional lawyers, we are not subject to these same constraints, at least not to the same degree (clients may insist that certain terms are "nonnegotiable"). Thus, positional bargaining in transactional negotiations can be more easily avoided, and transactional lawyers are freer to compromise to achieve a win-win result.

Sometimes you may be forced to engage in positional bargaining: your client may have a firm position from which it does not want to budge, or the other side may leave you no option but to dig in your heels. This can lead to deadlock, where no one wins.

---

*Illustration: **Positional Bargaining Leading to Deadlock***

You represent a client who has instructed you that it will not pay more than $400,000 to hire an executive employee. The executive demands no less than $600,000. If each side sticks to its position, no deal can be reached. If both parties really want the deal to get done, the lawyer needs to generate options to find a middle ground. Perhaps the client will agree to increase the salary incrementally over a period, or perhaps it can offer a performance bonus for the difference. Perhaps the executive would be willing to accept a lower salary for some other benefit or commitment. Without compromise, the two parties would be deadlocked.

Positional bargaining can also lead to the parties ending in a game of chicken, where each side threatens to walk away if the other side does not meet its demands.[3] For example: "If your client doesn't agree to these terms, my client is going to walk away," or "This issue is nonnegotiable for my client." If these are true, then you should let the other side know. Avoid making these types of statements if they are not genuine, however, as this tactic can backfire, resulting in the other party either calling your bluff or making counter-demands. At a minimum, it will not help inspire trust between the parties or promote cooperation.

Sometimes it is in a client's best interest to walk away from a deal if the other side is unwilling to meet its terms. But the transactional lawyer needs to keep working toward compromise and resolution to the extent possible until that point is reached.

Be Mindful of Anchoring and Other Techniques Used by the Other Side

Other lawyers will not always play fair. They can use tactics that make it difficult to engage in reasoned negotiations or to fully trust the other side. For instance, they might deliberately make unreasonable demands to get you to counter with what they are actually looking for. In making the unreasonable demand, the other side creates an "anchor point"—a starting point from which compromise is measured.[4] But this distorts what is being conceded, and the concession will appear greater than it is.

---

3. *See* Robert H. Mnookin, Scott R. Pepper & Andrew S. Tulumello, Beyond Winning: Negotiating to Create Value in Deals and Disputes 253–54 (2000).

4. *See* Korobkin & Ulen, *supra* Chapter 9, note 7, at 1100.

Illustration: **Anchoring**

The seller in a merger opens negotiations by stating that it does not want to make any representations regarding the ownership of its intellectual property. Counsel for the buyer pushes back, arguing that: (1) the seller must be able to provide some comfort on whether it owns the intellectual property it is purporting to sell, (2) the buyer needs to know it is acquiring all necessary intellectual property, and (3) the seller needs to confirm there are no potential infringement issues. The seller eventually agrees to represent that, to its knowledge, it owns the intellectual property listed in the agreement, but refuses to represent that the intellectual property listed constitutes all the intellectual property needed to operate the business, or whether it is aware of any infringement of third-party intellectual property rights. The buyer may be happy that it got the seller to back down from its initial position that it would not make any representations at all and be willing to accept this compromise. But what is the actual point of comparison? The buyer's initial position contained a request for three separate representations. When viewing the seller's compromise from this vantage point, it does not seem as reasonable.

When the other side offers a concession or makes a first offer, make sure you are evaluating it not from the other side's anchor point, but based on objective criteria.

One way to avoid anchoring by the other side is to try to control the draft of the relevant agreements. This can create additional legal costs for your client, but being the side to prepare the first draft allows you to set the anchor point and can outweigh cost concerns. It also lets you to select the language and style of the document, allowing you to preempt potential ambiguities and lack of clarity. Any comments or negotiations by the other side will be anchored to your initial draft, making it harder for the other side to justify making stylistic changes and substantive comments.

For example, assume you include in your initial draft a covenant that states: "The Seller will use *best efforts* to obtain all required consents *as promptly as possible.*" The seller might have started with a different anchor point, such as "*commercially reasonable efforts,*" or omit any reference to timing. Perhaps it would have used the term "*necessary*" instead of "*required.*" Once you have set the anchor point, however, it becomes harder for the seller to justify deleting "*as promptly as possible,*" and any changes the seller wants to make to the "*best efforts*" requirement will need to be negotiated; the seller will need to consider whether this is something worth negotiating, or whether it would rather focus its efforts on other issues.

If you are in a position where you are negotiating a draft prepared by the other side, prepare for the negotiation by comparing that draft to a form precedent that is neutral or drafted favorably to your side to determine how far off-center the other side's anchor point is.

FOR DISCUSSION:

You are charged with preparing the initial draft of a license agreement in a transaction. Should you start with a pro-licensor form, a pro-licensee form, or a neutral form? Why? Does it matter which side you represent? Are there any provisions you would prioritize in terms of negotiating?

Use the Negotiation to Gather Information From the Other Side

Don't focus on getting what you want to the point where you forget to listen to what the other side has to say. You risk missing information that could be vital to identifying potential compromises, issues, and weaknesses in the other side's arguments. The two components of effective information gathering are active listening and questioning. In listening and asking questions of the other side, strive to understand the interests that underlie the other side's position. For example, if opposing counsel is insisting on including an indemnity, don't be afraid to ask what his concerns are. You can even say you have no problem with adding the provision but are curious as to why he thinks it necessary. Questioning is of limited use without making sure you also listen to the response, clarifying as necessary. Pay attention to verbal and nonverbal cues that might help you adjust your strategy.

Know When and How to Speak Incompletely or Ambiguously

On occasion, you may not want to disclose sensitive information or details that might weaken your client's negotiation power. For example, as counsel for the seller of a business, you may not want to volunteer that the other side's offer is the highest offer you have received. You do not want to misrepresent facts (see discussion on ethical considerations below), but that does not mean you have to offer the information without being asked. If the buyer asks if you have other offers, you may want to respond in the affirmative without necessarily going into detail.

It can also be counterproductive to appear too eager to get the deal done. You will not serve your client's best interests if you tell the other side your client badly needs the deal or will do anything to get the deal done. Instead, you could suggest that your client believes the deal proposed is a good one and is very interested in seeing if the parties can reach a mutually satisfactory agreement.

As a junior associate, you may not be aware of the client's concerns regarding disclosing information. If in doubt, it is acceptable for you to say that you are not sure; avoid being lured into the trap of wanting to show that you are "in the know."

Ethical Considerations in Negotiations

Be wary of being lulled into believing that a negotiation tactic used by your client or the other side is acceptable. As lawyers, we are held to higher ethical standards than non-lawyers. It can be tempting to push the boundaries in a negotiation, but employing unethical or unreasonable negotiation tactics can create unintended adverse consequences, including harming the long-term relationship between the parties, your reputation and credibility; causing the other side to walk away; and engendering potential disciplinary action.

At what point does zealous advocacy in negotiations become unethical or unreasonable? Recognizing when your behavior crosses that line can be difficult. For instance, what is the difference, if any, between exaggeration or "puffery," and misrepresenting or withholding a fact? Knowing misrepresentation of a fact, including by omission, violates not only ethics rules but may also subject the lawyer to tort liability.

FOR DISCUSSION:

1. Model Rule 4.1(a) states that in representing a client: *"a lawyer shall not knowingly [ ] make a false statement of material fact or law to a third person. . . ."*[5] Comment (2) to Model Rule 4.1 clarifies that: *"in negotiation, certain types of statements ordinarily are not taken as statements of material fact."*[6]

   Consider the difference between telling the other side: "There is no way my client is going to agree to go that low on the purchase price" and "My client emailed me yesterday instructing me to reject any offer less than $500,000." Assume the client did not send an email but has told the lawyer she really doesn't want to go below $500,000. Do either of the lawyer's statements violate Rule 4.1(a) in light of comment (2)? Does it matter whether the fact is material?

2. What about a scenario in which the lawyer deliberately withholds the fact that her client is on the verge of bankruptcy? Would this violate Rule 4.1(a)? Comment (1) to Rule 4.1(a) states that *"[a] lawyer is required to be truthful when dealing with others on a client's behalf, but generally has no affirmative duty to inform an opposing party of relevant facts."* Does this alter your opinion?

3. Rule 8.4(c) charges a lawyer with misconduct if the lawyer *"engage[s] in conduct involving dishonesty, fraud, deceit or misrepresentation. . . ."*[7] Would any of the above actions fall under Rule 8.4(c)?

Scrivener's Errors

One type of ethical dilemma that can occur when negotiating is where one party inadvertently makes an error in a document that the other party knows is an error. For example, the buyer might state the purchase price as $3,000,000 when both parties know the deal to be worth $300,000. This error is an obvious one, and it would arguably be bad faith to try to hold the buyer to the erroneous $3,000,000 purchase price (and likely would not be successful in court). But what about less obvious errors, such as forgetting to input a change that was agreed upon, or stating that a representation made by the seller is qualified by the *buyer's* knowledge (instead of the *seller's)*? Look at Rule 4.4(b) of the Model Rules. This rule deals with receiving correspondence not intended for the recipient, but does the spirit of the rule suggest that it applies by analogy to a scrivener's error in a document?

The best practice is to err on the side of reasonableness and fairness. If something feels deceptive or unreasonable—if you find yourself questioning whether it is crossing the line—it probably is. The adage "if you cheat, you are only cheating yourself" holds true: by being unreasonable or deceptive, you may get away with scoring a negotiation point, but risk losing the other side's trust and willingness to collaborate, ultimately making it harder to negotiate the best deal for your client.

---

5. Rule 4.1 of the ABA Model Rules of Professional Conduct.
6. Comment (2) to Rule 4.1 of the ABA Model Rules of Professional Conduct.
7. Rule 8.4 of the ABA Model Rules of Professional Conduct.

Cross-Cultural Considerations

As with communications in general, cross-cultural negotiations can add a layer of interference that can impede the effectiveness of the negotiations and can inform your decisions as to the choice of form, style, and approach.

Choosing the Appropriate Form of Communication

When dealing with individuals from high-context cultures,[8] who rely more heavily on nonverbal cues and value relationships, in-person meetings can offer several advantages over telephone calls, emails, or other written communication when attempting to negotiate a transaction. In-person meetings can:

- Eliminate barriers to communication that might arise in a telephone conversation or written communication due to lack of nonverbal cues. This can be especially true where a language barrier is present. Being able to see the other person's expression can make it easier to recognize when that person has not understood something, and gestures can help give meaning to unfamiliar words.
- Build necessary rapport, which can often be instrumental in building trust and cooperation between the parties. Being able to look someone in the eye and shake his or her hand can make a person more comfortable than just speaking to a faceless voice over the telephone.

In some cases, although in-person meetings can help the parties develop a working relationship, they may not be the most effective means of reaching agreement. Depending on the culture and rhetorical preferences of the parties, it can be difficult to engage in actual negotiations of substantive deal points, either because the parties are reticent to offend the other side, or because of a cultural aversion to conflict. In these situations, it can be counterproductive to try to push for resolution at the meeting. Instead, focus on relationship-building during the meeting, and then follow up in writing with suggested resolutions to any issues discussed.

Adapting for Different Views of Conflict

The role of conflict is different across cultures. U.S. culture tend to be more adversarial: people are more comfortable with arguing and engaging in conflict. In cultures that are more conflict-averse, being argumentative can seem disrespectful. The emphasis in these cultures is on seeking harmony. When negotiating with lawyers from these types of cultures, interest-based negotiations can be more productive than positional bargaining. Similarly, a combative approach is more likely to offend, stymieing efforts to reach a deal.

Recognizing Differing views of Persuasiveness

Cultural preferences can influence how you are perceived. For example, in some cultures, looking the other person straight in the eye can convey sincerity; in others, it can be offensive and create mistrust. The same is true of directness: some cultures value directness, while others view it as lacking sufficient reasoning.

Understanding Gender Differences

We often overlook gender differences, but they are worth noting for two important reasons. First,

---

8. Refer to discussion in Chapter 5 on high- versus low-context cultures.

different cultures hold diverse attitudes toward gender differences, specifically with how women are treated. In some cultures, a woman in a negotiation might be given additional respect. In others, she may not be taken seriously. Men in the room might adopt a more formal, polite tone and vocabulary in the presence of a woman counterpart. This added politeness or formality does not necessarily translate into more effective negotiations, however, and in some cases can make it more difficult to reach agreement. Second, women and men tend to have different communication styles. This can skew a negotiation by accentuating the degree to which a party appears collaborative or combative (recall that communication style is perceived by the listener).

Exercise 14.1

For this exercise, your instructor will assign you a cultural identity. Working in pairs, negotiate the following issue, adhering to the stereotypical cultural preferences for your assigned culture.

Issue: A borrower is seeking to increase the repayment term on a loan provided by a finance lender. The borrower is willing to offer additional collateral.

Did you achieve the expected result? What surprised you? What difficulties did you encounter? How did you attempt to overcome these difficulties? Did you alter your behavior or language? Is there anything that seems would be the same regardless of cultural differences?

Negotiating with Difficult People

Negotiation, as with communication in general, is a two-way street. The effectiveness of your negotiation strategies and techniques will depend in part on the person with whom you are negotiating and how that person interprets and responds to what you say.

Sometimes you will have to deal with positional bargainers and other difficult people—people with character traits or behavior that hamper collaboration. They can be naturally cantankerous, have a quick temper, be noncommittal, like to bully others, thrive on conflict, or be reticent to share information. They can be unwilling to compromise and determined to win at all costs. They can brazenly push for more each time you make a concession or whittle surreptitiously away at each point before you realize how much you have conceded. Or they can be inexperienced, leaving them unwilling to concede a point out of fear of giving up something they should not. None of these are conducive to interest-based, cooperative negotiations.

How do you get a positional bargainer to engage in interest-based negotiations? As a first step, avoid mirroring the other side's behavior, especially if they are being combative. Instead, you can attempt one or more of the following techniques to steer the discussion toward interest-based negotiation:

- *Ask questions.* Use questions to identify the underlying interests of the other side.[9] For example: "*Why do you want an unlimited due diligence period? What is your concern with limiting it to a reasonable period?*" You can also frame the question in a way to force the other side to justify its position. For example: "*Why don't you want to represent that you own the intellectual property? Are there any concerns we should be aware of? Is there anything you perhaps need to*

9. Fischer & Ury, *supra* Chapter 13, note 11, at 117.

carve out that we can discuss?" This type of questioning can be effective in drawing out underlying interests or making the other lawyer recognize his demand is unreasonable.

- *Engage in active listening.* Pay attention to tone and nonverbal cues. Listen to what the speaker is *not* saying. Can you glean any clues as to what the underlying interests are? Also, by sensing and responding to the speaker, she may begin to feel placated and more open to compromise. For example: *"I see . . . . I understand . . . . So if I hear you correctly, you want to eliminate the indemnity and the termination provisions?"*

- *Refrain from arguing.* Arguing with someone who is already angry or emotional will only escalate their anger. Instead, seek to remain calm and control your own emotions.

- *Allow the other person to "save face."* The idea of "saving face" is a core social value in Asian cultures that has worked its way into most cultures; it signifies the need to allow a person to avoid humiliation and maintain dignity when conceding. In negotiations, it means providing the other person with a way to back down from his or her position without making it seem as if the person is backing down. It can be as subtle as saying: *"We can accept your point, but would you at least be willing to consider giving us [XYZ]?"* XZY can be something that you wanted all along, but this allows you to ask for it without making the other person appear weak.

- *Persist in trying to bridge the gap.* Avoid backing into your own position. Continue to seek ways to meet the other person halfway—to "bridge the gap" between your respective positions—by generating options that appeal to the underlying interests of both parties. But be mindful of anchoring your options to the other side's starting position (see page 203).

- *Finally, remember we are all human.* Focus on communicating, not on results; if negotiations are not getting anywhere, take a step back and try to reconnect. If you are unable to agree on a point, don't give up before trying to figure out *why*. For example: *"We seem to be at an impasse, perhaps we should take a step back and discuss your client's concerns."*

Debriefing the Negotiation

You have concluded negotiations. You may be more or less happy with the results. Either way, for the negotiation to have been worthwhile, you need to be able to synthesize the results and articulate the next steps. Nothing is less productive than a meeting that ends with everyone walking away without a clear idea of what was decided or any commitment for follow-up.

Making Sure You Know What Was Agreed

This first step starts before you end the negotiations. Take a few minutes at the end of a negotiation or meeting to recap your understanding of: (1) any agreements reached; (2) any items that still need to be agreed (often, we refer to these items as "open" issues or issues that are "parked" for further discussion); and (3) the agreed next steps (including who will be responsible for each step and the proposed timeframe). Taking notes during the meeting can help you prepare this summary.

In some instances, going through the process of recapping the negotiation might flush out lingering misunderstandings between the parties or additional issues that were not spotted during the negotiation. These can either be addressed then and there, or added to the list of parked issues for follow-up.

Debriefing the Partner and the Client

The next step is to update the partner or senior associate. Even if the partner or senior associate was present at the meeting, he or she may still expect you to prepare a summary for the file to memorialize what was agreed. As a deal progresses, memories fade as to what was decided weeks earlier; having a summary in the file provides a clear record. Depending on the partner's preferences, you may be expected to update her orally, in an email or bullet point summary, or in a short memo.

You also likely will need to debrief the client. Recall the discussion in Chapter 10 on how to convert a research memo into a client letter. The same principles and techniques apply here: your task is to take the summary prepared for the partner and tailor it as needed for your client. Most often, your summary for the client will be in an email or perhaps a brief memo.

Regardless of whether you are debriefing the partner or your client:

- Recall the three central characteristics of effective legal writing: conciseness, precision, and clarity, and other fundamental techniques.
- Keep your reader in mind:
  - If to the partner, what information does the partner need? What is she likely to do with the information?
  - If to the client, what does she need to know to make an informed decision (and what does she not need to know)? Are you advising the client, counseling her, or both?
  - What assumptions might your reader make regarding the relevance, accuracy, and completeness of the information you provide?
  - What are the rhetorical preferences of your reader? What is the appropriate tone, level of formality, and degree of directness?
  - How can you organize the information logically?
- If in an email, recall the techniques discussed in Chapters 7 and 10, such as keeping your summary to one page or less and using bullet points or other tabulation.

Conclusion

This chapter brings us to the close of our exploration of effective communication in transactional practice. It also brings us full circle: we started by using the fundamental writing techniques discussed throughout this text to communicate with the partner, the client, and lawyers on the other side, and ended by reporting back to the partner and the client.

We have also completed a full circle in experiencing the role of a junior associate, from responding to partner emails, conducting research, participating in client meetings, drafting and reviewing various forms of documents, to negotiating deal terms with opposing counsel. The communication and problem-solving skills you have developed, through illustration, discussion, and practice, are fundamental to any type of communication you may encounter.

I hope you have gained not only the practical skills, but the insight and confidence necessary to succeed as you embark on your transactional career, "practice-ready"!

SIMULATION EXERCISE #11: Debriefing a Negotiation

Julie Ryan

From: Julie Ryan jryan@ryanassoc.com
Sent: April __ 1:00 PM
To: Junior Associate
Subject: Debriefing Email to Client

Junior Associate,

Please draft an email to your client *briefly* summarizing the results of your negotiation. You should explain what issues were discussed, any options proposed or agreed, any issues tabled for later discussion, and any additional insight you think important for the client to know (facts that came out, particular concerns, etc.).

In drafting your email, keep in mind the three fundamental characteristics of effective legal correspondence: conciseness, precision, and clarity. Also, keep your reader in mind: (i) what does your reader need to know in order to make an informed decision (and what doesn't he/she need to know); (ii) what assumptions might your reader make regarding the relevance, accuracy, and completeness of the information you provide; (iii) what are the rhetorical preferences of your reader (e.g., appropriate tone/formality/directness); and (iv) how can you present the information in a format that is easy for the reader to grasp? Hint: keeping the email to one page or less, using bullet points or other tabulation, and plain English, are particularly useful techniques in drafting client emails.

Please email me your draft email within 48 hours. Please let me know if you have any questions.

Thanks,

Julie

Julie A. Ryan
Ryan & Associates
299 Valley Avenue
3rd Floor
Los Angeles, CA 90009
Tel: 213-510-5000
Email: jryan@ryanassoc.com

Glossary of Key Terms and Concepts

Glossary of Select Terms Used in This Text

Acquired Assets — The assets being purchased or sold in an Asset Purchase.

Acquisition — The purchase of a company's Stock or Assets.

Articles of Incorporation — The governing document required to form a corporation and filed with the applicable state registrar. Other terms include Certificate of Incorporation and Charter.

Asset — Something of value. Assets can be tangible or intangible. For example, Assets of a company can include its inventory, machinery, buildings, employees, intellectual property rights, accounts receivable, and goodwill.

Asset Purchase/Sale — The acquisition/sale of one or more Assets of a Target Company.

Assignment — The transfer of rights, interests, or benefits, sometimes coupled with the assumption of associated Liabilities.

Assumption of Liabilities/Assumed Liabilities — An entity or person (typically the Buyer in an Acquisition or Merger) stepping into the shoes of another entity or person with respect to the Liabilities of that other entity or person, such that the Buyer assumes the obligation to satisfy that Liability. This can be contractually agwreed or can occur by operation of law (such as in a Stock Purchase or Merger, or under the doctrine of Successor Liability).

Authorized Shares — The number of units (Shares) of Stock that a company can issue as stated in its Articles of Incorporation.

Baskets/Caps/Floors — These apply to Indemnities and limit the amount to which an indemnitor will be liable under the Indemnity. A Cap limits the total amount payable under the Indemnity. A Basket establishes a threshold below which an Indemnification claim would not be payable. A Basket can act as a deductible, where anything below the basket is not indemnifiable, or as a tipping Basket, where once the threshold is reached, everything in the Basket becomes indemnifiable. A Floor is similar to a Basket and usually refers to the minimum amount for a claim to be considered.

Blue Sky Laws — Individual state securities laws with their own registration, qualification, disclosure, and exemption requirements.

Board of Directors — A group of individuals who are elected to serve as representatives of the Stockholders of a Corporation to make major decisions on behalf of the Corporation.

Bridge Loan — A form of short-term financing, sometimes convertible into equity. Often, principal and interest are paid only upon maturity.

Broker-Dealer — As defined in Section 3 of the Securities Exchange Act, a Broker is "any person engaged in the business of effecting transactions in securities for the account of others," and a Dealer is "any person engaged in the business of buying and selling securities for his own account, through a broker or otherwise."[1] Most brokerage firms act as both brokers and dealers, hence the combined term. With limited exceptions, Broker-Dealers must be registered with the SEC and join a self-regulatory organization, such as FINRA.

Buyer — The purchaser or acquirer in an Acquisition.

By-laws — The administrative guidelines for a Corporation that control the timing, place, and procedure for Stockholder and Board of Director meetings, the appointment and duties of Officers, voting, and other matters not contained in the Articles of Incorporation.

Capital — At its most basic, Capital refers to money. It also refers to the Assets of a business, including cash and property that has value.

Capital Markets — The marketplaces in which Securities are traded for their value. See Practice Area Overview.

Capital Structure — The overall structure of a company's outstanding Debt and Equity. A company's Capital Structure is generally divided into senior debt, subordinated debt, and equity (common and preferred).

Capitalization — The amount of Stock issued and outstanding and the market value of that Stock, calculated by multiplying the price per Share by the number of issued and outstanding Shares. Companies with a high market capitalization are referred to as large cap. Companies with medium market capitalization are referred to as mid caps, and companies with small capitalization are referred to as small caps or emerging-growth companies. The initial funding of a company at its formation through the issuance of Stock to its Founders or other early investors is referred to as the company's initial Capitalization.

Certificate of Incorporation — See Articles of Incorporation.

Change of Control Clause — A provision in an agreement giving a party certain rights in the event of a change in ownership or management of the other party. A Change of Control Clause is comprised of two components: the trigger (typically the transfer of more than 50 percent of a party's Stock or substantially all its assets) and the consequence (for example, the right of the other party to terminate the agreement or to accelerate an obligation). Commonly used in conjunction with a No-Assignment Provision to avoid circumvention of that provision.

Charter — See Articles of Incorporation.

Closing — The consummation of a Transaction, typically involving the actual transfer of value and risk. In cross-border transactions, particularly in the United Kingdom, the Closing is referred to as Completion.

Closing Condition — A condition that must be satisfied on or prior to the Closing of the relevant transaction in order for the parties to have an obligation to proceed. Also called a condition precedent.

Collateral — Something of value that is pledged by a borrower to secure repayment of a loan or debt, which is forfeited if the loan or debt is not repaid. A security interest in Collateral typically should

---

1. 15 U.S.C. 78c(a)(4)–(5).

be perfected by a mortgage, UCC-1, or other notice filing, which then puts other creditors on notice.

Common Stock — The equity slice of the Capitalization that sits at the bottom of the Capital Structure. In most jurisdictions, the only protections for Common Stock holders are the Fiduciary Duties owed to them by the Board of Directors. Also called Ordinary Shares.

Confidentiality Agreement — An agreement to keep confidential the nonpublic information of another party. Two aspects are important to incorporate to ensure effective protection: (i) restrictions on disclosure and (ii) restrictions on use. See also NDA.

Consideration — Something of value given by both parties to a contract that induces them to enter into the agreement to exchange mutual performances. Money is a common form of Consideration in a Transaction, as are services.

Convertible Debt — Debt that converts into Equity upon certain trigger events. Conversion can be mandatory or optional, depending on the terms negotiated by the parties and the type of instrument. Common Convertible Debt includes Convertible Notes and Bridge Loans.

Convertible Note — See Convertible Debt.

Corporate Formalities — Steps and precautions that a Corporation (or other limited liability entity) must take to ensure that it remains legally distinct from its owners. The separation between management and ownership is what protects the owners from personal liability for the debts and obligations of the entity. Corporate formalities include regular board meetings to approve necessary decisions, annual shareholder meetings to elect directors, and maintaining minutes of those meetings. See Practice Area Overview.

Corporate Governance — The system of rules, practices, and processes by which a company is directed and controlled.

Corporate Veil — A "shield" that protects stockholders of a Corporation (or owners of other limited liability entity forms) from personal liability for the debts and actions of the Corporation. This veil can be "pierced," allowing creditors to seek recourse against the individual stockholders in certain circumstances, such as failure of the corporation to adhere to Corporate Formalities or failure to adequately Capitalize the company. The standard for piercing the Corporate Veil varies from state to state.

Corporation — A legal entity created by state statute that affords its owners limited liability. Corporations have a separate legal existence from their owners (Stockholders).

Creditor — An entity or individual that extends credit or loans money to another person who is under an obligation to repay it. Creditors can be secured or unsecured. A Secured Creditor typically receives an interest in Collateral to secure the repayment of the loan or credit, and has an interest that is prior to unsecured creditors (a secured lender has the right to be paid back ahead of any unsecured creditors, even if the secured lender loaned money after the unsecured creditors). In a Liquidation, Creditors' rights are prior to those of the Stockholders.

Cross-Border — Spanning more than one country.

De Facto Merger Doctrine — An exception to the presumption that a purchaser of Assets does not assume Liabilities of the Seller, unless expressly stated, that allows the court to look to substance over form when determining whether statutory merger law applies. Thus, where an Asset Purchase leads to the same result as a Merger, the court can find that the acquiror assumed the Liabilities of the Target Company by operation of law.

Debt — An amount of money due by contract, typically as a result of a loan or credit.

Direct Merger — A combination of two companies (the Buyer and the Target Company) pursuant to state statute.

Distribution — This term can have several meanings in the transactional context: (1) the sale of goods; (2) the public sale of Securities; and (3) the disbursement of profits or other money or Assets from a company to its owners.

Distribution Agreement — An agreement governing the purchase and resale of a company's products by another entity or individual in a specific territory. May also be known as a reseller agreement.

Distribution Waterfall — The agreed flow of Distributions from a company to its owners and the order in which each owner or investor receives its share, typically by category of owner. For example, in the event of a sale of an LLC for cash, investors in the LLC might receive an amount equal to their original investment plus a Preferred Return first, and then any remaining proceeds might be distributed equally among all Members.

Due Diligence — What parties to a transaction and their advisors do to learn about a company. A Buyer in an Acquisition (and its lawyers, bankers, and accountants) performs Due Diligence so it can understand what it is buying. The individual elements of Due Diligence may include commercial (markets, product, and customers), financial (balance sheets, income and loss, and taxation position), and legal (implications of litigation, title to assets, intellectual property issues, etc.). Due Diligence activities are broad and range from a review of relevant documents and financial statements to visits and interviews with management, outside accountants, counsel, customers, and suppliers.

Duty of Care — The Duty of Care is one of the two central Fiduciary Duties of directors under U.S. state corporation laws. The Duty of Care requires that, in making a decision, a member of the Board of Directors must use the same degree of care as a reasonable businessperson would do in the conduct of his or her own business affairs. The seminal Delaware case on the Duty of Care is *Smith v. Van Gorkom*, 488 A.2d 858 (Del. 1985).

Duty of Loyalty — The Duty of Loyalty encompasses both conflicts of interest (and how to guard against them) and the requirement that the Board of Directors act in good faith in what they believe is the best interests of the company and its shareholders. In the United States this is the second central Fiduciary Duty of the Board of Directors under state corporation laws.

Earn-out — A risk allocation mechanism used in an M&A transaction whereby a portion of the purchase price is deferred and is paid out based on the performance of the acquired business over a specified period following the Closing of the transaction.

Entity — A structure for a business that has its own independent existence; the generic term used to refer to Corporations, LLCs, and Partnerships.

Equity — A generic term referring to shares of Stock or other Security representing an ownership interest or right to receive an ownership interest.

Escrow — An arrangement with a neutral third party to hold funds or other Assets on behalf of the parties in a transaction. The funds are held by the escrow service until it receives the appropriate written or oral instructions to disburse. An Escrow is often established in M&A transactions where the purchase price is payable over time to ensure the funds are distributed as agreed.

Excluded or Retained Assets — These are the converse to Acquired Assets; any assets specifically not being acquired.

Excluded or Retained Liabilities — As with Excluded Assets, these are liabilities expressly disclaimed by the purchaser in an Asset Purchase.

Fiduciary Duty — An obligation imposed on a party by virtue of that person's role, which requires that party to act solely in the interests of another party. Officers and directors of a corporation serve as fiduciaries for the corporation's stockholders.

Financing — The securing of Capital to fund operations, expenses, Acquisitions, or other purposes. It can refer to Equity or Debt. The term is often used interchangeably with an Offering.

FINRA — The Financial Industry Regulatory Authority, an independent nonprofit regulator charged with regulating broker-dealers and other intermediaries and the conduct of their business with the investing public. The predecessor to FINRA was the NASD (National Association of Securities Dealers).

Flow-Through Entity — Also known as a pass-through Entity, a Flow-Through Entity is not subject to entity-level taxation. Instead, all items of income and loss "flow through" the entity and are allocated to the individual owners and reported on each owner's respective tax return. Partnerships and LLCs are Flow-Through Entities. A Corporation can also elect flow-through taxation by making an "S" election with the IRS.

Forward Triangular Merger — A Merger pursuant to which the Buyer forms a Subsidiary and merges the Target Company with and into that Subsidiary.

Founders — The individuals involved in the initial launch of a new company. The designation of someone as a Founder is agreed among the parties. Founders are typically considered entrepreneurs.

Goodwill — As a legal term, Goodwill refers to the reputation, customer loyalty, or brand identification of a business. As an accounting term, Goodwill is an intangible Asset in an Acquisition equal to the price paid for the acquired company minus the fair market value of its Assets, net of Liabilities. The legal and accounting definitions closely relate in that they both recognize value in excess of the tangible Assets of a business. Accounting for a portion of the purchase price in an Acquisition as Goodwill can create significant tax advantages and facilitate enforceability of non-compete restrictions. Thus, how the purchase price will be allocated between Goodwill and the tangible Acquired Assets can be heavily negotiated.

Hart-Scott-Rodino (HSR) — The Hart-Scott-Rodino Antitrust Improvement Act of 1976. This Act establishes the pre-merger notification program that requires parties involved in Mergers or Acquisitions that exceed certain dollar thresholds (adjusted annually) to seek prior approval from the Department of Justice or the Federal Trade Commission before consummating the transaction. The goal of the act is to allow the DOJ and the FTC to assess the potential effect on competition before the deal occurs.

Indemnification/Indemnity — A contractual remedy pursuant to which one party (the indemnitor) agrees to reimburse—or indemnify—the other party (the indemnitee) for certain losses incurred by the indemnitee. Often, indemnification is limited to losses incurred as a result of claims by third parties.

Indenture — A contract governing a Debt obligation, typically used in syndicated debt financings where a group of investors holding a series of notes or other Debt instrument are all parties to the same Indenture governing their collective rights and allowing for voting or other decision-making among the various holders.

Independent Contractor — An individual or entity that provides services to another individual or entity not as an employee. The line between Independent Contractor and employee can be difficult to draw, with most states using a factors test. Misclassifying a worker as an Independent Contractor can create significant tax and other liability for an employer.

Intellectual Property — A generic term applied to property that involves intangible creations of the mind, primarily embodied in copyrights, patents, and trademarks, as well as trade secrets, publicity rights, and moral rights. In transactions, the parties typically negotiate the definition of Intellectual Property to include any specific elements relevant to the transaction. Intellectual Property Rights refer to the type of ownership in the Intellectual Property and the right of the holder to protect the Intellectual Property from being used or misappropriated by another. For instance, a license to use software constitutes an Intellectual Property Right to use that software, but may not extend to the right to sell that software to someone else.

Joint Venture — A business or enterprise undertaken jointly by two or more parties that retain their distinct identities. Joint Ventures can be created as a contractual alliance (in which the parties' respective rights and obligations are governed by contract law) or by forming a Partnership (in which case the parties' relationship is governed by relevant state partnership law). A Joint Venture is treated for tax purposes as a partnership, unless the parties expressly state otherwise.

Jumpstart Our Business Startups (JOBS) Act — An act signed into law on April 5, 2012, that loosened restrictions on capital raising for small businesses, such as allowing general solicitation in certain private placements and legitimizing crowdfunding techniques. The majority of the provisions of this Act were codified in amendments to the Securities Act.

Letter of Intent (LOI) — A nonbinding expression of intent that may include binding provisions that would otherwise be included in a separate agreement and that outlines the terms of a transaction to allow the parties to negotiate definitive documentation. Term Sheets are often used as alternatives to LOIs. A Memorandum of Understanding (MOU) is another form often used in cross-border transactions.

Liabilities — In the legal sense, a Liability is a legal responsibility for something, such as expenses or harm caused to another person. In the accounting sense, a Liability is an outstanding obligation to another party incurred as a result of a past transaction or event that must be settled through the transfer of cash, services, or other Assets. Examples of accounting Liabilities include accounts payable, accrued expenses, wages payable, and taxes payable. Liabilities can be short-term or long-term. Both definitions are related in that they involve something owed to another party, but it is important to distinguish them.

License — A License is granted to permit or authorize a party to use something owned by the grantor, or to engage in an activity. Licenses are tools commonly used to grant parties the right to use Intellectual Property for a specific use. Payments under Licenses are called Royalties. Licenses can be revocable or irrevocable, perpetual or limited, and worldwide or confined to a specific territory.

Limited Liability — The concept in which the shareholders of a Corporation, members of an LLC, or limited partners in a limited Partnership are personally liable for the actions and debts of the Corporation, LLC, or Partnership, only to the extent of the loss of the value of their investment. Limited liability is created by statute, and stems from the underlying principle that each of these Limited Liability entities involves a separation of ownership and management, such that it would be unjust to hold the owners liable for the actions of the entity.

Limited Liability Company (LLC) — A hybrid statutory entity that allows for corporation-like limited liability and partnership-like flow-through tax treatment. LLCs are a relatively new form but are popular, particularly among Start-Ups, due to the ease of formation and the flexibility in structuring Distributions and decision-making.

Liquidated Damages — Contractually specified amount of damages used where it would be difficult to ascertain the amount of actual damages incurred in the event of a breach of contract. Liquidated Damages must bear some reasonable relation to the loss to be enforceable.

Liquidity — The degree to which an asset can be converted into cash. Liquidity can also refer to a company's ability to meet its near-term payments.

Manager — The person or entity responsible for managing the affairs of a Limited Liability Company. A Manager may (but need not) also be a Member of the LLC and can be an individual or another entity. LLCs can have more than one Manager, or even a board of Managers.

Mark-Up — Edits or revisions to a document that are made visible (either by marking by hand or by using a track-changes, redlining, or editing feature in a word-processing program) to allow the other side to view the proposed changes.

Material Adverse Change (MAC) — The absence of a Material Adverse Change is a common Closing Condition. What constitutes a Material Adverse Change is typically negotiated between the parties. In general, a MAC is a negative change in the operating or financial condition of a target company that would have a material effect on the value of what is being acquired.

Member — An owner of a Limited Liability Company.

Membership Interest — The ownership interest held by a Member in a Limited Liability Company. Membership is expressed either in terms of a percentage of the whole, or as a number of Units. A Membership Interest has two components: economic (the right to receive Distributions) and voting. These can be separated in most jurisdictions.

Merger — See Direct Merger.

Minutes — The record of a meeting of the Board of Directors or Shareholders, including items discussed, decisions and approvals, and actions to be taken.

MOU — A Memorandum of Understanding. See Letter of Intent.

NDA/Nondisclosure Agreement — A generic name for an agreement by one party not to disclose information provided by a second party. In M&A deals, NDAs are typically signed prior to the commencement of Due Diligence, and often even before an LOI is negotiated. NDAs are also used in employment contexts, particularly in technology or other highly competitive industries. NDAs are also sometimes referred to as Confidentiality Agreements.

No-Assignment Clause — A provision in a contract that prohibits the Assignment of the contract. The provision can be drafted as an absolute prohibition or to require the prior written consent of the other party. An attempt to assign a contract in violation of this clause typically results in the assignment being void. A No-Assignment Clause can be used in conjunction with a Change of Control Clause to ensure the parties cannot circumvent the restriction on Assignment by structuring a transaction as a Merger or Stock Purchase, each of which does not technically require Assignment of contracts. In the case of a Merger, there is no assignment because the contractual obligations of the merged entity transfer by operation of law. In the case of a Stock Purchase, there is no assignment because the contracting party does not change, just the owners.

Noncompete/Noncompetition — A negative covenant restricting a party's right to engage in activities competitive with another business, typically used in Acquisitions to ensure the Seller does not sell the business and then undermine the value of the business by competing against it. Noncompetes can also be used in employment contexts. Most jurisdictions disfavor Noncompetes and, in some jurisdictions (for example, California), Noncompetes are unenforceable by statute, subject to limited exceptions.

Nonsolicitation — A corollary to a Noncompete, a Nonsolicitation clause restricts a party from soliciting the employees, customers, or vendors of a business to cease working for or doing business with that company. Key aspects to consider when drafting or negotiating a Nonsolicitation clause are: the duration of the restriction, what constitutes "solicitation," and who falls within the protected category. Nonsolicitation clauses are generally more enforceable than Noncompetes and can be effective protection, especially when used in conjunction with a Nondisclosure Agreement or clause.

Offering — The issuance of Securities (usually for the purpose of raising Capital).

Officers — The individuals appointed by the Board of Directors of a Corporation to manage the day-to-day operations of the Corporation. LLCs can also have Officers, appointed by the Members or Managers.

Operating Agreement — The document governing the rights and obligations of the Members of a Limited Liability Company.

Ordinary Shares — See Common Stock.

Parent Company — An entity that owns a controlling ownership interest in another entity, referred to as a Subsidiary (or, where the Parent Company owns all of the ownership interest, a wholly-owned Subsidiary).

Partner — An owner in a Partnership.

Partnership — An association of two or more people who carry on business, and the default entity type for a business involving more than one person. Partnerships are flow-through entities for tax purposes, and thus are not subject to entity-level taxation. Partnerships can be general partnerships, limited partnerships (LPs), or limited liability partnerships (LLPs). Each of these vary slightly in terms of Fiduciary Duties owed and the liability of the Partners for the acts of the Partnership and the other Partners. See Practice Area Overview.

Pass-Through Entity — See Flow-Through Entity.

Piercing the Corporate Veil — A legal theory under which courts put aside limited liability and holds a Corporation's shareholders or directors personally liable for the Corporation's actions or debts. See Practice Area Overview.

Preferred Return — A minimum threshold return on its investment that an investor (typically a limited partner) must receive before the general partner receives its Distribution (known as carried interest or "carry"). The Preferred Return is usually expressed as a percentage return per year. The concept applies in a similar way to holders of Preferred Stock.

Preferred Stock — Preferred Stock sits between Debt and Common Stock in the Capital structure of a Corporation, and is commonly issued to outside investors in order to raise Capital. Preferred Stock has priority over Common Stock in a liquidation, either up to the amount of the initial investment (a "1x preference"), or a negotiated multiple of that amount (for example, a "2x preference"), and generally receives a fixed dividend (the equivalent of the interest paid on debt). Preferred Stock may also have certain negotiated voting or veto rights, as well as the right to appoint a director or observer to the Board of Directors. Preferred Stock can be participating (once it has received its preference, it shares in the remaining Distributions with Common Stock), or nonparticipating. Preferred Stock is convertible into Common Stock, either at the option of the holder or automatically upon certain trigger events. Outside of the United States, the terms Preferred Shares or Preference Shares are used.

Private Placement — An offering of securities that does not involve any public offering and hence falls within the Securities Act §4(a)(2) exemption from Section 5 Registration. In general, the hallmark of a private placement is the absence of general solicitation or advertising and a limited number of offerees. See Practice Area Overview.

Public Reporting Company — This term generally refers to issuers of securities subject to the periodic reporting requirements of the Exchange Act. Also referred to as public company.

Publicly Traded Company — A company whose stock is traded on a public exchange (NYSE, NAS-DAQ, etc.). Used synonymously with Public Reporting Company, but not all Public Reporting Companies are Publicly Traded.

Redline — See Mark-Up.

Regulation D — A regulation under the Securities Act that creates a series of safe-harbors for issuers seeking to rely on the Securities Act §4(a)(2) private placement exemption or the limited offering exemption.

Restrictive Covenants — Covenants—or agreements—to not do something. For example, a Non-compete is a restrictive covenant pursuant to which the party subject to the covenant agrees not to compete for a defined period.

Reverse Triangular Merger — A merger pursuant to which the Buyer forms a Subsidiary and merges the Subsidiary with and into the Target company.

Royalty — A payment owed under a License.

Safe-Harbor — A statutory provision specifying conduct that, if complied with, will be deemed not to violate a given rule.

Sarbanes-Oxley Act of 2002 — Federal legislation enacted in the wake of the Enron scandal comprised of a set of rules applicable to Public Reporting Companies (and some nonreporting companies) and their officers and directors, including additional disclosure, internal controls, and certification requirements.

Schedules — Attachments to an agreement referenced in the agreement. Typically, these contain additional information that is too bulky to be included in the agreement itself, such as lists of Assets, exclusions to representations and warranties, required disclosures, or inventory being acquired.

Section 5 Registration — The basic registration requirement for any offering of Securities in the United States. The disclosure document that must be filed with the SEC pursuant to Section 5 is called a registration statement (which consists of a prospectus and certain supplemental information). Different variations exist depending on the status of the issuer and the type of Offering.

Securities — Broadly defined, a Security is an investment of money made with the expectation of profits from the efforts of others and that can be traded for value (barring certain restrictions on transfer). The most recognized form of Security is Stock. Section 2(a)(1) of the Securities Act provides a nonexclusive laundry list of other forms of Securities.

Securities Act — The U.S. Securities Act of 1933, as amended, regulates the offer, sale, and registration of Securities to the public, with the goal of promoting full public disclosure and protecting the investing public against fraudulent and manipulative practices.

Securities Exchange Act — The U.S. Securities Exchange Act of 1934, as amended, was promulgated to regulate secondary trading in Securities, including regulation of Broker-Dealers, securities exchanges, and reporting obligations of Publicly Traded Companies. It also encompasses regulations regarding the solicitation of proxies, Tender Offers, and insider trading. The Securities Act and the Securities Exchange Act, and the rules and regulations promulgated under each of these, constitute the backbone of U.S. federal securities laws.

Securities Exchange Commission (SEC) — A U.S. government agency that oversees securities transactions, Capital Markets, and financial market intermediaries. Among other things, the SEC has rulemaking and enforcement powers with respect to the Securities Act and the Exchange Act.

Seller — The person or entity transferring Assets or ownership interests. In an Asset Purchase, the Seller is typically the Target Company. In a Stock Purchase, the Seller(s) are the individual Stockholders in the Target Company.

Shareholder — The holder of Shares of Stock of a Corporation, and as such, the owners of the Corporation. Also referred to as a Stockholder in certain jurisdictions.

Shares — A unit in the Stock of a Corporation. Shares are a form of Security.

Short-Form Merger — A Merger between a company and its majority equity holder (typically its Parent) that, by statute, does not require a vote of stockholders. For a Delaware corporation, subject to compliance with certain other statutory requirements, this can be accomplished so long as a majority Stockholder owns at least 90 percent or, in some instances, following a negotiated Tender Offer.

Spinoff — The creation of an independent company through the sale or distribution of new Shares of Stock of an existing business line or division of a parent company. A spinoff is a type of divestiture, typically when a company wants to streamline its operations or to sell off a portion of its business.

Start-Up — A newly formed company, usually in need of initial Capitalization.

Stepped-Up Tax Basis — A tax term referencing the readjustment of the value of an appreciated Asset for tax purposes upon purchase, determined to be the market value of the Asset at the time of purchase.

Stock — A type of corporate Security divided into Shares that allows a Corporation to raise Capital and gives the holder the potential to share in the Corporation's profits by way of dividends as well as the right to elect directors of the corporation and to vote on matters that will fundamentally change the structure or nature of the corporation.

Stock Purchases — The acquisition of Shares of Stock of a Target Company (or the acquisition of Shares pursuant to an original issuance).

Stockholder — See Shareholder.

Subsidiary — A company whose voting stock is more than 50 percent controlled by another company, usually referred to as the Parent Company or holding company. For the purposes of Liability, taxation, and regulation, Subsidiaries are distinct legal entities.

Successor Liability — An equitable common law doctrine (with some statutory law) that deems a purchaser to have assumed liabilities of a Target Company in certain circumstances.

Target Company — The company being acquired or holding the Assets that are being acquired. In a Merger, the Target Company is the entity that is being merged out of existence.

Tender Offer — A unilateral offer by a Buyer to purchase a Target Company's Securities directly from the owners of those Securities, usually for all cash. Tender offers are subject to regulation under the Williams Act (codified at Sections 14(d) and (e) of the Exchange Act). There is no bright-line test for what constitutes a tender offer; rather, the courts look at a variety of factors.

Term Sheet — A nonbinding agreement in bullet point or tabular form setting forth the basic terms and conditions under which a transaction will be structured. A term sheet serves as a template to develop more detailed legal documents. See also Letter of Intent.

Underwriter — The investment bank that buys Securities in the initial purchase from the issuer and then immediately resells them to the public in a public offering.

Valuation — The process of determining the current worth of a Security, other Asset, or a company, often to determine the price per Share in an Offering.

Vesting — A technique commonly used in relation to stock options or Founders' Stock to incentivize the holders to remain with the company, whereby the rights to exercise the options or to own the Stock are released over time.

APPENDIX A

....

Practice Area Overview

This section provides a brief "primer" on some of the practice areas and topics referenced in this text and that you will likely encounter in practice. It is not intended as a comprehensive study. Instead, the goals are to:

- expose you to the terminology, concepts, and basic construct, as well as a big picture view of the breadth and scope of transactional practice;
- provide you with a concrete practice-area context in which to consider the various concepts discussed throughout the text;
- get you thinking about practice areas you may want to explore in greater depth; and
- provide helpful background for the simulation exercises.

Mergers & Acquisitions (M&A)

M&A Defined

M&A is a broad practice area that involves the buying, selling, and combining of assets or ownership of companies. Mergers involve two companies combining into one. Acquisitions typically involve a larger company purchasing a smaller company, or a subsidiary, division, or assets of another company.

> **Key Terminology:**
>
> The entity acquiring the assets or ownership is referred to as the **acquiror** or **buyer**. The entity whose assets or ownership are being acquired is the **seller** or **target**. In a merger, the resulting company is referred to as the **surviving entity**. In a hostile takeover, the entity seeking to acquire the target company's shares is known as the **bidder** or **shark**.

How an M&A deal is structured, and the lawyer's role, will depend on a variety of factors, including the nature and identity of the parties, the business expectations, and the underlying motivation (i.e., what is driving the transaction). For example:

- Does the transaction involve private or public companies?
- Are you representing a strategic buyer looking to expand its existing business, or a financial buyer looking to make an investment, such as a venture capital group?
- Is the transaction friendly (negotiated), or hostile (such as a tender offer)?
- Is the transaction being driven by corporate efficiencies, the need to acquire technology or other specific assets, tax advantages, globalization, or other reasons?

You should have an idea of the answers to each of these before you begin drafting or negotiating any documents.

Structuring an M&A Transaction

Asset purchases, stock purchases, mergers, tender offers, and hostile takeovers are some of the more common forms of M&A. Others you might encounter include consolidations, leveraged buy-outs, spin-offs, and partnership or membership interest purchases.

223

Friendly (Negotiated) Transactions. The three basic structural alternatives for a negotiated M&A deal are summarized below:

Structure	Who is the seller?	What is acquired?	Consequences?
Asset Purchase	Target company	Individual specified assets and liabilities	Target remains its own legal entity. Any assets not specifically acquired remain with target
Stock Purchase	Individual shareholder(s)/ parent company	Ownership interest in target company (e.g., shares, LLC interests)	No change in ownership of assets; buyer acquires assets indirectly; seller becomes subsidiary of buyer
Merger	Shareholders of Target (and in some cases of buyer[1])	Entire assets and liabilities of target are subsumed into merged entity	Assets are consolidated by operation of law, either into surviving entity or into a newly created entity. In either case, target is "merged out" of existence

Several sub-species of mergers exist:

- **Forward Triangular Merger**—the acquirer forms a wholly owned subsidiary and the target company is merged into that subsidiary, forming a "triangle" between the acquirer, its subsidiary, and the target.
- **Reverse Triangular Merger**—here, the forward triangular merger operates in reverse. The acquirer forms a subsidiary but then merges that subsidiary into the target.
- **Short-form Merger**—available in most states for mergers between a parent and a subsidiary, allowing for streamlined shareholder approval.

Hostile Takeovers. Hostile takeovers refer to when the acquirer negotiates (often against the target company's wishes) directly with the target company's shareholders to purchase their shares, or to solicit proxies (a proxy is the right to vote a shareholder's shares).

By obtaining shares or proxies from the requisite number of shareholders, the bidder obtains sufficient voting power to control decisions of the shareholders, such as which directors to appoint to the board, or whether to vote to approve a proposed merger or other corporate action. Once the bidder is able to control the board through the appointment of directors friendly to its goals, it can proceed to obtain appropriate board approval that may otherwise not have been forthcoming.

Hostile takeovers can be achieved in several different ways, including combining one or more of the following approaches:

---

1. For example, where the consideration consists of shares of stock of the acquiror, the buyer is "selling" or "exchanging" its shares for the shares or assets of the target company.

Approach	Steps Involved	Consequences
Bear Hug	Bidder notifies the target by letter of its interest in acquiring target and its willingness to pursue a hostile bid.	Target company can either agree to negotiate or refuse the offer, in which case the bidder will proceed with one of the approaches below.
Tender Offer	Bidder offers to buy all or substantially all of the publicly held shares of target from target's shareholders at a specified price.	May not acquire 100%, although typically conditioned on acquiring percentage of the shares sufficient to control election of the board of directors and/or shareholder approval of a subsequent acquisition or merger (see below). Target may employ defensive strategies to attempt to block.
Two-Step Merger	The bidder starts with a tender offer (Step 1). Bidder then causes the target company to approve a short-form merger to complete acquisition of all the shares (Step 2).	Bidder ends up owning 100% of the shares of target.
Consent Solicitation/ Proxy Fight	Bidder seeks to effect a change by obtaining support from the requisite number of target's shareholders needed to vote to elect board members or other change.	Once accomplished, bidder advances its acquisition offer to the new board.

M&A Deal Process

Typical steps in a negotiated M&A transaction include:

1. Initial Negotiations:
   - Confidentiality agreement
   - Standstill agreement
   - No shop agreement
   - Letter of intent
2. Due diligence
3. Drafting and negotiating the acquisition or merger agreement and ancillary documents
4. Obtaining board approval and signing definitive agreement
5. Obtaining shareholder approval
6. Obtaining any regulatory approval and third-party consents
7. Closing
8. Making any filings (e.g., the articles of merger), transferring operations, and ensuring performance of any post-closing obligations

In a hostile takeover, typical steps include:

1. Bear hug or commencement of tender offer/proxy solicitation
2. Defensive strategies by target company
3. Individual shareholders decide whether to sell their shares
4. Second step merger if needed (which will include Steps 3–8 above).

Role of the Transactional Lawyer in M&A

An M&A lawyer acts as a quarterback, overseeing the various aspects involved in consummating an M&A deal, including:

- Advising and counseling client on appropriate structure (including the legal and practical consequences of each structure)
- Drafting and negotiating any preliminary documents, such as LOI and NDA
- Preparing and managing the closing checklist
- Conducting and reporting on due diligence
- Drafting and negotiating the acquisition or merger agreement
- Determining, drafting, and negotiating necessary ancillary documents: assignment and assumption agreements; third-party consents; bills of sale, etc.
- Coordinating input from subject-matter experts
- Preparing internal office memos on relevant legal issues
- Ensuring compliance with corporate, securities, antitrust, and other laws and regulations
- Preparing any necessary regulatory filings and communicating with relevant regulatory bodies

Relevant Laws

M&A is not a discrete body of law. Rather, it includes the interplay of:

- Corporate law: requisite corporate formalities for approving the transaction
- Securities law: implicated any time shares or other securities are being acquired or form part of the consideration,[2] as well as potential compliance issues for publicly traded companies
- Contract law: documentation should properly reflect the intent of the parties and be legally enforceable in the relevant jurisdiction(s)
- Tax law: potential tax advantages—and minimizing adverse tax consequences—are often a key determinant in structuring an M&A deal
- Antitrust law: implicated in deals that meet certain thresholds (including the pre-merger notification filing required under Hart-Scott-Rodino (HSR))
- Employment law: how employees and employee benefits will be handled, as well as any potential regulatory constraints

---

2. Parties often overlook the need to comply with securities laws on the buyer's side if shares or other securities of the buyer are being used as part of the consideration.

- Regulatory law:
  - Industry-specific regulations: the parties may be subject to specific disclosure or consent requirements if their business activities are governed by a regulatory agency
  - Regulations on foreign investment: where one of the parties to an M&A transaction is outside of the United States, this can trigger additional regulatory requirements such as CFIUS regulations[3]
  - Foreign regulations: cross-border transactions will need to comply with the regulatory requirements of all relevant jurisdictions. For example, a merger with a French company would be subject to the EU Merger Regulations in addition to U.S. antitrust laws

Key Takeaways

Following are key points to keep in mind when approaching an M&A transaction:

- **Both federal and state laws are relevant.** You may also need to comply with the laws of more than one state. For example, in a merger between a Delaware corporation and a California corporation, you will need to determine corporate governance and filing requirements under both Delaware and California law, and comply with applicable federal, Delaware, and California securities, employment, tax, and other laws.

- **Each structure has specific legal and practical consequences.** For example, what happens to the liabilities of the target company following consummation of an acquisition or merger? What approvals or consents are needed? What are the tax consequences? It depends which structure is used and what the documents say. The lawyer's role is to make sure the client understands the legal and practical significance of the selected structure and that the documentation reflects the parties' expectations and intent.

- **Deals involving public companies are subject to specific disclosure and other rules.** These need to be factored into the deal process. For example, at what point does the transaction need to be announced to the public? When and how do shareholders need to be given notice of the proposed transaction? Is the transaction subject to the tender offer rules?

- **A good closing checklist is critical to ensuring all documents and actions are completed.** An M&A deal involves many moving parts. A comprehensive closing checklist can help keep track of each piece and keep the deal on schedule.

---

3. CFIUS is the Committee on Foreign Investment in the United States, a multi-agency government body chaired by the Secretary of the Treasury that reviews foreign investment for national security considerations. The mandate of CFIUS was recently strengthened by FIRRMA (Foreign Investment Risk Review Modernization Act of 2018) signed into law in August 2018.

Corporate Governance

Corporate Governance Defined

Corporate governance relates to the formalities entities must adhere to in connection with their formation, operation, transferring of ownership or assets, and dissolution. Although it uses the term "corporate," corporate governance applies in the generic sense to any entity type. Each entity type has its own set and degree of formalities and statutory requirements, predominantly governed by the state in which the entity is formed.

> **Key Terminology:**
>
> To appreciate the importance of corporate governance, you need to understand the concepts of **limited liability** and **fiduciary duty**. Limited liability refers to the liability of the entity's owners and requires sufficient separation between the company's ownership and management. The owners of a company who enjoy limited liability are only liable to the extent of their investment in that company (referred to as their capital contribution). In certain circumstances, such as the failure to adhere to applicable corporate formalities, the limited liability shield can be **pierced**, exposing the owners to full liability.
>
> The separation of ownership and management that justifies this limited liability also requires that the directors of the company be accountable to the owners. This concept is referred to as **fiduciary duty**. There are two fiduciary duties owed: the **duty of care** and the **duty of loyalty**. A **covenant of good faith and fair dealing** is also recognized in most states.

Corporate Formalities

The consequences for failing to adhere to the applicable formalities can vary. Some of the more significant consequences include:

- *Inability to enforce contracts with third parties.* This can result, for example, if an entity was not properly formed at the time it entered into the contract, or if the contract was not properly authorized.
- *Piercing of the corporate veil.* This doctrine can expose shareholders of corpora-

tions to liability for the debts of the corporation if corporate formalities are not observed, including failure to adequately capitalize the company.[4]

- *Fines and penalties.* These can be imposed by the relevant jurisdiction's corporate and/or tax regulator.
- *Liability for breach of fiduciary duty.* A corporation's officers, directors, and controlling shareholders owe varying degrees of fiduciary duty to the corporation, depending on the jurisdiction in which it is formed and the corporation's governing documents. Similar fiduciary duties apply to managers and members of LLCs and general partners in a partnership.

Entity Types

The three forms of entity used in the United States that offer limited liability are corporations, limited liability companies (LLCs), and limited partnerships. Partners in a general partnership (and the general partner of a limited partnership) do not enjoy limited liability protection.

The separation of ownership and management is structured as follows for each of the three main entity types offering limited liability:

	Corporation	LLC	Limited Partnership
Management:	Directors Officers	Manager(s)/Board of Managers [Officers]	General Partner
Owners:	Shareholders	Members	Limited Partners

Formation and Governing Documents

The different formation formalities and principal governing documents for the various entity types are summarized below. Note which documents typically are required to be filed with the Secretary of State, and which are contractual agreements between the parties:

Document	Purpose/ Key Elements	Filed with State?
CORPORATIONS:		
Charter[5]	Brings corporation into existence Referred to as Certificate or Articles of Incorporation Most jurisdictions require minimum mandatory information	✓
Statement of Information	Most jurisdictions require initial and annual or biannual filing Typically contain names of officers, directors, and agent for service	✓

---

4. Adequate capitalization refers to the requirement that the founders of a company contribute and maintain sufficient funds in the company to ensure the company has the ability to pay its liabilities when due.

5. The Secretary of State's website will often contain templates for use, as well as links to the relevant statutory provisions governing mandatory and optional provisions. *See, e.g.,* https://corpfiles.delaware.gov/incstk09.pdf; http://bpd.cdn.sos.ca.gov /corp/pdf/articles/arts-gs.pdf

By-laws	Establish procedures for:
	Shareholders: procedures for noticing and conducting meetings; rules for voting; quorum; procedures for action by written consent
	Directors: size of board; elections and meetings; quorum; action by written consent; committees and delegation of authority
	Officers: basic positions and authority; appointment procedures
Action of Sole Incorporator	Appoints the initial directors and adopts the by-laws. This relieves the initial incorporator of any ongoing fiduciary duties
Initial Meeting of Board	Typically handled by unanimous written consent
	Initial actions including ratifying the by-laws, appointing initial officers, issuance of initial stock to founding shareholders, approving any stock option plan, opening a bank account, etc.
	Statutory requirement in some jurisdictions (e.g., Del. Gen. Corp. L. §108)

LIMITED LIABILITY COMPANIES:

Articles of Organization[6]	Brings LLC into existence	✓
	Simple form in most jurisdictions	
Statement of Information	Most jurisdictions require	✓
	Frequency can vary but often biannual	
Operating Agreement	Governs the ownership, management, and distributions of profits of the LLC	
	Combines the charter and by-laws of a corporation	
	Optional in some jurisdictions; others may allow for oral agreement	
Initial Meeting of Managers/ Members	Not required but common — tracks the initial meeting of a corporation	

PARTNERSHIPS:

Certificate of Limited Partnership	Some jurisdictions, such as Delaware, require a certificate to be filed for a limited partnership to come into existence	✓
	General partnerships do not typically require any formal filing and are formed by default when two or more persons engage in a business	
Fictitious Name Statement	Required if the partnership's name is other than the last names of the partners and the jurisdiction does not require a certificate	✓
Partnership Agreement	Depending on the jurisdiction, may be mandatory and/or required to be in writing	
	Governs all aspects of the ownership, management, and distribution of profits	

6. As with corporations, templates are typically available on the relevant Secretary of State's website. *See, e.g.*, ca.gov /corp/pdf/articles/arts-gs.pdf

ALL ENTITY TYPES:

Name reservation	Recommended to ensure that the desired name is available to avoid having the initial filing rejected	✓
Qualification to Do Business	Needed in any jurisdiction in which the entity does business *other* than its state of organization	✓
EIN Application	Filed with the IRS and necessary in order to open a bank account, hire employees, and to establish the separate identity of the entity	✓

Ongoing Management and Governance

Decision-making:

- Day-to-day operations typically managed by the officers, managers, or general partner
- Fundamental decisions require approval of the board of directors and shareholders (or managers and members in an LLC or the limited partners in a limited partnership)
- Shareholders, members, and limited partners generally have only certain prescribed rights to interfere in the management and operation of the company
- In LLCs, decision-making responsibility depends on whether the LLC is formed as a manager-managed or member-managed LLC. In a manager-managed LLC, the day-to-day operations of the LLC are left to one or more managers, who may or may not be members

Voting:

- Typical default vote required to approve any action of the board of directors or shareholders (or the corollary manager, member, or limited partner vote) is a majority of the ownership interests entitled to vote (i.e., >50%)
- A quorum is typically required in order for a vote to be valid. Most states set default quorum requirements

Documenting Decision-making:

- Depending on the statutory requirements and the governing documents, voting will occur either at a meeting or by written consent
- Meetings of the board of directors (or managers of an LLC) and shareholders (or members or limited partners) should be documented by preparing detailed minutes of the meeting (or written consent)
- All minutes and written consents, together with any notices and waivers, should be included in the company's minute books
- Proper documentation of decision-making can be critical for demonstrating compliance with fiduciary duties

Role of the Transactional Lawyer in Advising Clients on Corporate Governance Matters

A corporate lawyer advising companies on any matter, whether initial formation, raising capital, or an M&A transaction, needs to be familiar, and ensure compliance, with applicable corporate governance.

Examples of how corporate governance is relevant include:

Sample matter	Key corporate formalities to be observed	Potential consequence(s) if not observed
Entering into an exclusive supply contract	Depending on size of deal, may need board approval: • Comply with voting, notice, and meeting requirements per the charter/by-laws • Draft necessary board resolutions approving the transaction	• Could be unenforceable • Could give rise to a breach of contract claim if there is also a representation that the parties are duly authorized
Hiring an accountant	Charter or by-laws may mandate process: • Comply with charter/by-law requirements May trigger fiduciary duty concerns, especially if accountant is a related party to any director • Ensure decision and documentation consistent with fiduciary duties of due care and loyalty	• Accountant may not have proper authority to act • If issues arise due to accountant's actions, shareholders may have cause of action • Officer and director liability for breach of fiduciary duty (especially if there is a conflict of interest)
Entering into a merger agreement	Most states require both board and shareholder consent, as well as specific notice periods: • Comply with voting, notice, and meeting requirements to obtain proper board and shareholder consent • Draft necessary resolutions Shareholders may be entitled to appraisal/dissenters' rights: • Comply with statutory requirements Various potential fiduciary duty concerns: • Ensure decision and documentation consistent with fiduciary duties of due care and loyalty • Observe any relevant case law governing fiduciary duties in M&A (e.g., Revlon duties)	• Potentially unenforceable • Breach of contract • Shareholder cause of action
Issuing shares of stock, membership interests, or other equity	Typically requires board and possibly shareholder approval • Confirm any specific requirements in charter/by-laws and prepare appropriate documentation Corporations must have authorized sufficient shares for each class: • Ensure sufficient number and type of equity authorized in the charter or other applicable organizational document • If not sufficient, prepare charter amendment and obtain necessary board/shareholder approval to amend	• Potential rescission remedy • Breach of fiduciary duty

Relevant Laws

Corporate governance is determined by state law and entity type. Each state will have its own statutory requirements governing the relevant entity type. For example, in Delaware, the relevant code provisions are:

- Corporations: Delaware General Corporations Law.[7]
- Limited Liability Companies: Delaware Limited Liability Company Act.[8]
- Partnerships: Delaware Revised Uniform Partnership Act and the Delaware Revised Uniform Limited Partnership Act.[9]

Case law can also be relevant in certain circumstances, especially in determining how to apply standards.

Key Takeaways

Following are key points to keep in mind when advising a client on formation or corporate governance matters in general:

- *Know your jurisdiction: internal affairs doctrine applies.* The laws of the state in which you incorporate or form the entity will govern formation and ongoing corporate governance. Thus, it is important to be familiar with that state's requirements for formation, as well as any provisions that will apply to ongoing governance. For example, does your state of formation require a written operating agreement for an LLC? Are there annual statement of information filing requirements? Being familiar with the statutory defaults helps ensure you include any required opt-outs into the company's organizational documents.

- *Choice of entity and jurisdiction are important to discuss with the client.* Different entity types offer diverse advantages and disadvantages, ranging from tax treatment to ease of transferability of ownership and cost of formation. These advantages and disadvantages should be weighed against the client's concerns and goals. For example, if the client is most concerned with minimizing taxes, an LLC or partnership (which do not have entity-level taxation) may be the best fit. But if the client is also concerned with having a clear delineation between shareholders and management, a corporation may be the best choice.

  In addition, different jurisdictions take different approaches to corporate governance. For example, in Delaware, the fiduciary duty of care for directors can be waived completely; in California, it can be waived only in certain circumstances.

- *It matters where the company does business.* A company does not necessarily need to be formed in the state in which it operates (or in which its primary business operations are located). However, to the extent it has operations in states other than the state of incorporation, it may need to: (i) qualify to do business in those other states (typically a form that must be filed with the Secretary of State), and (ii) comply with the corporate governance requirements of the other states.[10] Make sure you ascertain from your client where they will be doing business and survey the relevant state statute(s).

---

7. Del. Code Ann. Tit. 8 § 1-101 *et seq.*

8. Del. Code Ann. Tit. 6 § 18-101 *et seq.*

9. Del. Code Ann. Tit. 6 § 15-101 *et seq.* and § 17-101 *et seq.*

10. For example, California's long-arm statute, Cal. Corp. Code. §2115, imposes on non-California corporations portions of California's corporations laws if the corporation is privately held, more than fifty percent of its shareholders are resident in California, and on average more than fifty percent of its payroll, property, and sales are in or derived from California.

Capital Markets

Capital Markets Defined

Capital markets practice encapsulates any transaction involving the purchase or sale of securities, including original issuances and resales of securities. Capital markets is somewhat synonymous with securities law, and these two practice areas can often be conflated within a firm. It also overlaps with M&A to some degree.

What differentiates capital markets as a separate practice area is its focus on securities *as a means of raising money* ("capital"). Capital markets refers to the marketplaces in which this occurs; that is, where securities are traded for their value. These markets can be public, private, primary, or secondary. Stock exchanges are part of the public market.

Although M&A practice also often involves the buying and selling of securities (such as in a stock purchase or where the consideration for a transaction consists of securities of the buyer), in an M&A transaction, the securities are merely the *currency* for buying and selling businesses.

In securities law, the focus is more on *the regulatory aspect* of securities; however, a capital markets lawyer must have a firm understanding of securities laws to be able to advise a client on a capital market transaction, and the two areas are inexorably intertwined.

> ### Key Terminology:
>
> Capital markets transactions typically have three types of players: the **issuer** (the company seeking to raise capital by issuing new securities), the **investors** or **purchasers** who will be acquiring the securities, and banks or investment banks that facilitate the sale of securities, known as **underwriters, broker-dealers**, or **placement agents**. Where professional investors are investing a significant amount in a start-up or young company, the capital raised is **venture capital**. Often, these venture capital investors (known colloquially as VCs) will pool together the funds needed to invest in a **venture capital fund**.
>
> Once an investor or purchaser acquires securities, she becomes a **security holder**. When security holders seek to resell securities they have purchased, this is referred to as a **secondary market transaction**. The sale of new securities by an issuer is referred to as an **issuance** or an **offering** of securities and is conducted on the **primary market**. Primary and secondary markets can be **public** or **private**.

Components of a Capital Markets Transaction

The main components of any capital markets transaction are:

- Determining the market on which the securities will be issued or sold (public, private, primary, secondary)
- Structuring the transaction
- Identifying and complying with relevant securities regulations
- Performing due diligence
- Drafting and reviewing disclosure documents
- Drafting and negotiating the purchase agreement (the form can vary depending on structure)

Core Underlying Securities Law Premises

To fully understand capital markets and how they function, keep in mind the following core premises of U.S. securities law:

1. Any time a security is offered or sold, the issuer or selling security holder must either register the offering or find an exemption from registration.
2. A "security" includes: (a) any instrument commonly known as securities (such as stocks and bonds), (b) interests or instruments expressly defined as securities by statute (such as oil and gas interests), and (c) any "investment contract" (a contract where an investor invests money or other consideration in a common enterprise with the expectation of a profit from the significant efforts of others, including, in some cases, LLC interests).

These two premises govern when a transaction constitutes a capital markets transaction, how it is structured, and the relevant securities laws that will apply.

Common Forms of Capital Markets Transactions

Following is some of the more common nomenclature used to categorize capital markets transactions. Some are described in terms of the relevant securities law exemption, while others are more generic. Thus, some overlap exists. The key is to recognize the type of transaction and where it falls in the securities law spectrum.

- *Public Offerings.* From a capital markets standpoint, a public offering is one that is conducted using an underwriter, investment banker, or broker-dealer to either generate a public market for the securities or to sell securities to the public. The quintessential public offering is an initial public offering (IPO). Public offerings must be registered with the SEC (see Premise #1 above).
- *Private Placements.* This broadly refers to offerings by issuers in which securities are bought and sold in a privately negotiated transaction (as opposed to being sold on the open market to the public). Typically, private placements are exempt from registration.[11]

---

11. Private placements are often referred to as Section 4(a)(2) offerings, after the Securities Act provision that creates a statutory exemption for non-public offerings. However, much of the guidance on complying with this exemption has been developed through common law.

- *Reg D Offering.* An offering of securities relying on a statutory safe-harbor from registration known as Regulation D.[12] Regulation D is comprised of three separate exemptions, each with its own set of requirements. The most common is Rule 506(b), which is known as the private placement safe-harbor. It essentially codifies the common law that has evolved around the private placement exemption described above. Other exemptions include Rule 504, which provides an exemption for "limited offerings," and Rule 506(c), which provides an exemption where the offering is limited to "accredited investors."[13]

- *Equity Financing.* This is a broad category that encompasses any offering, public or private, that involves the sale of equity securities. Typically, equity financing refers to the issuance of equity by an issuer to raise capital. Types of equity securities that can be offered include common stock, preferred stock, and securities convertible into equity, such as warrants and options. Most equity financings are private placements.

- *Debt Financing.* Debt financing refers to offerings that involve the sale of debt securities to raise capital, such as secured or unsecured notes, syndicated loans, and convertible notes (convertible into equity upon certain events). Not all debt financings are offerings of securities.

- *Initial Capitalization/Founders' Stock.* When a corporation, LLC, or partnership is formed, the initial ownership interests are granted to the founders in exchange for value, such as an initial cash contribution or services. In most cases, the issuance of these initial interests is considered an issuance of securities; thus Premise #1 above applies.

- *Series Seed Financing.* A series seed financing is a round of equity financing (or, in some cases, convertible debt) conducted at a relatively early stage in a company's development. Typically, series seed investors receive preferred stock. Sometimes, a seed round may be preceded by a "friends and family" round (where the founders of the company receive money from close friends and family). In other instances, the series seed round will be the first round of financing. The funds raised in a series seed financing are referred to as seed capital and are used to fund start-up expenses. Series seed financings range from $500,000 to $5,000,000. Series seed investors are sometimes referred to as "angel investors."

- *Preferred Stock Financing.* A preferred stock financing typically follows a series seed round. A company may conduct several preferred stock rounds. Each round involves the issuance of a new "series" of preferred stock (or, in some cases, convertible notes). The price per share in these rounds is negotiated based on the company's "pre-money valuation": the higher the valuation, the fewer shares that need to be issued for the same amount of investment, and the less dilution of existing shareholders. Investors in a preferred stock financing typically negotiate certain preferences and other rights, such as the right to nominate a member of the board of directors, to receive a preferred return on their investment, to approve certain major decisions, and to receive periodic financial information.

- *Venture Capital Financing.* This encompasses Series Seed and Preferred Stock financings. The term venture capital financing tends to be used when the investment comes from a fund with pooled money, as opposed to individual investors investing their own funds. Accordingly, it tends to signify a more institutional-type investment round. Venture capital investors will invest in companies only when they expect to receive a certain minimum return on their investment (known as an IRR), and when they have a clear exit strategy, such as a sale of the company or an IPO.

---

12. 17 C.F.R. . §230.500 *et seq.*

13. Accredited investors refer to investors who meet certain minimum criteria such that they are deemed to need less protection under the securities laws. 17 C.F.R. §230.501.

- *Private Equity.* Private equity transactions involve investments by pooled funds that seek to acquire 100 percent ownership or majority interest in the companies in which they invest. As a result, the private equity fund is in total control of the company after the investment. A private equity fund is managed by an investment manager. Private equity is often its own practice area within a larger firm.

- *Institutional Offerings.* These are offerings of securities to large, institutional investors, known as "qualified institutional buyers" or "QIBs." Types of QIBs include banks, pension funds, insurance companies, and large hedge and mutual funds.

- *Private Resales/Secondary Market Transactions.* Resales are sales of securities by existing security holders. Private resales relate to resales of securities that were originally sold in reliance on an exemption from registration, and therefore cannot be freely traded. Secondary market transactions include these private resales, as well as resales of publicly traded securities.

- *Rule 144 Resales.* Rule 144 is a statutory safe-harbor allowing security holders to resell restricted securities (e.g., securities that have not been registered) publicly, without the need for registration. Rule 144 imposes minimum holding and certain other requirements. Rule 144 is commonly used as a means of reselling shares of privately held but well-known companies.

- *Crowdfunding.* A relatively new form of capital markets transaction, crowdfunding relies on a specific exemption to bridge the gap between a public offering and a private placement, allowing issuers to raise up to $1 million in a 12-month period using a financial intermediary.[14]

- *Other.* Many other types of transactions exist. Terminology you might encounter includes PIPEs (private investment in public equity), cross-border financing, high-yield debt financings, bridge financings, convertible notes, derivatives, mezzanine financing, and stock exchange listing.

Each of these transactions will require compliance with either the registration requirements or an applicable exemption from registration under U.S. federal and relevant state securities laws, as well as any applicable securities laws in other countries.

Role of the Transactional Lawyer in Capital Markets

The lawyer's role will depend on whether the lawyer is serving as the issuer's, underwriter's, or, in private transactions, investor's counsel, and whether the transaction is private or public.

---

14. Securities Act Section 4(a)(6), 17 C.F.R. Part 227. Regulation A+, created pursuant to the Jumpstart our Businesses Act of 2012, also offers a form of limited public offering.

Client/Type of Offering	Private Placement	Public Offering
Representing the Issuer, you may be involved in:	• Advising and counseling client on available securities law exemptions • Drafting and negotiating any preliminary documents, such as an LOI or term sheet • Preparing and managing the closing checklist • Conducting and reporting on due diligence (to confirm accuracy of disclosures) • Drafting any private placement memorandum or similar disclosures • Drafting and negotiating the purchase agreement • Determining, drafting, and negotiating necessary ancillary documents • Ensuring compliance with securities laws • Determining any tax, employment law, regulatory, or other considerations • Preparing any necessary securities law filings	• Corporate governance clean-up • Preparing necessary board approval • Advising on engagement of underwriter • Conducting and reporting on due diligence • Drafting the preliminary registration statement • Overseeing the printing of the preliminary registration statement • Ensuring company complies with restrictions on offering and sales during the "quiet period" (the time between filing and effectiveness of the registration statement) • Reviewing and responding to SEC comments • Filing any amendments to the registration statement • Preparing necessary paperwork for listing on national exchange • Establishing corporate governance procedures • Preparing ongoing periodic and annual reporting • Advising on securities law compliance
Representing the Underwriter (public offering) or Broker-Dealer:	• Draft and negotiate the agent agreement with the issuer • Assist in drafting the private placement memorandum • Prepare any permitted marketing materials • Advise on securities law compliance • Advise on any broker-dealer regulatory requirements	• Draft and negotiate the representation agreement and any firm commitment letter • Commenting and assisting in the drafting of the registration statement, particularly in connection with the marketing aspects • Preparing and advising on the conduct of the road show (where the investment bank starts to market the offering) • Advising on securities laws • Closely coordinating with issuer's counsel throughout the process
Representing the Investor:	• Prepare and negotiate the term sheet • Conduct and report on due diligence • Draft and negotiate the purchase agreement • Determine, draft, and negotiate necessary ancillary documents • Determine any tax or other considerations	• Not generally applicable

Relevant Laws

The starting point for any capital markets transaction is with applicable securities laws, including:

- Securities Act of 1933
- Securities Exchange Act of 1934
- Securities Act and Exchange Act rules
- State securities laws (referred to as "Blue Sky" laws)
- Sarbanes-Oxley Act of 2002
- Dodd-Frank Wall Street Consumer Protection Act of 2010
- Jumpstart our Business Startups Act of 2012
- Internal Revenue Code of 1986 and other tax laws

Key Takeaways

Following are key points to keep in mind when approaching a capital markets transaction:

- **How a capital markets transaction is structured can significantly affect the rights and obligations of the seller and purchaser of securities.** For example, if you are representing the investor, will your client be able to resell the securities? What voting, liquidation, or other rights will your client receive? If you represent the issuer, what rights are you giving to the investors? What will the issuer's ongoing obligations be? Regardless of whom you represent, what are the tax implications?

- **In any transaction involving the offer or sale of securities, you must identify and ensure compliance with relevant securities laws.** You need to consider both federal securities laws as well as the securities laws of any state in which the securities are offered or sold ("Blue Sky" laws). For cross-border transactions, you will also need to identify any applicable securities laws in other jurisdictions.

- **A good understanding of securities laws is critical to avoid inadvertent consequences.** Any time you are advising a client that is offering, buying, selling, or facilitating a purchase or sale of securities, you must be able to identify all potentially applicable securities laws and regulations and what steps are needed to comply with each. This analysis is important to conduct early in the transaction, as failure to miss a step can have significant adverse consequences. For example, once an issuer has engaged in general solicitation, it can no longer rely on the private placement exemption. Thus, you need to determine early on which exemptions might be available and establish appropriate guidelines for the client.

- **Don't forget to address any tax law and other regulatory issues; seek expert advice.** It can be easy to overlook the tax consequences of a capital markets transaction if you are not a tax lawyer. Tax laws and how they apply to a transaction can drive the decision as to how it should be structured. The best practice is to bring in a tax lawyer to advise on these issues early on (and to "bless" any proposed transaction structure before it is finalized). She may identify issues you have not thought of and eliminate unintended consequences. The same is true for any other specific regulatory areas, such as antitrust or ERISA if they are implicated. For international regulations, you may need to seek advice from local counsel.

Commercial Transactions

Commercial Transactions Defined

A commercial transaction is any transaction involving commercial law, ranging from technology licensing and franchise agreements, to loans, supply contracts, and employment agreements.

Commercial law can overlap with banking, bankruptcy, credit transactions, secured transactions, real estate, and other practice areas. At its most fundamental, commercial transactions practice is the practice of drafting and negotiating commercial agreements or contracts.

Commercial law can be distinguished from business law by its focus: commercial law focuses primarily on the sale and distribution of goods, as well as financing of certain transactions; business law focuses on the other aspects of business, including forming a company, mergers and acquisitions, and shareholder rights. However, the two share commonalities and frequently overlap.

> **Key Terminology:**
>
> A commercial agreement can be **B2B** (business-to-business) or **B2C** (business to consumer). Commercial agreements involving the sale of goods are subject to the **UCC** (Uniform Commercial Code) or, if involving cross-border deals, the **CISG** (Convention on the International Sale of Goods, also known as the Vienna Convention). Each party to a commercial agreement will have obligations that need to be **performed**, including **delivery** of goods or services.

Common Forms of Commercial Transactions

Common categories of commercial transactions include:

- Licensing
- Franchising
- Software development
- Marketing
- Technology services
- Supply of goods and services

- Financial services
- Distribution
- Shipping
- Entertainment
- Real estate

Common Forms of Commercial Agreements

Commercial agreements that might be used in connection with these activities include:

Agreement	Description
License	Used as a means of sharing or transferring the right to use technology and other intellectual property, such as software, patents, trademarks, and copyright in exchange for royalties. License can be inbound (obtaining a license) or outbound (granting a license).
Franchise Agreement	Governs the rights and obligations of the franchisor (owner) of a business concept and the franchisee, who operates a business using that concept. Typically, franchise agreements incorporate a license to use the franchisor's trademark and branding.
Loans and Other Finance Agreements	The documentation for these types of transactions will vary depending on the type of loan or financing, but can include documents such as loan agreements, promissory notes, security agreements, collateral agency agreements, indentures, assignment of proceeds, and deeds. In addition, you may encounter UCC-1 or other filings used to perfect a creditor's security interest in collateral used to secure the loan.
Development Agreement	A generic term for an agreement in which one party is engaging another to develop a product or service. Most often, this term is used in the context of software development, but is also used in the real estate and fundraising contexts.
Service Agreement	A broad category of agreements used when one party is agreeing to provide services to another party. Independent contractor agreements, consulting agreements, and professional services agreements are all common forms. A relatively new form of service agreement is a SAAS agreement (SAAS stands for "software as a service") used by enterprise software companies in which software is licensed on a subscription basis.
Supply Agreement	Used to govern the terms of the sale of goods, often on a B2B basis.
Employment Contract	Although employment law is a separate practice area in many firms, employment agreements are a form of commercial agreement, governing the provision of services in exchange for compensation and other benefits.
Joint Venture Agreement	An agreement between two or more parties where the parties are collaborating in a business and even combining resources but want to retain their separate identities. A joint venture agreement is the contractual equivalent of a partnership relationship.

Distribution Agreement	Governs the relationship between a manufacturer or owner of goods and a buyer of those goods who then resells them to end-users. Other related agreements include wholesale agreements and reseller agreements. Distribution agreements typically specify the territory in which the distributor may resell products.
Vendor Agreement	Like a supplier agreement, a vendor agreement governs the sale of products on a B2B basis.
Manufacturing Agreement	Another example of a B2B contract. As its name suggests, a manufacturing agreement governs the manufacture of goods. Often used where a manufacturer of goods outsources certain components or the assembly of a product.
Private Label Agreement	Used where a company wants to sell another company's products under its own brand. Grocery stores commonly sell private-label goods.
Marketing Agreement	Defines the marketing activities that one party will provide to another, or in which two or more parties collaborate (a joint-marketing agreement).
Film and Television Contracts	Collaboration, film or music distribution, financing, production, and merchandising contracts used in the entertainment industry to govern the rights of authors, talent, producers, directors, and others. Drafting and negotiating these specific forms of commercial contracts is typically handled by lawyers who specialize in entertainment law.
Nondisclosure Agreement	Nondisclosure agreements (NDAs) are both corporate and commercial contracts, used by parties to a transaction to protect from misuse or disclosure to third parties nonpublic information that needs to be disclosed in order to effectively negotiate the transaction.
Noncompetition Agreement	Noncompetition agreements (or noncompetes) can be stand-alone agreements or provisions incorporated into another agreement, such as an employment agreement. Noncompetes must be carefully drafted in terms of scope, duration, and geographic range to be enforceable, depending on the jurisdiction.
Installment Contract	An agreement to provide or purchase goods or services over time, or to pay over time.
Real Property Purchase Agreement or Lease	Agreements governing the buying, selling, and leasing of real property are forms of commercial agreements. Most real property transactions involving transactional lawyers relate to commercial real estate.

Common Characteristics in Commercial Agreements

To varying degrees, all commercial agreements are created using the basic contractual building blocks described in Chapter 11. The following components are singularly important in commercial transactions, regardless of form:

Item:	Location in Contract (Building Block):	Example:
The timeframe of the contract	Operative Provisions or Term/Termination	• The period during which services will be provided in a service agreement • The end date of the parties' contractual relationship in a joint-venture agreement or license
A description of the goods or service being provided	Operative Provisions	• The goods being supplied in a vendor agreement • The intellectual property being licensed (and the type of grant) • The title and job duties in an employment agreement
Consideration, such as amounts payable and details of payment dates, including any interest or other remedies triggered by late payment	Operative Provisions	• The quarterly royalty payments in a franchise agreement • The interest charged on a late payment of a loan or installment contract • The base salary and contingent compensation due under a production contract
The delivery date for goods or services	Operative Provisions	• The agreed delivery date of goods under a supply agreement • The agreed completion date in a manufacturing agreement • The completion of development milestones in a development agreement
Insurance and indemnification	Covenants and Deal Protection Devices (Remedies)	• Indemnification for defects in manufacturing • Indemnification for claims of infringement in a license • Minimum insurance requirements in a private label agreement • Indemnification for undisclosed environmental issues in a commercial lease
Allocation of the risk of loss	Covenants	• Agreement as to when risk of loss of goods passes to purchaser in a supply agreement • The ability to raise fees or royalty rates in a franchise agreement • The ability to adjust prices for inflation in a supply agreement
Termination	Deal Protection Devices (Termination)	• The ability of the buyer to cancel a private label agreement • The ability of an employer to terminate an employee • The ability of a licensor to terminate a license
Remedies for breach	Deal Protection Devices	• Termination of an employment agreement for cause • The right to equitable relief for a breach of a non-compete • The right to restitution for unpaid goods in a vendor agreement

Role of the Transactional Lawyer in Commercial Transactions

The role of the transactional lawyer in a commercial transaction is similar to that of a lawyer in M&A and other business transactions. Responsibilities might include:

- Advising and counseling client on appropriate form of agreement
- Drafting and negotiating the relevant agreement as well as any ancillary agreements, such as bills of sale, terms and conditions, or other documentation
- Coordinating input from subject-matter experts as necessary
- Preparing internal office memos on relevant legal issues
- Ensuring compliance with applicable laws and regulations
- Preparing any necessary filings

Relevant Laws

Uniform Commercial Code (UCC). In addition to basic contract law and other common law, all states have adopted a form of the Uniform Commercial Code (UCC). The UCC applies primarily to the sale of goods, but can also apply to other commercial transactions such as certain leasing and secured transactions. The main provision of the UCC relating to the sale of goods is Article 2. Article 2A deals with leases, and Article 9 with secured transactions. Lawyers advising clients on commercial transactions need to be familiar with the UCC and mindful of the situations in which it might apply.

Convention for the International Sale of Goods (CISG). The CISG is an international treaty that provides a uniform set of laws governing the sale of goods across different countries. The CISG applies to any contract for the sale of goods where the countries involved are signatories to the CISG, unless the parties expressly opt out in the agreement. In the United States, the CISG is treated as a federal law that trumps state laws, including the UCC. Commercial lawyers differ as to whether it is better to opt out of the CISG, depending on the jurisdictions involved and the predictability and favorability of local law.

Other. Commercial transactions are generally governed by state statutory and common law, including general contract principles, although some federal laws may also apply in specific types of transactions. Examples of federal laws include the Fair Labor Standards Act, the Equal Protection Act, and the Comprehensive Environmental Response Compensation and Liability Act (CERCLA).

Key Takeaways

Following are key points to keep in mind when approaching a commercial transaction:

- **Deal protection devices are essential.** It is easy in a commercial transaction to focus on the commercial aspects of the transaction: what the parties are agreeing to sell, provide, or buy, and for how much. But what happens when the other side breaches the agreement? One of your goals as a transactional lawyer is to help your client avoid litigation. One of the most effective ways to do this in a commercial agreement (or any contract) is to use deal protection devices to create a deterrent to breach. For example, you might include a unilateral right to terminate a service agreement if the services do not meet agreed standards. If you represent the service provider, you might include the right to receive any fees earned but unpaid as of termination. In either case, you may negotiate indemnification or liquidated damages. Insurance can be another effective tool to mitigate risk.

- **Understand the scope of applicable laws and regulations.** As you are structuring a commercial transaction or drafting documentation, consider what other areas of law might apply. Will the UCC or CISG apply, for example? Many forms of commercial transactions are governed by other specific regulations as well. For example, a franchise must comply with mandatory disclosure rules, loans are subject to usury and other banking regulations, and installment contracts must comply with state truth-in-lending laws. Other examples might include employment law issues, intellectual property concerns, or environmental issues. Be prepared to identify relevant regulations and to bring in specialized counsel as necessary.

- **Identify the business issues.** Make sure you have a clear understanding of business issues before recommending a form of agreement or commencing drafting a commercial agreement. Often, there is more than one way to structure a commercial transaction. What are the advantages and disadvantages of each structural alternative considering your client's business concerns? Similarly, once you begin drafting or negotiating an agreement, what are the specific business issues you need to address?

APPENDIX B

Appendix B contains samples of some of the forms of documents referenced in this book. These documents are included primarily for illustration purposes but are also intended to serve as precedent forms you can use when completing the various exercises and simulations in this book. In some instances, the exercise or simulation will direct you to a particular form. In others, you can draw on any of the samples that may be relevant.

Note, these samples are just that—samples. They do not represent the only way to draft these documents, nor are they intended to be perfect. Rather, they are designed to expose you to a realistic view of typical documents in various stages of drafting and negotiation, and to prompt you to review with a critical eye, as you should any precedent you encounter in practice.

Appendix B-1

This sample closing checklist relates to an asset purchase transaction in which a new entity is being formed to acquire the assets. Depending on the structure of the transaction, the items included will vary.

ABC, Inc.
Acquisition of Assets of Crest Design Group, Ltd.

CLOSING CHECKLIST

Updated as of 2/19/2019 ◄

> Helpful to have date update automatically to avoid confusion as to current version

Parties

ABC Holding	Parent
ABC, Inc.	Buyer
Buyer's US Counsel, Arnold, Lime, and Gold	ALG
Crest Design Group, Ltd.	Target
Escrow Agent, Bankers Trust Company	Escrow
Seller's US Counsel, Green and Dunn	GD
Seller's Accountants, Krausse LLP	Accountant

> Identify parties up front for ease of reference and assignment of responsibility

Document/Action	Agreement Section Reference	Responsible Party	Signatory	Status/ Comments
1. Pre-Signing of Definitive Agreement				
1.1. Letter of Intent dated Dec. 5, 2018		ALG	Buyer, Target, Key Employee	Executed and Delivered
1.2. Mutual Nondisclosure Agreement		ALG/GD	Buyer, Target, Key Employee	TBC
1.3. Discuss transaction structure with tax advisors		Buyer/Target/ ALG/GD	--	TBC
1.4. Conduct financial due diligence		Buyer, Accountant	--	TBC

> Critical to keep status updated

Document/Action	Agreement Section Reference	Responsible Party	Signatory	Status/Comments
1.5. Conduct legal due diligence		ALG	--	Additional responses pending from Seller
1.6. Prepare and file articles of incorporation of Buyer		ALG	Buyer	Completed 1/9/18
1.7. Prepare by-laws of Buyer		ALG	--	
1.8. Prepare and execute Parent and Buyer resolutions approving negotiations		ALG	Board of Parent and Buyer	Completed 2/4/18
1.9. Prepare and execute Target resolution approving negotiations		GD	Board of Target	
2. Definitive Agreement and Contemporaneous Documentation				
2.1. Asset Purchase Agreement ("APA")		ALG	Buyer, Target, Parent	Executed 2-5-18
2.2. Exhibits to APA				
2.2.1. Form of Offer Letter	Ex A	ALG	--	Completed
2.2.2. Form of Employee Confidentiality Agreement	Ex B	ALG	--	Completed
2.2.3. Form of Assignment & Assumption Agreement	Ex C	ALG		Completed
2.2.4. Form of Assignment of Contracts	Ex D	ALG		TBD
2.2.5. Form of Bill of Sale	Ex E	ALG		Completed
2.2.6. Form of IP Assignment	Ex G	ALG		Completed

Signature column is helpful when it comes time to circulate signature pages

Note that each exhibit will appear twice: once in form, and again at Closing to reflect the need to have it signed

Document/Action	Agreement Section Reference	Responsible Party	Signatory	Status/ Comments
2.2.7. Form of Notice of Assignment of Contracts (notice and/or consent, as required, for each contract listed on Schedule __)		GD		ALG to approve template, any departures from template; Target/GD to give notice and/or secure consents
2.2.8. Form of notice and/or consent, as required, for each software license listed on Schedule __		GD		ALG to approve template, any departures from template; Target/GD to give notice and/or secure consents
2.2.9. Form of TM assignment	Ex H	ALG		To be filed with the USPTO
2.2.10. Form of Escrow Agreement	Ex F	ALG	--	Completed
2.2.11. Form of Termination of unvested options agreement		ALG	--	N/A
2.2.12. [Form of Holder Release]		ALG	--	To release Buyer from any claims held by former shareholders of Target (or option holders) — TBC
2.2.13. Form of Target Key Officer Certificate			--	N/A
2.2.14. Form of Target Counsel opinion				N/A
2.2.15. Allocation of Purchase Price among Acquired Assets	3.4/ Sched 3.4	Target/Buyer	--	Preliminary Allocation agreed
2.3. Disclosure Schedules to the APA		Target/GD	--	Completed

The documents and actions needed will depend on the specific transaction. When using a precedent form, make sure you modify to match your transaction

Document/Action	Agreement Section Reference	Responsible Party	Signatory	Status/ Comments
2.4. Other Ancillary Documentation Required Prior to or Contemporaneous with Signing of APA				TBD
2.5. Prepare and file HSR pre-merger notification (if applicable)		Buyer/Target/ ALG/GD		N/A
3. Actions between Signing of Acquisition Agreement and Closing				
3.1. Obtain all third-party consents and UCC termination statements		Target, GD	TBD	Pending
3.2. Give notices and request and obtain third-party consents, as required, for assignment and assumption of contracts and other rights and obligations		Target, GD		As applicable — TBD
3.3. [Allow HSR waiting period to expire]				N/A
3.4. [Distribute satisfaction and discharge agreements relating to third-party loans being terminated at Closing] as applicable		Target, GD, ALG		TBD
3.5. Select Escrow Agent		Target & Buyer	Target, AcquisitionSub, Buyer, EA	SRS Acquiom selected. Pending KYC review
3.6. Prepare Estimated Closing Adjustment Statement		Target/GD		N/A
3.7. Prepare and obtain Target written consent approving Acquisition		GD	Target Share- holders	
3.8. Prepare and obtain written consent of Parent (as sole shareholder of Buyer) approving Acquisition		ALG	Parent	

Document/Action	Agreement Section Reference	Responsible Party	Signatory	Status/ Comments
3.9. Prepare funds flow memo		Buyer and Target	--	
3.10. Conduct lien and judgment searches		Buyer/ALG	--	Completed
3.11. Completion of Buyer due diligence		Buyer/ALG	--	Pending additional responses from Seller
3.12. Prepare updates to Disclosure Schedules		Target/GD		
3.13. Certificates of good standing of Target in its jurisdiction of organization and the various foreign jurisdictions in which it is qualified	4.4			dated no earlier than 5 business days prior to the Closing
4. Closing				
4.1. Deliver Closing Amount	Art 3	Buyer	--	
4.2. Deliver Holdback to Escrow Agent	Art 3	Buyer	--	
4.3. Execute and deliver all other assignments. Consents, and deliverables				See Items in 2.2 above
4.4. Execute and deliver Escrow Agreement	Art 3	ALG	Buyer, Target, EA, Seller	
4.5. Execute and deliver Key Employee Offer Letters	4.4	ALG	SE, KE Employees, Selling Member	
4.6. Execute and deliver Holder releases (if any)		ALG	Target, Holders	TBD
4.7. Execute and deliver Termination Agreements			TBD	N/A
4.8. Execute and deliver Target Officers' certs		ALG/GD	Target Officers	N/A

Document/Action	Agreement Section Reference	Responsible Party	Signatory	Status/ Comments
4.9. [Execute and deliver Buyer Secretary and Incumbency Cert certifying resolutions of the Board of Buyer authorizing the Acquisition]		ALG	Buyer Secretary	
4.10. [Execute and deliver AcquisitionSub Secretary and Incumbency Cert certifying resolutions of the Board of AcquisitionSub and sole shareholder authorizing the Acquisition]		ALG	Buyer Secretary	
4.11. [Execute and deliver Target Secretary and Incumbency Cert certifying resolutions of the Board of Target authorizing the Acquisition]		GD	Target Secretary	
4.12. Deliver UCC termination statements and Satisfaction and Discharge Agmts as applicable				N/A
4.13. Deliver third-party consents necessary for Acquisition		Target, GD		Including software assignment
4.14. Request/apply for/ obtain governmental approvals/permits				Determine extent to which these are required
4.15. Execute and deliver legal opinion of Target counsel		GD	GD	N/A
4.16. [Execute and deliver resignation letters of officers and directors of Target]		Target/GD		TBD

Document/Action	Agreement Section Reference	Responsible Party	Signatory	Status/ Comments
4.17. Deliver Estimated Working Capital	Certified by officer of Target	Target		N/A
4.18. [Other actions relating to assets/contracts not to be transferred (such as terminations of certain agreements, resignation of auditor)]				
4.19. [Any actions related to extinguishing of existing debt (such as payoff letters)]				
4.20. [Obtain releases from victims or indemnities from seller (and possible seller indemnitors) with respect to potential tort liabilities discovered during due diligence.]				Subject to continuing due diligence.
4.21. Employment/Human Resources Matters				TBD
4.22. [Obtain resignations from all other officers and directors of Target]				TBC
4.23. Prepare press release as applicable		Buyer, ALG, Target, GD		

> Post-closing actions are often overlooked but are critical to follow-through

5. Post-closing

Document/Action	Agreement Section Reference	Responsible Party	Signatory	Status/ Comments
5.1. Arrange for filing of UCC Termination Statements (if applicable)		ALG		N/A
5.2. Arrange for filing of TM Assignment with USPTO		ALG		
5.3. Prepare and deliver Closing Adjustment Statement		Buyer		N/A

Document/Action	Agreement Section Reference	Responsible Party	Signatory	Status/ Comments
5.4. Deliver notice of Purchase Price Adjustment		ALG	Buyer	N/A
5.5. Distribute Holdback Funds	8.6			
5.6. Apply to qualify to do business in jurisdictions in which Target had been qualified to do business and Buyer is not		ALG		TBD
5.7. Payment of Retention Bonuses	7.12	Buyer		TBD
5.8. Payment of Milestones	3.3; 7.14	Buyer		

This sample checklist is just that: a sample. The specific items will vary depending on the type of deal, the structure, the parties, and a variety of other factors.

Appendix B-2

The memos below illustrate the differences and similarities between a litigation focused memo and transactional-focused memo. For readability purposes, some sections and footnotes are omitted.

MEMORANDUM
[Litigation]

To: Senior Associate
From: Junior Associate
Date: February 14, 20__
Re: NPD—Client No. 2614-00—"commercial activity" exception of Foreign Sovereign Immunities Act

INTRODUCTION

The Norwegian Petroleum Directorate (NPD), an agency of the Norwegian government, has hired us to advise it concerning a potential breach of contract claim by TechMex S.A., a Mexican manufacturer with offices in Mexico and the United States. You have asked me to research whether NPD could claim immunity from suit under the Foreign Sovereign Immunities Act (FSIA) or whether it would be prevented from doing so by the so-called "commercial activities" exception. As instructed, I have focused my analysis on the third prong of the commercial activities exception and have assumed that TechMex can show that the threatened lawsuit is based upon an act outside the territory of the United States. I have also assumed that NPD is a "foreign state." Finally, I am not to address any other exceptions under the FSIA, or breach of contract, choice of law, minimum contacts, or personal jurisdiction issues.

MEMORANDUM
[Transactional]

To: Senior Associate
From: Junior Associate
Date: February 14, 20__
Re: NPD Client No. 2614-001—Protection from breach of contract—claim under Foreign Sovereign Immunities Act

You have asked me to analyze to what extent the Norwegian Petroleum Directorate (NPD), an agency of the Norwegian government, would be able to rely on the Foreign Sovereign Immunities Act (FSIA) to protect it against potential claims filed in the United States in the event it agrees to provide a guaranty on behalf of TransNorge ASA, a Norwegian company, in favor of TechMex S.A., a Mexican manufacturer with offices in Mexico and the United States. As described in more detail in Part I below, although the FSIA does provide immunity in certain circumstances, engaging in a commercial activity, such as the issuance of a guaranty in a commercial transaction, generally precludes reliance on the FSIA. Accordingly, this memorandum adopts a conservative approach. Part I sets out the general rules governing FSIA immunity. Part II discusses structural recommendations and alternative safeguards.

[Litigation]

[Transactional]

QUESTIONS PRESENTED

[Not necessary—general question incorporated into Introduction]

A.   Does failure to arrange a letter of credit required under a guaranty qualify as being "in connection with a commercial activity outside of the United States" when the guaranty was issued by a government entity to promote private-sector participation in environmental protection, but private parties often provide guaranties and the underlying transaction involved the sale of goods?

B.   [*Omitted*]

BRIEF ANSWERS/RECOMMENDATION

[Incorporated into Introduction]

A.   Likely yes. The failure to arrange the letter of credit required under the guaranty likely was "in connection with a commercial activity" because, even though the government entity may have been acting as a market regulator when it issued the guaranty, guaranteeing a contract for the sale of goods – in this case, boom – is an action engaged in by private players and thus likely was commercial in nature.

B.   [Omitted]

STATEMENT OF FACTS

In analyzing the issue, I have relied on the following facts and assumptions:

On January 1, 2011, the Norwegian Petroleum Directorate, an agency of the Norwegian government, breached a guaranty that it had provided to TechMex, S.A., a Mexican company with offices in the United States and Mexico, by failing to arrange a standby letter of credit required under the guaranty. The guaranty was issued by NPD from Norway in November 2010 on behalf of TransNorge, ASA, a Norwegian oil and gas company, as a condition of a contract entered into between TransNorge and TechMex. The purpose of the guaranty was to secure the payment obligations of TransNorge under the contract.

The contract, which was executed in New York, called for TechMex to design and manufacture one

- NPD is a "foreign state" for purposes of the FSIA;
- the purpose of the guaranty is to secure the payment obligations of TransNorge under its proposed contract with TechMex for the manufacture by TechMex of flotation boom to be used by TransNorge in its North Sea operations;
- the parties have agreed to meet in New York to execute the proposed contract;
- NPD issues guaranties to help it achieve its mission to promote the participation of private oil and gas companies in environmental protection; the applicant must be engaged in a qualifying environmental-protection activity which

[Litigation]

and a half tons of flotation boom meant to protect coastlines from accidental oil spills at sea. TransNorge intended to use the boom along parts of the Norwegian coastline that could be affected by a spill from one of the company's offshore wells. The total purchase price for the design and manufacture of the boom was U.S. $30 million, payable by TransNorge in a series of wire transfers directly into TechMex's bank account in Mexico City.

Under the terms of the guaranty, NPD was to arrange a standby letter of credit at Citywide Bank in New York in the amount of U.S. $15 million, on or prior to January 1, 2011; failure to timely arrange the letter of credit was an express breach of the guaranty. The purpose of the letter of credit was solely to secure the guaranty; thus, payment under the letter of credit was required only in the event of nonpayment under the contract and the guaranty.

On January 15, 2011, TransNorge unilaterally terminated the contract and refused to pay TechMex for work performed prior to termination of the contract. TechMex therefore sought payment under the guaranty, which NPD is now refusing to honor. Because NPD failed to arrange the letter of credit, TechMex cannot seek payment under the letter of credit.

NPD issues guaranties to help it achieve its mission to promote the participation of private oil and gas companies in environmental protection; the applicant must be engaged in a qualifying environmental-protection activity which NPD determines will create a "significant benefit to the country as a whole." The NPD guaranty is a standard-type commercial form; TransNorge could have sought a similar guaranty from its parent company.

[Transactional]

NPD determines will create a "significant benefit to the country as a whole;" and

· the NPD guaranty is a standard-type commercial form.

DISCUSSION

Under the Foreign Sovereign Immunities Act, a foreign state is immune from suit in the United States unless one of several enumerated exceptions applies. Republic of Arg. v. Weltover, Inc., 504 U.S. 607, 610-11 (1992). One of the principal exceptions is the "commercial activity" exception, set forth in § 1605(a)(2) of

I. FSIA requirements and exceptions

The Foreign Sovereign Immunities Act, [*footnote citation to statute omitted*] provides a foreign state immunity from suit in the United States unless one of several enumerated exceptions applies. [*footnote citation omitted*]. The relevant exception in our case is the "commercial activity" exception [*footnote citation omitted*].

[Litigation]

the FSIA. Id. at 611. Under this exception, a foreign state is not immune from suit when the lawsuit is based on (1) "a commercial activity carried on in the United States by the foreign state;" (2) "an act performed in the United States in connection with a commercial activity of the foreign state elsewhere;" or (3) "an act outside . . . of the United States in connection with a commercial activity of the foreign state elsewhere and that act causes a direct effect in the United States." Id.

This memorandum focuses on the third prong of § 1605(a)(2) and addresses only whether the described act was in connection with a commercial activity of NPD outside of the United States and had a "direct effect" in the United States.

A. In Connection with a Commercial Activity

For an act to be "in connection with a commercial activity" of a foreign state there must be an underlying commercial activity. See id. at 614. Whether a foreign state's activity is "commercial" for purposes of the FSIA turns on whether the state is acting as a regulator of a market or as a private player in the market. Id. The character of an activity is determined by its nature, not its purpose. Id. at 612. For instance, the foreign state need not have a profit motive, as long as the particular actions are of the type engaged in by private players. Id. at 612, 616. In Weltover, the Argentine government's unilateral rescheduling of the maturity date of bonds it had issued was in connection with a commercial activity outside of the United States because the issuance of bonds is a commercial activity. Id. at 615. The bonds, which were issued from Argentina, were a normal type of debt instrument that could be held and traded by private players; the fact that the Argentine government had issued them for the purpose of stabilizing Argentina's currency, and not for profit, was irrelevant. Id. Similarly, in Texas Trading & Milling Corp. v. Federal Republic of Nigeria, 647 F.2d 300, 310 (2d Cir. 1981), the purchasing of cement by the Nigerian government was a commercial activity even though the purpose was to help build infrastructure, an otherwise sovereign act; the cancellation of the cement-purchase contracts was thus in connection with a commercial activity.

[Transactional]

[footnote listing other exceptions omitted]. Under this exception, a foreign state is not immune from suit when the lawsuit is based on (1) "a commercial activity carried on in the United States by the foreign state;" (2) "an act performed in the United States in connection with a commercial activity of the foreign state elsewhere;" or (3) "an act outside . . . of the United States in connection with a commercial activity of the foreign state elsewhere and that act causes a direct effect in the United States." Presumably, the guaranty would be issued outside of the United States. Thus, the main inquiry turns on whether the issuance of the guaranty would be considered an act "in connection with a commercial activity" that causes a "direct effect" in the United States.

A. In Connection with a Commercial Activity

Whether an act is "in connection with a commercial activity" turns on whether the state is acting as a regulator or a private player in the market. [footnote citation omitted]. The character of an activity is determined by its nature, not its purpose. [footnote citation omitted]. For instance, the foreign state need not have a profit motive, as long as the particular actions are of the type engaged in by private players. In Weltover, [footnote citation] the Argentine government's unilateral rescheduling of the maturity date of bonds it had issued was in connection with a commercial activity outside of the United States because the issuance of bonds is a commercial activity. The bonds, which were issued from Argentina, were a normal type of debt instrument that could be held and traded by private players; the fact that the Argentine government had issued them for the purpose of stabilizing Argentina's currency, and not for profit, was irrelevant. Id. Similarly, in Texas Trading & Milling Corp. v. Federal Republic of Nigeria, [footnote citation], the purchasing of cement by the Nigerian government was a commercial activity even though the purpose was to help build infrastructure, an otherwise sovereign act; the cancellation of the cement-purchase contracts was thus in connection with a commercial activity.

[Litigation]	[Transactional]

[Litigation]

Conversely, an activity that is by its nature uniquely sovereign is not "commercial" for purposes of the FSIA. See Anglo-Iberia Underwriting Mgmt. Co. v. P.T. Jamsostek, 600 F.3d 171, 177-78 (2d Cir. 2010). In Anglo-Iberia, an Indonesian state-owned social security insurer was not engaged in a commercial activity by providing health insurance because it did not sell insurance to workers as a private company would, but rather provided default coverage for all workers and ensured compliance by private companies with government-mandated insurance requirements; thus, the negligent supervision of its employees was not in connection with a commercial activity. Id.

In this case, NPD's failure to arrange the letter of credit may not have been in connection with a commercial activity because the issuance of the guaranty may have been a uniquely sovereign act. NPD issues guaranties only in transactions that benefit its mission of promoting private companies' participation in environmental protection, similar to Anglo-Iberia, in which the insurer's issuance of default health insurance was part of its mission to ensure basic insurance coverage. This suggests that NPD was not competing in the marketplace for guaranties but rather acting in its sovereign capacity as a market regulator.

On the other hand, NPD's failure to arrange the letter of credit was likely in connection with a commercial activity because even if the guaranty was part of NPD's regulatory function, guaranteeing a contract for the sale of goods is an action typically engaged in by private players and thus is commercial in nature. The contract for the boom was a contract for the sale of goods. Private parties often guarantee third-party payment obligations under contracts for the sale of goods, just as they often issue bonds, as in Weltover, and purchase cement, as in Texas Trading, activities that were found to be commercial in nature. The fact that NPD was providing the guaranty for an otherwise sovereign purpose is irrelevant, as was the fact in Texas Trading that the government was using the concrete to help build the country's infrastructure.

Thus, even though the purpose of issuing the guaranty may have been a sovereign one, because the letter of credit was in connection with the issuance of a guaranty in Norway and the issuance of guaranties is commercial in nature, NPD's failure to arrange the letter of credit was likely in connection with a commercial activity outside of the United States.

[Transactional]

Conversely, an activity that is by its nature uniquely sovereign is not "commercial" for purposes of the FSIA. [footnote citation omitted]. In Anglo-Iberia, an Indonesian state-owned social security insurer was not engaged in a commercial activity by providing health insurance because it did not sell insurance to workers as a private company would, but rather provided default coverage for all workers and ensured compliance by private companies with government-mandated insurance requirements; thus, the negligent supervision of its employees was not in connection with a commercial activity. [NOTE: some or all of RE can be placed in a parenthetical or a footnote]

Arguably, the issuance of the guaranty by NPD may not be "in connection with a commercial activity" given that NPD issues guaranties only in transactions that benefit its mission of promoting private companies' participation in environmental protection. Similar to Anglo-Iberia, in which the insurer's issuance of default health insurance was part of its mission to ensure basic insurance coverage, NPD could argue that it is not competing in the marketplace for guaranties but rather acting in its sovereign capacity as a market regulator. To further bolster this position, we would want to ensure NPD's mission is clearly stated on the guaranty and perhaps limit some of the more commercial terms in the guaranty, as discussed below.

However, even if the guaranty is part of NPD's regulatory function, guaranteeing a contract for the sale of goods is an action typically engaged in by private players and thus is commercial in nature. The contract for the boom is a contract for the sale of goods. Private parties often guarantee third-party payment obligations under contracts for the sale of goods, just as they often issue bonds, as in Weltover, and purchase cement, as in Texas Trading, activities that were found to be commercial in nature. The fact that NPD is providing the guaranty for an otherwise sovereign purpose likely will be irrelevant, as was the fact in Texas Trading that the government was using the concrete to help build the country's infrastructure.

Thus, even though the purpose of issuing the guaranty may be a sovereign one and even if we take the the steps described above, because the underlying contract is commercial in nature, the guaranty likely would be deemed "in connection with a commercial activity."

[Litigation]

B. Direct Effect

[Omitted]

[*Typically, litigation memo does not include option-generation, other than in the form of a recommendation, generally incorporated into Brief Answer*]

[Transactional]

B. Direct Effect

[*Omitted*]

II. Recommended Structure and Alternative Safeguards

Based on the above analysis, in order to minimize the risk of triggering the "commercial activity" exception, the client should adhere to the following guidelines in structuring its guaranty:

- Include a stipulation in the form of the guaranty stating that the guaranty is not a commercial guaranty but is a guaranty of last resort.
- Require TransNorge to certify that it is unable to obtain a commercial guaranty.
- Limit the commercial language in the guaranty.

Moreover, assuming the issuance of the guaranty may be deemed to be in connection with a commercial activity [that has a direct effect in the United States], we should also recommend the following alternative safeguards:

- Require that the contract and the guaranty be fully executed outside of the United States.
- Require that the contract be governed by the laws of either Mexico or Norway.
- Seek to obtain a release from TechMex.
- Consider making the guaranty one of payment, not performance.

Please let me know if you have any questions or would like me to review any of the above in greater detail.

J.A.

CONCLUSION

NPD's breach of the guaranty was likely in connection with a commercial activity, given that guaranteeing a contract for the sale of goods is an action typically engaged in by private players and thus is commercial in nature. [conclusion regarding Direct Effect omitted]. Therefore, the "commercial activities" exception likely will apply.

Note: *The [footnote citation] references in the transactional memo refer to citations that would be included as footnotes, as opposed to in-text. For purposes of this comparison, the footnotes have been omitted.*

Appendix B-3

The following memorandum is a sample memo analyzing a statute-based transactional legal issue.

MEMORANDUM

Date: May 13, 20__
To: Senior Associate
From: Junior Associate
Re: [Client] — Company and Officer Reporting Obligations

You have asked me to research the rules that govern (i) which employees of [Client], Inc. (the "Company") are and will be subject to the reporting obligations under Section 16(a) of the Securities Exchange Act of 1934, as amended (the "Exchange Act") and (ii) the reporting and disclosure obligations of the Company under the Exchange Act with respect to both compensatory agreements or arrangements between the Company and its existing and impending employees and changes in the beneficial ownership of equity securities (including derivatives) of the Company by certain of its officers. This memorandum briefly summarizes the provisions of Section 16 (and the Forms 3, 4 and 5 required thereunder), Regulation 14A (proxy statements), Form 10-K and Form 8-K which are relevant to these issues. We have not, in this memorandum, sought to apply the rules to specific individuals in the Company.[1]

The reporting and disclosure obligations of the Company and its employees are dependent, in part, on the definitions of "officer," "executive officer" and "named executive officer" set forth in the applicable regulations and the Company's determination as to which employees are appropriately classified under each such designation. The applicable definitions are as follows:

- "Officer" means a company's president, principal financial officer, principal accounting officer (or if none, controller), a vice president in charge of a principal business unit, division or function (such as sales, administration or finance), an officer who performs a significant policy-making function or any other person who performs similar significant policy-making functions for the company. Of-

---

1. Please note that we also have not addressed any particulars of the Company's insider trading policy as it may apply differently to "officers," "executive officers" and other persons.

263

ficers of a company's parent(s) or subsidiaries are deemed to be officers of the company if they perform significant policy-making functions for the company.[2]

- "Executive officer" means a company's president, any vice president in charge of a principal business unit, division or function (such as sales, administration or finance), any other officer who performs a policy-making function, or any other person who performs similar policy-making functions for the company. Executive officers of subsidiaries of a company are deemed to be executive officers of the company if they perform such policy-making functions for the company.[3]

- The "named executive officers" of a company are all individuals serving as chief executive officer or in a similar capacity during the last completed fiscal year, the four other most highly compensated executive officers who were serving as executive officers at the end of the last completed fiscal year and an additional two individuals for whom disclosure would have been provided had they been serving as an executive officer at the completion of the last completed fiscal year.[4]

__Appendix A__ summarizes the reporting and disclosure obligations of the Company regarding its "officers," "executive officers" and "named executive officers" that are discussed in greater detail in this memorandum.

Discussion

Section 16(a)

Under Section 16(a) of the Exchange Act, each director, "officer" and beneficial owner of more than 10% of any class of equity securities of the Company (also known as a Section 16 reporting person) must file reports with the SEC detailing their transactions in, and holdings of, the Company's equity securities. The reporting requirements extend to all of the Company's equity securities in which a reporting person has a direct or indirect beneficial interest, including "derivative securities" such as stock options, puts and calls, convertible securities, securities owned by immediate family members,[5] corporations, partnerships and certain trusts in which reporting persons have an interest. The list of "officers" required to file beneficial ownership reports under Section 16(a) does not necessarily include all the persons who hold an officer title and is often co-extensive with the officers listed as executive officers in the Company's annual proxy statement.

The initial ownership report by a reporting person must be filed on a Form 3 and provide information about all classes of equity securities (including options and other derivative securities) of the Company beneficially owned by that person. The Form 3 must be filed within ten days of the event by reason of which the person becomes a reporting person.

A Form 4 must be filed with the SEC upon a reportable change in such beneficial ownership. In addition to market purchases and sales, this includes most transactions between a director or "officer" and the Company. Examples of these transactions include: (i) grants of stock options, restricted stock, or other equity compensation awards; (ii) dispositions to the Company, including tax withholding of shares, the tender of stock upon exercise, and any routine purchase of shares by the Company to fund tax payments; and (iii) most derivative securities transactions, including exercises, cancellations, and

---

2. See Rule 16a-1(f) of the Exchange Act.
3. See Rule 3b-7 of the Exchange Act.
4. See Item 402(a)(3) of Regulation S-K.
5. The family members to whom this rule extends are any of the following who live in the insider's household: children, stepchildren, grandchildren, parents, stepparents, grandparents, spouse, siblings, mother-in-law, father-in-law, sons-in-law, daughters-in-law, brothers-in-law and sisters-in-law. Adoptive relationships are included.

regrants of stock options (including repricings). The Form 4 must be filed within two business days of the execution date of the transaction.

In the case of new hires, assuming that the new hires are deemed to be "officers" as described above and that the new hires receive options as part of their compensation, the Form 4 is typically filed concurrently with the Form 3.

A Form 5 must be filed within 45 days after the Company's fiscal year end to disclose transactions and holdings exempt from prior reporting, as well as transactions and holdings that should have been reported previously but were not.

Forms 3, 4 and 5 must be filed electronically via the SEC's EDGAR system. Although the responsibility for complying with the reporting requirements of Section 16(a) rests solely with the reporting person, the Company must post reports on its website and has certain disclosure obligations relating to delinquent reports. Specifically, the Company is required to disclose in its proxy statement the names of all of its reporting persons who reported transactions late or failed to file required reports during the Company's fiscal year. The cover page of the Form 10-K will also indicate that Company reporting persons have made delinquent Section 16 filings.

Annual Report on Form 10-K

- [omitted]

Report on Form 8-K

Form 8-K requires that the entering into of management contracts or compensatory plans, contracts or arrangements of the types described above with regard to reports on Form 10-K, or any amendments to the same, be reported on Form 8-K within four business days of their adoption or execution.[6] Any such Form 8-K must disclose the following information:

- the date on which the agreement or amendment was entered into;
- the identity of the parties;
- any material relationship which exists between the parties other than the agreement or amendment which is the subject of the Form 8-K; and
- a brief description of the terms of the agreement or amendment that are material to the Company.

The filing of the actual agreement or amendment as an exhibit can be delayed until the Company's next periodic report, which may be on Form 10-Q or Form 10-K.

Recent SEC guidance and informal commentary regarding Form 8-K has expanded what are properly considered to be "management contracts or compensatory plans, contracts or arrangements." Presently, the prudent course is to summarize any oral compensatory arrangement with a "named executive officer" and, except where immaterial in amount or significance, any "executive officer," with the written summary filed as an exhibit to the Company's next periodic report. In addition, the Company should also file as exhibits written summaries of (i) perquisites awarded (if the value of the perquisite is material) and (ii) the initial and annual setting of compensation in "at-will" employment

---

6. Please note that in addition to the types of management contracts and compensatory plans, contracts or arrangements previously described herein, recent SEC guidance has stated that unless shareholder approval is required by the plan, the adoption of a cash bonus plan in which named executive officers are eligible to participate, the setting of performance goals under such plan and the payment of a bonus under the plan that is not in accordance with previously disclosed criteria are all events which trigger an 8-K filing obligation.

arrangements (in each instance where the employee involved is a "named executive officer" or, except where immaterial in amount or significance, an "executive officer").

Form 8-K also requires the filing of a report when a new principal executive officer, president, principal financial officer, principal accounting officer, principal operating officer or person performing similar functions is appointed. In such circumstances, the Form 8-K must disclose the following information with respect to the new appointee:

- his or her name, position, age, term of office and date of appointment;
- a brief description of any arrangement or understanding between the newly appointed officer and any other person pursuant to which the former was selected as an officer;
- any family relationship which may exist between the newly appointed officer and any director or executive officer of the Company;
- a brief description of the business experience of the newly appointed officer for the previous five years; and
- disclosure regarding certain business transactions between the Company or one of its subsidiaries and the newly appointed officer or a member of his or her immediate family since the beginning of the Company's last fiscal year.

Proxy Statement

- *[omitted]*

Please let me know if you would like me to proceed with applying these rules to specific employees at [Client], or if you would like me to research any of the above in greater depth.

Appendix A

The following table summarizes the reporting and disclosure obligations of the Company with respect to its officers, executive officers and named executive officers.

Type of Employee	Event	Type of Filing	Additional Notes
Officers	*New hire is awarded beneficial ownership of equity securities (including derivatives) of the Company as part of compensation package*	Employee must concurrently file Forms 3 and 4	
	Change in an employee's beneficial ownership of equity securities (including derivatives) of the Company	Employee must file Form 4	
	Failure of employee to file Forms 3 or 4	Employee must file a Form 5 after the end of the Company's fiscal year regarding transactions and holdings that were exempt from prior reporting on Forms 3 and 4 or that should have been reported on Forms 3 and 4 but were not	While the responsibility to file Forms 3, 4 and 5 is technically that of the employee involved, the Company's annual proxy statement must disclose those officers who filed late or did not file required Forms 3 or 4 and the cover page of the Company's Form 10-K will also indicate that officers have made delinquent filings
Named Executive Officers	*Company enters into new or amended management contract or compensatory plan, contract or arrangement (written or oral) or awards perquisites in material amounts or sets initially or annually the compensation of "at will" employees*	1. Form 8-K disclosure of the particulars of the written agreement or, if none, oral arrangement (4-day deadline) 2. The written agreement or, if none, a written summary of any oral arrangement can be filed as an exhibit to the Form 8-K disclosing such agreement or arrangement or the Company can delay filing the exhibit until its next periodic report, which may be on Form 10-Q or Form 10-K	Please note: any compensatory plan, contract or arrangement that is not approved by the Company's stockholders and which may award equity securities of the Company must be disclosed on Form 8-K (regardless of which employees participate) and filed as an exhibit to the Form 8-K or the Company's next periodic report

Type of Employee	Event	Type of Filing	Additional Notes
Named Executive Officers, (*continued*)	*Company files its annual report on Form 10-K*	Disclosure on Form 10-K re: 1. Compensatory contracts or arrangements 2. Executive compensation 3. Security ownership Company also required to file compensatory contracts or arrangements as exhibits (unless any such compensatory contract or arrangement has already been filed as an exhibit to the Form 8-K disclosing its adoption or on an earlier Form 10-Q)	
	Company files its proxy statement	Disclosure in the annual proxy statement or the proxy statement for a special meeting in lieu of an annual meeting re: 1. Compensatory contracts or arrangements 2. Executive compensation 3. Security Ownership (the same disclosure as required under the Form 10-K, other than exhibits)	Please note: these disclosures only required if certain enumerated matters are being voted on by securityholders (as discussed under "*Proxy Statement*")

[Remainder of table omitted]

Appendix B-4

The following is an example of a short-form memo for use in Exercises 7.1 and 10.1.

RYAN & ASSOCIATES, LLP

TO: Partner
FROM: Associate
RE: Sale of CCPL's Interests in CCE, LLC
DATE: March 14, 20__

You have asked me to analyze whether the proposed sale by Century Circle Partners Landlord, LLC ("CCPL") of all of its membership interests (the "LLC Interests") in CCE, LLC (the "Company") will constitute a sale of "securities" for purposes of U.S. securities laws; and if so, what are the minimum requirements for structuring and conducting the offer and sale of the interests in compliance with relevant securities laws.

Assumptions

My analysis is based on the following assumptions: (1) CCPL is not a manager or managing member of the Company; (2) under the terms of the operating agreement for the Company, the day-to-day management of the Company is vested in a managing member; and (3) the operating agreement contains a number of controls intended to prevent the managing member from mismanaging the Company's business, including veto rights of the other members with respect to "major decisions," annual budget requirements, and provisions allowing for the removal of the managing member upon the occurrence of certain events.

Analysis

A. Whether the LLC Interests are Securities

Although the definition of a "security" under federal securities laws does not expressly include limited liability company interests,[1] the sale of the LLC Interests could reasonably be deemed to be "securities" for purposes of U.S. securities laws under both the *Howey* test, as a form of "investment contract," and by comparison to other limited liability entity forms.

1. *Howey* Test. Under the *Howey* test, an "investment contract" exists where there is a contract, transaction or scheme whereby a person (1) invests money, (2) in a common enterprise, and (3) is led to expect profits solely from the efforts of the promoter or a third party.[2] In the case

---

1. *See* Section 2(a)(1) of the Securities Act of 1933, as amended, 15 U.S.C. §77a *et seq.*
2. *SEC v. Howey*, 328 U.S. 293 (1946).

of the LLC Interests, there is arguably a common enterprise and an investment of money. The analysis therefore turns on the third factor: whether the investor is led to expect profits solely from the efforts of another. The current standard adopts a liberal interpretation of "solely" and focuses on whether the efforts of a third party are "significant ones" and whether the third party's "management efforts . . . affect the failure or success of the enterprise." The Supreme Court has endorsed the relaxation of this requirement, by omitting the word "solely" from its restatements of the *Howey* test. Some courts have gone even further, defining the issue to be whether an investor, as a result of the investment agreement itself or the factual circumstances that surround it, is left unable to exercise "meaningful control" over his investment.[3] Cases in which the courts have found there to be no security interest tend to involve initial joint venture partners who are actively involved in the day-to-day operations of the company or have the power to exert significant control over the manager.

The courts may also look beyond the operating agreement to other documents such as promotional materials, the experience and knowledge of the investor with respect to the business being conducted, and to the practical possibility of the members exercising the powers provided pursuant to the operating agreement.[4]

In our case, although the members each have some control over decision-making and are experienced investors, they deliberately vested the day-to-day management of the Company in the managing member, and the controls in the operating agreement may not sufficiently limit the managing member's ability to "affect the failure or success" of the Company. Unlike in *Robinson v. Glynn* and other cases in which the investors had an active role in management, CCPL is not involved in day-to-day management, suggesting that CCPL is relying on the efforts of the managing member. Thus, the LLC Interests may fall within the scope of an "investment contract."

2. **Comparison to other limited liability forms.** A strong presumption exists against characterizing general partnership interests as securities, regardless of whether the *Howey* factors are present. Arguably, due to similarities between general partnerships and limited liability companies, this presumption should also apply in the case of limited liability company interests.[5] Like general partners, limited liability members are generally permitted to be an active participant in management and thus are not passive investors in need of protection under securities laws.

However, limited liability companies differ from general partnerships in several respects. For instance, members of limited liability companies are entitled to limited liability, and, depending on the terms of the operating agreement, the members of the LLC tend to be less involved in the management of the enterprise than partners in a general partnership. To date, courts have generally declined to adopt a blanket presumption for limited liability companies in either direction. Thus, despite the potential similarities, the LLC Interests may be deemed to be securities under this approach as well,

Thus, unless we are provided with additional facts showing CCPL is actively involved in the

---

3. *Robinson v. Glynn*, 349 F.3d 166 (4th Cir. 2003). The investor in this case had meaningful control when he not only had the power to appoint two of the board members, but he himself assumed one of the board seats and was named as the board's vice-chairman. The board, in turn, delegated extensive responsibility to a 4-person committee of which the investor was a member. *Distinguished by Haddad v. Rav Bah., Ltd.*, 431 F. Supp 2d 1278 (S.D. Fla 2006) (distinguished on the basis that the interests were referred to as securities).

4. *See Williamson v. Tucker*, 645 F.2d 404 (5th Cir. 1981).

5. *See, e.g., Ribstein, Form and Substance in the Definition of a Security: The Case of Limited Liability Companies,* 51 Wash & Lee L. Rev. 807 (1994).

management and decision-making for the Company, the LLC Interests will likely be considered securities.

B. Structuring the Offering in Compliance with U.S. Securities Laws

Assuming the offering of the LLC Interests (the "**Offering**") will constitute an offer and sale of securities, the Offering must either be registered in accordance with the Securities Act and applicable state securities laws or be exempt from registration.

Based on the information we have been provided, we can probably structure the Offering to comply with the exemption from registration of the Securities Act for transactions "by any person not involving an issuer, underwriter or dealer" (Section 4(a)(1) of the Securities Act), provided that CCPL adhere to the restrictions on publicity outlined below.

Section 4(a)(1) permits the resale of restricted securities, provided that neither the seller nor any other participant in the transaction is an underwriter. The definition of an underwriter for purposes of Section 4(a)(1) turns on whether the transaction involves a "distribution." The term "distribution" has been equated with the term "public offering" used in Section 4(a)(2) of the Securities Act. Accordingly, where the transaction does not amount to a distribution or a public offering under Section 4(a)(2) but rather is a private resale, the restricted securities may be sold in reliance on Section 4(a)(1). Thus, CCPL should comply with the requirements of Section 4(2) and/or Regulation D,[6] to ensure the ability of the Section 4(a)(1) exemption.[7]

The principal elements required to satisfy Section 4(a)(2) or Regulation D are as follows:

- Sophistication. Any purchaser that is not an accredited investor should have such knowledge and experience in financial and business matters, either alone or with his advisors, that he is capable of evaluating the merits and risks of the prospective investment and be able to bear such risks. Each purchaser should be provided with or have access to the type of material financial information that would be included in a registration statement and be afforded the opportunity to ask questions and to receive answers concerning the terms and conditions of the Offering and their investment in the LLC Interests.
- No general solicitation. General solicitation or advertising includes, but is not limited to, (i) the offer or sale of securities by means of any advertisement, article, notice or other communication publishing in any newspaper, magazine or similar media or broadcast over television or radio, and (ii) any seminar or meeting whose attendees have been invited by any general solicitation or advertising. Under some circumstances, posting information on the Company's website could constitute a general solicitation. Ideally, CCPL should have a pre-existing business or "substantive relationship" with each offeree.
- No distribution. Precautions should be taken to determine each investor is acquiring the offered securities for its own account and not with a view to distribution or resale. This is generally achieved by requiring the investors to certify in the representation letter that they are acquiring the securities for investment purposes and not with a view to reselling their shares.
- Limited number of U.S. investors. As the number of offerees increases, so does the risk that the offered sale of the securities will not satisfy the Section 4(a)(2) exemption. Typically, private placements are limited to no more than 100 offerees. Under Regulation D, if there are

---

6. Rule 506 of Regulation D under the Securities Act. By complying with the requirements of this safe-harbor, the Offering would be deemed to be a private placement under Section 4(2). In addition, compliance with Regulation also facilitates compliance with state securities laws in most states.

7. This traditionally is referred to as the 4(a)(1½) exemption. This exemption has also recently been codified as new section 4(a)(7) of the Securities Act.

unaccredited investors, certain minimum financial and other information must be provided. Accordingly, I recommend limiting the Offering to accredited investors only.

Failure to properly comply with the relevant exemption and publicity restrictions can give rise to civil or criminal penalties, including rescission and 10(b)(5) liability.

Conclusion

CCPL should comply with the provisions of Section 4(a)(1) and 4(a)(2) of the Securities Act to ensure that the sale of their LLC Interests does not inadvertently violate federal securities laws.

In addition, we should also examine the relevant state securities laws once purchasers have been identified to ensure that the offering complies with those state laws.

* * * *

Please let me know if you would like me to perform any additional research or do anything else on this matter.

J.A.

Appendix B-5

This sample client letter is excerpted in Chapter 10.

RYAN & ASSOCIATES, LLP
299 Valley Avenue, 3rd Floor
Los Angeles, CA 90009

March 15, 20___

James Ogden
Chief Financial Officer
Hudson Equity Group
1200 Company Way
Middletown, NY 11104

Re: Employee participation in securities offerings

Dear James:

It was a pleasure speaking with you last week. As requested, set out below is a summary of broker-dealer issues relating to using employees of Hudson Equity Group to solicit additional investors for one of your real estate investment funds. As discussed, this is a complex area of securities laws. Thus, we recommend engaging in additional research and establishing clear guidelines prior to any employee engaging in this type of activity.

Background

Our understanding is that the employees in question, some of whom are officers or directors, are employed by Hudson Equity and that Hudson Equity is a member of the investment fund that will be issuing the securities. We further understand that these employees will be limiting their activities to emailing potential investors with whom they have had previous business relations to inform them about the investment opportunity. Finally, we understand that the securities will be offered to individuals both within and outside of California in one or more private placements in accordance with relevant exemptions from registration.

Analysis

The principal issue is whether the employees are required to be licensed as broker-dealers. Because the offering of securities will be made to potential investors inside and outside of California, both state and federal securities laws will apply. Generally, under both regimes, a person is acting as a broker-dealer and subject to licensing if the person "engages in the business of effecting transactions in securities for the account of others." This definition tends to be viewed broadly.

Limited exemptions from licensing are available under both federal and California law. Following is a description of the relevant exemptions, as well as a discussion of general considerations.

California law — exception from definition of broker-dealer

Under California law, an employee of an issuer is not required to be licensed as a broker-dealer as long as that employee is (1) acting on behalf of the issuer and (2) is receiving special compensation related to the offering of securities. The special compensation must be payment over and above any regular salary or bonus payment, such as a commission. In other words, the employee must be acting as an "agent" of the issuer, separate from his or her normal role within the company.

Provided you are planning on paying your employees some form of commission based on their sales efforts, they should qualify as agents under California law. However, there are several important caveats:

- The exception does not apply to offerings that are exempt from registration under California Corporations Code §25102(f) (the common exemption for private placements). Thus, to ensure your employees are exempt from broker-dealer licensing, you will need to rely on an alternative exemption from registration. One possible alternative is to structure the offering to comply with Regulation D, which eliminates the need to rely on §25102(f). Regulation D is a safe-harbor exemption for private placements under federal securities laws. If you do decide to proceed, we can advise you in terms of complying with this exemption.
- Technically, the employees in question are not employed by the issuer (the fund) but by Hudson Equity, a member of the issuer. Thus, the employee-agent exception may not apply. We could argue that the fund does not directly employ any individuals; rather, the manager of the fund (Hudson Equity) employs the individuals on behalf of the fund. We would need to conduct additional research on this, however.
- Finally, having an employee-agent subjects the issuer to certain reporting, supervisory, and training requirements. This regulatory burden should be taken into account. At a minimum, employee-agents should be required to adhere to clearly defined guidelines. If you decide to proceed, we would recommend establishing appropriate guidelines. We can assist you with this if and when you decide to proceed.

Federal law — safe-harbor from broker-dealer definition

Under federal securities laws, an "associated person" of an issuer (which would include officers and directors), is not considered to be acting as a broker-dealer solely by participating in an offering of securities of the issuer, provided, however, that the associated person receives no special compensation relating to the offering. This requirement directly contradicts the specific requirement under California law that the employee receive special compensation.

In addition, to be exempt under federal law, an associated person's activities must be limited. For instance, the sale of securities must not be the person's primary duty, the person should not otherwise be a broker-dealer, the person should not participate in more than one offering per year, or the person's participation should be limited to preparing and sending out printed materials or other ministerial function.

Options/Recommendations

Intrastate offering. One option is to structure the offerings as intrastate offerings to California residents only. This way, the federal broker-dealer licensing requirements may not apply. We should discuss further if you would like to pursue this option.

Seek no-action relief. If you do not want to limit the offering to California only, you have two possible options: (1) we can seek no-action relief from the SEC confirming that the proposed use of the employees to solicit investors in compliance with the California exemption will not violate the federal broker-dealer licensing requirements; or (2) research further to see if any existing SEC no-action relief might be applicable. No-action relief is an informal opinion of the SEC in which it confirms whether it will recommend enforcement action based on a particular set of facts. Seeking no-action relief will obviously delay the offering. In addition, prior no-action relief is not necessarily binding; thus, it cannot completely eliminate the risk of inadvertent violation of the federal broker-dealer licensing requirements. Thus, we recommend caution in relying on prior relief and, if possible, submitting our own request for no-action.

Penalties and other considerations

Failure to comply with the broker-dealer licensing requirements can result in both civil and criminal penalties for the employees and for the company. In addition, under California law, if the employees are found to have been required to be licensed, investors may have a right of rescission.

Further, while ensuring compliance with the elements of either the state exemption or the federal safe-harbor creates a presumption that the employee is not acting as a broker, this presumption may be challenged. On the other hand, the failure to completely satisfy either the exemption or the safe-harbor (or both) does not necessarily mean that the employee is acting as a broker, although it will be more likely. Thus, regardless, some risk of inadvertent violation cannot be avoided.

As a final note, our analysis presumes as a threshold matter that the actions of the employees will rise to the level of a broker-dealer. It may be possible to argue that the activities of the employees do not satisfy this threshold. However, the SEC and the California Commissioner of Corporations tend to view this definition very broadly. We have not researched this issue in any depth, but would be happy to do so if you would like us to.

Conclusion

In conclusion, you may be able to use employees to solicit investors in an intrastate offering, without having them register as broker-dealers with careful structuring and strict guidelines. Expanding the offering beyond California will likely increase the risk of inadvertent violation of broker-dealer licensing requirements; thus, expansion of the offering should be carefully weighed against this risk.

Given your time and cost constraints, the above represents only a brief overview of the potential issues, however, and is not a complete analysis of the law in this regard. Thus, we recommend analyzing these issues in greater detail before taking any action.

Please let us know whether and how you would like to proceed. In the meantime, please let me know if you have any questions.

Sincerely,

/s/ Julie Ryan

Julie Ryan

Enclosures

Cc: Mary Jones

Appendix B-6.1

This sample asset purchase agreement is an example of a pro-buyer first draft, annotated to illustrate the common contractual "building blocks" referred to in Chapter 11 and common provisions typically included in a mid-sized transaction. Names of parties and other details have been redacted, but typically would be included in the first draft if known. It is common for the buyer in a transaction to prepare the first draft. Depending on the value of the transaction, the type of business, and the parties involved, the provisions may vary. The seller may also seek to negotiate some of the provisions by adding qualifications, softeners, or exceptions, or by adding, modifying, or deleting language.

Compare the provisions and structure of this agreement to the sample share purchase agreement in Appendix B-6.3. Note the similarities and differences.

Confidential
Draft for discussion purposes __/__/2010

ASSET PURCHASE AGREEMENT

This Asset Purchase Agreement (this "*Agreement*"), dated January___, 2010 is by and among (i) [   ], LLC a limited liability company organized under the laws of the state of New Jersey ("*Buyer*"), (ii) [   ], Inc., a California corporation ("*Company*" *or* "*Seller*"), and (iii) [   ], individuals and sole shareholders of Company (individually each a "*Shareholder*" and collectively "*Shareholders*," and jointly and severally together with Company "*Seller Parties*").

Preamble

R E C I T A L S:

A. Shareholders own all the issued and outstanding stock of Company;

B. Company develops, manufactures, imports, sells and distributes [   ] under the [   ] brand name (the "*Business*");

C. Seller Parties desire to sell, and Buyer desires to purchase, substantially all the assets of the Business, in accordance with the terms and conditions set forth herein.

D. SE ("*SE*") and Buyer are entering into, concurrently with and as a condition to the execution of this Agreement, an Employment Agreement ("*Employment Agreement*") pursuant to which, among other things, SE will be employed full time by Buyer for a period of one year from the date of Closing, after which continued employment by Buyer of SE shall be on an "at will" basis.

Recitals

AGREEMENT:

NOW, THEREFORE, in consideration of the premises and the mutual promises herein made, and in consideration of the representations, warranties, and covenants contained herein, Buyer and Seller Parties agree as follows:

ARTICLE 1.
PURCHASE AND SALE OF ASSETS; ASSUMPTION OF LIABILITIES

Operative
Provisions — the
Transaction

1.1   Acquired Assets. Seller Parties shall sell, transfer and assign to Buyer and Buyer shall purchase from Seller Parties, free and clear of all liens and encumbrances, the Acquired Assets. For purposes of this Agreement, "*Acquired Assets*" shall mean all the assets of Seller Parties related to the Business other than the Excluded Assets (defined below), including but not limited to, the assets set forth on Schedule 1.1.

1.2   No Assumed Liabilities. Subject to Section 1.3 below, Buyer shall not assume any liabilities of Seller Parties whatsoever, direct or indirect, fixed, contingent or otherwise, known or unknown, whether relating to the Acquired Assets, the Business or otherwise.

1.3   Assumed Contracts. Notwithstanding Section 1.2, following the Closing Date, subject to the receipt of all third-party consents and approvals deemed necessary or advisable by Buyer, Buyer will assume and become obligated to perform the obligations of Company under any contract listed on Schedule 1.3 hereto (the "*Assumed Contracts*,") but only to the extent such obligations (i) arise after the Closing Date; (ii) do not arise from or relate to any breach of any Seller Party of any provision of any Assumed Contract; (iii) do not arise from or relate to any event, circumstance or condition occurring or existing on or prior to the date hereof that, with notice or lapse of time, would constitute a breach of any of the Assumed Contracts; and (iv) are ascertainable in nature and amount solely by reference to the express terms of the Assumed Contracts; provided that in no event shall the obligations assumed hereunder include any liability of any person under the Assumed Contracts, except for Company, any liability of Company to any Seller Party or to any affiliate or related party of any Seller Party, or any tax liability.

ARTICLE 2
PURCHASE PRICE

Operative
Provisions —
Consideration
and Closing
Mechanics

2.1   Purchase Price. In consideration of the sale, transfer, conveyance and delivery of the Acquired Assets and associated good will, and in reliance upon the representations and warranties made herein by Seller Parties, Buyer shall pay to Company the aggregate purchase price of Eighteen Million Dollars ($18,000,000.00), as adjusted pursuant to Section 2.2, plus the amount set forth in Section 2.1(c) (the "*Purchase Price*"), payable as set forth below. Unless otherwise indicated, all payments shall be made in cash or by wire transfer to an account or accounts designated by Seller. The Purchase Price shall be allocated among the Acquired Assets in accordance with the mutual agreement of the parties hereto.

(a) The sum of ten million dollars ($10,000,000.00) shall be paid at Closing (the "*Closing Amount*").

(b) The sum of eight million dollars ($8,000,000.00) shall be delivered by Buyer to the Escrow Agent (the "*Deposit*"), to be held and disbursed by the Escrow Agent pursuant to the terms and conditions of an escrow agreement substantially in the form attached hereto as Exhibit [   ] (the "*Escrow Agreement*").

(c) As additional consideration for the Acquired Assets, subject to Section 2.2 and Section 8.3, Buyer shall pay to Company or its designee within thirty (30) days of the end of each fiscal quarter following the Closing Date, for a period of three (3) years following the Closing (the "*Earn-Out Period*"), an amount equal to ten percent (10%) of Net Sales generated during the fiscal quarter then ended (each such payment being an "*Earn-Out Amount*"). Any Earn-Out Amount shall be payable only with respect to amounts actually received by Company. In the case of a fiscal quarter which falls only partially within the Earn-Out Period, the

2

Earn-Out Amount shall be calculated with respect to Net Sales generated during the portion of that fiscal quarter that falls within the Earn-Out Period only. For purposes hereof, "*Net Sales*" means the total of gross amounts directly or indirectly invoiced or charged to [   ] Customers for the sale of [   ] health and beauty products, including any and all Trade Discounts (as defined below), less returns, chargebacks or markdown money issued by or given to [   ] Customers, shipping costs, cost of goods, warranty claims and commissions payable in respect of sales to [   ] Customers. For purposes hereof, "*Trade Discounts*" shall mean reductions in the wholesale list price that are customary in the trade. "*[   ] Customers*" shall mean those customers listed at Schedule 2.1(b) hereto (to be provided at Closing).

2.2   **Adjustments.** The Purchase Price will be subject to the following adjustments (the "*Purchase Price Adjustments*"):

(a)   <u>Closing Statement.</u> Promptly, but in any cvcnt within ninety (90) days after the Closing, Buyer shall furnish to Seller a written statement (the "*Closing Statement*") setting forth its calculation of (i) the Working Capital as of the close of business on the last Business Day immediately preceding the Closing Date (the "*Closing Working Capital*"), and (ii) the calculation of the final Purchase Price and the Final Closing Payment resulting therefrom, all as determined in accordance with this Agreement. The Closing Statement and Closing Working Capital shall be prepared in accordance with the Accounting Principles. Following receipt of the Closing Statement, Seller and its representatives shall be afforded a period of thirty (30) calendar days to review the Closing Statement. At or before the end of the 30-day review period, Seller shall either (i) accept the Closing Statement in its entirety or (ii) deliver to Buyer a written notice (a "*Dispute Notice*") setting forth a detailed explanation of those items in the Closing Statement that Seller disputes, including the amount thereof (to the extent such information is available) (each, an "*Item of Dispute*") provided, that the only basis on which Seller shall be permitted to submit an Item of Dispute is that such Item of Dispute was not prepared in accordance with the terms of this Agreement or contains a mathematical or clerical error or errors. If Seller does not deliver a Dispute Notice to Buyer within the 30-day review period, Seller shall be deemed to have accepted the Closing Statement in its entirety. If Seller delivers a Dispute Notice in which some, but not all, of the items in the Closing Statement are properly disputed, Seller shall be deemed to have accepted all of the items not disputed other than those not directly disputed but which are affected by an Item of Dispute. The Parties shall and shall cause their respective Affiliates to reasonably cooperate with Buyer in connection with the preparation of the Closing Statement. After the delivery of the Closing Statement, Buyer shall, and shall cause its Affiliates to, reasonably cooperate with Seller in connection with the review of the Closing Statement including by providing Seller reasonable access during business hours to materials used in the preparation of the Closing Statement.

(b)   <u>Dispute Resolution by the Parties.</u> If Seller deliver a Dispute Notice to Buyer within the required 30-day period, Buyer and Seller shall use best efforts to resolve their differences concerning the Items of Dispute, and if any Item of Dispute is so resolved, the Closing Statement shall be modified as necessary to reflect such resolution. If all Items of Dispute are so resolved, the Closing Statement (as so modified) shall be conclusive and binding on all Parties.

(c)   <u>Determination by Independent Accounting Firm.</u> If any Item of Dispute remains unresolved for a period of thirty (30) calendar days after Buyer's receipt of a Dispute Notice, then either Buyer or Seller may, within thirty (30) calendar days after Buyer's receipt of such Dispute

Notice, submit the dispute to [_____]¹, or, if such firm shall decline or is unable to act or is not, at the time of such submission, independent of Seller or Buyer, to another independent nationally recognized certified public accounting firm mutually acceptable to Seller and to Buyer (either [_____] or such other accounting firm being referred to herein as the "*Independent Accounting Firm*"). If Buyer and Seller are unable to mutually agree upon an accounting firm within such 10-day period, then Buyer and Seller shall, within five (5) calendar days thereafter, each select a nationally recognized certified public accounting firm. Within five (5) calendar days after such selection, those two accounting firms shall jointly select a third nationally recognized certified public accounting firm, which third accounting firm shall act as the Independent Accounting Firm. Such third nationally recognized accounting firm shall not be an accounting firm that has performed accounting or similar services for Buyer or Seller in the past three (3) years. Buyer and Seller shall each provide their respective calculations of the Items of Dispute in writing to the Independent Accounting Firm and shall request that the Independent Accounting Firm render a written determination, which determination (i) shall be based solely on whether each such Item of Dispute was prepared in accordance with the terms of this Agreement or whether each such Item of Dispute contains a mathematical or clerical error or errors and (ii) shall not be resolved so the final amount determined by the Independent Accounting Firm is more favorable to Seller than the calculation(s) presented in any Item of Dispute delivered by Seller or more favorable to Buyer than the calculation(s) delivered by Buyer, as to each unresolved Item of Dispute as soon as reasonably practicable, but in no event later than thirty (30) days after its retention, and the Parties shall cooperate fully with the Independent Accounting Firm so as to enable it to make such determination as quickly and as accurately as practicable. The Independent Accounting Firm's determination as to each Item of Dispute submitted to it shall be in writing and shall be conclusive and binding upon the Parties, absent manifest error or willful misconduct. Buyer and Seller shall bear the costs and expenses of the Independent Accounting Firm based on the percentage which the portion of the contested amount not awarded to each party bears to the amount actually contested by or on behalf of such party, and Seller and Buyer shall each pay one-half of any retainer required by the Independent Accounting Firm at the initiation of the engagement, such amount to be reallocated and credited or reimbursed by the other party depending on the final award of the contested amount by the Independent Accounting Firm.

(d) <u>Final Closing Payment Adjustment.</u> If the amount of the Final Closing Payment as reflected on the Final Closing Statement is less than the Closing Amount, then Seller shall pay to Buyer an amount equal to such shortfall; provided, however, that Buyer shall have the right (but not the obligation) to satisfy such payment obligation from the Escrow Fund and, in such event, upon the written request of Buyer, Seller shall (i) authorize any payment in respect of such claims. If the amount of the Final Closing Payment as reflected on the Final Closing Statement is greater than the Closing Amount, then Buyer shall pay to Seller an amount equal to such excess. Any such payment shall be made within five (5) Business Days after the Closing Statement becomes final and binding upon the Parties

2.3   Closing. The Closing of the purchase and sale of the Acquired Assets (the "*Closing*") will take place at the offices of Buyer in _____, California, commencing at ____ a.m., local time, on _____, 2010 or such other date as Buyer and Seller Parties may mutually determine in writing (the date on which Closing actually occurs being the "*Closing Date*").

---

1. NTD: Parties to agree upon mutually acceptable independent accountant.

2.4   **Deliveries at Closing. At Closing:**

(a) Seller Parties shall deliver to Buyer: (i) originals of any Assumed Contracts in effect as of the Closing Date, including without limitation, the Lease; (ii) all original books and records relating to the Business as set forth under Section 1.1(i), and all tangible Acquired Assets not otherwise located on the Leased Premises, including, without limitation, any and all product formulations, training manuals, marketing materials, artwork and brochures; (iii) a general assignment agreement in the form attached hereto as Exhibit "___", and such other assignment documents necessary to ensure proper transfer to and ownership by Company of the Acquired Assets, including the Assumed Contracts any and all Intellectual Property (including, without limitation, the confirmatory assignments set forth under Exhibit "___"; (iv) all customer lists and databases; (v) a duly executed counterpart of the Employment Agreement; and (vi)other deliverables as appropriate.

Operative provision — Deliverables

(b) Buyer shall deliver to Company: (i) the Closing Amount; and (ii) a duly executed counterpart of the Employment Agreement.

(c) The parties shall also deliver to each other the agreements, closing certificates and other documents and instruments required to be delivered pursuant to this Agreement.

ARTICLE 3.
REPRESENTATIONS AND WARRANTIES OF BUYER

3.1   **Representations and Warranties of Buyer.** Buyer warrants to Seller Parties that the statements contained in this ARTICLE 3 are correct and complete as of the date of this Agreement and will be correct and complete as of the Closing Date (as though made then and, except as expressly provided in a representation or warranty, as though the Closing Date were substituted for the date of this Agreement throughout this ARTICLE 3).

Representations and Warranties — note use of qualifiers and softeners in 3.4 and 3.6

3.2   **Entity Status.** Buyer is a limited liability company duly organized, validly existing and in good standing under the laws of New Jersey. Buyer has the requisite power and authority to own or lease its properties and to carry on its business as currently conducted. There is no pending or threatened claim, suit, demand, action, litigation, arbitration, inquiry, investigation or other proceeding, or injunction or final judgment relating thereto ("Action") (or basis therefor) for the dissolution, liquidation, insolvency, or rehabilitation of Buyer.

3.3   **Power and Authority; Enforceability.** Buyer has the power and authority to execute and deliver this Agreement each ancillary agreement, document, schedule and certificate necessary or advisable for the consummation of the transactions contemplated hereunder and thereunder (collectively, the "*Transaction Documents*"), and to perform and to consummate the transactions contemplated hereunder and thereunder (the "*Transactions*"). Buyer has taken all action necessary to authorize the execution and delivery of each Transaction Document to which it is party, the performance of its obligations thereunder, and the consummation of the Transactions. Each Transaction Document to which Buyer is a party has been duly authorized, executed and delivered by, and is enforceable against, Buyer.

3.4   **No Violation.** To Buyer's Knowledge, the execution and delivery of the Transaction Documents to which Buyer is a party by Buyer and the performance and consummation of the Transactions by Buyer will not (i) breach any law or order to which Buyer is subject or any provision of its organizational documents; (ii) breach any Contract, order, or permit to which Buyer is a party or by which it is bound or to which any of its assets is subject; or (iii) require any consent of any third party.

3.5   **Brokers' Fees.** Buyer has no liability to pay any compensation to any broker, finder or agent with respect to the Transactions for which Seller Parties could become liable.

3.6   Representations Complete. Except as and to the extent set forth in this Agreement, and in the absence of fraud, Buyer makes no representations or warranties whatsoever to Seller Parties and hereby disclaims all liability and responsibility for any representation, warranty, statement, or information not included herein that was made, communicated, or furnished (orally or in writing) to Seller Parties or their respective representatives (including any opinion, information, projection, or advice that may have been or may be provided to Seller Parties by any director, officer, employee, agent, consultant, or representative of Buyer).

ARTICLE 4.
REPRESENTATIONS AND WARRANTIES OF SELLER PARTIES

4.1   Representations and Warranties of Seller Parties. Seller Parties jointly and severally represent and warrant to Buyer that the statements contained in this ARTICLE 4 are correct and complete as of the date of this Agreement and will be correct and complete as of the Closing Date (as though made then and, except as expressly provided in a representation or warranty, as though the Closing Date were substituted for the date of this Agreement throughout this ARTICLE 4).

4.2   Status of Seller Parties. Each Shareholder is an individual with the requisite competence and authority to execute and deliver this Agreement and any and all other Transaction Documents to which it is a party, and to perform and to consummate the Transactions. Company is a corporation duly incorporated, validly existing, and in good standing under the laws of California and is duly authorized to conduct its business and is in good standing under the laws of each jurisdiction where such qualification is required. Company has the requisite power and authority necessary to own or lease its properties and to carry on its businesses as currently conducted. Shareholders are the sole beneficial and legal owners of all of the issued and outstanding stock of Company. Schedule 4.2 lists the Company's directors and officers. Seller Parties have delivered to Buyer correct and complete copies of Company's organizational documents, as amended to date. There is no pending or threatened Action (or basis therefor) for the dissolution, liquidation, insolvency, or rehabilitation of Company.

4.3   Power and Authority; Enforceability. Seller Parties have taken all actions necessary to authorize the execution and delivery of each Transaction Document, the performance of Seller Parties' obligations thereunder, and the consummation of the Transactions. Each Transaction Document has been duly authorized, executed, and delivered by, and is enforceable against, each Seller Party.

4.4   No Violation. To Seller Parties' Knowledge, the execution and the delivery of the Transaction Documents by Seller Parties and the performance and consummation of the Transactions by Seller Parties will not (i) breach any law or order to which any Seller Party is subject or any provision of any of the Company's organizational documents, (ii) breach any Contract, order, or Permit to which either Seller or Company is a party or by which either Seller or Company is bound or to which any of Company's assets is subject, or (iii) except as set forth on Schedule 4.4, require any consent of any third party or governmental or regulatory entity.

4.5   Brokers' Fee. Seller Parties acknowledge that any liability to pay any compensation to any broker, finder, or agent with respect to the Transactions is the responsibility of Seller Parties and will indemnify and hold harmless Buyer any compensation to any broker, finder, or agent with respect to the Transactions for which Buyer could become directly or indirectly liable.

4.6   No Subsidiaries. Company does not own, in whole or in part, and has no interest of any nature in, any other entity or person.

4.7   **Financial Statements.** Set forth on <u>Schedule 4.7</u> are the following financial statements (collectively the "***Financial Statements***"):

  (a) Unaudited balance sheets, cash flows and statements of income for Company as of and for the year ended December 31, 2008 and December 31, 2009 (the latter being the "***Balance Sheet Date***").

  (b) The Financial Statements have been prepared in accordance with applied on a consistent basis throughout the periods covered thereby, present fairly the financial condition of Company as of such dates and the results of operations of Company for such periods, are correct and complete, and are consistent with the books and records of Company, subject to normal year-end adjustments (which will not be material individually or in the aggregate). Since the Balance Sheet Date Company has not effected any change in any method of accounting or accounting practice, except for any such change required because of a concurrent change in.

[. . . .]

ARTICLE 5.
COVENANTS

The parties agree as follows:

5.1   **General.** Each party will use its reasonably commercial efforts to take all actions and to do all things necessary, proper, or advisable to consummate, make effective, and comply with all of the terms of this Agreement and the Transactions applicable to it (including satisfaction, but not waiver, of the Closing conditions for which it is responsible or otherwise in control, as set forth in <u>ARTICLE 6</u>).

Covenants —
note use of
softeners

5.2   **Notices and Consents.** Seller Parties will promptly give any notices to third parties, and will use their best efforts to obtain any third party consents necessary or advisable in order to consummate the Transactions contemplated hereunder, or that Buyer reasonably may otherwise request. Seller Parties will give any notices to, make any filings with, and use their best efforts to obtain any consents of governmental bodies, if any, required or reasonably deemed advisable pursuant to any applicable law in connection with the Transactions.

5.3   **Operation of Business; Prohibited Actions.** Seller Parties shall not, and will cause Company to not, between the date of this Agreement and the earlier of the Closing Date and the Termination Date, engage in any practice, take any action, or enter into any transaction outside the ordinary course of business or engage in any practice, take any action, or enter into any transaction of the sort described in Section 4.8 above or similar actions.

5.4   **Preservation of Business.** Without limiting the foregoing, Company will use its best efforts to keep its business and properties substantially intact, including its present operations, physical facilities, and working conditions, and relationships with lessors, licensors, suppliers, customers, and employees.

5.5   **Personnel.** In the case of any employees of Company that are retained or rehired by Buyer, Company shall be responsible for paying all costs and expenses associated with accrued but unpaid salary, wages, bonuses and health benefits for the period prior to the Closing Date for such employees. Seller Parties shall jointly and severally indemnify and hold harmless Buyer, its affiliates and their respective shareholders, members, managers, directors, officers, managers, employees, agents, attorneys and successors-in-interest from and against any and all Losses which Buyer may incur relating to or arising from any termination of any employee of Company prior to Closing. Nothing contained in this Agreement shall confer upon any employees of Company any right with respect to continuance of employment, nor shall anything herein interfere with the right of Buyer to hire or terminate the employment of any such employee at any time, with or without cause, or restrict Buyer in the exercise of its independent business judgment in modifying any of the terms and conditions of the employment of any such employee. No provision of this Agreement shall create any third party beneficiary rights in any employee of the Company.

5.6   **Full Access.** Company will permit representatives of Buyer (including financing providers) to have full access at all reasonable times, and in a manner so as not to interfere with the normal business operations of Company, to all premises, properties, personnel, books, records, Contracts and documents pertaining to Company and will furnish copies of all such books, records, Contracts and documents and all financial, operating and other data, and other information as Buyer may reasonably request; provided, however, that no investigation pursuant to this Section 5.6 will affect any representations or warranties made herein or the conditions to the parties' obligations to consummate the Transactions.

5.7   **Tax Covenants.** All transfer, documentary, sales, use, stamp, registration and other such Taxes, and all conveyance fees, recording charges and other fees and charges (including any penalties and interest) incurred in connection with consummation of the transactions contemplated by this Agreement shall be paid by Seller Parties when due, and Seller Parties will, at their own expense, file all necessary tax returns and other documentation with respect to all such Taxes, fees and charges, and, if required by applicable law, Buyer will join in the execution of any such tax returns and other documentation.

5.8   **Confidentiality; Publicity.** Each of the parties, on behalf of itself and its constituent entities and their respective affiliates, hereby agrees that it is in all of their best interests to keep the economic provisions of this Agreement confidential. To this end, each party agrees that it (and its agents and affiliates) will not, without the prior written consent of the other party, take any action or conduct itself in a fashion that would disclose to third parties any aspect of the economic provisions of this Agreement, unless required to do so in order to comply with a court order or any applicable law. The provisions of this Section 5.8 shall not prohibit any party from communicating any information to its attorneys, accountants and other advisors or which is reasonably necessary for the conduct of the affairs of such party, provided that each person to whom such information is disclosed shall be advised of the confidential nature of the information. Seller Parties will not, and will cause Company to not, issue any press release or other public announcement related to this Agreement or the Transactions without Buyer's prior written approval. The provisions of this Section 5.8 shall survive the expiration or termination of this Agreement.

5.9   **Transfer of Domain Names.** Seller Parties shall, on or prior to Closing, take all actions necessary to ensure that all domain names as set forth on Schedule 4.15 remain in effect and are duly transferred and assigned to Buyer.

5.10   **Exclusivity.** No Seller Party shall (i) solicit, initiate or encourage the submission of any proposal or offer from any person or entity relating to the acquisition of any capital stock or other voting securities, or any substantial portion of the assets of Company (including by way of merger, consolidation or otherwise) or (ii) participate in any discussions or negotiations regarding, furnish any information with respect to, assist or participate in, or facilitate in any other manner any effort or attempt by any person or entity to do or seek any of the foregoing. Seller Parties will notify Buyer immediately if any Person makes any proposal, offer, inquiry or contact with respect to any of the foregoing.

5.11   Transition of Business. For a period of six (6) months following the Closing (the "*Transition Period*"), SE agrees to provide consulting services without additional consideration hereunder with respect to (a) the integration of the Business into the Buyer's operations, (b) the transition of customers and suppliers to the Buyer's operations, (c) the operation of the Business as it existed prior to the Closing Date and (d) such other services as mutually agreed (collectively, the "Consulting Services"). In addition, each Seller Party agrees to refer all customer, supplier and other inquiries relating to the Business of Company to Buyer. The parties acknowledge and agree that Seller Parties shall not be entitled to any additional consideration in connection with any of the foregoing covenants.

5.12   Name Change. As of the Closing Date, Seller Parties shall cease to use or to have any rights or interest in or to the name "[   ]" or any other Intellectual Property or other Acquired Asset, and shall take such action as is necessary to amend its corporate name and withdraw its fictitious business name registration.

5.13   Bank and Merchant Accounts. The parties expressly acknowledge and agree that Seller Parties are not agreeing to sell or transfer or to cause to be sold or transferred to Buyer any of Company's cash in bank, merchant or reserve accounts or cash on hand.

5.14   Further Assurances. In case at any time after Closing any further action is necessary to carry out the purposes of this Agreement, each party will take such further action (including executing and delivering such further instruments and documents) as any other party reasonably may request, all at the requesting party's sole cost and expense (unless the requesting party is entitled to indemnification therefor under ARTICLE 8). After Closing Buyer will be entitled to possession of all documents, books, records, agreements, and financial data of any sort relating to the Business.

5.15   Restrictive Covenants; Non-Competition. Each Seller Party acknowledges that the consideration received pursuant to this Agreement is at least equal to the fair market value of the Acquired Assets, reflecting, among other things, the value of all of the goodwill of Business as a going enterprise, and that the covenants of each Seller Party in this Section 5.15 (the "*Restrictive Covenants*") are intended to preserve and protect the value of the goodwill of Business and the Acquired Assets for the benefit of Buyer. Each Seller Party further acknowledges that they have devoted substantial time, effort and resources to developing Company's trade secrets and its other confidential and proprietary information as well as Company's relationships with customers, suppliers, employees and others doing business with Company; that such relationships, trade secrets and other information are vital to the successful conduct of the Business in the future; that Seller Parties would be in a unique position to divert business from Buyer and to commit irreparable damage to the Business and the Acquired Assets were Seller Parties to be allowed to compete with Buyer or to commit any of the other acts prohibited below; that the enforcement of the Restrictive Covenants against each Seller Party would not impose any undue burden upon such Seller Party; that none of the Restrictive Covenants is unreasonable as to period or geographic area; and that the ability to enforce the Restrictive Covenants against each Seller Party is a material inducement to the decision of Buyer to consummate the Transactions. Each Seller Party acknowledges that Buyer would not purchase the Acquired Assets or assume the Assumed Contracts but for the agreements and covenants of Seller Parties contained in this Section 5.15. Accordingly, each of the Seller Parties and Company, jointly and severally, covenants and agrees as follows:

(a) **Nondisclosure.** From and after the Effective Date, Seller Parties shall keep secret and retain in strictest confidence, and shall not shall not directly or indirectly use for the personal benefit of Seller Parties, or disclose, communicate or divulge to, or use for the direct or indirect benefit of any person or entity other than Buyer, any Proprietary Information of any nature whatsoever and existing and/or stored in any medium whatsoever. As used herein, "*Proprietary Information*" includes all Intellectual Property and other confidential and/or proprietary information relating to the Business which is not lawfully known or readily accessible to the general public or others in the health and beauty product industry, which may include product specifications, research, customer and supplier lists and contact information, pricing policies, operational methods, marketing plans or strategies, product development techniques or plans, business acquisition plans, budgets and unpublished financial statements, new personnel acquisition plans, technical processes, and projects and other information relating to the Business, or the operations or activities of the Business learned by the Seller Parties heretofore or hereafter.

(b) **Covenant Not to Compete.** From the Effective Date until three years after the Closing Date (or, in the case of SE, if later, for so long as she is employed by Buyer or otherwise receiving compensation under the Employment Agreement) (in each case, the "*Non-Compete Period*") none of the Seller Parties shall, without the prior written consent of Buyer, in its sole discretion, directly or indirectly, alone or as a partner, joint venturer, officer, director, member, employee, consultant, agent, independent contractor or equity interest holder of, or as lender to, any person or business, engage in the business of developing, importing, manufacturing, distributing or selling health and beauty products, anywhere in the United States, so long as Buyer, or any successor in interest of the Buyer, remains engaged in the Business.

(c) **Covenant Not to Induce.** From the Effective Date until three years after the Closing Date (or, in the case of SE, if later, until two years after termination of her employment with Buyer) (in each case, the "*Restricted Period*"), Seller Parties shall not directly or indirectly (A) induce or attempt to influence any customer, vendor, lessor or supplier of Buyer to terminate their relationship with Buyer or to enter into any contract with or otherwise patronize any business directly or indirectly in competition with the Business; (B) canvass, solicit, or accept from any person or entity who is or was within the preceding six (6) months a customer, vendor, supplier or lessor of Company, any such Business; or (C) request or advise any person or entity who is or was a customer, vendor, supplier or lessor of the Business, to withdraw, curtail, or cancel any such customer's, vendor's, supplier's or lessor's business with Buyer.

(d) **Covenant Not to Solicit.** During the Restricted Period, Seller Parties shall not, directly or indirectly, (A) solicit for employment or other similar relationship with any Seller Party, its affiliates or anyone else, any employee or then currently active independent contractor of Buyer, or any person who was an employee or then currently active independent contractor of Buyer, within the six-month period immediately preceding such solicitation of employment, other than such person who independently responded to a general solicitation for employment by such Seller Party or such Seller Party's affiliate; or (B) induce or attempt to induce, any employee or independent contractor of Buyer, to terminate such employee's employment or independent contractor's active contractual relationship with Buyer.

(e) **Covenant Not to Hire.** During the Restricted Period, Seller Parties shall not, directly or indirectly employ or knowingly permit any affiliate of any Seller Party to employ any person whom Buyer employed within the prior six months.

(f) **Non-disparagement.** Each of the parties agrees that, during the Restricted Period, none of Buyer, on the one hand, or the Shareholders, on the other, will knowingly and intentionally make statements or representations, or otherwise communicate, directly or indirectly, in writing, orally, or otherwise, or knowingly and intentionally take any action which may, directly or indirectly, disparage the other or their respective officers, trustees, directors, employees, advisors, businesses or reputations. Notwithstanding the foregoing, nothing in this Agreement shall preclude the parties from making (i) truthful statements, (ii) disclosures that are required by applicable law, regulation or legal process (iii) disclosures in connection with any legal or arbitration proceedings.

(g) **Specific Performance.** If any Seller Party breaches, or threatens to commit a breach of, any of the provisions of the Restrictive Covenants, in addition to any other available remedies, Buyer shall have the right and remedy to have the Restrictive Covenants specifically enforced by any court having equity jurisdiction, all without the need to post a bond or any other security or to prove any amount of actual damage or that money damages would not provide an adequate remedy, it being acknowledged and agreed that any such breach or threatened breach will cause irreparable injury to Buyer and that monetary damages alone will not provide an adequate remedy to Buyer.

(h) **Severability.** If any court determines that any of the Restrictive Covenants, or any part thereof, is invalid or unenforceable, the remainder of the Restrictive Covenants shall not thereby be affected and shall be given full effect, without regard to the invalid portions. If any court determines that any of the Restrictive Covenants, or any part thereof, is unenforceable because of the duration of such provision or the area covered thereby, such court shall have the power to reduce the duration or area of such provision and, in its reduced form, such provision shall then be enforceable and shall be enforced. Seller Parties hereby waive any and all right to attack the validity of the Restrictive Covenants on the grounds of the breadth of their geographic scope or the length of their term.

(i) The parties acknowledge and agree that the foregoing restrictive covenants are in addition to and not in lieu of the restrictive covenants set forth in the Employment Agreement, and that separate consideration has been received for each set of restrictive covenants.

ARTICLE 6.
CONDITIONS

6.1   **Conditions Precedent to Obligation of Buyer.** Buyer's obligation to consummate the Transactions contemplated to occur in connection with Closing and thereafter is subject to the satisfaction of each condition precedent listed below. Unless expressly waived pursuant to this Agreement, no representation, warranty, covenant, right or remedy available to Buyer in connection with the Transactions will be deemed waived by any of the following actions or inactions by or on behalf of Buyer (regardless of whether any Seller Party is given notice of any such matter): (i) consummation by Buyer of the Transactions, (ii) any inspection or investigation, if any, of any Company or Seller, (iii) the awareness of any fact or matter acquired (or capable or reasonably capable of being acquired) with respect to Company or Seller, or (iv) any other action, in each case at any time, whether before, on, or after the Closing Date.

Conditions

(a) **Accuracy of Representations and Warranties.** Each representation and warranty set forth in ARTICLE 4 must be accurate and complete in all material respects as of the Closing Date, as if made on the Closing Date.

(b) **Compliance with Obligations.** Seller Parties must have performed and complied with all of their covenants to be performed or complied with at or prior to Closing (singularly and in the aggregate) in all material respects.

(c) **No Material Adverse Change or Destruction of Property.** Since the Balance Sheet Date hereof there must have been no event, series of events or the lack of occurrence thereof

11

which, singularly or in the aggregate, could reasonably be expected to have a material adverse effect on the Business or the Acquired Assets.

(d) **Consents.** The parties shall have received all approvals and consents required from all third parties necessary in order to consummate the Transactions contemplated hereunder.

(e) **Due Diligence.** Buyer must have satisfactorily completed its reasonable due diligence review of the Business.

(f) **Deliverables.** The deliverables set forth in Section 2.4 shall have been duly executed and delivered by all parties thereto.

6.2   **Conditions Precedent to Obligation of Seller Parties.** Each Seller Party's obligation to consummate the Transactions contemplated to occur in connection with the Closing and thereafter is subject to the satisfaction of each condition precedent listed below. Unless expressly waived pursuant to this Agreement, no representation, warranty, covenant, right, or remedy available to any Seller Party in connection with the Transactions will be deemed waived by any of the following actions or inactions by or on behalf of any Seller Party (regardless of whether Buyer is given notice of any such matter): (i) consummation by Seller Parties of the Transactions, (ii) any inspection or investigation, if any, of Buyer, (iii) the awareness of any fact or matter acquired (or capable or reasonably capable of being acquired) with respect to Buyer, or (iv) any other Action, in each case at any time, whether before, on, or after the Closing Date.

(a) **Accuracy of Representations and Warranties.** Each representation and warranty set forth in ARTICLE 3 must be accurate and complete in all material respects as of the Closing Date, as if made on the Closing Date.

(b) **Compliance with Obligations.** Buyer must have performed and complied with all its covenants and obligations required by this Agreement to be performed or complied with at or prior to Closing (singularly and in the aggregate) in all material respects.

ARTICLE 7.
TERMINATION

7.1   **Termination of Agreement.** The parties may terminate this Agreement as provided below:

Remedies

(a) Buyer and Seller Parties may terminate this Agreement by mutual written consent at any time prior to Closing.

(b) Buyer may terminate this Agreement by giving written notice to Seller Parties at any time prior to the Closing if any of the Seller Parties have breached any representation, warranty, or covenant contained in this Agreement in any material respect, or in the event the conditions precedent set forth in Section 6.1 are not satisfied or waived on or prior to the date specified.

(c) Seller Parties may terminate this Agreement by giving notice to Buyer at any time prior to the Closing if Buyer has breached any representation, warranty, or covenant contained in this Agreement in any material respect, or in the event the conditions precedent set forth in Section 6.2 are not satisfied or waived on or prior to the date specified.

7.2   **Effect of Termination.**

(a) Except for the obligations under Section 5.8, 5.10, 5.15, this ARTICLE 7, ARTICLE 8, and ARTICLE 9, if this Agreement is terminated under this ARTICLE 7 then, except as provided in this ARTICLE 7, all further obligations of the parties under this Agreement will terminate.

(b) Nothing in this ARTICLE 7 shall relieve either party of any willful breach of this Agreement which occurs prior to the date of termination.

12

ARTICLE 8.
INDEMNIFICATION

8.1   Indemnity. For purposes of this Agreement, "*Losses*" shall mean all damages (other than incidental or consequential), awards, judgments, assessments, fines, sanctions, penalties, charges, costs, expenses, payments, diminutions in value and other losses, however suffered or characterized, all interest thereon, all costs and expenses of investigating any claim, lawsuit or arbitration and any appeal therefrom, all actual attorneys' fees incurred in connection therewith, whether or not such claim, lawsuit or arbitration is ultimately defeated and all amounts paid incident to any compromise or settlement of any such claim, lawsuit or arbitration. In addition to any indemnification obligations provided elsewhere in this Agreement or the Transaction Documents, Seller Parties shall indemnify, defend and hold harmless Buyer, its affiliates and their respective shareholders, members, directors, officers, managers, employees, agents, attorneys and representatives, assigns and successors in interest, from and against any and all Losses which may be incurred or suffered by any such party and which may arise out of or result from: (a) the operation of the Business prior to the Closing Date; (b) any breach of any representation, warranty, covenant or agreement of Seller Parties contained in this Agreement or in any other Transaction Document, or failure of Seller Parties to fully transfer to Buyer any Acquired Assets; (c) any liability of Company which is not expressly assumed hereunder by Buyer, including any liability that becomes a liability of Buyer under operation of law or otherwise. The liability of Seller Parties under this Section 8 shall be joint and several and shall survive the expiration or termination of this Agreement. Buyer shall have the right, in its sole discretion, to waive or delay in enforcing its rights as to one or more of Seller Parties without losing or affecting any of its rights to proceed against the other Seller Party(-ies).

8.2   Survival of Representations and Covenants of Seller Parties. Notwithstanding any right of Buyer fully to investigate the affairs of Company and notwithstanding any knowledge of facts determined or determinable by Buyer pursuant to such investigation or right of investigation, Buyer shall have the right to rely fully upon the representations, warranties, covenants and agreements of Seller Parties contained in this Agreement or in any Transaction Document. Each representation, warranty, covenant and agreement of Seller Parties contained herein shall survive the execution and delivery of this Agreement and the Closing.

8.3   Set Off Rights. Buyer will have the option of setting off all or any part of any Losses Buyer suffers against any Earn-Out Amount owed by Buyer under this Agreement. Without limiting the foregoing, any breach by Seller Parties of the covenants contained in Sections 5.12 or 5.16 shall excuse payment by Buyer of all or a portion of the Earn-Out Amount.

ARTICLE 9.
MISCELLANEOUS

9.1   Schedules. If there is any inconsistency between the statements in the body of this Agreement and those in the Schedules (other than an exception expressly set forth as in the Schedules with respect to a specifically identified representation or warranty), the statements in the body of this Agreement will control.

9.2   Entire Agreement. This Agreement, together with the Exhibits and Schedules hereto and the certificates, documents, instruments and writings that are delivered pursuant hereto, constitutes the entire agreement and understanding of the parties in respect of its subject matters and, in the absence of fraud, supersedes all prior understandings, agreements, or representations by or among the parties, written or oral, to the extent they relate in any way to the subject matter hereof or the Transactions. There are no third party beneficiaries having rights under or with respect to this Agreement.

"Boilerplate"

9.3   Successors. All of the terms, agreements, covenants, representations, warranties, and conditions of this Agreement are binding upon, and inure to the benefit of and are enforceable by, the parties and their respective successors.

9.4   Assignments. No party may assign either this Agreement or any of its rights, interests, or obligations hereunder without the prior written approval of the other; provided, however, that Buyer may (a) assign any or all of its rights and interests hereunder to one or more of its affiliates and (b) designate one or more of its affiliates to perform its obligations hereunder (in which case Buyer nonetheless will remain responsible for the performance of all of its obligations hereunder).

9.5   Notices. All notices, requests, demands, claims and other communications hereunder will be in writing. Any notice, request, demand, claim or other communication hereunder will be deemed duly given if (and then three business days after) it is sent by registered or certified mail, return receipt requested, postage prepaid, and addressed to the intended recipient as set forth below:

If to Buyer:
Copy to (which will not constitute notice):
If to Seller Parties:
And to:

Any party may send any notice, request, demand, claim, or other communication hereunder to the intended recipient at the address set forth above using any other means (including personal delivery, expedited courier, messenger service, telecopy, telex, ordinary mail, or electronic mail), but no such notice, request, demand, claim, or other communication will be deemed to have been duly given unless and until it actually is received by the intended recipient. Any party may change the address to which notices, requests, demands, claims, and other communications hereunder are to be delivered by giving the other parties notice in the manner herein set forth.

9.6   Time. Time is of the essence in the performance of this Agreement.

9.7   Counterparts. This Agreement may be executed in two or more counterparts, each of which will be deemed an original but all of which together will constitute one and the same instrument.

9.8   Headings. The article and section headings contained in this Agreement are inserted for convenience only and will not affect in any way the meaning or interpretation of this Agreement.

9.9   Governing Law. This Agreement and the performance of the Transactions and obligations of the parties hereunder will be governed by and construed in accordance with the laws of California, without giving effect to any choice of law principles.

9.10   Amendments and Waivers. No amendment, modification, replacement, termination or cancellation of any provision of this Agreement will be valid, unless the same will be in writing and signed by Buyer and Seller Parties. No waiver by any party of any default, misrepresentation, or breach of warranty or covenant hereunder, whether intentional or not, may be deemed to extend to any prior or subsequent default, misrepresentation, or breach of warranty or covenant hereunder or affect in any way any rights arising because of any prior or subsequent such occurrence.

9.11   Severability. The provisions of this Agreement will be deemed severable and the invalidity or unenforceability of any provision will not affect the validity or enforceability of the other provisions hereof; provided that if any provision of this Agreement, as applied to any party or to any circumstance, is adjudged by a governmental body, arbitrator, or mediator not to be enforceable in accordance with its terms, the parties agree that the governmental body, arbitrator, or mediator making such determination will have the power to modify the provision in a manner consistent with its objectives such that it is enforceable, and/or to delete specific words or phrases, and in its reduced form, such provision will then be enforceable and will be enforced.

9.12 **Expenses.** Except as otherwise expressly provided in this Agreement, each party will bear its own costs and expenses incurred in connection with the preparation, execution and performance of this Agreement and the Transactions including all fees and expenses of agents, representatives, financial advisors, legal counsel and accountants.

9.13 **Obligations of Seller Parties Joint and Several.** The obligations of Seller Parties hereunder are joint and several.

9.14 **Remedies.** Except as expressly provided herein, the rights, obligations and remedies created by this Agreement are cumulative and in addition to any other rights, obligations, or remedies otherwise available at law or in equity. Except as expressly provided herein, nothing herein will be considered an election of remedies.

9.15 **Attorneys Fees.** In the event that any action or arbitration proceeding is brought to enforce any of the provisions of this Agreement and such action results in the award of a judgment for money damages or in the granting of any injunction or other equitable relief in favor of one of the parties to this Agreement, the prevailing party shall be entitled to reimbursement for all expenses, including reasonable attorneys' fees.

IN WITNESS WHEREOF, the parties have executed this Agreement as of the date first above written.

BUYER

By: _____

Name:_____

Title: _____

SHAREHOLDERS

By: _____

Name:, an individual _____

By: _____

Name:, an individual _____

COMPANY
[   ], Inc.,

By: _____

Name:_____

Title: _____

By: _____

Name:_____

Title: _____

15

Schedules & Exhibits

Appendix B-6.2

This sample distribution agreement is for use with Exercise 11.3.

DISTRIBUTION AGREEMENT

This Distribution Agreement ("AGREEMENT") is entered into as of the ____ day of _____, 20__ by and between Organa Corp. ("SUPPLIER") and [   ] ("DISTRIBUTOR")

RECITALS

A. SUPPLIER is the producer of certain organic snack foods from the state of California as more particularly identified on the price list attached hereto, and made a part hereof, as schedule A (hereinafter referred to as the "Products");

B. DISTRIBUTOR desires to secure from SUPPLIER, and SUPPLIER is willing to grant to DISTRIBUTOR, the exclusive right to sell and distribute SUPPLIER'S Products in the United States of America with the exception of the state of *STATE* and direct retail, airline or consumer sales and sales exported out of the country from SUPPLIER's facility (hereinafter referred to as the "Territory").

NOW THEREFORE, it is mutually agreed as follows:

AGREEMENT

1. SUPPLIER hereby appoints DISTRIBUTOR as its sole and exclusive distributor for the term of this Agreement for the sale and distribution of the Products in and throughout the Territory. DISTRIBUTOR will maintain, or cause to be maintained, a sales staff for the distribution of products handled by DISTRIBUTOR, including the Products, and DISTRIBUTOR shall use its best efforts to promote the sale and distribution of SUPPLIER'S Products.

2. SUPPLIER will not ship the Products, or any other products bearing the same or similar trademark, signature or identification anywhere on the package, to the Territory except under the order or by the direction of DISTRIBUTOR. It will refer to DISTRIBUTOR any and all orders or inquiries for the Products that it may receive for shipment to the Territory, or orders which are intended for eventual shipment to the Territory.

3. SUPPLIER will fill promptly and to the best of its ability all orders for the Products received from DISTRIBUTOR. The price to DISTRIBUTOR shall be based on delivery to DISTRIBUTOR'S

293

warehouse and shall include a mutually negotiated delivered price to said warehouse. SUPPLIER and DISTRIBUTOR shall negotiate any price increases for the Products at least 60 days prior to the effective date of any such increase. DISTRIBUTOR shall have the right to order one month's supply of the Products at the current price prior to any increase. Payment in U.S. dollars shall be made by DISTRIBUTOR 90 days from the date of delivery to DISTRIBUTOR'S warehouse.

4. DISTRIBUTOR and SUPPLIER shall agree on an annual basis, or more frequently if required, as to the prices at which DISTRIBUTOR shall sell the Products to its customers. SUPPLIER will furnish to DISTRIBUTOR, promptly upon request, any and all authorizations that may be required by any governmental authority in connection with the sale and distribution of the Products in the Territory, provided that SUPPLIER is responsible for obtaining or maintaining said authorizations.

5. Pursuant to paragraphs 3 and 4 hereof, SUPPLIER and DISTRIBUTOR shall agree on SUPPLIER'S price to DISTRIBUTOR and DISTRIBUTOR'S price to its customers. In the event that SUPPLIER and DISTRIBUTOR cannot agree on either price within 30 days of commencement of the negotiations, the prices then in effect for each of said prices will be increased by an amount equal to the change in the Consumer Price Index-All U.S. over a period of months equal to the number of months since the last price increase for each price.

6. SUPPLIER warrants, represents and agrees that all shipments of the Products sold or shipped under this Agreement shall be of first quality, suitable for consumption, properly packaged in California, free from foreign matter, whether or not prejudicial to health, and will be packaged in conformity with applicable laws, regulations and requirements in effect within the Territory.

7. SUPPLIER will, upon demand, promptly execute such documents and perform such acts as may be necessary so as to prevent any products labeled in imitation or simulation of the Products from being distributed in the Territory.

8. The term of this Agreement shall be for a period of three years commencing on
January 1, 20__, and terminating on December 31, 20___, and shall thereafter continue in effect unless either party shall notify the other of its intention to terminate this Agreement by giving at least 12 months written notice prior to any specified termination date. Either party shall have the option to terminate this Agreement after six months of the notice period by paying to the other party a sum equal to one-half of the case volume of the previous calendar year multiplied by $*DOLLAR* per case. However, in the event of a breach of any of the terms and provisions of this Agreement, either party may terminate this Agreement by giving the other party 90 days written notice provided said notice shall set forth the breach being claimed as the basis for termination. If the offending party cures the breach being claimed within said 90-day period, the notice of termination shall be void and this Agreement shall continue in full and force and effect.

9. Notwithstanding the provisions of paragraph 7 hereof, SUPPLIER shall have the right to terminate this Agreement upon 60 days written notice in the event that DISTRIBUTOR shall:

a. be declared bankrupt or enter a voluntary petition for bankruptcy or in any way enter into a compromise or agreement for the benefit of its creditors;

b. fail to meet at least 90 percent of the mutually agreed upon sales performance goals set forth in Schedule B, attached hereto and made a part hereof;

c. fail to maintain in good standing all Federal and state licenses and permits necessary for the proper conduct of its business;

d. change or in any way be affected by a change in the majority ownership of its business

e. sells all or substantially all of its assets to a third party.

10. DISTRIBUTOR, upon request from SUPPLIER, will furnish SUPPLIER with available sales and depletion reports and details of all promotional and sampling programs with respect to the Products. DISTRIBUTOR will discuss with SUPPLIER any proposed changes in its distributor network at least 30 days prior to any such change.

11. Upon termination of this Agreement by either party, SUPPLIER shall repurchase, or cause its successor representative to purchase, as of said termination date, DISTRIBUTOR'S then existing inventory of SUPPLIER'S Products at DISTRIBUTOR'S laid-in cost, provided DISTRIBUTOR has properly stored and maintained the inventory of the Products in a saleable condition.

12. This Agreement is the entire agreement between the parties, cannot be changed orally, and neither party has made any representations or promises to the other which are not expressed in this Agreement.

13. No waiver of a breach of the terms of this Agreement shall be effective unless made in writing, and no such waiver shall be deemed a waiver of any other existing or subsequent breach. No modification of this Agreement shall be of any effect unless set forth in writing.

14. All the provisions of this Agreement are made subject to all applicable laws, regulations, rules or requirements of the Government of the United States of America or agencies of said Government, and in the performance of this Agreement, each of the parties hereto agrees to comply therewith.

15. All notices shall be sent prepaid either by mail or facsimile addressed to the respective parties at the address hereinabove set forth, unless they shall otherwise notify in writing.

16. This Agreement is a California contract and shall be governed by and construed in accordance with the laws of the state of California. Any controversy or claim arising out of or relating to this Agreement or the breach thereof shall be settled by arbitration in California in accordance with the rules of the American Arbitration Association then in effect, and judgment upon the award rendered by the arbitrator or arbitrators shall be final and binding upon the parties hereto.

17. If arbitration is required to enforce or to interpret a provision of this Agreement, or otherwise arises with respect to the subject matter of this Agreement, the prevailing party shall be entitled, in addition to, other rights and remedies that it may have, to reimbursement for its expenses incurred with respect to that action, including court costs and reasonable attorneys' fees at trial, on appeal;, and in connection with any petition for review.

18. This Agreement shall not be assigned by either party hereto without the prior written consent of the non-assigning party. For purposes of this Agreement, a "change in control" (including by any change in the ownership of more than fifty percent (50%) of the voting capital stock of a party in one or more related transactions, mcrger (whether or not such party is the surviving corporation), operation of law or any other manners) shall be deemed an assignment.

IN WITNESS WHEREOF, the parties hereto have caused this Agreement to be executed as of the day and year first above written.

SUPPLIER   DISTRIBUTOR

By: _____   By: _____

Name: Name:

Title: Title:

Appendix B-6.3

This sample share purchase agreement is an example of a pro-buyer first draft illustrating the common provisions typically included in a mid-sized transaction. Note the provisions left blank at this stage, a fairly common practice. Depending on the value of the transaction, the type of business, and the parties involved, the various provisions may vary. For example, in the acquisition of a company that designs software or other technology, you would likely see more extensive representations regarding intellectual property. As with the asset purchase agreement in Appendix B-6.1 Seller may also seek to negotiate some of the provisions by including additional qualifications, softeners, or exceptions, or by adding, modifying, or deleting language.

Compare the provisions and structure of this agreement to the sample asset purchase agreement in Appendix B-6.1. Note the similarities and differences in structure and style.

SHARE PURCHASE AGREEMENT

This Share Purchase Agreement (this *"Agreement"*), dated _____, 2011 (the *"Effective Date"*), is by and among (i) [   ], **LLC**, a company organized under the laws of California, with its registered office at [   ], New York, 10022, U.S.A. (*"Buyer"*), (ii) [   ], *an individual residing at _____ ("Seller"), and (iii) [   ]* **UK Ltd.**, a private limited company (registered in England and Wales under company Number [   ]), the registered office of which is at [   ], England (the *"Company"*, *and, together with Seller, the "Seller Parties"*).

Preamble

RECITALS:

A. Seller is the legal and beneficial owner of all of the outstanding shares of the Company (the *"Shares"*).

B. Buyer desires to purchase from Seller, and Seller desires to sell to Buyer the Shares, in accordance with the terms and conditions set forth herein.

Recitals

AGREEMENT:

NOW, THEREFORE, in consideration of the premises and the mutual promises herein made, and in consideration of the representations, warranties, and covenants contained herein, Buyer and Seller agree as follows:

ARTICLE 1.
DEFINITIONS

"*Affiliate*" or "*Affiliated*" with respect to any specified Person, means a Person that, directly or indirectly, through one or more intermediaries, controls or is controlled by, or is under common control with, such specified Person. For this definition, "*control*" (and its derivatives) means the possession, directly or indirectly, of 50% or more of the voting equity interests of a Person, or the power, directly or indirectly, to vote 50% or more of the voting equity interests of a Person.

"*Encumbrance*" means, with respect to an interest in an asset, any mortgage, pledge, security interest, charge, lien, hypothecation, proxy coupled with an interest, option, preferential right to purchase, or other similar instrument, device or power, or any agreement to create any of the foregoing.

"*Proprietary Information*" means and includes any and all trade secret, confidential proprietary and/or Intellectual Property and/or knowledge, data or information relating to, or used, conceived, discovered or developed in connection with, the business of the Company, of any nature whatsoever and existing and/or stored in any medium whatsoever, including any work-for-hire performed by Seller, and any information regarding plans for development, new products, marketing and selling, business plans, budgets and unpublished financial statements, licenses, prices and costs, supplier and customer lists, and names and addresses or any data on or relating to prospective customers or clients, information regarding the skills compensation and benefits of employees, domain names, corporate name, and any other confidential information relating to or dealing with the business, operations or activities of the Company. Intellectual Property includes without limitation, any and all copyrights, trademarks, trade names, patents, inventions, improvements, processes, procedures, other works of authorship, know-how, discoveries, drawings, engineering, and designs (*"Intellectual Property"*).

Other terms defined elsewhere in this Agreement include:

"*Agreement*"	is defined in the Preamble.
"*Buyer*"	is defined in the Preamble.
"*Company*"	is defined in the Preamble.
"*Effective Date*"	is defined in the Preamble.
"*Lease*"	is defined in Section 5.3.
"*Required Consent*"	is defined in Section 3.1.
"*Restricted Period*"	is defined in Section 5.6(a).
"*Seller*"	is defined in the Preamble.
"*Seller Parties*"	is defined in the Preamble.
"*Shares*"	is defined in Recital A.
"*Transaction Documents*"	is defined in Section 3.1(a).

ARTICLE 2.
PURCHASE AND SALE OF SHARES

2.1 **Purchase and Sale of Shares.** On and subject to the terms and conditions of this Agreement, effective as of the Effective Date, Buyer agrees to purchase from Seller, and Seller agrees to sell to Buyer, all of the Shares fully paid up and free from any Encumbrance, together with all rights which, as of the Effective Date or subsequently, attach to them, for the consideration specified in <u>Section 2.2.</u>

2.2 **Consideration.**

(a) As consideration for the Shares and the goodwill associated therewith, Buyer shall pay to Seller the Purchase Price set forth on Schedule 2.2. The parties hereby acknowledge and agree that no additional consideration is due for the purchase of the Shares hereunder. Seller further acknowledges and agrees that, as of the Effective Date, Seller shall cease to have any rights with respect to the Shares and/or the assets of the Company, including any rights to receive dividends or distributions or any revenue-sharing or profit-sharing rights. Furthermore, the parties acknowledge that any and all compensation, dividends, distributions or other amounts, including without limitation all salary, bonus and other benefits of any nature, earned by Seller or otherwise payable to Seller by Company for services rendered by Seller to the Company prior to the Effective Date, have been paid in full, and no other or additional compensation or benefits are payable and/or may accrue or become payable to Seller hereunder in respect of the period prior to the Effective Date.

(b) The parties acknowledge and agree that Buyer shall have the right to set off from the Purchase Price all or a portion of any outstanding principal and interest owed by Seller to Buyer under any loans provided by Buyer to Seller.

2.3   **Taxes.** In respect of United Kingdom or United States stamp duty or other documentary or transfer taxes payable in relation to this Agreement or the transfer of the Shares pursuant to this Agreement, Buyer shall be responsible for the payment of such amount of stamp duty or other documentary or transfer taxes as determined by the relevant tax authority.

2.4   **Deliverables.** Concurrent with the execution and delivery of this Agreement, the parties shall execute and/or deliver the following:

(i)   Seller shall deliver any and all certificates representing the Shares, duly endorsed in blank, together with a duly executed stock transfer in registrable form;

(ii)   Seller shall deliver his resignation from any directorship or officership, employment or other position within the Company;

(iii) Seller Parties shall deliver to Buyer all originals books and records of the Company, including without limitation, the certificate of incorporation or registration, all share registers, minute books and other statutory books, and any leases and other contracts in effect as of the Effective Date;

(iv)   Seller Parties shall deliver to Buyer a duly completed authority for the alteration of signatories of every bank account of the Company as required by Buyer;

(v)   Seller Parties shall deliver to Buyer any assignment documents necessary to ensure proper transfer to and ownership by the Company of any and all tradenames, trademarks or other Intellectual Property associated with the business of the Company;

(vi)   Seller Parties shall deliver to Buyer:

(a)   an Officers' certificate of the Company, substantially in the form of Exhibit A, duly executed on the Company's behalf;

(b)   a Secretary's certificate of the Company, substantially in the form of Exhibit B, duly executed on the Company's behalf;

(c)   the resignation, effective as of the Closing, of each the Company's directors and officers;

(d)   pay-off letters, dated as of the Effective Date, from each lender to the Company, evidencing that all indebtedness owed to such lender has been paid in full; and

(e)   all Required Consents obtained on or prior to the Effective Date; and

(vii) Buyer shall deliver to Seller Parties:

(f) $ _____ in cash, via wire transfer;

(g)   an Officers' certificate of Buyer, substantially in the form of Exhibit C, duly executed on Buyer's behalf;

Operative
Provisions —
Deliverables

3

(h) a Secretary's certificate of Buyer, substantially in the form of Exhibit D, duly executed on Buyer's behalf; and

(i) [other — to be determined]; and

(viii) The Company and each employee of the Company to be retained by the Company after the Effective Date shall deliver executed counterparts of an Employment Agreement in substantially the form of Exhibit E; and

(ix) The parties shall also deliver to each other the agreements, including without limitation any accompanying escrow agreement, and other documents and instruments required to be delivered pursuant to this Agreement

ARTICLE 3.
REPRESENTATIONS AND WARRANTIES

Representations and Warranties.

3.1   Representations and Warranties of Seller Parties. Seller Parties jointly and severally represent and warrant to Buyer that the statements contained in this Section 3.1 are correct and complete as of the Effective Date:

(a) **Status of Seller.** Seller is an individual with the requisite competence and authority to execute and deliver this Agreement and each other document deliverable pursuant to Section 2.4 above (collectively, the "*Transaction Documents*"), and to perform and to consummate the transactions contemplated hereunder and thereunder.

(b) **Power and Authority; Enforceability.** Seller has the requisite competence and authority to execute and deliver each Transaction Document to which he or she is a party, and to perform and to consummate the transactions described therein. Seller has taken all actions necessary to authorize the execution and delivery of this Agreement and each Transaction Document, the performance of Seller's obligations hereunder and thereunder, and the consummation of the contemplated transactions. This Agreement and each Transaction Document has been duly authorized, executed, and delivered by, and is enforceable against, Seller.

(c) **No Violation.** The execution and the delivery of the Agreement and/or the Transaction Documents by Seller and the performance and consummation of the transactions contemplated herein and therein by Seller will not (i) breach any law or order to which Seller is subject or any provision of any of the Company's articles or by-laws, (ii) breach any contract, order, or permit to which Seller or the Company is a party or by which Seller or the Company is bound or to which any of the Company's assets is subject, or (iii) require any consent of any third party. Seller has not breached any contract to which Seller is a party or by which Seller is bound or any of its assets is subject.

(d) **Shares.** Seller holds of record and owns beneficially _____ Shares, representing all of the issued and outstanding shares of the Company, free and clear of any Encumbrances. Seller is not a party to any contract that could require Seller to sell, transfer, or otherwise dispose of any Shares (other than this Agreement).

(e) **Brokers' Fee.** Seller has no liability to pay any compensation to any broker, finder, or agent with respect to the transactions contemplated by the Transaction Documents for which Buyer or the Company could become directly or indirectly liable.

3.2   Representations and Warranties of Buyer.

Buyer warrants to Seller Parties that the statements contained in this Section 3.2 are correct and complete as of the Effective Date:

(a) **Entity Status.** Buyer is a company duly organized, validly existing and in good standing

4

under the laws of California. Buyer has the requisite power and authority to own or lease its properties and to carry on its business as currently conducted. There is no pending or threatened action (or basis therefor) for the dissolution, liquidation, insolvency, or rehabilitation of Buyer.

(b) **Power and Authority; Enforceability.** Buyer has the power and authority to execute and deliver the Agreement and each Transaction Document to which it is party, and to perform and consummate the transactions contemplated hereunder and thereunder. Buyer has taken all action necessary to authorize the execution and delivery of this Agreement and each Transaction Document to which it is party, the performance of its obligations thereunder, and the consummation of the transactions. This Agreement and each Transaction Document to which Buyer is a party has been duly authorized, executed and delivered by, and is enforceable against, Buyer.

(c) **No Violation.** The execution and delivery of this Agreement and/or the Transaction Documents to which Buyer is a party by Buyer and the performance and consummation of the contemplated transactions by Buyer will not (i) breach any law or order to which Buyer is subject or any provision of its organizational documents; (ii) breach any contract, order, or permit to which Buyer is a party or by which it is bound or to which any of its assets is subject; or (iii) require any third party consent.

(d) **Brokers' Fee.** Buyer has no liability to pay any compensation to any broker, finder, or agent with respect to the transactions contemplated by the Transaction Documents for which Seller could become directly or indirectly liable.

(e) **Representations Complete.** Except as and to the extent set forth in this Agreement, and in the absence of fraud, Buyer makes no representations or warranties whatsoever to any Seller Party and hereby disclaims all liability and responsibility for any representation, warranty, statement, or information not included herein that was made, communicated, or furnished (orally or in writing) to any Seller Party or its representatives (including any opinion, information, projection, or advice that may have been or may be provided to any Seller Party by any director, officer, employee, agent, consultant, or representative of Buyer or any Affiliate thereof).

ARTICLE 4.
REPRESENTATIONS AND WARRANTIES
CONCERNING THE COMPANY

Seller Parties jointly and severally represent and warrant to Buyer that the statements contained in this <u>ARTICLE 4</u> are correct and complete as of the Effective Date:

4.1   **Company Status.** The Company is duly incorporated, validly existing, and in good standing under the laws of England and Wales. The Company is duly authorized to conduct its business and is in good standing under the laws of each jurisdiction where such qualification is required. The Company has the requisite power and authority necessary to own or lease its properties and to carry on its businesses as currently conducted. Seller has delivered to Buyer correct and complete copies of the Company's organizational documents, as amended to date. The Company is not in breach of any provision of its organizational documents. There is no pending or, to Seller Parties' knowledge, threatened action (or basis therefor) for the dissolution, liquidation, insolvency, or rehabilitation of the Company.

4.2   **Power and Authority; Enforceability.** The Company has the power and authority necessary to execute and deliver this Agreement and each Transaction Document to which it is a party. The

> Note use of qualifiers and exceptions in this Section

Company has taken all action necessary to authorize the execution and delivery of this Agreement and each Transaction Document to which it is a party, the performance of its obligations hereunder and thereunder, and the consummation of the transactions contemplated herein and therein. This Agreement and each Transaction Document to which the Company is party has been duly authorized, executed, and delivered by, and is enforceable against, the Company.

4.3   No Violation. The execution and the delivery of the applicable Transaction Documents by the Company and the performance of its obligations hereunder and thereunder, and consummation of the transactions contemplated hereby and thereby by Seller will not (a) breach any law or order to which the Company is subject or any provision of the organizational documents of the Company; (b) breach any contract, order, or permit to which the Company is a party or by which it is bound or to which any of its assets is subject; (c) require any consent of any third party necessary or desirable in order for the Company to continue after the Effective Date to enjoy all of the rights, powers and benefits available to and/or enjoyed by the Company prior to the Effective Date ("*Required Consents*"), other than any Required Consents which have been obtained or made as of the Effective Date; (d) trigger any rights of first refusal, preferential purchase, or similar rights; or (e) cause the recognition of gain or loss for tax purposes with respect to the Company or subject the Company or its assets to any tax.

4.4   Brokers' Fees. The Company does not have any liability to pay any compensation to any broker, finder or agent with respect to the transactions contemplated by the Transaction Documents for which Buyer or the Company could become directly or indirectly liable.

4.5   Capitalization. All of the issued and outstanding Shares of the Company (A) have been duly authorized, are validly issued, fully paid, and nonassessable, (B) were issued in compliance with all applicable securities laws, (C) were not issued in breach of any commitments, and (D) are held of record and owned beneficially by Seller. No commitments exist with respect to any equity interest of the Company and no such commitments will arise in connection with the contemplated transactions.

4.6   Records and Accounts. The copies of the Company's books and records and statutory accounts provided to Buyer hereunder are accurate and complete and reflect all amendments made through the Effective Date. The statutory accounts have been prepared in accordance with U.K. GAAP applied on a consistent basis throughout the periods covered thereby, present fairly the financial condition of the Company as of such dates and the results of operations of the Company for such periods, are correct and complete, and are consistent with the books and records of the Company, subject to normal year-end adjustments (which will not be material individually or in the aggregate). Since the date of the most recent balance sheet, there has been no significant subsequent event that could reasonably be expected to have a material adverse effect on the Company or its financial condition.

4.7   Liabilities. The Company has no liability (and there is no basis for any present or future action or order against it giving rise to any liability), except for (a) liabilities quantified on the face of the statutory accounts (rather than in any notes thereto) and not heretofore paid or discharged, and (b) liabilities that have arisen after the date of the most recent balance sheet in the ordinary course of business which, individually or in the aggregate, are not material and are of the same character and nature as the liabilities quantified on the face of the statutory accounts (rather than any notes thereto) none of which results from or relates to any breach of contract, breach of warranty, tort, infringement, or breach of law, or arose out of any action or order.

4.8.   Legal Compliance. To the Seller Parties' knowledge, the Company and its predecessors and its Affiliates have complied with all applicable laws, and no action is pending or threatened (and there is no basis therefor) against it alleging any failure to so comply. No material expenditures are, or based on applicable law, will be required of the Company for it and its business and operations to remain in compliance with applicable law.

4.9   Tax Matters. The Company has paid all taxes levied against the Company in respect of all periods prior to the Effective Date (except for taxes not yet due).

4.10   Title to and Condition of Assets. The Company has good marketable title to, or a valid leasehold interest in, all buildings, machinery, equipment and other tangible assets located on their premises, included in the statutory accounts, or acquired since the date of the most recent balance sheet, except for those disposed of in the normal course of business, free and clear of all Encumbrances. Each such tangible asset is free from defects (patent and latent), has been maintained in accordance with normal industry practice, is in good operating condition (subject to normal wear and tear), and is suitable for the purposes for which it is currently used and currently is proposed to be used. None of the assets shown in the Company's books and records or statutory accounts or used by the Company is the subject of any lease, lease hire agreement, hire purchase agreement or capital lease or is the subject of any license or factoring arrangement.

4.11   Intellectual Property and other Proprietary Information. As of the date of this Agreement, the Company owns, or has validly licensed or otherwise has the right to use, all Proprietary Information used or held for use in connection with its business and all goodwill associated therewith. Seller has assigned, or promptly upon execution of this Agreement will assign, to the Company all of its right, title and interest in and to any and all Proprietary Information. To the knowledge of the Seller Parties, none of the Intellectual Property of Seller infringes on the intellectual property rights of any third party. There is no currently pending or threatened claim by Seller against any person or entity for infringement, misuse or misappropriation of any Intellectual Property nor is Seller aware of any such infringement, misuse or misappropriation.

4.12   Company Filings. All particulars, resolutions and other documents which the Company is required pursuant to the Companies Act of 1985 or by other law to file with or deliver to any authority in any jurisdiction have been correctly made up and filed or, as the case may be, delivered.

4.13   Contracts. Schedule 4.13 lists and describes briefly all material contracts to which the Company is a party or is otherwise bound.

4.14   Real Property. Schedule 4.14 lists and describes briefly all real property owned or leased by the Company.

4.15   Environmental. To Seller Parties' knowledge, the Company is not in violation of any applicable environmental law.

4.16   Litigation. There is no suit, action or other proceeding, or injunction or final judgment relating thereto pending, or to Seller Parties' knowledge, threatened against the Company, in which it is sought to restrain or prohibit or to obtain damages or other relief in connection with this Agreement or the consummation of the transactions contemplated hereby, or which could have a material adverse effect on the Company, and to the knowledge of the Seller Parties, no investigation that might result in any such suit, action or proceeding is pending or threatened.

4.17   Employee Matters/Employee Benefits. [*to be confirmed based on due diligence/consultation with UK counsel*]

4.18   Environmental, Health and Safety Matters. [*to be confirmed based on due diligence and UK environmental regs*]

4.19   Licenses, Permits and Consents. The Company has all necessary licenses, consents, permits and authorities necessary to carry on its business in the places and in the manner in which its business is now carried on, all of which are valid and subsisting. To the knowledge of Seller Parties, there is no reason why any of those licenses, consents, permits and authorities should be suspended, cancelled, revoked or not renewed on the same terms. The transactions contemplated by the Transaction Documents will not adversely affect the validity of any such license, consent or permit or cause a cancellation of or otherwise adversely affect such license, consent or permit.

4.20   **Foreign Corrupt Practices Act Compliance.** No Seller Party has, directly or indirectly, in connection with the Company's business, made or agreed to make any payment to any person or entity connected with or related to any governmental body, except payments or contributions required or allowed by applicable law. The internal accounting controls and procedures of the Company are sufficient to cause the Company to comply with the US Foreign Corrupt Practices Act.

ARTICLE 5.
COVENANTS

Covenants — note use of softeners

The parties agree as follows:

5.1   **General.** Each party will use its reasonably commercial efforts to take all actions and to do all things necessary, proper, or advisable to consummate, make effective, and comply with all of the terms of this Agreement and the transactions applicable to it.

5.2   **Confidentiality; Publicity.** Seller recognizes that he has had access to certain Proprietary Information that are valuable, special and unique assets of the Company and/or Buyer or Buyer's Affiliates or licensors, and Seller shall not use for Seller's personal benefit, or divulge to, or use for the direct or indirect benefit of, any person, firm, corporation, association or other entity, for any purpose or reason whatsoever, any Proprietary Information relating to the Company, Buyer or Buyer's Affiliates or licensors. The provisions of this paragraph shall be in addition to (and not a limitation of) any legally applicable protections of Company's interest in its confidential information, trade secrets and the like. Except as may be required by applicable law, or as otherwise expressly contemplated herein, no party or their respective Affiliates, employees, agents, and representatives will disclose to any third party the existence of this Agreement or the subject matter or terms hereof.

5.3   **Assignment of Lease.** The parties acknowledge and agree that the Company is currently a party to that certain lease dated _____ for the warehouse facilities located at _____, England (the "*Lease*"). The parties shall each use commercially reasonable efforts to cause the Lease to be assigned to Seller. In the event the parties are unable to obtain the necessary consent of the landlord to such assignment, the parties agree to enter into a mutually acceptable sub-lease (to the extent permitted by and in compliance with the terms of the Lease), pursuant to which the Company will sub-lease to Seller the premises under the Lease, and Seller will pay to the Company and assume the rent and all other obligations becoming due under the Lease from and after the closing of the transaction contemplated under this Agreement.

5.4   **Proprietary Information.** Seller shall take or cause to be taken all actions within Seller's control necessary or advisable to perfect and protect the Company's rights to the Proprietary Information, including but not limited to executing assignments and documents and providing all information and assistance required to achieve Company ownership of the Proprietary Information. In the event Seller fails to sign any such necessary assignment, applications or other documents, then Seller hereby irrevocably designates and appoints the Company and its duly authorized officers and agents as its agent and attorney in fact, to act for and in its behalf and stead to execute and file any such assignments, applications and documents and to do all other lawfully permitted acts to further the prosecution and issuance of letters patent or copyright registrations with the same legal force and effect as if executed by Seller.

5.5   Further Assurances. In case at any time after Closing any further action is necessary to carry out the purposes of this Agreement, each party will take such further action (including executing and delivering such further instruments and documents) as any other party reasonably may request, all at the requesting party's sole cost and expense. After completion, Buyer will be entitled to possession of all documents, books, records, agreements, and financial data of any sort relating to the Company.

5.6   Non-competition. To assure that Buyer will realize the benefits of the transactions contemplated hereunder, and as part of the consideration for the Purchase Price, Seller hereby agrees with Buyer:

Negative Covenants

(a) From the Effective Date and for a period of two (2) years following the Effective Date (the "*Restricted Period*"), Seller shall not, without the prior written consent of Buyer, in its sole discretion, directly or indirectly engage in (as principal, shareholder, partner, director, officer, agent, employee, consultant or otherwise) or be financially interested in any competing business of the Company that sells lift gate products within the U.K.; provided, however, nothing contained in this section shall prevent Seller from holding for investment no more than five percent (5%) of any class of equity securities of a company whose securities are publicly traded on a national securities exchange or in a national market system.

(b) During the Restricted Period, Seller shall not, directly or indirectly (A) induce any person or entity that is a customer of the Company to enter into any contract with or otherwise patronize any business directly or indirectly in competition with the Company; or (B) request or advise any person or entity who is a customer, vendor, or lessor of the Company, to withdraw, curtail, or cancel any such customer's, vendor's, or lessor's business with the Company; provided, however, that a general solicitation or advertisement originating outside of, and not specifically targeted to or reasonably expected to target, the territory as to which such Seller is restricted from engaging in such competitive business as provided above under this Agreement at such time, will not be deemed in and of itself to violate the prohibitions of (A) or (B) of this subparagraph.

(c) Any and all writings, inventions, improvements, processes, procedures and/or techniques which Seller made, conceived, discovered or developed, either solely or jointly with any other person or persons, at any time they were affiliated with the Company, which relate to or are useful in connection with any business now or hereafter carried on or contemplated by Company, including developments or expansions of its present fields of operations, shall remain the sole and exclusive property of Company and shall be deemed to have been performed as a "work-for-hire," and Seller holds no right, title or interest in or to any such work and expressly waives any existing or future moral or other rights of any nature whatsoever in or to such work.

(d) Seller agrees and acknowledges that the restrictions in Section 5.2 and this Section 5.5 are reasonable in scope and duration and are necessary to protect Buyer and the Company after the Closing. If any provision of Section 5.2 or this Section 5.6, as applied to any party or to any circumstance, is adjudged not to be enforceable in accordance with its terms, the same will in no way affect any other circumstance or the enforceability of the remainder of this Agreement. The parties agree and acknowledge that the breach of Section 5.2 or this Section 5.6 will cause irreparable damage to Buyer and the Company and upon breach of any provision of this Section 5.6, Buyer and/or the Company will be entitled to injunctive relief, specific performance, or other equitable relief without bond or other security; provided, however, that the foregoing remedies will in no way limit any other remedies which Buyer and/or the Company may have. The provisions of Section 5.2 and this Section 5.6 shall

9

survive any termination of this agreement and completion of the contemplated transactions.

(e) Seller acknowledges that (i) the goodwill associated with his ownership and management of the Company prior to the purchase of the Shares hereunder is an integral component of the value to the Company and is reflected in the consideration to be received by Seller in the purchase, and (ii) Seller's covenants as set forth herein are necessary to preserve the value for the Company following the purchase.

5.7   Repayment of Lines of Credit. To the extent that all lines of credit of the Company are not paid down to $0 as of the Effective Date and the transactions contemplated by Article 2 of this Agreement are nevertheless consummated, Sellers shall as soon as possible after the Effective Date pay down such lines of credit to $0 and shall be jointly and severally liable to Buyer for all amounts outstanding thereunder to the extent that they fail to do so.

5.8   Affiliated Transactions. Seller Parties will cause all contracts and transactions by and between any Seller or any Affiliate of any Seller, on the one hand, and the Company, on the other hand, to terminate effective immediately, without any cost or continuing obligation to the Company or Buyer, and will deliver to Buyer evidence of such terminations that is reasonably acceptable to Buyer.

ARTICLE 6.

INDEMNIFICATION

Remedies

6.1   Indemnification Provisions for Buyer's Benefit. Sellers, jointly and severally, will indemnify and hold Buyer harmless from and pay any and all damages resulting from, relating to, arising out of, or attributable to any one of the following:

(a) Any breach of any representation or warranty any Seller Party has made in this Agreement.

(b) Any breach by any Seller Party of any covenant or obligation of any Seller Party in this Agreement.

(c) Any actions taken by any Seller Party prior to the Effective Date which may have a material adverse effect on the Company, its operations, or its financial condition.

6.2   Indemnification Provisions for Sellers' Benefit. Buyer will indemnify and hold the Sellers harmless from and pay any and all damages, directly or indirectly, resulting from, relating to, arising out of, or attributable to any of the following:

(a) Any breach of any representation or warranty Buyer has made in this Agreement;

(b) Any Breach by Buyer of any covenant or obligation of Buyer in this Agreement.

(c) The operation and ownership of the Company subsequent to the Effective Date.

6.3   Survival. The provisions of this Article 6 shall survive termination of this Agreement and/or completion of the transactions contemplated hereunder for a period of two (2) years following such termination and/or completion.

ARTICLE 7.

MISCELLANEOUS

7.1   Entire Agreement. This Agreement, together with the exhibits and schedules hereto and the certificates, documents, instruments and writings that are delivered pursuant hereto, constitutes the entire agreement and understanding of the parties in respect of its subject matters and, in the absence of fraud, supersedes all prior understandings, agreements, or representations by or among the parties, written or oral, to the extent they relate in any way to the subject matter hereof or the Transactions.

10

7.2   **Successors.** All of the terms, agreements, covenants, representations, warranties, and conditions of this Agreement are binding upon, and inure to the benefit of and are enforceable by, the parties and their respective successors.

7.3   **Assignments.** No party may assign either this Agreement or any of its rights, interests, or obligations hereunder without the prior written approval of the other; provided, however, that Buyer may (a) assign any or all of its rights and interests hereunder to one or more of its Affiliates and (b) designate one or more of its Affiliates to perform its obligations hereunder.

7.4   **Notices.** All notices, requests, demands, claims and other communications hereunder will be in writing. Any notice, request, demand, claim or other communication hereunder will be deemed duly given if (and then three business days after) it is sent by registered or certified mail, return receipt requested, postage prepaid, and addressed to the intended recipient at the address set forth in the preamble to this Agreement, with, in the case of Buyer, a copy to: [law firm].

Any party may send any notice, request, demand, claim, or other communication hereunder to the intended recipient at the address set forth above using any other means (including personal delivery, expedited courier, messenger service, telecopy, telex, ordinary mail, or electronic mail), but no such notice, request, demand, claim, or other communication will be deemed to have been duly given unless and until it actually is received by the intended recipient. Any party may change the address to which notices, requests, demands, claims, and other communications hereunder are to be delivered by giving the other parties notice in the manner herein set forth.

7.5   **Counterparts.** This Agreement may be executed in two or more counterparts, each of which will be deemed an original but all of which together will constitute one and the same instrument.

7.6   **Headings.** The article and section headings contained in this Agreement are inserted for convenience only and will not affect in any way the meaning or interpretation of this Agreement.

7.7   **Governing Law.** This Agreement and the performance of the obligations of the parties hereunder will be governed by and construed in accordance with the laws of California, without giving effect to any choice of law principles, the parties hereto hereby submit to jurisdiction in Los Angeles County in the State of California, U.S.A.

7.8   **Amendments and Waivers.** No amendment, modification, replacement, termination or cancellation of any provision of this Agreement will be valid, unless the same will be in writing and signed by each of the parties hereto. No waiver by any party of any default, misrepresentation, or breach of warranty or covenant hereunder, whether intentional or not, may be deemed to extend to any prior or subsequent default, misrepresentation, or breach of warranty or covenant hereunder or affect in any way any rights arising because of any prior or subsequent such occurrence.

7.9   **Severability.** The provisions of this Agreement will be deemed severable and the invalidity or unenforceability of any provision will not affect the validity or enforceability of the other provisions hereof; provided that if any provision of this Agreement, as applied to any party or to any circumstance, is adjudged by a governmental body, arbitrator, or mediator not to be enforceable in accordance with its terms, the parties agree that the governmental body, arbitrator, or mediator making such determination will have the power to modify the provision in a manner consistent with its objectives such that it is enforceable, and/or to delete specific words or phrases, and in its reduced form, such provision will then be enforceable and will be enforced.

7.10   **Construction.** The parties have participated jointly in the negotiation and drafting of this Agreement. If an ambiguity or question of intent or interpretation arises, this Agreement will be construed as if drafted jointly by the parties and no presumption or burden of proof will arise favoring or disfavoring any party because of the authorship of any provision of this Agreement. Words

11

"include," "includes," and "including" will be deemed to be followed by "without limitation." Pronouns in masculine, feminine, and neuter genders will be construed to include any other gender, and words in the singular form will be construed to include the plural and vice versa, unless the context otherwise requires. The words "this Agreement," "herein," "hereof," "hereby," "hereunder," and words of similar import refer to this Agreement as a whole and not to any particular subdivision unless expressly so limited. The parties intend that each representation, warranty, and covenant contained herein will have independent significance. If any party has breached any representation, warranty, or covenant contained herein in any respect, the fact that there exists another representation, warranty or covenant relating to the same subject matter (regardless of the relative levels of specificity) which the party has not breached will not detract from or mitigate the fact that the party is in breach of the first representation, warranty, or covenant.

7.11 **Incorporation of Exhibits, Annexes, and Schedules.** The exhibits, annexes, schedules, and other attachments identified in this Agreement are incorporated herein by reference and made a part hereof.

7.12 **Remedies.** Except as expressly provided herein, the rights, obligations and remedies created by this Agreement are cumulative and in addition to any other rights, obligations, or remedies otherwise available at law or in equity. Except as expressly provided herein, nothing herein will be considered an election of remedies.

[Signatures follow]

IN WITNESS WHEREOF, the parties have executed this Agreement as of the date first above written.

BUYER

[   ], LLC

By: _____

Name:_____

Title:_____

SELLER

[   ]

By: _____

Name:, [   ], an individual

By: _____

Name:,   an individual _____

COMPANY

By: _____

Name:_____

Title:_____

[Signature page to Share Purchase Agreement]

ATTACHMENTS

Exhibits

Exhibit A   Form of Company Officers' Certificate

Exhibit B   Form of Company Secretary's Certificate

Exhibit C   Form of Buyer Officers' Certificate

Exhibit D   Form of Buyer Secretary's Certificate

Exhibit E   Form of Employment Agreement

Schedules

Schedule 2.2   Purchase Price

Schedule 4.13   Material Contracts

Schedule 4.14   Real Property

Appendix B-6.4

This sample strategic alliance agreement illustrates the use of standard contractual building blocks to reflect a unique business deal—in this case, a joint venture in which services would be provided by one party in exchange for a share of profits on sales of products by the other party. The title of the agreement defines the structure; alternative structures could also be used to reflect this type of arrangement, such as a consulting agreement, service agreement, or other.

Note the use of footnotes to flag issues for client input, and brackets to identify information that still needs to be determined.

STRATEGIC ALLIANCE AGREEMENT

THIS STRATEGIC ALLIANCE AGREEMENT ("Agreement") is made as of October __, 2018 (the "**Effective Date**") between **MRD, Inc.** (**d/b/a MRD Devices**), a Delaware corporation with offices at _____ ("**MRD**"), and RB Services, Inc., a [   ] corporation with offices at _____ ("**RB**"). Each of MRD and RB may be referred to herein as a "**Party**" and together as the "**Parties.**"

RECITALS

A.   MRD develops, manufactures, markets, and sells certain MRD® branded occupational therapy devices and related accessories and products identified on Schedule 1 (the "Products") for various uses, including the treatment of sprains, tendonitis, and pain.

B.   RB has significant experience and a positive reputation in marketing, endorsing and influencing the purchase of similar products.

C.   The Parties desire to collaborate in a strategic alliance to further commercialize, market, and sell the Products on the terms and conditions set forth in this Agreement.

NOW, THEREFORE, in consideration of the foregoing, the mutual agreements contained herein, and other good and valuable consideration, the receipt and sufficiency of which are acknowledged, the Parties hereto, intending to be legally bound, hereby agree as follows:

1.   **General**

1.1.   <u>Strategic Alliance; Scope</u>. Pursuant to the terms and conditions of this Agreement, the Parties hereby form a strategic alliance, purely contractual in nature, and not to be construed as a partnership or joint venture of any kind for any reason whatsoever, all as set forth in and subject to the terms and conditions of this Agreement (the "**Strategic Alliance**"). Except as otherwise mutually agreed by the Parties, the primary objectives of the Strategic Alliance shall be the [design, development, marketing, promotion, exploitation, and expansion of retail sales of the Products] (the "**Business**").

1.2.   <u>Relationship of the Parties.</u> The relationship of the Parties pursuant to this Agreement is that of independent contractors. Nothing in this Agreement is intended or will be deemed to constitute a joint venture, partnership, agency or employer-employee relationship between the Parties. Neither Party shall have any express or implied right or authority to assume or create any obligations on behalf of or in the name of the other party or to bind the other party to any contract, agreement or undertaking with any third party.

1.3.   <u>Obligations of RB</u>. Subject to the terms and conditions of this Agreement, during the Term of this Agreement, RB will use its [best efforts] to diligently perform the services described on Schedule 2, as the same may be revised from time to time by mutual agreement of the Parties (the "Services").

1.4.   <u>Obligations of MRD</u>. In order to allow RB to perform the Services in accordance with Section 1.3, during the Term of this Agreement, MRD agrees to: (a) devote sufficient resources, substantially comparable to those employed as of the date of this Agreement, to the development, manufacture, marketing, distribution, and sale of the Products subject to this Agreement; (b) maintain sufficient inventory of Products to ensure timely fulfillment of all sales; (c) make available to RB such information and materials regarding the Products, pricing, marketing strategies, customers, and other information or materials as reasonably requested, including, without limitation, information with respect to any planned promotional activities; and (d) keep RB informed of any Product changes and/ or developments and such other information as is reasonably necessary for RB to comply with its obligations hereunder.

1.5.   <u>Collaboration between the Parties</u>. During the Term of this Agreement, [both Parties will act in good faith to cooperate in developing the Business of this Strategic Alliance]. [All decisions relating to the Business will be mutually agreed in advance by the Parties, including, without limitation, any creative decisions [such as _____], marketing strategy, marketing and advertising budget, discounts and promotions, changes to return policy, and [other]].[Alt: have certain actions be subject to RB reasonable approval?]. MRD will provide RB with a copy of its annual budget, including an estimate of quarterly manufacturing and marketing plan. [do you want approval rights?] [MRD shall submit to RB for prior approval, any marketing or sales materials it intends to use or distribute in connection with the advertising or marketing of the Products].[1]

1.6.   <u>Other Business Activities</u>. Except as expressly provided herein, nothing in this Agreement will, or will be deemed by implication to: (a) restrict MRD's development, marketing, and sale of Products in the non-retail market or otherwise outside of the scope of the Business; or (b) restrict RB or its owners, officers, directors, or affiliates from, at any time, endorsing products or providing other services to other parties, in each case so long as such activities do not infringe upon any Intellectual Property of the other Party, use any work product developed for or on behalf of this Strategic Alliance, or involve the disclosure or use of any proprietary or confidential information of the other Party.

2.   **Payments**

2.1.   <u>Consulting Fee.</u> In consideration for the Services provided hereunder, in addition to the

---

1. Note to client: Let's discuss what you want here and what is feasible.

other covenants and obligations set forth in this Agreement, MRD agrees to pay to RB the amounts set forth on Schedule 3.

2.2.   Taxes. RB will be solely responsible for and will file, on a timely basis, all tax returns and payments required to be with or made to any federal, state or local tax authority with respect to RB's performance of Services and receipt of fees under this Agreement.

3.   Reports and Records; Audit Rights.

3.1.   Books and Records. MRD agrees that throughout the term of this Agreement it shall keep complete and accurate financial records and books of account in sufficient detail to permit verification of Gross Sales, Net Revenues, and the amounts payable to RB hereunder. All such books and records shall be maintained and kept accessible and available to RB for inspection for at least two (2) years after the date such records were created by MRD.

3.2.   Reports. Without limiting the foregoing, MRD will provide to RB, within thirty (30) days of the end of each calendar quarter:

3.2.1.   A written statement in a form reasonably agreed by the Parties that sets forth, for the quarter then ended, the RB Consulting Fee for that quarter, with the supporting calculation and facts in reasonable detail broken down by category of Product and type of sale, including (i) Gross Sales; (ii) Marketing Expenses; (iii) a breakdown of Products sold; and (iv) such other information as reasonably requested.

3.2.2.   A written notice of any (a) any developments with respect to any current or proposed new Products; (b) any material event that could adversely impact Retail Sales; and (c) significant departures from or proposed changes to the Annual Budget.

3.3.   Audit Rights. RB shall have the right to have an independent certified public accountant reasonably acceptable to MRD to have access during normal business hours, and upon reasonable prior written notice, to such of the records of MRD as may be reasonably necessary to verify the accuracy of the calculation of Net Revenues, the RB Retail Amount, or the Success Fee for any calendar quarter ending not more than five (5) years prior to the date of such request, and provided, however, that, RB will have the right to conduct no more than one such audit in any six (6) month period. In the event that such inspection reveals a discrepancy in the RB Retail Amount or Success Fee owed RB from what was actually paid, MRD shall promptly pay such discrepancy. RB will bear all costs of such audit, unless the audit reveals a discrepancy in RB's favor of more than [10%], in which case MRD will bear the cost of the audit.

3.4.   Defined Terms. Capitalized terms used in this Section 3 and not otherwise defined have the meaning ascribed there to in Schedule 3 (Payments).

4.   Term and Termination

4.1.   Term. This Agreement will continue in effect from the Effective Date until the [first] anniversary thereof (the "**Term**"), unless earlier terminated in accordance with this Section 4.[2]

4.2.   Termination. This Agreement may be terminated prior to the expiration of the Term Date under the following circumstances:

4.2.1.   By either Party by written notice to the other Party, in the event of a material breach by the other Party of any of its representations, covenants or obligations hereunder, unless such breach is cured (i) with respect to a breach of any monetary obligations hereun-

---

2. Note to client: do you want to build in auto-renewal or the right to renew?

der, within five (5) days following the date of such notice or (ii) for all other obligations, with thirty (30) days following the date of such notice;[3]

4.2.2. By either Party by delivery of written notice to the other Party in the event the other Party makes an assignment for the benefit of creditors or has a petition in bankruptcy filed for or against it that is not dismissed within sixty (60) days of such filing;

4.2.3. By RB in the event MRD takes any action which RB reasonably believes may threaten or harm RB's reputation;

4.3.   Effect of Termination. Upon termination of this Agreement in accordance with this Section 4, neither party shall have any further rights or obligations hereunder, and all rights and obligations of the Parties under this Agreement shall terminate except as follows:

4.3.1. MRD shall prepare a final accounting, which shall indicate any accrued but unpaid amounts due to RB under Section 2 as of the date of termination. Such final accounting shall be delivered to RB within thirty (30) days after expiration or termination of this Agreement. All payments to be made pursuant to this Section shall be made within thirty (30) days of expiration or termination.

4.3.2. Each Party will promptly return or destroy all relevant records and materials in its possession or control containing the other Party's proprietary or confidential information with respect to which the former Party does not retain rights hereunder; provided, however, that each Party may retain one archival copy of such records and materials solely to be able to monitor and perform its obligations that survive under this Agreement.

4.3.3. Termination or expiration of this Agreement will not relieve MRD from its payment obligations pursuant to Section 2 with respect to (i) any Retail Sales made prior to or within [90] days[4] following such expiration or termination, and (ii) any reimbursement of expenses incurred prior to the date of expiration or termination.

4.4.   Survival. Any provisions of this Agreement which by their nature are intended to survive termination shall survive termination of this Agreement and shall remain in full force and effect for the greater of seven (7) years and the maximum period permitted by applicable law, including, without limitation, the provisions set forth in this Section 4 and Sections 1, 6.3, 7, and 8.

4.5.   No Willful Breach. Notwithstanding any of the foregoing, nothing herein shall relieve either party of a willful breach of this Agreement which occurs prior to the date of termination.

5. Representations and Warranties

5.1.   Mutual Representations and Warranties. Each Party represents and warrants to the other Party that:

5.1.1. it has full power, authority, and right to perform its obligations under the Agreement;

5.1.2. this Agreement constitutes a legal, valid, and binding obligation of each Party, enforceable against it in accordance with its terms (except as may be limited by bankruptcy, insolvency, moratorium, or similar laws affecting creditors' rights generally and equitable remedies);

5.1.3. entering into this Agreement does not conflict with and will not violate the charter or bylaws of the respective Party or any material contract to which that Party is also a party

---

3. Note to client: Do you want to add the right to terminate if the economics are not making sense, or for any reason?
4. Note to client: We should discuss tail period.

or by which that Party is otherwise bound, and does not violate any law or regulation of any court, governmental body or administrative or other agency having authority over such Party;

5.1.4. no person or entity has or will have, as a result of the transactions contemplated by this Agreement, any right, interest or valid claim against or upon such Party for any commission, fee or other compensation as a finder or broker because of any act by such Party or its agents; and

5.1.5. as of the Effective Date, there are no actions, suits or proceedings pending or, to the best of the Party's knowledge, threatened against such Party, at law or in equity, at or before any federal, state, municipal or other governmental agency or authority (i) relating to such Party's intellectual property that is expected to be used in connection with this Agreement; (ii) relating to the transactions contemplated by this Agreement; relating to any claims of personal injury resulting from the use of any Product; or (iv) that could reasonably be expected to materially affect the ability of such Party to enter into this Agreement or to perform its obligations hereunder.

5.2.   Additional Representations and Warranties of MRD. MRD represents and warrants to RB that:

5.2.1. it is the sole and exclusive owner of all intellectual property used in the Business, including, without limitation, all trademarks, trade names, service marks, copyright, patents, and trade secrets and other know-how (the "Intellectual Property"); and, to its knowledge the use of the Intellectual Property in the Business does not and will not infringe on or misappropriate any intellectual property or other rights of any third party;

5.2.2. any financial and other information provided to RB, including, without limitation, any financial records or other documents provided under Section 3, are, to MRD's knowledge, true and correct in all material respects and, with respect to financial information, fairly reflect the financial condition and operations of MRD.

5.3.   Additional Representations and Warranties of RB. RB represents and warrants to MRD that:

5.3.1. all Services to be provided by RB will be performed in a competent and professional manner, by qualified personnel in accordance with applicable law, regulation, and industry self-regulation; and

5.3.2. to its knowledge, no deliverables, information or materials, other than those provided or made available by MRD to RB, nor the performance of the Services by RB or its delegee hereunder, will infringe upon or violate the rights of any third party.

5.4.   Disclaimer of Additional Warranties. EXCEPT AS EXPRESSLY SET FORTH HEREIN, NEITHER PARTY MAKES ANY WARRANTIES EXPRESS OR IMPLIED, AS TO ANY MATTER WHATSOEVER, INCLUDING, WITHOUT LIMITATION, THE MERCHANTABILITY OF THE PRODUCTS OR THEIR SUITABILITY FOR ANY PURPOSE, OR WITH RESPECT TO THE SUCCESS OF THIS STRATEGIC ALLIANCE. Nothing contained in this Agreement shall be construed as MRD's obligation to file any patent application, to secure any patent or to maintain any patent in force, or its obligation to bring or prosecute actions or suits against third parties for infringement.

6.   Intellectual Property; Approvals

6.1.   MRD's Intellectual Property Rights. As between MRD and RB, MRD retains all ownership rights in its social media platforms, software, websites and technology, including any updates, enhancements, and modifications thereto ("Company Platforms") and other Intellectual Property.

MRD hereby grants RB a limited, nonexclusive, non-transferable license to access and use MRD's Intellectual Property and Company Platforms solely as necessary to provide the Services as set forth herein.

6.2. <u>RB's Content and Attributes.</u> With respect to the Services which RB is providing under this Agreement and without limiting MRD's ownership as specified above, subject to Section 6.3, RB gives MRD the limited right and license to use any work product or other video, photo, written or verbal content RB shares or provides related to the Services in any manner, in whole or in part, and for any purpose in any and in any and all media, including and without limitation, on Company Platforms, any advertising materials, publications, marketing materials, and/or presentations, and in any and all other media. Subject to RB's prior written approval, any statements, posts and/or feedback that RB provides may be paraphrased, amplified, shortened and/or put into conversational form.

6.3. <u>Use of Name/Likeness.</u> Notwithstanding anything in Sections 6.1 or 6.2 to the contrary, the Parties acknowledge and agree that RB has the right to protect the RB brand. Accordingly, RB will have the right to approve, in its sole discretion, any appearance, statement, and endorsement by RB and the specifics thereof (including content, script, parameters of use, etc.), and any use of RB's name, voice, biography, other identifying characteristics, or likeness, in any and all media. Nothing herein constitutes a waiver of any moral rights. The Parties acknowledge that any breach of this provision may result in irreparable damage for which (1) an adequate monetary remedy does not exist and (2) available remedies at law may prove to be inadequate. Accordingly, in the event of any actual or threatened breach RB shall be entitled to seek injunctive relief in addition to other available remedies, without need to post any bond or security.

7. Indemnification

7.1. <u>Indemnification by MRD.</u> MRD will defend, indemnify and hold RB and its affiliates, and each of their respective directors, officers, employees, and agents harmless from and against any and all third-party claims, suits or demands for liability, damages, losses, costs and expenses (including the reasonable costs and expenses of attorneys and other professionals) (collectively, "Claims") arising from or related to:

    (a) MRD's breach of any of its representations, warranties or covenants in this Agreement;

    (b) the gross negligence or willful misconduct of MRD;

    (c) the alleged infringement upon or misappropriation of any third-party intellectual property rights;

    (d) the sale or use of any of the Products, including but not limited to any third-party consumer product liability claims or from any injury to any third-party consumer;

7.2. <u>Indemnification by RB.</u> RB will defend, indemnify and hold MRD and its Affiliates, and each of their respective directors, officers, and employees, and agents harmless from and against any and all third-party Claims arising from or related to:

    (a) RB's breach of any of its representations, warranties or covenants in this Agreement; or

    (b) the gross negligence or willful misconduct of RB in the performance of its Services hereunder.

7.3. <u>Procedure.</u> Any party seeking indemnification with respect to any Liabilities (the "Indemnified Party") will promptly notify the party required to provide indemnity hereunder (the "Indemnifying Party"); provided that the failure to give such notice will not affect the right of the Indemnified Party to indemnification except to the extent the failure to give notice directly prejudices the Indemnifying Party to contest any claim. The Indemnifying Party will defend and/or settle any actions or proceedings with counsel reasonably satisfactory to the Indemnified Party. If the Indemnifying Party does not promptly defend or settle any such claims, the Indemnified Party will have the right to control any defense or settlement, at the expense of the Indemnifying Party. No claim will be settled or compromised without the prior written consent of each party to be affected, with such consent not being unreasonably withheld or delayed. The Indemnified Party will at all times also have the right to participate fully in the defense at its own expense.

8.   Miscellaneous

8.1.   Assignments. No party may assign either this Agreement or any of its rights, interests, or obligations hereunder without the prior written approval of the other; provided, however, that RB may (a) assign any or all of its rights and interests hereunder to one or more of its affiliates and (b) designate one or more of its affiliates to perform its obligations hereunder (in any or all of which cases RB will nonetheless will remain responsible for the performance of all of its obligations hereunder). Subject to the foregoing, this Agreement shall be binding upon and inure to the benefit of the successors and permitted assigns of the parties hereto.

8.2.   Notices. All notices required or permitted under this Agreement shall be in writing, shall reference this Agreement and shall be given by: (i) delivery in person (ii) a nationally recognized next day courier service, (iii) first class, registered or certified mail, postage prepaid, (iv) facsimile or (v) by electronic mail to the address of the party specified in this Agreement or such other address as either party may specify in writing.

8.3.   Governing Law; Venue. This Agreement and any disputes arising hereunder are governed by the laws of the State of California, without regard to principals of conflict of laws. The sole jurisdiction and venue for actions related to the subject matter hereof shall be the state and federal courts located in the Los Angeles, California and both parties hereby consent to such jurisdiction and venue.

8.4.   Use of Names. Except as otherwise expressly provided herein, neither Party will have any right, express or implied, to use in any manner the name or other designation of the other Party or any other trade name or trademark of the other Party for any purpose without the prior written consent of the other Party.

8.5.   Public Announcement. No announcement, news release, public statement, publication, or presentation relating to the existence of this Agreement, or the terms hereof, will be made by either Party or its affiliates without the other Party's prior written approval. Each of the Parties agrees not to disclose to any third party the terms and conditions of this Agreement without the prior approval of the other Parties, except to its advisors (including attorneys, financial advisors and accountants).

8.6.   Severability. All terms and provisions of this Agreement shall, if possible, be construed in a manner which makes them valid, but in the event any term or provision of this Agreement is found by a court of competent jurisdiction to be illegal or unenforceable, the validity or enforceability of the remainder of this Agreement shall not be affected if the illegal or unenforceable provision does not materially affect the intent of this Agreement.

8.7.   Waiver. The waiver of, or failure to enforce, any breach or default hereunder shall not constitute the waiver of any other or subsequent breach or default.

8.8.   Expenses. Except as otherwise specifically provided herein, each Party shall bear its own fees and expenses incurred in connection with the preparation, execution, and performance of this Agreement.

8.9.   Entire Agreement; Amendment. This Agreement, along with all exhibits and schedules, sets forth the entire Agreement between the parties and supersedes any and all prior proposals, agreements and representations between them, whether written or oral. This Agreement may be amended only by mutual agreement of the parties in writing.

8.10. <u>Further Assurances</u>. Subject to the terms and conditions of this Agreement, each Party will use its commercially reasonable efforts to take, or cause to be taken, all actions and to do, or cause to be done, all things necessary or desirable under applicable laws and regulations to consummate the transactions contemplated by, and to realize the objectives of, this Agreement.

8.11. <u>Headings</u>. The headings in this Agreement are for convenience of reference only and shall not control or affect the meaning or construction of any provisions hereof.

8.12. <u>Counterparts.</u> This Agreement may be executed in any number of counterparts (via facsimile, PDF copy, electronic signature, or otherwise), each of which shall be an original with the same effect as if the signatures thereto and hereto were upon the same instrument.

8.13. <u>No Partnership Relationship</u>. Nothing in this Agreement shall be construed as establishing or implying any partnership relationship between or among the Parties.

8.14. <u>Third Parties</u>. The Parties acknowledge and agree that a Party shall not be held in breach for failure of performance of its obligations hereunder if such failure is a result of actions or inactions of the other Party, third parties (excluding actions or inactions of such Party's own independent contractors or other engaged agents), and events or circumstances (i.e., acts of God, war and terrorist activity) that are beyond the control of such Party.

[Signature page follows]

IN WITNESS WHEREOF, the parties have executed this Agreement as of the date first above written.

MRD   **RB**

MRD, Inc. (d/b/a MRD Devices)   RB Services, Inc.

By: _____   By: _____

Name: _____   Name: _____

Title: _____   Title: _____

[Signature page to Strategic Alliance Agreement]

Schedule 1

Products

[To be confirmed]

[Schedules to Strategic Alliance Agreement]

Schedule 2

Services

[To be discussed]

[Schedules to Strategic Alliance Agreement]

Schedule 3

Consulting Fee

[To be discussed]

[Schedules to Strategic Alliance Agreement]

Appendix B-7

The following sample letter of intent is used in Exercise 11.4.

ABC, Inc.

September __, _____

Sam Smith
CEO
Organa Corp.
5 Main Street
Los Angeles, CA 90046

Re: Proposal to Purchase Substantially All Assets of Organa Corp.

Dear Mr. Smith:

This letter (this "Letter of Intent") is intended to summarize the principal terms of a proposal being considered by ABC, Inc., or its designated assignee ("Buyer") regarding its possible acquisition of substantially all the assets, and certain specified liabilities, of the organic snack-food business of Organa Corp. ("Seller"). The possible acquisition of the Business is referred to as the "Transaction" and Buyer and Seller are referred to collectively as the "Parties." Except as specifically set forth in Section VI below, the Parties understand and agree that this Letter of Intent is non-binding.

I. Structure of Transaction

      A. Subject to the satisfaction of the conditions described in this Letter of Intent, at the closing of the Transaction and pursuant to a definitive asset purchase agreement to be provided by Buyer's legal counsel (the "Purchase Agreement"), Buyer would acquire (i) substantially all of the assets, and certain specified liabilities, of the Business (the "Assets"), free and clear of all encumbrances, at the purchase price set forth in Section II below and (ii) only the specific liabilities of Seller identified in the Purchase Agreement (the "Assumed Liabilities", along with the Assets, the "Business") with the Seller otherwise retaining and being responsible for discharging all other liabilities, whether known or unknown, including, but not limited to, any pre-closing indebtedness and liabilities of the Seller (the "Retained Liabilities").

II.   Outline of Terms of Purchase

A.   Purchase Price. The purchase price to be paid to the Seller would be up to $20,000,000, subject to the adjustments set forth in this Letter of Intent (as adjusted pursuant to the terms hereof, the "Purchase Price"). The Purchase Price will be allocated among the assets of the Business in the Purchase Agreement. The Purchase Price would be paid as follows:

1.   Initial Purchase Price. $10,000,000 would be paid to the Seller upon the consummation of the Transaction (the "Closing").

2.   Deferred Purchase Price. Subject to certain provisions set forth below Buyer would pay to the Seller an amount equal to $5,000,000 (the "Initial Deferred Purchase Price") within thirty (30) days after the first anniversary of the Closing, and an additional $5,000,000 (the "Second Deferred Purchase Price", and collectively with the Initial Deferred Purchase Price, the "Deferred Purchase Price" on the second anniversary of the Closing.]

3.   Earn-out/Supplemental Purchase Price. In addition there may be up to $5.0 million of contingent payments, based on the following hurdles:

(i) In the year to December 31, 20__, the Business must achieve EBITDA of $3 million to trigger a payment of $1.75 million, rising at a linear rate to $2.5 million on achieving EBITDA of $3.5 million.

(ii) In the year to December 31, 20__, the Business must achieve EBITDA of $4 million to trigger a payment of $1.75 million, rising at a linear rate to $2.5 million on achieving EBITDA of $4.5 million;

(iii) Of this $5.0 million contingent payment up to $2.0 million payment would be paid in cash and up to $3.0 million would be satisfied by the issuance of Petrochem shares of that value.

4.   Escrow. $2.0 million to be deposited with a mutually agreeable escrow agent and subject to the terms of a separately negotiated and mutually agreed upon escrow agreement, to be held for a period of two (2) years after the closing, in order to secure the performance of Seller's post-closing obligations under the definitive purchase agreement.

B.   Adjustments to Purchase Price.

1.   Working Capital. Working capital at the closing of the Transaction is $[AMOUNT], calculated in accordance with US GAAP, consistently applied. The Purchase Price payable at closing would be increased or decreased based on changes in the working capital of the Business, on a dollar-for-dollar basis.

2.   Indebtedness Discharged, Payments to be Made Prior to or at Closing. For the sake of clarity, any and all indebtedness of Seller not expressly assumed by Buyer shall be paid, satisfied and discharged by the Seller before or at the Closing.

III.   Purchase Agreement.

A.   General. As soon as reasonably practicable after the execution of this Letter of Intent, the Parties shall negotiate the definitive Purchase Agreement, to be drafted by Buyer's counsel. The Purchase Agreement would contain the terms summarized in this Letter of Intent and other representations, warranties, conditions, covenants, indemnities and other terms that are customary for transactions of this kind and are not inconsistent with this Letter of Intent. The Parties shall also commence to negotiate ancillary agreements to be drafted by Buyer's counsel, including (i) an escrow agreement, (ii) a bill of sale, and (iii) an assignment and assumption agreement. The Purchase

Agreement will also include confidentiality, non-competition, non-solicitation, non-accept, non-piracy and non-hiring covenants applicable to the Seller.

B.   Provisions.

   1. Representations and Warranties.

      a. The Purchase Agreement would contain representations and warranties of Buyer customary for transactions of this nature with respect to due organization and good standing, due authorization to conduct business and full power and authority to enter into and perform obligations under the Purchase Agreement.

      b. The Purchase Agreement would contain representations and warranties of the Seller, customary for transactions of this nature or as otherwise required by Buyer, relating to the Seller, including without limitation a representation that Seller owns all intellectual property used or held for use by the Seller in connection with the Business, and there is no third-party claim that challenges the ownership of Seller of such intellectual property. Such representations and warranties would survive the Closing.

   2. Indemnification. The Seller would indemnify and defend the Buyer with respect to all losses, claims and expenses ("Claims") relating to or arising out of, among other things: (a) any misrepresentation or breach of warranty or covenant made by them in the Purchase Agreement; (b) in the case of the Seller, the operation of the Business prior to the Closing; and (c) such other specific indemnity line items as set forth in the Purchase Agreement. The Deferred Purchase Price and the Earn-Out/Supplemental Purchase Price would be subject to, at the Buyer's option, set-off to satisfy any indemnification obligations of the Seller.

   3. Conditions. Buyer's obligation to close the proposed Transaction will be subject to customary conditions, including:

      (a) Buyer's satisfactory completion of due diligence;

      (b) Buyer's receipt of cash proceeds from financing transactions in an amount necessary to finance the Transaction, pay related fees and expenses and provide adequate ongoing working capital and on the terms and conditions satisfactory to Buyer;

      (c) the Board of Directors and stockholders of Buyer and Seller approving the Transaction;

      (d) the Parties' execution of the Purchase Agreement and the ancillary agreements;

      (e) the receipt of any regulatory approvals and third party consents, on terms satisfactory to Buyer;

      (f) each of [NAMES OF KEY EMPLOYEES] entering into employment agreements with Buyer on terms agreed with Buyer;

      (g) Seller and its affiliates entering into restrictive covenants, in a form acceptable to Buyer, agreeing not to: (i) compete with the Business for five (5) years following the closing, and (ii) hire or solicit any employee of the Business or encourage any such employee to leave such employment for a period of five (5) years following the closing; and

      (h) there being no material adverse change in the business, results of operations, prospects, condition (financial or otherwise) or assets of the Business.

IV.   <u>Due Diligence.</u> Upon execution of this Letter of Intent, Buyer shall proceed with its due diligence review. From and after the date of this Letter of Intent, Seller will (i) permit Buyer and its advisors full access to the facilities, records, key employees, customers, suppliers and advisors of the Business for the purpose of completing Buyer's due diligence review and (ii) disclose and make available to Buyer and its advisors all books, agreements, papers and records relating to the ownership of the Seller and its operations. The due diligence investigation will include, but is not limited to, a complete review of the financial, legal, tax, environmental, intellectual property and labor records and agreements of the Business, and any other matters as Buyer's accountants, tax and legal counsel, and other advisors deem relevant.

V.   <u>Employment Arrangements.</u>

A.   Buyer would offer employment to substantially all of the employees of the Business on an "at will" basis (other than the Key Employees) and would expect the Seller's management to use its reasonable best effort to assist Buyer to employ those individuals.

B.   <u>Other Employee Matters.</u> Pending due diligence, the parties will determine whether Buyer will maintain the Seller's existing employee benefits plans following the Closing. Notwithstanding the foregoing, the Seller's existing 401(k) plan will be terminated and the participants employed by the Business would be afforded the opportunity to contribute their assets from such plan to the Buyer 401(k) plan, in each case, to the extent permitted by the terms thereof and applicable law. All such employees would be entitled to participate in the Buyer benefit plans and 401(k) plan, consistent with employee benefit policies of Buyer, immediately upon closing, to the extent permissible by the terms of the plans, policies and applicable law. In terms of benefit plans (including 401(k) participation and vesting), to the extent permitted by the terms of the plans, all employees would be granted service credit for their employment at the Seller.

VI.   <u>Binding Provisions.</u>

A.   <u>Exclusivity.</u>

1.   In consideration of the fees, costs and expenses incurred by Buyer in the Transaction, including having its counsel draft the Purchase Agreement and negotiate the terms of this Letter of Intent and the Purchase Agreement, beginning on the date of execution of this Letter of Intent and for a period of ninety (90) days thereafter/the termination of this Letter of Intent pursuant to the terms hereof (the "Exclusivity Period")], neither the Seller nor any of its affiliates, representatives, officers, employees, directors, stockholders, partners, and agents (the "Seller Representatives") will, directly or indirectly, (i) solicit, initiate, encourage or discuss any proposal or offer, enter into any agreement, or accept any offer, with or from any third party other than Buyer or an affiliate of Buyer (an "Acquisition Proposal"), relating to any merger, consolidation, purchase or sale of assets or equity interests of the Seller or any of its subsidiaries, or any similar transaction or business combination involving the Seller, its subsidiaries or their businesses or acquisition of any portion of the Assets, whether by merger, purchase of stock, purchase of assets, tender offer or otherwise, or (ii) furnish any information with respect to, assist or participate in, or in any other manner facilitate any effort or attempt by any third party to do or seek to do any of the foregoing.

2.   Seller agrees to immediately notify Buyer if any member of the Seller Representatives receives any indications of interest, requests for information or offers in respect of an Acquisition Proposal, and will communicate to Buyer in reasonable detail the terms of

any such indication, request or offer, and will provide Buyer with copies of all written communications relating to any such indication, request or offer. Immediately upon execution of this Letter of Intent, Seller shall, and shall cause the Seller Representatives to, terminate any and all existing discussions or negotiations with any person or group of persons other than Buyer and its affiliates regarding an Acquisition Proposal. Seller represents that no member of the Seller Representatives is party to or bound by any agreement with respect to an Acquisition Proposal other than under this Letter of Intent.

3. Buyer shall have the right to equitable remedies, including, but not limited to, injunctive relief, should the Seller violate any covenants contained in this Section VI.A.

4. In addition to the foregoing, if within the Exclusivity Period, Seller does not execute definitive documentation for the Transaction reflecting the material terms and conditions for the Transaction set forth in this Letter or material terms and conditions substantially similar thereto (other than as a result of either the mutual agreement by Buyer and Seller to terminate this Letter or to change such material terms and conditions in any material respects or the unilateral refusal of Buyer to execute such definitive documentation), then Seller shall pay to Buyer an amount equal to the reasonable out-of-pocket expenses (including the reasonable fees and expenses of legal counsel, accountants and other advisors and whether incurred prior to or after the date hereof) incurred by Buyer in connection with the proposed Transaction, which amount shall be payable in same day funds on the day that is the first business day after the Exclusivity Period.

B.   Confidentiality. The mutual nondisclosure (confidentiality) agreement executed on [•] between the parties remains in full force and effect, is binding on each party thereto, and shall remain in full force and effect until specifically terminated. In addition, Seller agrees not to disclose, and each will cause its respective officers, directors, stockholders, partners, agents and employees not to disclose: (i) the terms and conditions discussed in this Letter of Intent; (ii) any information about the Transaction discussed by the parties hereto; or (iii) the terms, conditions or other facts relating to any business relationship between the parties hereto, including, but not limited to, the fact that discussions are taking place with respect thereto or the status thereof. Buyer shall have the right to equitable remedies, including, but not limited to, injunctive relief, should the other party violate any covenants contained in this Section VI.B.

C.   Expenses. All fees and expenses incurred in connection with the Transaction, including, but not limited to, all fees and expenses of attorneys, accountants and other representatives employed by any party, shall be borne solely by the party that has incurred such expenses.

D.   Nature of Letter of Intent.

1. This Letter of Intent is intended to be a guide in the preparation of the Purchase Agreement in a form satisfactory to the parties, and nothing herein shall be deemed or construed to (i) require that the parties enter into a Purchase Agreement (or other definitive agreement) or (ii) preclude other provisions that are consistent with the terms of the transactions outlined herein from being included in any of such agreements; provided such other provisions are satisfactory to all parties thereto. Except for the provisions of this Section VI (including all subparagraphs thereof), which upon execution of this Letter of Intent will be binding on the parties hereto, this Letter of Intent is not a binding or enforceable agreement, or an offer (including an offer to enter into a binding agreement), and no other provisions of the Letter of Intent shall be binding or enforceable.

5

2. This Letter of Intent does not contain all material terms upon which the parties intend to agree and is only intended to provide a basis on which to begin to work on the Purchase Agreement (and other related agreements). A binding commitment will only be made pursuant to the execution of a definitive purchase agreement, and other related agreements, mutually acceptable to the parties thereto, and only after the conditions set forth therein have been satisfied, and no past or future action, course of conduct or failure to act relating to the Transaction, or relating to the negotiation of, or the failure to negotiate, the terms of the Purchase Agreement or Transaction, will give rise to any obligation or other liability on the part of any party hereto.

E.   Governing Law. This Letter of Intent is, and the Purchase Agreement and any agreements relating to the Transaction will be, governed by the laws of _____ without regard to whatever laws might otherwise apply under applicable principles of conflicts or choice of laws.

F.   No Third Party Beneficiaries. Except as specifically set forth or referred to herein, nothing herein is intended or shall be construed to confer upon any person or entity other than the Parties and their successors or assigns, any rights or remedies under or by reason of this Letter of Intent.

G.   Miscellaneous. This Letter may be executed in counterparts, each of which shall be deemed to be an original, but all of which together shall constitute one agreement. The headings of the various sections of this Letter of Intent have been inserted for reference only and shall not be deemed to be a part of this Letter of Intent.

[Remainder of page intentionally blank; signatures on following page]

Please acknowledge your acceptance of this Letter of Intent by signing in the space provided below. This Letter of Intent will terminate effective September __, _____, if unsigned by you.

ABC, Inc.

By: *Audrey Allen*   Date: _____

Name: Audrey Allen
Title: President

Accepted and Agreed:

Organa Corp.

By: _____   Date: _____
Name: Sam Smith
Title: President

Appendix B-8

The following sample nondisclosure agreement (NDA) is used in Simulation Exercise #9. Note Simulation Exercise #9 refers to a confidentiality agreement. The two terms are used interchangeably, especially by clients. Although the principal focus of each is slightly different, in practice, the scope is typically similar and, in many instances, identical.

NONDISCLOSURE AGREEMENT

THIS AGREEMENT (the "**Agreement**") is entered into on this 24th day of _____, 20__ by and between GTI, located at 2200 Marine Center Drive, Long Beach, California (the "**Disclosing Party**"), and KL Shipping Berhad, with and address at 10 Jalan Semantan, Kuala Lumpur, Malaysia (the "**Recipient**" or the "**Receiving Party**").

The Recipient hereto desires to participate in discussions regarding the potential acquisition of all or substantially all of the assets of Disclosing Party (the "**Transaction**"). During these discussions, Disclosing Party may share certain proprietary information with the Recipient. Therefore, in consideration of the mutual promises and covenants contained in this Agreement, and other good and valuable consideration, the receipt and sufficiency of which is hereby acknowledged, the parties hereto agree as follows:

1. **Definition of Confidential Information.**

For purposes of this Agreement, "**Confidential Information**" means any data or information that is proprietary to the Disclosing Party or its parent company and not generally known to the public, whether in tangible or intangible form, whenever and however disclosed, including, but not limited to: (i) any marketing strategies, plans, financial information, or projections, operations, sales estimates, business plans and performance results relating to the past, present or future business activities of such party, its affiliates, subsidiaries and affiliated companies; (ii) plans for products or services, and customer or supplier lists; (iii) any scientific or technical information, invention, design, process, procedure, formula, improvement, technology or method; (iv) any concepts, reports, data, know-how, works-in-progress, designs, development tools, specifications, computer software, source code, object code, flow charts, databases, inventions, information and trade secrets; and (v) any other information that should reasonably be recognized as confidential information of the Disclosing Party. Confidential Information need not be novel, unique, patentable, copyrightable or constitute a trade secret in order to be designated Confidential Information. The Receiving Party acknowledges that the Confidential Information is proprietary to the Disclosing Party, has been developed and obtained through great efforts by the Disclosing Party and that Disclosing Party regards all of its Confidential Information as trade secrets.

2. Disclosure of Confidential Information.

From time to time, the Disclosing Party may disclose Confidential Information to the Receiving Party. The Receiving Party will: (a) limit disclosure of any Confidential Information to its directors, officers, employees, or agents (collectively "**Representatives**") who have a need to know such Confidential Information in connection with the current or contemplated business relationship between the parties to which this Agreement relates, and only for that purpose; (b) advise its Representatives of the proprietary nature of the Confidential Information and of the obligations set forth in this Agreement and require such Representatives in writing to keep the Confidential Information confidential; (c) shall keep all Confidential Information strictly confidential by using a reasonable degree of care, but not less than the degree of care used by it in safeguarding its own confidential information; and (d) not disclose any Confidential Information received by it to any third parties (except as otherwise provided for herein).

Each party shall be responsible for any breach of this Agreement by any of their respective Representatives.

3. Use of Confidential Information.

The Receiving Party agrees to use the Confidential Information solely in connection with the current or contemplated business relationship between the parties and not for any purpose other than as authorized by this Agreement without the prior written consent of an authorized representative of the Disclosing Party. No other right or license, whether expressed or implied, in the Confidential Information is granted to the Receiving Party hereunder. Title to the Confidential Information will remain solely in the Disclosing Party.

4. Term.

This Agreement shall remain in effect until the earlier of (a) the expiration of a two-year term (subject to a one year extension if the parties are still discussing and considering the Transaction at the end of the second year) and (b) the closing of the Transaction.

5. Remedies.

Both parties acknowledge that the Confidential Information to be disclosed hereunder is of a unique and valuable character, and that the unauthorized dissemination of the Confidential Information would destroy or diminish the value of such information. The damages to Disclosing Party that would result from the unauthorized dissemination of the Confidential Information would be impossible to calculate. Therefore, both parties hereby agree that the Disclosing Party shall be entitled to injunctive relief preventing the dissemination of any Confidential Information in violation of the terms hereof. Such injunctive relief shall be in addition to any other remedies available hereunder, whether at law or in equity. Disclosing Party shall be entitled to recover its costs and fees, including reasonable attorneys' fees, incurred in obtaining any such relief. Further, in the event of litigation relating to this Agreement, the prevailing party shall be entitled to recover its reasonable attorney's fees and expenses.

6. Return of Confidential Information.

Receiving Party shall immediately return and redeliver to the other all tangible material embodying the Confidential Information provided hereunder and all notes, summaries, memoranda, drawings, manuals, records, excerpts or derivative information deriving there from and all other documents or materials ("Notes") (and all copies of any of the foregoing, including "copies" that have been converted to computerized media in the form of image, data or word processing files either manually or by image capture) based on or including any Confidential Information, in whatever form of storage or retrieval, upon the earlier of (i) the completion or termination of the dealings between the parties contemplated hereunder; (ii) the termination of this Agreement; or (iii) at such time as the Disclosing Party may so request; provided however that the Receiving Party may retain such of its documents as is necessary to enable it to comply with its document retention policies. Alternatively, the Receiving Party, with the written consent of the Disclosing Party may (or in the case of Notes, at the Receiving Party's option) immediately destroy any of the foregoing embodying Confidential Information (or the reasonably nonrecoverable data erasure of computerized data) and, upon request, certify in writing such destruction by an authorized officer of the Receiving Party supervising the destruction).

7. Notice of Breach.

Receiving Party shall notify the Disclosing Party immediately upon discovery of any unauthorized use or disclosure of Confidential Information by Receiving Party or its Representatives, or any other breach of this Agreement by Receiving Party or its Representatives and will cooperate with efforts by the Disclosing Party to help the Disclosing Party regain possession of Confidential Information and prevent its further unauthorized use.

8. No Binding Agreement for Transaction.

The parties agree that neither party will be under any legal obligation of any kind whatsoever with respect to a Transaction by virtue of this Agreement, except for the matters specifically agreed to herein. The parties further acknowledge and agree that they each reserve the right, in their sole and absolute discretion, to reject any and all proposals and to terminate discussions and negotiations with respect to a Transaction at any time. This Agreement does not create a joint venture or partnership between the parties. If a Transaction goes forward, the nondisclosure provisions of any applicable transaction documents entered into between the parties (or their respective affiliates) for the Transaction shall supersede this Agreement. In the event such provision is not provided for in said transaction documents, this Agreement shall control.

9. Warranty. Each party warrants that it has the right to make the disclosures under this Agreement. **NO WARRANTIES ARE MADE BY EITHER PARTY UNDER THIS AGREEMENT WHATSOEVER.** The parties acknowledge that although they shall each endeavor to include in the Confidential Information all information that they each believe relevant for the purpose of the evaluation of a Transaction, the parties understand that no representation or warranty as to the accuracy or completeness of the Confidential Information is being made by either party as the Disclosing Party. Further, neither party is under any obligation under this Agreement to disclose any Confidential Information it chooses not to disclose. Neither Party hereto shall have any liability to the other party or to the other party's Representatives resulting from any use of the Confidential Information except with respect to disclosure of such Confidential Information in violation of this Agreement.

10. Miscellaneous.

    (a) This Agreement constitutes the entire understanding between the parties and supersedes any and all prior or contemporaneous understandings and agreements, whether oral or written, between the parties, with respect to the subject matter hereof. This Agreement can only be modified by a written amendment signed by the party against whom enforcement of such modification is sought.

(b) The validity, construction and performance of this Agreement shall be governed and construed in accordance with the laws of California applicable to contracts made and to be wholly performed within such state, without giving effect to any conflict of laws provisions thereof.

(c) This Agreement is personal in nature, and neither party may directly or indirectly assign or transfer it by operation of law or otherwise without the prior written consent of the other party, which consent will not be unreasonably withheld. All obligations contained in this Agreement shall extend to and be binding upon the parties to this Agreement and their respective successors, assigns and designees.

IN WITNESS WHEREOF, the parties hereto have executed this Agreement as of the date first above written.

Disclosing Party	Receiving Party
By: Global Tankers, Inc.	By: KL Shipping Berhad
/s/ George Lamar	/s/ Esther Buckley
Name: George Lamar	Name: Esther Buckley
Title: CEO	Title: President

Appendix B-9

This sample mark-up of a share purchase agreement is used in Simulation Exercise #10. Irrelevant portions of the agreement have been omitted. This mark-up has been creating using "redlining."

SHARE PURCHASE AGREEMENT

This Share Purchase Agreement (this "*Agreement*"), dated _____, 2015 (the "*Effective Date*") is by and among (i) Shaw Holdings, LLC, a company organized under the laws of California, with its registered office at 5555 Slauson Avenue, Santa Fe Springs, California 90671, U.S.A. ("*Buyer*"), (ii) Sofia Laudon, an individual residing at _____ ("*Seller*"), and (iii) Cayman Yachts (BVI) Ltd., a private limited company (registered in the British Virgin Islands under company number 6627420, the registered office of which is at ~~27 Skippon Way~~ 5 Commonwealth Lane, Tortola, B.V.I., West Indies (the "*Company*").

Deleted: 27 Skippon Way

R E C I T A L S:

A. Seller is the legal and beneficial owner of all of the outstanding shares of the Company (the "*Shares*").

B. Buyer desires to purchase from Seller, and Seller desires to sell to Buyer the Shares, in accordance with the terms and conditions set forth herein.

AGREEMENT:

NOW, THEREFORE, in consideration of the premises and the mutual promises herein made, and in consideration of the representations, warranties, and covenants contained herein, Buyer and Seller agree as follows:

ARTICLE 1.
DEFINITIONS

"*Affiliate*" or "*Affiliated*" with respect to any specified Person, means . . . .
"*Encumbrance*" means. . . .
"*Proprietary Information*" means . . . .

ARTICLE 2.
PURCHASE AND SALE OF SHARES

2.1 Purchase and Sale of Shares. On and subject to the terms and conditions of this Agreement, effective as of the Effective Date, Buyer agrees to purchase from Seller, and Seller agrees to sell to Buyer, all of the Shares fully paid up and free from any Encumbrance, together with all rights which, as of the date hereof or subsequently, attach to them, for the consideration specified in Section 2.2.

2.2. Consideration.

(a)   As consideration for the Shares and the goodwill associated therewith, Buyer shall pay to Seller the Purchase Price set forth on Schedule 2.2. The parties hereby acknowledge and agree that no additional consideration is due for the purchase of the Shares hereunder. Seller further acknowledges and agrees that, as of the Effective Date, Seller shall cease to have any rights with respect to the Shares and/or the assets of the Company, including any rights to receive dividends or distributions or any revenue-sharing or profit-sharing rights.

(b)   The parties acknowledge and agree that Buyer shall have the right to set off from the Purchase Price all or a portion of any outstanding principal and interest owed by Seller to Buyer under any loans provided by Buyer to Seller.

2.3. Taxes. In respect of B.V.I. or United States stamp duty or other documentary or transfer taxes payable in relation to this Agreement or the transfer of the Shares pursuant to this Agreement, Buyer shall be responsible for the payment of such amount of stamp duty or other documentary or transfer taxes as determined by the relevant tax authority. Purchaser agrees to pay all Solicitor and Accountancy fees incurred by the Seller.

2.4. Deliverables. Concurrent with the execution and delivery of this Agreement, the parties shall execute and/or deliver the following:

(i)   Seller shall deliver any and all certificates representing the Shares, duly endorsed in blank, together with a duly executed stock transfer in registrable form;

(ii)   Seller shall deliver her resignation from any directorship or officership, employment or other position within the Company;

(iii)   Seller shall deliver to Buyer all originals books and records of the Company, including without limitation, the certificate of incorporation or registration, all share registers, minute books and other statutory books, and any leases and other contracts in effect as of the date hereof;

(iv)   Seller shall deliver to Buyer a duly completed authority for the alteration of signatories of every bank account of the Company as required by Buyer;

(v)   Seller shall deliver to Buyer any assignment documents necessary to ensure proper transfer to and ownership by the Company of any and all tradenames, trademarks or other Intellectual Property associated with the business of the Company; and

(vi)   other deliverables as appropriate or necessary to enable the parties to comply with their obligations under this Agreement.

ARTICLE 3.
REPRESENTATIONS AND WARRANTIES

3.1. Representations and Warranties of Seller. Seller represents and warrants to Buyer that the statements contained in this Section 3.1 are correct and complete as of the date hereof:

(a)   **Status of Seller.** Seller is an individual with the requisite competence and authority to execute and deliver this Agreement and each other document deliverable pursuant to Section 2.4 above (collectively, the "*Transaction Documents*"), and to perform and to consummate the transactions contemplated hereunder and thereunder.

(b) **Power and Authority; Enforceability.** Seller has taken all actions necessary to authorize the execution and delivery of this Agreement and each Transaction Document, the performance of Seller's obligations hereunder and thereunder, and the consummation of the contemplated transactions. This Agreement and each Transaction Document has been duly authorized, executed, and delivered by, and is enforceable against, Seller.

(c) **No Violation.** The execution and the delivery of the Agreement and/or the Transaction Documents by Seller and the performance and consummation of the transactions contemplated herein and therein by Seller will not (i) breach any law or order to which Seller is subject or any provision of any of the Company's articles or by-laws, (ii) breach any contract, order, or permit to which Seller or the Company is a party or by which Seller or the Company is bound or to which any of the Company's assets is subject, or (iii) require any consent of any third party.

(d) **Shares.** Seller holds of record and owns beneficially ⸺ 100 Shares, representing all of the issued and outstanding shares of the Company, free and clear of any Encumbrances.

Deleted: ⸺

3.2. Representations and Warranties of Buyer.

Buyer warrants to Sellers that the statements contained in this Section 3.2 are correct and complete as of the date hereof:

(a) **Entity Status.** Buyer is a company duly organized, validly existing and in good standing under the laws of California. Buyer has the requisite power and authority to own or lease its properties and to carry on its business as currently conducted. There is no pending or threatened action (or basis therefor) for the dissolution, liquidation, insolvency, or rehabilitation of Buyer.

(b) **Power and Authority; Enforceability.** Buyer has the power and authority to execute and deliver the Agreement and each Transaction Document to which it is party, and to perform and consummate the transactions contemplated hereunder and thereunder. Buyer has, upon due inquiry and reasonable belief, taken all action necessary to authorize the execution and delivery of this Agreement and each Transaction Document to which it is party, the performance of its obligations thereunder, and the consummation of the transactions. This Agreement and each Transaction Document to which Buyer is a party has been duly authorized, executed and delivered by, and is enforceable against, Buyer.

(c) **No Violation.** The execution and delivery of this Agreement and/or the Transaction Documents to which Buyer is a party by Buyer and the performance and consummation of the contemplated transactions by Buyer will not, to Buyer's knowledge, upon due inquiry and reasonable belief, (i) breach any law or order to which Buyer is subject or any provision of its organizational documents; (ii) breach any contract, order, or permit to which Buyer is a party or by which it is bound or to which any of its assets is subject; or (iii) require any third party consent.

ARTICLE 4.
REPRESENTATIONS AND WARRANTIES
CONCERNING THE COMPANY

Seller represents and warrants to Buyer that the statements contained in this ARTICLE 4 are correct and complete as of the date hereof:

4.1. Company Status. The Company is duly incorporated, validly existing, and in good standing under the laws of the British Virgin Islands, a British Territory. The Company is duly authorized to conduct its business and is in good standing under the laws of each jurisdiction where such qualification is required. The Company has the requisite power and authority necessary to own or lease its properties and to carry on its businesses as currently conducted. Seller has delivered to Buyer correct and complete copies of the Company's organizational documents, as amended to date. The Company is not in breach of any provision of its organizational documents. ~~There~~ To the Company's knowledge, there is no pending or threatened action (or basis therefor) for the dissolution, liquidation, insolvency, or rehabilitation of the Company.

Deleted: There

4.2. Power and Authority; Enforceability. The Company has the power and authority necessary to execute and deliver this Agreement and each Transaction Document to which it is a party. The Company has taken all action necessary to authorize the execution and delivery of this Agreement and each Transaction Document to which it is a party, the performance of its obligations hereunder and thereunder, and the consummation of the transactions contemplated herein and therein. This Agreement and each Transaction Document to which the Company is party has been duly authorized, executed, and delivered by, and is enforceable against, the Company.

4.3. Capitalization. All of the issued and outstanding Shares of the Company (A) have been duly authorized, are validly issued, fully paid, and nonassessable, (B) were issued in compliance with all applicable securities laws, (C) were not issued in breach of any commitments, and (D) are held of record and owned beneficially by Seller. No commitments exist with respect to any equity interest of the Company and no such commitments will arise in connection with the contemplated transactions.

4.4. Records and Accounts. The copies of the Company's books and records and statutory accounts provided to Buyer hereunder are accurate and complete and reflect all amendments made through the date hereof. The statutory accounts have been prepared in accordance with ~~U.K.~~ GAAP applied on a consistent basis throughout the periods covered thereby, present fairly the financial condition of the Company as of such dates and the results of operations of the Company for such periods, are correct and complete, and are consistent with the books and records of the Company, subject to normal year-end adjustments (which will not be material individually or in the aggregate). Since the date of the most recent balance sheet, there has been no significant subsequent event that could reasonably be expected to have a material adverse effect on the Company or its financial condition.

Deleted: [
Deleted: .]

4.5. Liabilities. The Company has no liability (and there is no basis for any present or future action or order against it giving rise to any liability), except for (a) liabilities quantified on the face of the statutory accounts (rather than in any notes thereto) and not heretofore paid or discharged, and (b) liabilities that have arisen after the date of the most recent balance sheet in the ordinary course of business which, individually or in the aggregate, are not material and are of the same character and nature as the liabilities quantified on the face of the statutory accounts (rather than any notes thereto) none of which results from or relates to any breach of contract, breach of warranty, tort, infringement, or breach of law, or arose out of any action or order.

4.6. Contracts. Schedule 4.10 lists all material contracts to which the Company is a party or is otherwise bound.

ARTICLE 5.
COVENANTS

The parties agree as follows:

5.1.   General. Each party will use its reasonably commercial efforts to take all actions and to do all things necessary, proper, or advisable to consummate, make effective, and comply with all of the terms of this Agreement and the transactions applicable to it.

5.2.   Confidentiality; Publicity. Seller recognizes that he has had access to certain Proprietary Information that are valuable, special and unique assets of the Company and/or Buyer or Buyer's Affiliates or licensors, and Seller shall not use for Seller's personal benefit, or divulge to, or use for the direct or indirect benefit of, any person, firm, corporation, association or other entity, for any purpose or reason whatsoever, any Proprietary Information relating to the Company, Buyer or Buyer's Affiliates or licensors. The provisions of this paragraph shall be in addition to (and not a limitation of) any legally applicable protections of Company's interest in its confidential information, trade secrets and the like. Except as may be required by applicable law, or as otherwise expressly contemplated herein, no party or their respective Affiliates, employees, agents, and representatives will disclose to any third party the existence of this Agreement or the subject matter or terms hereof.

5.3.   Assignment of Lease. The parties acknowledge and agree that the ~~Company~~ Seller is currently a party to that certain lease dated _____ for the warehouse facilities located at _____, Tortola, B.V.I. (the "*Lease*"). The parties shall each use commercially reasonable efforts to cause the Lease to be assigned to ~~Seller~~ Buyer. In the event the parties are unable to obtain the necessary consent of the landlord to such assignment, the parties agree to enter into a mutually acceptable sub-lease (to the extent permitted by and in compliance with the terms of the Lease), pursuant to which the ~~Company~~ Seller will sub-lease to ~~Seller~~ Buyer the premises under the Lease, and ~~Seller~~ Buyer will pay to the ~~Company~~ Seller and assume the rent and all other obligations becoming due under the Lease from and after the closing of the transaction contemplated under this Agreement.

. . . .

5.6.   Non-competition. To assure that Buyer will realize the benefits of the transactions contemplated hereunder, and as part of the consideration for the Purchase Price, Seller hereby agrees with Buyer:

(a)   From the date hereof and for a period of two (2) years following the date hereof (the "Restricted Period"), Seller shall not, without the prior written consent of Buyer, in its sole discretion, directly or indirectly engage in (as principal, shareholder, partner, director, officer, agent, employee, consultant or otherwise) or be financially interested in any competing business of the Company that designs and builds custom yachts within the West Indies; provided, however, nothing contained in this section shall prevent Seller from holding for investment no more than five percent (5%) of any class of equity securities of a company whose securities are publicly traded on a national securities exchange or in a national market system.

(b)   During the Restricted Period, Seller shall not, directly or indirectly (A) induce any person or entity that is a customer of the Company to enter into any contract with or otherwise patronize any business directly or indirectly in competition with the Company; or (B) request or advise any person or entity who is a customer, vendor, or lessor of the Company, to withdraw, curtail, or cancel any such customer's, vendor's, or lessor's business with the Company; provided, however, that a general solicitation or advertisement originating outside of, and not specifically targeted to or reasonably expected to target, the territory as to which such Seller is restricted from engaging in such competitive busi-

---

Deleted: Company

Deleted: Seller

Deleted: Company

Deleted: Seller

Deleted: Seller

Deleted: Company

5

ness as provided above under this Agreement at such time, will not be deemed in and of itself to violate the prohibitions of (A) or (B) of this subparagraph.

(c) Any and all writings, inventions, improvements, processes, procedures and/or techniques which Sellers made, conceived, discovered or developed, either solely or jointly with any other person or persons, at any time they were affiliated with the Company, which relate to or are useful in connection with any business now or hereafter carried on or contemplated by Company, including developments or expansions of its present fields of operations, shall remain the sole and exclusive property of Company and shall be deemed to have been performed as a "work-for-hire," and Seller holds no right, title or interest in or to any such work and expressly waives any existing or future moral or other rights of any nature whatsoever in or to such work.

(d) Seller agrees and acknowledges that the restrictions in Section 5.2 and this Section 5.5 are reasonable in scope and duration and are necessary to protect Buyer and the Company after the Closing. If any provision of Section 5.2 or this Section 5.6, as applied to any party or to any circumstance, is adjudged not to be enforceable in accordance with its terms, the same will in no way affect any other circumstance or the enforceability of the remainder of this Agreement. The parties agree and acknowledge that the breach of Section 5.2 or this Section 5.6 will cause irreparable damage to Buyer and the Company and upon breach of any provision of this Section 5.6, Buyer and/or the Company will be entitled to injunctive relief, specific performance, or other equitable relief without bond or other security; provided, however, that the foregoing remedies will in no way limit any other remedies which Buyer and/or the Company may have. The provisions of Section 5.2 and this Section 5.6 shall survive any termination of this agreement and completion of the contemplated transactions.

(e) Seller acknowledges that (i) the goodwill associated with his ownership and management of the Company prior to the purchase of the Shares hereunder is an integral component of the value to the Company and is reflected in the consideration to be received by Seller in the purchase, and (ii) Seller's covenants as set forth herein are necessary to preserve the value for the Company following the purchase.

ARTICLE 6.
INDEMNIFICATION

6.1. **Indemnification Provisions for Buyer's Benefit.** Seller hereby agrees to indemnify and hold the Buyer harmless from and pay any and all claims, losses, damages and expenses resulting from, relating to, arising out of, or attributable to; (a) any breach of any representation or warranty Seller has made in this Agreement; (b) any breach by Seller of any covenant or obligation of Seller in this Agreement; or (c) any actions taken by Seller prior to the date hereof which may have a material adverse effect on the Company, its operations, or its financial condition.

6.2. **Indemnification Provisions for Sellers' Benefit.** Buyer will indemnify and hold Seller harmless from and pay any and all claims, losses, damages and expenses resulting from, relating to, arising out of, or attributable to (a) any breach of any representation or warranty Buyer has made in this Agreement; (b) any breach by Buyer of any covenant or obligation of Buyer in this Agreement; or (c) operation and ownership of the Company subsequent to the date hereof.

6.3. **Survival.** The provisions of this Article 6 shall survive termination of this Agreement and/or completion of the transactions contemplated hereunder for a period of two (2) years following such termination and/or completion.

ARTICLE 7.
MISCELLANEOUS

7.1.   Entire Agreement.

7.2.   Successors.

7.3.   Assignments.

7.4.   Notices.

7.5.   Counterparts.

7.6.   Headings.

7.7.   **Governing Law.** This Agreement and the performance of the obligations of the parties hereunder will be governed by and construed in accordance with the laws of ~~California~~ the British Virgin Islands, without giving effect to any choice of law principles, ~~the parties parties hereto hereby submit to jurisdiction in Los Angeles County in the State of California, U.S.A.~~

7.8.   **Amendments and Waivers.**

7.9 .   Severability.

7.10.   Construction.

7.11.   Remedies.

Deleted:
California

Deleted:
the parties parties hereto hereby submit to jurisdiction in Los Angeles County in the State of California, U.S.A

IN WITNESS WHEREOF, the parties have executed this Agreement as of the date first above written.

BUYER

Shaw Holdings, LLC

By: _____

Name: _____

Title: _____

SELLER

Sofia Lauden

By: _____

Name: Sofia Laudon, an individual

COMPANY

By: _____

Name: _____

Title: _____

Schedule 2.2
Purchase Price

The Purchase Price shall be _____, less any offset pursuant to Section 2.2.

Index

A

acquisitions, 51, 175n, 184, 211, 215, 220, 223
    letters of intent in, 152fig
    noncompete in, 217
    structure of, 22–23
    See also mergers & acquisitions
active listening, 99, 100, 102–106, 108, 120, 141, 194fig
    with clients, 111, 113, 114, 120
    in negotiations, 187, 204, 208
adverse parties, as term, 159
advising, 13, 21–22, 111, 116–118, 124, 127n5
agendas, 120, 121, 122fig, 193
agreements, 22, 35–36, 140, 189, 203, 241. *See also* commercial agreements
ambiguity, 46, 48, 48n
American Bar Association, 31
analysis. *See* legal analysis
anchor points, 194fig, 202, 203, 208
angel investors, 237
antitrust law, 226, 240
articles of incorporation, 211, 212, 230
articles of organization, 231
assets, 22–23, 212, 214, 215, 220
    purchase of, 78, 211, 219, 224
assignability, 190
associates. *See* junior associates
Association of Corporate Counsel, 31
assumption of liabilities, 211
Attorney Work Product, 127, 127n5
audience, 141, 163
    in writing, 43, 49–50, 87, 126, 127, 133–134

B

banks, 235, 238
baskets, 211
BATNA (best alternative to a negotiated agreement), 191, 195fig
bcc, in email, 95

bear hug, 225, 226
best alternative to a negotiated agreement. *See* BATNA
bidder, 223–225
Binder, David A., 112n
Bishop, K., 173n4
Blue Sky laws, 211, 240
board of directors, 96, 115ex, 218, 224, 225, 237
    in corporate governance, 113, 123, 211–215, 230–233
boilerplate, 190
bridge loans, 212, 213, 238
Brief Answer, in memos, 71–72fig, 71n4, 82
bright-line test, 220
broker-dealers, 28–32, 212, 219, 235, 236, 239
building blocks, in contracts, 141, 142fig, 143, 152–153
bulk transfer laws, 33
bullet points, 46, 81, 82, 94, 121, 170, 209
bullet point summaries, 86–87, 91, 93, 162
business issues, 14–15, 17, 21, 23, 77, 186, 246
business law, 18–19, 241
buyer's counsel, 160
buy-outs, 224
by-laws, 212, 231, 233

C

California, 78n8, 217, 227, 234, 234n10
California Corporations Code, 115ex, 234n10
California Rules of Professional Conduct, 10
capitalization, 212, 213, 220, 230n4, 237
capital markets, 9, 10, 212, 219, 235–240
capital structure, 212, 213, 218
carried interest, 218
case law, 31, 77, 130, 131fig
cc, in email, 95
CERCLA. *See* Comprehensive Environmental Response Compensation and Liability Act
certificate of incorporation, 230